WATCHING THE OLYMPICS

Global sporting events involve the creation, management and mediation of cultural meanings for consumption by massive media audiences. The apotheosis of this cultural form is the Olympic Games. This challenging and provocative new book explores the Olympic spectacle, from the multi-media bidding process and the branding and imaging of the Games to security, surveillance and control of the Olympic product across all of its levels.

The book argues that the process of commercialisation, directed by the IOC itself, has enabled audiences to interpret its traditional objects in non-reverential ways and to develop oppositional interpretations of Olympism. The Olympics have become multi-voiced and many themed, and the spectacle of the contemporary Games raises important questions about institutionalisation, the doctrine of individualism, the advance of market capitalism, performance, consumption and the consolidation of global society.

With particular focus on the London Games in 2012, the book casts a critical eye over the bidding process, Olympic finance, promises of legacy and development, and the consequences of hosting the Games for the civil rights and liberties of those living in their shadow. Few studies have offered such close scrutiny of the inner workings of Olympism's political and economic network, and therefore this book is indispensible reading for any student or researcher with an interest in the Olympics, sport's multiple impacts, or sporting mega-events.

John Sugden is Professor of the Sociology of Sport at the University of Brighton, UK, and has researched and written widely around topics concerned with the politics and sociology of sport. He is Academic Leader of the Sport and Leisure Cultures subject group and Director of Football for Peace, an international collaborative project based in Israel.

Alan Tomlinson is Professor of Leisure Studies at the University of Brighton, UK. He is Deputy Chair of the University Research Degrees Committee and Director of Research in the Chelsea School, teaching predominantly in the social history of sport, the sociology of leisure and cultural studies.

WATCHING THE OLYMPICS

Politics, power and representation

*Edited by John Sugden
and Alan Tomlinson*

Routledge
Taylor & Francis Group

LONDON AND NEW YORK

First published 2012
by Routledge
2 Park Square, Milton Park, Abingdon, Oxon OX14 4RN

Simultaneously published in the USA and Canada
by Routledge
711 Third Avenue, New York, NY 10017

Routledge is an imprint of the Taylor & Francis Group, an informa business

British Library Cataloguing in Publication Data
A catalogue record for this book is available from the British Library

Library of Congress Cataloging in Publication Data
Watching the Olympics : politics, power and representation / edited by
John Sugden and Alan Tomlinson.
    p. cm.
  1. Olympics—Sociological aspects. 2. Olympics—Political aspects.
  3. Olympics—History. 4. Mass media and sports. I. Sugden, John Peter.
  II. Tomlinson, Alan.
  GV721.5.W33 2012
  796.48—dc22   2011008099

ISBN: 978–0–415–57832–5 (hbk)
ISBN: 978–0–415–57833–2 (pbk)
ISBN: 978–0–203–85220–0 (ebk)

Typeset in Goudy
by Swales & Willis Ltd, Exeter, Devon

Printed and bound in Great Britain by
CPI Antony Rowe, Chippenham, Wiltshire

The editors and numerous among the other contributors to this volume owe an intellectual debt to John Hargreaves, who died in 2010.

John was Visiting Professor of Sociology, in the Sport and Leisure Cultures Area, Chelsea School Research Centre, for several years up to 2000–2001. We dedicate this book to the memory of his wide influence and global impact in the sociology and politics of sport.

TABLE OF CONTENTS

CONTRIBUTORS

Lincoln Allison is Visiting Professor in the Politics of Sport and a member of the Centre for Sport Research at the University of Brighton, UK.

Daniel Burdsey is a Senior Lecturer and a member of the Centre for Sport Research at the University of Brighton, UK.

Thomas F. Carter is a Senior Lecturer and a member of the Centre for Sport Research at the University of Brighton, UK.

Jayne Caudwell is a Senior Lecturer and a member of the Centre for Sport Research at the University of Brighton, UK.

Shane Collins is a Lecturer in the School of Applied Social Sciences at Durham University, UK.

Barrie Houlihan is Professor of Sport Policy in the School of Sport, Exercise and Health Sciences at Loughborough University, UK.

P. David Howe is a Senior Lecturer in the School of Sport, Exercise and Health Sciences at Loughborough University, UK.

Marc Keech is a Principal Lecturer and a member of the Centre for Sport Research at the University of Brighton, UK.

Ian McDonald is a Principal Lecturer and a member of the Centre for Sport Research at the University of Brighton, UK.

Graham McFee is Professor of Philosophy and a member of the Centre for Sport Research at the University of Brighton, UK; and in the Department of Philosophy at California State University, Fullerton.

Jim McKay is Professor in the School of Tourism and Hospitality Management at Southern Cross University, Australia; and Centre for Critical and Cultural Studies, The University of Queensland, Australia.

Catherine Palmer is Reader in the School of Applied Social Sciences at the Durham University, UK.

Mark Perryman is a Research Fellow and a member of the Centre for Sport Research at the University of Brighton, UK

David Rowe is a Professor at the Centre for Cultural Research, College of Arts, University of Western Sydney, Australia.

Rob Steen is a Senior Lecturer and a member of the Centre for Sport Research at the University of Brighton, UK.

John Sugden is Professor of the Sociology of Sport and a member of the Centre for Sport Research at the University of Brighton, UK.

Holly Thorpe is a Senior Lecturer in the Department of Sport and Leisure Studies at The University of Waikato, New Zealand.

Alan Tomlinson is Professor of Leisure Studies and a member of the Centre for Sport Research at the University of Brighton, UK.

Belinda Wheaton is a Senior Research Fellow and a member of the Centre for Sport Research at the University of Brighton, UK.

PREFACE

Watching the Olympics: the critical social scientific gaze

Ever since the Olympic Games secured financial independence in the 1980s, when its marketing strategy attracted exclusive corporate partners to complement the media revenues that the USA network companies in particular were willing to pay, a minor offshoot of its survival and prosperity has been the academic study of the Olympics itself. Centres for the study of the Olympics had been established prior to those boom years, sometimes sanctioned or supported by organizing committees and the International Olympic Committee (IOC) itself. These have produced valuable scholarship and reflection, in Canada, Spain/Catalonia, Australia, and Norway for instance, but not all have had long-term impact and profiles.

Nevertheless, and now more than ever, each Olympics generates a torrent of academic analysis of the Games. And much of this is produced in the national context of the host city. Economists discuss and evaluate financial impact; political scientists explore the citizenship issues and persisting expressions of nationalism; sociologists theorise on social and cultural meanings, values and ideologies; anthropologists and media scholars comment on the experience and mediation of the rituals and ceremonies that in any other context would seem wacky, antiquated, and contrived; historians tell us that we've all been there before, and that De Coubertin's Olympism certainly wasn't the only show in town for much of its early history. And that's just the mainstream disciplines. Cultural studies specialists explore Olympic identities; policy analysts review the cultural and social impacts of Olympic policy; environmentalists interrogate the IOC's commitment to the environment; urban studies scholars check up on infrastructural legacies; and sport studies generates individuals, groups, and teams who have either studied the Olympic phenomenon for some time or feel that their particular specialism has something to say to an Olympics that has turned up on their doorstep. Research into high-level performance and the making of Olympic champions has also provided widespread opportunities for sport scientists in their home nations, and in some countries less ethical scientists have been willing to apply their science to the use of performance-enhancing substances and processes.

This book is to some extent the product of an established sport studies team. Of the 19 contributors, all have worked in sport studies groups or departments. A dozen or so have written on the Olympics before July 2005 when London won the 2012 Games at the IOC meeting in Singapore. And of the 19, all but 4 have worked or spent time as a researcher or visiting scholar at the University of Brighton's Chelsea School, in the Sport and Leisure Cultures (SLC) group. The book is therefore also a product of Brighton's approach to the socio-cultural study of sport, labelled by some as critical interpretivism (Gratton and Jones 2004). This approach was outlined in a previous collaborative product (Sugden and Tomlinson 2002), and need not be repeated here. But the core elements of that Brighton approach characterise this book's principles for critical Olympic scholarship: a healthy disrespect for disciplinary boundaries; an adventurous cross-cultural curiosity; and a commitment to critical social scientific scholarship not beholden to patrons, agencies or sponsors. The colleagues lining up alongside the Brighton and Brighton-linked contributors, those from Durham, Loughborough, and Western Sydney, share these principles.

As editors, we have asked all contributors to focus upon their topic and write in as accessible a fashion as possible to produce informed and well-evidenced accounts and analyses that take us beyond taken-for-granted notions of Olympism and its values and institutions. This is not to say that we all think the Olympics are a bad thing. The Olympics are in fact a hugely complex socio-cultural phenomenon. They offer hope, whatever the hyperbole and the rhetoric; they accelerate infrastructural development and even transformation, but at a cost to displaced communities; they speak of ideals in an ideologically soiled world. We have sought no party line on this, and have asked contributors to keep an open mind as they have investigated their individual themes and topics.

So if our underlying methodological principles are so general, and the theoretical frameworks varied and open-minded, what in fact holds this book together? The answer is in the title – 'watching' the Olympics. We conceive the academic's role as that of the disinterested critical observer, informed by appropriate theory, and focusing upon the construction of Olympic phenomena at each stage of their remaking. In asking all contributors to turn their own critical gaze upon particular themes and issues, the volume as a whole becomes a form of watching and interpreting, asking what the Olympics actually means, what sustains the Games, what ideological purposes the Olympic phenomenon serves. In doing this, as the subtitle says, authors concentrate as appropriate upon historical and sociological dimensions of politics, power and representation. Chapters 1–4 question many of the assumptions about the meaning of the Games and the ways in which past Games have been understood, and Olympic ideals and values appropriated and remade: London's three Games were very different things, sought for very different reasons; whatever De Coubertin wrote and thought, certain core themes have endured in modern understandings of Olympism; a fundamental philosophical or intrinsic meaning to Olympism may account for the hold of the phenomenon on the global imagination; and the implicit internationalism of the Olympic idea raises intriguing issues of sovereignty. Chapters 5–7 address specific policy issues, as they bear upon the cultural politics of Olympic events: urban and social regeneration and multiculturalism; governmental policies on legacy/participation; and the threat that will not go away – drug-use and anti-doping policy. Chapters 8–10 look at cultural forms and practices generated by and within the Olympics: official Olympic films; the torch relay; and the cultural Olympiad. Chapters 11–13 focus the critical gaze upon the athletes and their performing Olympian bodies: the anomalies and injustices of sex-testing; the criteria relating to and the framing of disability in the Paralympics; and the targeting of young, stylish and attractive bodies by the IOC in its changes to the competitive agenda of the Games. Chapters 14–16 address in varied ways issues of representation and politics: the construction of the notion of Team GB in a political climate of devolution; the pressures and constraints upon the campaigning journalist in Olympic settings; and the rise and rise of surveillance and security at the Olympics.

This book is in many ways a response to the fact of London 2012. But it is also an accumulation of independent scholarship that has subjected the Olympics, and diverse other sporting events, practices, and institutions, to the critical social scientific gaze. In an afterword, we develop some of the overarching themes that arise from subjecting the Games to this kind of interrogative scrutiny, drawing too upon some of the work of the late John Hargreaves. The latter's seminal book *Sport, Power and Culture* signposted an intellectual journey for a generation of critical social scientists of sport. In locating London 2012 within a broader historical narrative as well within the contemporary politics of global culture, we are proud to be able to carry a torch fuelled by the spirit of John Hargreaves's interdisciplinary and critical scholarship.

References

Gratton, C. and Jones, I. (2004) *Research Methods for Sports Studies*, London: Routledge.
Sugden, J. and Tomlinson, A. (eds) (2002) *Power Games: A Critical Sociology of Sport*, London: Routledge.

John Sugden and Alan Tomlinson
Centre for Sport Research
University of Brighton
January 2011

ACKNOWLEDGEMENTS

We are grateful to the University of Brighton for supporting the production of this book, in two specific ways: for financial support for a symposium held in March 2010, at which authors were invited to deliver drafts and outlines of their chapters; and for funding that enabled the manuscript to be formatted and checked prior to submission to the publisher. Colleagues in the Centre for Research and Development, Faculty of Arts, University of Brighton made their conference room wholly available to us for the two-day symposium, at no cost, in a gesture of collegiality and generosity that makes the University of Brighton such a good place in which to work.

Our gratitude is owed too to Routledge's commissioning editor, Simon Whitmore, and to his colleague Joshua Wells: the former believed in our conception of the book and encouraged us to deliver it as early as possible; the latter chased us as our deadlines slipped, but did so with unfailing courtesy and good humour. We are also pleased to acknowledge the six anonymous referees whose reports on the proposal were insightful and valuable, and whose points have been borne in mind in the production of the book. The Afterword benefits from extended conversations and collective thinking on the London 2012 Olympics between Jim McKay and Alan Tomlinson.

Myrene McFee brought her inimitable sharpness and rigour to the home-stretch task of smartening up both prose and presentation, and her outstanding skills will have made the publisher's job a lot smoother than if the manuscript had come only via the editors' hands.

John Sugden and Alan Tomlinson
January 2011

1

LORDING IT

London and the getting of the Games

Alan Tomlinson

Introduction

In 2012 London will become the only city to have staged the Summer Olympic Games more than twice (the so-called interim Games in Athens in 1906 are largely dismissed from recognised and authoritative records of the Games). For much of the 2012 bidding process up to July 2005, it seemed that Paris would win the race to be a three-times host, especially as its two previous Games were in the first quarter of the twentieth century, in 1900 and 1924. Athens, arrogantly and incorrectly assuming a sentimental vote for the centenary 1996 event, eventually hosted its second Games in 2004, and thereby helped precipitate its country's economic crisis. Los Angeles, with a half century between its 1932 and 1984 events, is the only other city to have held the Summer Games twice. Others have tried including Tokyo and Berlin. Some major cities have sought the Games but without success: New York, Istanbul, Madrid. The latter, along with Chicago and Tokyo, lost out in the final bidding round for the 2016 Games, awarded in October 2009 to Rio de Janeiro. Much has changed since Los Angeles laid down its ultimatum to the IOC for the 1984 Games, effectively rewriting the rules of engagement for any host city, allowing levels of commercialisation of the event not previously seen: the sponsoring of the Olympic torch relay being one particularly controversial initiative. And since then, television rights, sponsorship programmes, and the attraction of hosting an event claimed to deliver the world's largest-ever television audience have sustained the Olympics through crises of corruption (by officials and administration), cheating (the use of banned drugs for performance-enhancement), and economic volatility. It is remarkable that, for all these problems, the Olympics continues to stimulate bidding wars. What draws cities, states, and corporate allies in to this dynamic and towards this aspiration, and how is the prize won? It is these simple questions that underlie the consideration in this chapter of London's successful bid for 2012, and the wider mechanics of the bidding process. As a prelude to this it is illuminating, for the purposes of comparison, to reflect on the city's previous Summer Olympics.

London 1908 and 1948

1908

The first modern Games were held in cities on the basis of the networks of the founder of the modern Olympics as we know them, Pierre de Coubertin, and the pragmatics of innovation: make the event and then document its history. They were small-scale: Athens 1896 involved a mere 245 or so competitors from 14 nations, competing in 43 events. Paris in 1900 had double the number of nations and a little over 1,000 competitors competing in 75 events, but the transatlantic venue of St. Louis 1904 exposed the European anchorage of Olympian inter-nationalism, more than halving the number of competitors, at a Games that spread out over four and a half months and was the least representative of any in the history of the event, with just 7 European countries participating (Wallechinsky and Loucky 2008). Chicago had actually been awarded the event, but the organisers of the 1904 World's Fair (the Louisiana Purchase Exhibition) gained the support of US president Theodore Roosevelt to get this decision reversed. De Coubertin had little option than to accept this. With such a fragmented, scarcely international event – Tswana tribesmen at the Fair as part of a Boer War exhibition were hauled in to compete in the marathon and add international spice – the Olympic initiative looked to have derailed. Greece organised its own Athenian Games, what has become known as an 'interim' Olympics for 1906, with 20 nations and 847 athletes, and planned four-yearly celebrations intended to dovetail with the Olympics. Rome (chosen over Berlin: see *Revue Olympique* 1904: 72 for an account of this decision at the fourth session of the IOC in London) had been allocated the 1908 Games, but a fragile national economy, competing city factions across the country, and lack of support from the national Italian govern-ment in 1906 caused De Coubertin to doubt the strength of the commitment.

British fencer Lord Desborough (see Box 1) had competed in Athens in 1906, doubling up as King Edward VII's 'British Representative . . . on the same auspicious occasion'. With the uncertainties in Rome, and the future of the De Coubertin project in doubt: 'It was therefore with every prospect of success that the suggestion was made that the Games of 1908 should be celebrated in England . . . Lord Desborough was able to carry out that suggestion, not only because of the personal influence he possessed, but also because the Central Organisation from which the management of these games might be created had already come into existence in this country' (Cook 1909: 19).

The fourth IOC session in London in June 1904 proved palatable to all concerned: meetings with sportsmen C.B. Fry and W.G. Grace; the Lord Mayor's reception in Mansion House; dinner at the Corporation of Fishmongers' splendid

BOX 1: LORD DESBOROUGH

Beckett (2004) summarises: *'For all his public duties, Grenfell [Desborough] was probably best-known by contemporaries for his sporting prowess. He had represented Harrow at cricket and Oxford in fencing, athletics, and rowing. He made two appearances in the university boat race in 1877 and 1878: the first was a dead heat and the second a victory for Oxford. He won the Thames punting championships for three successive years (1888–90), stroked an eight across the channel, sculled the London–Oxford stretch of the Thames in a crew of three in twenty-two consecutive hours, and rowed for the Leander club in the Grand Challenge Cup at Henley while an MP. Having won foils at both Harrow and Oxford, Grenfell also represented Britain, and became founding president of the Amateur Fencing Association. He twice swam Niagara, crossing the pool just below the falls, and he ascended the Matterhorn by three different routes. In one eight day period he ascended the Matterhorn, the little Matterhorn, Monte Rosa, the Rothorn, and the Weisshorn. On one occasion he was lost for three days in the Rocky Mountains. He was also a keen horseman, hunter, and fisherman. He went big-game shooting in India, Africa, and British Columbia, and caught tarpon off Florida. He had been master of the draghounds at Oxford and maintained his own harriers at Taplow Court, which had formerly been hunted by King Edward VII as prince of Wales. An excellent whip, he was president of the Coaching Club and the Four-in-Hand Club. One of the conservators of the Thames, he was the founding chairman of the Thames Salmon Association. Three times acting president of the Life Saving Society, he was also president and chairman of the Bath Club from 1894 to 1942. At various times Desborough was also president of both the Marylebone Cricket Club and the Lawn Tennis Association as well as being president of the Olympics held in London in 1908. He was chairman of the Pilgrims of Great Britain from 1919 to 1929 and president of the Amateur Athletic Association from 1930 to 1936.'* See too Rebecca Jenkins (Jenkins 2008: 4–5), on Desborough as a symbol of the contemporary ideal of amateur all-round excellence. He was also a student at Balliol College, Oxford, personifying in its athleticist and sporting version what incoming British prime minister Herbert Asquith called in 1908 the Balliol man's 'tranquil consciousness of an effortless superiority' (Matthew 2004). Baker (2008: 89) notes that Desborough at one particular point of his busy life is said to have sat on 115 committees.

hall by London Bridge; visits to the MCC/Lord's and the Toxophilite Society; a reception hosted by the Prince of Wales in Marlborough House; and a detailed tour of the palace of Westminster. All this made favourable impressions on both sides. In under a year, the British Olympic Association had been formed (May 1905) at a meeting at the House of Commons, with Lord Desborough as its President. This was the 'Central Organisation' to which the 1908 report referred.

The following year Desborough was lobbying in Athens, Rome was abandoned (the tragic eruption of Mount Vesuvius in April 1906 provided a rationale for Rome/Italy's withdrawal), lobbying within the IOC for Budapest was proving relatively ineffective (IOC minute, 1905). So London's first Olympics was handed to it on a silver platter, with the Games planned as a core element of the Franco-British Exhibition, whose 'organisers . . . were powerful advocates of the Olympic Movement and intended to make the Games the centrepiece of the festival' (Miller 2008: 58).

Desborough was a typical champion of the amateur and athleticist ideal. Under his leadership London gained the1908 Games via a combination of networking (three Great Britain members on a small and malleable IOC), backroom diplomacy, get-up-and-go confidence, and a degree of *hauteur* characteristic of the sporting elite of the time. This aristocratic networking included use of the stateroom in Lord Howard de Walden's yacht moored in Athens's Bay of Phlerum (Kent 2008: ch. 2).

1948

Another prominent English Lord played a central role in securing London's second Olympics. David George Brownlow Cecil, sixth Marquess of Exeter, or Lord Burghley (see Box 2), had been a prominent Olympian in the 1920s (the model for the aristocratic Lord Lindsay in the 1981 Oscar-winning film *Chariots of Fire*), and was chairman and chief executive of the London Organising Committee.

BOX 2: LORD BURGHLEY

Janie Hampton writes: *'In the chair was 43-year-old Lord Burghley, formerly a Conservative MP and Governor-General of Bermuda, who had won a gold medal in the 1928 Olympics. Educated at Eton and Cambridge, he owned a pack of fox hounds and had recently divorced his wife, the daughter of a duke. "On the maiden voyage of the Queen Mary, for the gratification of H.G. Wells and Lord Camrose he ran 400 yards after dinner, in evening dress, round the upper deck in 58 seconds",* wrote the Observer . . . *Handsome and articulate, calm and genial, Burghley successfully torpedoed opposition to the Games with charm and persuasion'.* (Hampton 2008: 27)

Burghley's words at the closing ceremony of the London 1948 Olympics, displayed on the stadium scoreboard, evoked quintessential Olympic and Coubertinesque ideals: 'The spirit of the Olympic Games, which has tarried here a while, sets forth once more. May it prosper throughout the world, safe in the keeping of all those who have felt its noble impulse in this great Festival of Sport'

(Organising Committee 1951). Burghley was president of the British Olympic Association for 30 years from 1936, and his idealism was based on the principles of tolerance, understanding, friendship (and an associated cultivation of cross-cultural relations among young people) as essential to the post-war world order. London had in fact been allocated the 1944 Games before the war (Tokyo was to have hosted the 1940 event) and in November 1944 Burghley and fellow British Olympic Association stalwart Lord Aberdare, along with a third member Sir Noel Curtis-Bennett, issued a statement that the first post-war Games should be in London. In October 1945 Burghley travelled to Stockholm to meet the vice-president and acting president of the IOC, Sigfrid Edström, a fellow veteran Olympian and long-term president of the International Amateur Athletics Association. From his base in Sweden Edström had sustained IOC contacts throughout the war, and after the death in 1942 of incumbent president Count Henri de Baillet-Latour, he became IOC president by acclamation in 1946. He had already written to Lord Aberdare, in May 1945: '[Avery] Brundage [then president of the US Olympic Committee] and I have agreed that we shall have the next Games in London' (Phillips 2007: 6). Burghley's trip to Sweden was mere protocol, and was followed up by a formal letter from the Lord Mayor of London seeking approval to stage the Games; in March 1946 a postal vote formally 'allotted' (Burghley's words, see Organising Committee 1951: 17) the 1948 Games to London.

Forty years on from London's first Olympics, the second was landed without an open vote (there's little evidence of voting in the 'postal vote' referred to by Burghley); by agreement among networks of elites (McWhirter 2004); with the promise of the restoration of Olympian idealism; and with an assumption that even in the havoc and the austerity of the post-war context (Bolz 2010; Hampton 2008), Britain could do it, could step in and save the day.

London 2012

Sixty years after Burghley's securement of what he saw as London's right, the Games had to be worked-for in a completely different kind of bidding process. Soured by revelations of corrupt administration and unethical practices by bureaucrat and official alike (Jennings 1996; Jennings and Sambrook 2000; Lenskyj 2000; Symson and Jennings 1992), the IOC needed internal reform and more transparency in its decision-making processes. Juan-Antonio Samaranch's successor as IOC president, Jacques Rogge, president from 2001, has established and consistently reaffirmed the restrictions on hospitality and gift-giving that are intended to rid the bidding process of bribery and corruption, and sponsors concerned with the tarnished image of a corrupt IOC at the turn of the millennium have continued their partnerships, though after Beijing 2008 three North American giants – Manulife, Johnson and Johnson, and Kodak – terminated their support. Nevertheless, media rights have held their value, and the outcome of bidding processes can produce responses verging on hyperbole: 'Rarely in peacetime have Londoners celebrated together with so much emotion at the heart of the city' (Lee 2006: 192) may be an unsubstantiatable assertion, but there is no doubt that in London and some parts of the UK beyond England's capital, the announcement by Rogge on July 6th 2005 that London had pipped Paris to get the 2012 Games generated enthusiastic, even joyful, responses. Mike Lee describes the Paris bidding team's response in Singapore as 'dumbstruck and dejected', before the tears started to flow. So how did London do it?

Lee, the London bid's Director of Communications and Public Affairs, describes factors crucial to the success of the London bid: a united message emerging under inspired leadership; an emphasis on youth – and this was brilliantly and pithily evoked in the London presentational video (Tomlinson 2008: 73–4) – and legacy; and the presence of prime minister Tony Blair in Singapore for several days before the vote. But crucially, regardless of the cleaned-up bidding process, and the restraints on favours and incentives, the London bid was anchored in a sustained and intensive process of lobbying, incalculable in terms of visible or actual costs. It is widely recognised that the Paris bid was weakened by internal divisions in leadership, and by the arrogance and assumptions of the country's president, Jacques Chirac, who arrived at the last minute in Singapore confident that this third successive bid from Paris/France was won, and would deliver him an international success and legacy to match his internal monument, the Millau viaduct at the southern edge of the Massif Central. London played the bidding game more successfully than many had expected: a member of the bid team asked on the journey from the team hotel to the announcement venue, 'What the hell are we going to do if we win?'; an experienced member of the administration at London's City hall has conceded that no real budget was done, it was literally back-of-envelope jobs, so convinced was the Mayor of London's office that the bid would not succeed.

There are over 100 members of the IOC with voting rights and they constitute a scattered range of individuals, traditionally aristocratic, male, and privileged, though the committee has accepted women members from 1981, and its age-range has been widened by the inclusion of former athletes. The committee is capable of producing surprising results, but at the same time has often rewarded perseverance, awarding the event to a city that has come relatively close in previous bids. In part, this accounts for France's over-confidence in 2005. But it is widely agreed that the Paris bid took success for granted, neglecting the context of the bidding process. In the next, central section of this chapter, I peer more closely at the culture and context of bidding, lobbying, and decision-making relationships and dynamics, on the basis of my discussions with a veteran observer of international Olympic politics, whom I will call Voo (Veteran Observer of the Olympics). [1]

How a bidding team succeeds – or fails

Make the right contacts and get into knowledge channels: Voo reminds Olympic outsiders and onlookers that journalistic experts feed the corridors of power of

Olympic professionals and world sport governance, and also act as a means for bodies such as the IOC to inform the outside world. For many years this role was fulfilled by the circular/publication *Sport Intern*, and the equivalent source of information and communication on all matters Olympic in the multi-media age – and in relation to other international sporting powerbrokers such as at FIFA, the governing body of world football – is the subscription website *Around the Rings* (AtR), the brainchild of Ed Hula. This, says Voo, 'has become just about the only source of information for the IOC and its members'. The home page of AtR includes puffs from powerplayers of international sport (Around the Rings 2010). IOC member and president of Europe's Olympic Committees, Patrick Hickey sees it as 'essential reading' giving 'an insider view from the corridors of power in Olympic sport'; USA gymnastics executive director Steve Penny sees it as an industry 'must-read' willing 'to assist stakeholders without sacrificing . . . journalistic integrity'; Olympic ceremony guru Ric Birch uses AtR as his 'primary source of specialist Olympic background information . . . For anyone who needs to stay in touch with developments in Lausanne, AtR is essential'.

Voo gets to the heart of the AtR operation, observing that Ed Hula and his team at AtR get referred to by all the big cities in the bidding process, though international companies that look to use him can quickly become dependent upon him. Cities and companies 'subscribe as an insurance, so that they don't get bad publicity. It's almost like a knowledge or PR protection racket'. Ed Hula and his team, therefore, have unusual levels of access to all levels of the bidding process. Tony Blair was pictured with Hula in 2005. On its website AtR featured a piece by *Evening Standard* journalist Adrian Warner, his copy complemented by a photograph of Blair leaning forward out of his armchair, towards Ed Hula, in concentrated focus on the AtR owner's advice. The AtR website captioned this piece with its own puff: 'As bidding for the Games has become an increasingly important part of the process, world leaders have come to recognise the critical role *Around the Rings* plays in communicating information about their bid', before quoting Warner's copy:

> *Jumping Through Mr. Hula's Hoops*
> "Tony Blair's decision to give an exclusive interview to Ed Hula, the head of the Olympic newsletter *Around the Rings*, at Downing Street last week shows how the Government has learned to fight the campaign internationally. Culture Secretary Tessa Jowell and Sports Minister Richard Caborn have arranged their diaries around the bid. It was this kind of support that was missing during the failed bids of Birmingham and Manchester. Expect France President Jacques Chirac to be on the phone to Hula quite soon." Adrian Warner, *The Evening Standard*, May 31, 2005. (Around the Rings 2010)

President Chirac may have heeded the advice about Hula, but far too late, as within days London won the IOC vote over Paris. AtR acts as a cross between a knowledge-broker and an intelligence agency. Voo adds that all the bid committees file a report to the IOC on what worked in the bidding process, on what could have been done better. Frequently they complain informally or in undocumented exchanges about sources of information, and the IOC asks them to register such complaints in the report. None of them ever does. They fear potential negative coverage in AtR.

Why are usually powerful and confident communications and marketing professionals muted and neutered in this way? Voo observes: 'US journalists, AP and Reuters use AtR, quoting it as the authoritative and informative source. Local journalistic sources have not got the experience or the expertise with which to compete. Information via these websites are [sic] now becoming the norm for what passes as reliable knowledge on international sport politics'. Successful bidding cities know this and mobilise these information sources and flows.

Newspeople and the IOC: The IOC clamps down on newspeople and Voo contends that the news media and Olympic writers are being seriously undermined. Steve Wilson is a senior writer on the Olympic beat but often he doesn't get contacted and then the locals are called/sent in.[2] TV covers the Olympics just once every two years, and it's the written media that keeps the Olympics in the news. 'But you see loads of mistakes in local/national papers, a piece that you might go to because you think it's reliably sourced, you then see that it's totally wrong. The IOC needs a certain core of people who at least write the truth. People claiming to be Olympics experts, at say some West Georgia University and in other American universities, do no more than recycle this stuff that's unreliable in the first place'.

Blair, Mills and 2012: making friends: Voo is emphatic that it was not the support and presence of Blair alone that tipped the balance London's way. The British prime minister was just the final feather. Sir Keith Mills (knighted the year after London won the race to win the 2012 Games) made success possible for Blair, lobbying for support from IOC members; and influential others had already added their weight. 'Mills was worth, personally, 150 million, he's the Air Miles tycoon, and had the availability to talk very easily with people. He's very relaxed – in many bids businessmen, corporate businessmen, don't work. Barbara Cassani at the beginning of the bid brought in the valuable corporate experience that set up the team.[3] But she couldn't play the lobby bars and sit up until 2 in the morning. Seb Coe came in and they didn't need to go outside to anyone else. He did a great job'. (see Lee 2007: 63–4). Cassani moved on, to Marks and Spencer, and then the Jury's Inn hotel chain. Bose (2010) confirms that 'for all her considerable business skill, she did not fancy the job of hanging round the world's hotels wooing the mainly old men who make up the IOC'. But Coe could woo well, regularly dining with former IOC president Samaranch (see Box 3).

Voo characterises what Mills brought to the bidding table as 'entrepreneurial flair and impact. The entrepreneurial player doesn't fall into jargon or nonsense,

---

BOX 3: LORD COE

Sebastian 'Seb' Coe became Lord Coe in 2000. A highly successful Olympic middle-distance runner in the 1980s, winning gold at the 1980 and 1984 Olympics, this graduate of Loughborough University moved into politics and was a Conservative Member of Parliament in the UK for 5 years in the 1990s, serving a spell later as chief of staff to Conservative Party leader William Hague. He took over as chair of the London 2012 bidding company in 2004, becoming chair of the London 2012 organising committee. Coe accepted the chairmanship of world football governing body FIFA's ethics committee in 2006, though has never spoken publicly of his contribution to that organisation and of the cases and processes over which he presided, and has stonewalled journalistic approaches. When doorstepped by investigative reporter Andrew Jennings – 'Lord Coe, what's the point of an independent ethics committee if you won't talk about FIFA's scandal? (Jennings 2007) – Coe ignored the query, consistent with his refusal to grant the BBC an interview on his FIFA role. Pointing to his involvement in the English FA's bid for the 2018 World Cup, he stood down from the FIFA role in March 2010. (Owen 2010). Coe makes no secret of his focused determination to succeed, and this makes him for some a credible candidate for the most powerful positions in world sport (Bose 2010). Coe backed the bid of West Ham United Football Club to take over the Olympic Stadium, and retain an athletics facility, telling BBC Radio 5 Live (23rd January 2011) that London 2012 had a 'moral obligation' to retain a multi-sport legacy. 'I hope the decision supports a community legacy. I think it can work, it's the one we took to Singapore'. Not guaranteeing this legacy would 'trash our reputation', Coe stated, making it 'very difficult for us to be taken seriously in the corridors of world sport, and arguably beyond'. Coe was speaking a few days after the IAAF president, Senegal's Lamine Diack, had said that the dismantling of the Olympic Stadium – the option favoured by Coe's colleague Keith Mills – would make 'a big lie' of the original bid.

---

he has to convince someone, act effectively as a salesman. A corporate man is not a salesman. It's a sort of high-level Arthur Daley that's needed.[4] In Athens 2004 Mills had a boat there and secretly saw IOC members. He set up a comfortable feeling. Obviously this won't show in any accounts, you'll never find the full costs of a bid. He probably saw a dozen or more IOC members, and worked on them with his ability to listen, rather than talk *to* or *at* them. They want to feel important, the IOC member does not like being lectured. Many don't realise that the person you're talking to may be thick as two short planks, but he has a vote. The role of a bid city is to be suppliant'.

Voo reflects on what helped London snatch the victory: 'Paris's bid was dogged by too much left-right political infighting. You can't run a successful bid without governmental assistance, but you'll lose if a government has too much direct influence. The government in the UK took orders from the bid. Blair responded to that very successfully. Two or three days before going to Singapore he called in three journalists/consultants, including Steve Wilson of AP, and another from Reuters Singapore, and asked them some general questions at Downing Street. They had a cup of tea and a biscuit, with a young woman in the room with them and Blair, and had 20–30 minutes, and told him that his biggest threat was Madrid not Paris. If Madrid had been in the final vote it would have won. And there was, remember, a mistake in voting when Madrid was knocked out'.

Norwegian industrialist Gerhard Heiberg, IOC member who was head of the organising committee for Lillehammer's 1994 Winter Games, has said explicitly that a lot of it counts on the relationship built up in the lobbying: 'It's like Billy Payne for Atlanta, who did a superb job', says Voo. Payne 'recognised that "we have to make friends with these people. If they're not sure, they'll vote for their friend". Atlanta brought in a surgeon, say, and housed him with another surgeon in a local family. They linked members with types of people, and offered great Southern hospitality. Not like the Japanese, who are too timid. And you've got to make friends early on. It's no good coming in like that too late'.

Sochi (Russia) learnt a lot for the 2014 Winter Games bidding process and clearly impressed IOC members with its political heavyweights. The rules might have changed but you can still build up a relationship. And that's what Mills and Coe did. They were friendly, sociable, put in the effort to make the effort work. The years of this sort of work meant that when Blair arrived in Singapore, he might just be able to tip it over the top. Mills and Coe had formed a formidable, and robust, partnership, agreeing on the plane to Singapore that should the bid be successful they would see the project through together right to the end, to the closing ceremony (Sale 2010). This did not stop Mills dabbling in other interests, and in his capacity as a director of Tottenham Hotspur football club was backing a plan, in January 2011, to knock down the Olympic stadium and replace it with a football-only ground. Asked by the BBC's Rob Bonnett (*Today* programme, BBC Radio 4, 21st January 2011) whether, given his position within the London Organising Committee for the Olympic Games (LOCOG), this was a resignation issue, Mills simply said that LOCOG had nothing to do with the legacy strategy and the stadium decision, and that therefore his business interests in the stadium site were of no relevance to his LOCOG position. He has also condemned the stranglehold on the America's Cup of entrepreneurs even richer than himself , but with little impact (Alexander 2009).

The Putin effect is what all bidders are after, and Blair showed a little of that: the massive impact of the Russian prime minister's support for Sochi, in winning the 2014 Winter Olympics, without doubt shifted the balance against the South Korean rival. Says Voo, 'Sochi won even though there'd been nothing there in their bid except promises and commitment. Bid cities don't always get it because they're the best. Nobody's ever won by being the best bid, they may have been, but that's not the point'. Putin, along with billionaire Roman Abramovich, has become a major figure in international sport politics, as Russia's smooth and predictable victory in the 2018 football World Cup bidding process showed in December 2010.

You never know how it works at the end, acknowledges Voo. Paris thought victory was theirs and stopped listening. Chirac just gave a reception, late on, and it was hard for anyone to talk with him. Blair had 20-minute sessions with individual IOC members up in his room.

Wading in – how not to get the votes: Voo emphasises the pitch of the bidding approach, the relational dimensions of the lobbying process; you've got to get the tone right. 'Michelle Obama in Copenhagen approached a royal IOC member with "Are you going to vote for us?". This stifled any conversation. Never ask an IOC member "what are you going to vote?". Only Austin Sealey (Barbados) and the Malaysian Imran would tell you what they're going to vote, they're the only ones who act with that individual independence. And Imran – a lovely man, a great singer of pop from 60s classics, is Malaysian royalty (HRH Prince Tunku Imran, an English-qualified barrister and former Malaysian national squash champion). You could ask these and maybe some others if they might cast their second vote for you. But mostly, don't ask directly for a vote'.

In October 2009, Rio de Janeiro secured the 2016 Summer Games. To Voo, it was quite clear given 'what was coming out of the Chateau, that Rio would be good. The Chicago business model was seen as fatally flawed; if the word "ambitious" is used in an evaluation report, you've had it. And the USOC (United States Olympic Committee) mess didn't help. Obama pissed people off in the end – he's coming, he's not coming, times for in and out changed. Some knew a couple of weeks before what his schedule was, and let Ed Hula know. It was all over the LA Times and everywhere. "That will kill Chicago", we/they were saying. The secret service had to do its bit and lock people in an hour before his arrival, the IOC people had to get up at 6am and make do with room service. Members were waiting for an hour, and then the speech was pretty pathetic. Mayor Daley was aware that Chicago was in deep trouble. The USOC painted a rosier picture than the reality'.

Without any doubt, Obama's advisers, the Chicago bid team, and the USOC, underestimated the momentum of rival bids, and Chicago was eliminated in the first round. There were only two US members of the IOC, and they and the bid had clearly failed to generate any serious widespread support. So-called experts were of no help here either. Peter Ueberroth, the man behind LA '84' did not help, Voo notes, in the build-up. '"If it wasn't for us", he was saying, "there'd be no Olympics". But that was 26 years ago. Saying "you owe us" for the Chicago bid was hopeless. He's known as the dinosaur, lecturing people on change. The USOC was resented for approaching NOCs around the world, putting those countries under pressure. They were simply not understanding IOC politics. IOC members were joking in the lobby about the Americans, punning Opera House with Oprah Winfrey. One said "What's so special, there's an Opera House in Sydney, an Opera in Paris, an Opera in London. Who are you trying to impress?". There was a huge fanfare for Winfrey. Some wives were thrilled to have their picture taken with her, they might have lived in the US for a while. But who's heard of Oprah in Italy, in France, in Germany, in Japan? It didn't bring a single vote'.

For Voo, 'we've never seen a decision as clear as the Rio one'. And this is related to the position of IOC president, Jacques Rogge, who has never been as powerful. In his third period as president, he does not need and is not pursuing re-election, and 'a lot of people owe him. He can do what he wants. When he hints at Rio so clearly, members listen'. In the lobbying circles of the Olympic bidding game, to veterans such as Voo, with years on the Olympic circuit and the international sports beat, the Chicago bid and the country's presidential pitch looked naïve and unconnected to the networks and dynamics of international sporting power and status. In December 2010, when FIFA's executive committee awarded the 2022 World Cup to Qatar (13 votes) rather than the USA (9 votes), the veteran's observations looked like predictions rather than one-off commentary.

5. Conclusion

There are threats to the mega-event roller coaster: Athens 2004 was a financial disaster, and the Olympic facilities lie neglected and unwanted beyond the edge of the city; the cost of Beijing 2008 can never be known. But the queue to host 'the world's longest commercial' (Payne 2005: 169) still forms, despite the range of charges that could be levied, during Samaranch's presidency, against the bidding process: these included prejudice, commercial opportunism, and financial corruption via demands or inducements (Miller 1992: 219). Perhaps some of the worst of these excesses have been reined in to some extent, at least those discernible to the public eye. But who really knows quite what offers might be made, for example, by the likes of Roman Abramovich on behalf of his mentor Vladimir Putin, on the 21st century equivalents of Lord de Walden's private yacht?

The London 2012 bidding victory was rooted in lobbying processes and potentially beneficial mutual interests – or at least networks of likely personal advancement and aggrandisement – and an awareness of the importance of knowledge networks such as insider organs like *Around the Rings*. Reflection on London's three Olympic Games, and the route to getting them, is a reminder of the importance of the study of elites, of the motivation of influential players in international sport politics. These might have changed over time: Lords Desborough and Burghley were patrons, rich aristocrats whose sense of public service chimed with their personal passion for sport and athletics; Lord Coe is a careerist, possibly with an eye on the presidency of the IAAF (the former International Amateur Athletics Federation, renamed the International Association of Athletics Federations) as it approaches its centenary year in 2012, the anniversary of its formation by fourth IOC president Sigfrid Edström. We can usually call upon theories of policy communities and policy networks to account for the outcomes of decision-making processes within particular societies or national political contexts, or even within international bodies such as the European Union or the United Nations. But such frameworks are less successful in accounting for the profile or bidding impact of one city or another in the race to stage and host an Olympic Games.

In Olympic circles, decisions and outcomes are less about policy than status, power, and prestige. London's successful 2012 bid combined the entrepreneurial flair and interpersonal skills of Sir Keith Mills with the naked ambition of the socially mobile and sometimes oleaginous Lord Coe, to extraordinarily successful effect. Whether the benefits or impact of the event will justify the costs of its staging will not hamper the career trajectories of such operators: the Athens disaster has not curtailed the international profile of numerous of its organisers and leaders; Billy Payne of the widely criticised Atlanta Olympics is comfortable in his role as chairman of the Augusta National Golf Club and the Master's golf major tournament, and secure in his knowledge that few are interested any longer in the cost and the impact of Atlanta 1996.

In the aftermath and afterglow of the closing ceremony in Beijing's Bird's Nest stadium in 2008, LOCOG's chairman Lord Coe looked forward to London's turn (Coe 2008). Asked what effect Great Britain's Olympic success (4th in the medal table, ahead of Germany and Australia) had on the British public's support for London 2012, he responded that the vast majority 'was captivated by Team GB and Paralympics GB's achievements . . . the welcome they received during October's Heroes Parade in London reflected that'. But London is not the 'vast majority of the nation'. Coe's abiding memories were of the 'mind-boggling . . . spectacular venues', and the 'welcome afforded to us by the people of Beijing'. The combination of genuine Chinese hospitality and volunteer grooming will be difficult to replicate in London 2012, when eager volunteers have already been disillusioned by the banal and mundane experiences that it seems might reward their keenness to volunteer. And Coe was most impressed by the 'attention to detail' in Beijing, both in the global public eye of the opening and closing ceremonies, and in the background day-to-day business of the athletes' village; there would be much to oversee in a London with no such command economy and culture on which to depend.

Getting the Games has been motivated by changing motives throughout the Olympic story. London's three Lords – Desborough, Burghley, and Coe – were all well-networked former top athletic competitors, but the first two inhabited completely different cultural worlds to that of Coe. Desborough was at his competitive peak before the modern Games were really established, while Burghley and Coe share the distinction of being champions and gold medallists of their time. But neither Desborough nor Burghley had need of a prime minister's presence in their bidding delegations. Coe embodies a different world from that of the earlier Lords, one in which Olympic hosting is not just a part of the sporting calendar, but a key element in a wider social, political, and economic project. [5] As this book went to press in 2011, 34 cities were stating an interest in bidding for the 2020 Summer Olympics. Despite doubts about national and worldwide economies, continuing concerns over the sophisticated sciences of performance-enhancement, and the sheer scale and cost of the Games, cities continue to queue for the opportunity to stage the event. Doha, in Qatar, was one of the 34, and in the wake of its triumph in gaining the 2022 men's football World Cup, that was not mere posturing. Of course, staging the biggest multi-sport event in history with 17,000 competitors and 20,000 journalists, competing in and covering 26 sports, is a very different prospect to organising a single sports event for 32 national football squads. But all evidence shows that the attraction of getting the Games in the 21st century is not diminishing, despite the bogus nature of many arguments for the benefits of staging international sporting events (DCMS 2001).

At current estimate London 2012 may be costing £11.3 billion [6], but specialist retail consultants at Washington DC's Urban Land Institute confirm the benefits of mega-events if the strategy fits the location and the moment (ULI 2011)[7]. For Russia, with its Winter Olympics at Sochi in 2014 and the men's World Cup in 2018, Prime Minister Putin can escalate his 2011 sporting budget dramatically – US$25 million in 2010 up to 1.3 billion for boosting participation, 4.3 million in 2010 up to 83.4 million for sports medicine to get Russia higher up the winter medal table on home ground than its placing in Vancouver 2010 (Grayson 2010). And enough sponsors continue to come on board despite world recession and its effects. Joel Seymour-Hide, director of sports marketing consultancy Octagon, trusts in the deep commitment that people have to sports: 'Sport tends to be relatively recession proof . . . It's an irrational love which creates more loyalty and resilience' (quoted in Black 2009: 40). This is the message from the marketeers, to sponsors ready to associate themselves with the powerful and persistent emotions of such irrationalism. London 2012 had played a memorable game in landing the event, but the burden of delivery is heavy. As Lord Coe gazed upwards, tight-lipped and pensive, at the fireworks at the Bird's Nest extravaganza that closed Beijing 2008, no prime ministerial heavyweight by his side, he looked as if he were wondering just what he had let himself in for.

Notes

1 All unreferenced direct quotations in the following section are from this source.
2 Steve Wilson is a veteran sport writer and reporter who has covered numerous Olympic Games, many for AP (Associated Press).
3 USA businesswoman Barbara Cassani, graduate of Princeton University's Master's programme in international relations, successfully initiated British Airway's budget airline, Go, before private equity owners sold it on to Easyjet. She was an acclaimed and award-winning international manager when appointed, in June 2003, to lead London's bid for the 2012 Olympics. Less than a year later she stepped down, tactfully noting that Sebastian Coe's sporting profile would be more effective in the run-in to the decision than her own managerial and administrative experience. When the IOC criticised early plans, she 'faced considerable flak for being an American fronting a British bid' (Bridge 2009).
4 UK television fans and viewers may recall that Arthur Daley was the name of the London rogue played by George Cole in the television series *Minder*. For Mills's rise from a council house in Essex to entrepreneurial heights, see Hussain (2009).

5   In sociological terms, the ascribed status of Lords Desborough and Burghley embraced a culture of duty and patronage whereby the Games were their gift to the world. The achieved status of Coe has no such rootedness, but matches the spirit of the commercialised, corporatised and controlled contemporary event, in which the Games are a gift to the host city, and, potentially, to those (often) self-aggrandising individuals who run the event. The comparison between Coe and the two earlier Lords and their times might also be usefully illuminated by the use of Bourdieu's (1986) core concept of habitus, in that the three Lords operated within circumstances and relationships that reflect not just the dominant values of their time, but the appropriateness of the specific nuances and experiences of their individual biographies.

6   See http://city-of-london.com/london-olympics-2012.html [accessed 23rd January 2011].

7   In its report *Urban Investment Opportunities of Global Events*, ULI (2011) identifies 6 key benefits for getting these events, should 'a key variable' be in place: 'the capability of the actors and managers in securing the optimum impact through focused and careful alignment of the event and its amenities with the long-term development requirements of the city'. The report also specifies 10 principles that best underpin attempts to use global events to attract urban investment, the foremost of these being the appropriate choice of event and the focus upon specific legacy or legacies right from the start.

References

Alexander, S. (2009, 17th November) 'Sir Keith Mills turns attention to America's Cup', *The Independent*, http://www.independent.co.uk/sport/general/sailing/sir-keith-mills-turns-attention-to-americas-cup-1821686.html [accessed 21st January 2011].

Around the Rings (2010) 'About us', http://www.aroundtherings.com/about-us.aspx [accessed March 28th 2010].

Baker, K. (2008) *The 1908 Olympics*, Cheltenham: SportsBooks.

Beckett, I.F.W. (2004) 'Grenfell, William Henry, Baron Desborough (1855–1945)', *Oxford Dictionary of National Biography*, Oxford University Press, Sept 2004; online edn, May 2009 [http://www.oxforddnb.com/view/article/33566, accessed 23 March 2010].

Black, E. (2009, 7th December) 'How sports fans can turn defeat into a victory for the economy', *London Evening Standard*, p. 40.

Bolz, D. (2010) 'The 1948 Olympics: The eve of Europe's reconstruction', presentation at symposium on 'Sport and the Transformation of Modern Europe', *Sport in Modern Europe Network*, Pembroke College, Cambridge, England, http://www.sport-in-europe.group.cam.ac.uk/symposium3summaries.htm [accessed 26th March 2010].

Bose, M. (2010, 9th February) 'The big interview: Lord Coe interview', *London Evening Standard, standard.co.uk*, http://www.thisislondon.co.uk/standard-sport/article-23803707-the-big-interview-lord-coe.do [accessed 21st January 2011].

Bourdieu, P. (1986) *Distinction: A Social Critique of the Judgement of Taste*, London: Routledge and Kegan Paul.

Bridge, S. (2009, 12th July) 'The interview: Barbara Cassani', *Financial Mail Women's Forum*, http://www.fmwf.com/features/2009/07/the-interview-barbara-cassani/ [accessed 21st January 2011].

Coe, S. (2008, October-November-December) 'Sebastian Coe: LOCOG Chairman' (an interview) in 'Legacy' section, *Olympic Review: Official Publication of the Olympic Movement*, Issue 69: 87.

Cook, T. A. ['drawn up by'] (1909) *The Fourth Olympiad Being The Official Report of the Olympic Games of 1908 Celebrated in London Under the Patronage of His Most Gracious Majesty King Edward VII And by the Sanction of The International Olympic Committee, drawn up by Theodora Andrea Cook and issued under the authority of The British Olympic Council, Published by The British Olympic Association*, London.

DCMS (2001) Examination of Witness Professor Alan Tomlinson, House of Commons Select Committee on the Staging of International Sporting Events, Thursday March 8th 2001, www.culture.gov.uk/pdf/cm5288.pdf [accessed March 23rd 2010].

Grayson, M. (2011, 18th January) 'Spending skyrockets for Russian sports development', *Around the Rings*, 18th January.

Hampton, J. (2008) *The Austerity Olympics: When the Games Came to London in 1948*, London: Aurum Press Ltd.

Hussain, A. (2009, 13th September) 'Fame and fortune: Sir Keith Mills', *The Sunday Times*, http://www.timesonline.co.uk/tol/money/investment/article6831849.ece [accessed 21st January 2011].

Jenkins, R. (2008) *The First London Olympics 1908*, London: Piatkus Books.

Jennings, A. (1996) *The New Lords of the Rings: Olympic Corruption and How to Buy Gold Medals*, London: Simon & Schuster.

Jennings, A. and Sambrook, C. (2000) *The Great Olympic Swindle: When the World Wanted its Games Back*, London: Simon & Schuster.

Jennings, A. (2007, 22nd October) 'FIFA and Coe', *Panorama*, London: BBC.

Kent, G. (2008) *Olympic Follies: The Madness and Mayhem of the 1908 London Games: A Cautionary Tale*, London: JR Books.

Lee, M. (2006) *The Race for the 2012 Olympics: The Inside Story of How London Won the Bid* (with Adrian Warner and David Bond), London: Virgin Books Ltd.

Lenskyj, H. J. (2000) *Inside the Olympic Industry: Power, Politics, and Activism*, Albany, NY: State University of New York Press.

McWhirter, N. (2004) 'Cecil, David George Brownlow, sixth Marquess of Exeter (1905–1981)', *Oxford Dictionary of National Biography*, Oxford University Press, 2004; online edn, Oct 2005 [http://www.oxforddnb.com/view/article/30910, accessed 26 March 2010].

Matthew, H. C. G. (2004) 'Asquith, Herbert Henry, first Earl of Oxford and Asquith (1852–1928)', *Oxford Dictionary of National Biography*, Oxford University Press, 2004; online edn, Jan 2011 [http://www.oxforddnb.com/view/article/30483, accessed 18 Jan 2011].

Miller, D. (1992) *Olympic Revolution: The Olympic Biography of Juan Antonio Samaranch*, London: Pavilion Books Ltd.

Miller, D. (2008) *The Official History of the Olympic Games and the IOC: Athens to Beijing, 1894–2008*, Edinburgh and London: Mainstream Publishing.

(The) Organising Committee for the XIV Olympiad London 1948 (1951) *The Official Report of the Organising Committee for the XIV Olympiad*, London.

Owen, D. (2010, 17th March) 'Exclusive: Coe replaced as head of FIFA Ethics Commission', *Inside the Games: The Inside Track on World Sport*, http://www.insidethegames.biz/summer-olympics/2012/9216-coe-replaced-as-head-of-fifa-ethics-commission [accessed 21st January 2011].

Payne, M. (2005) *Olympic Turnaround: How the Olympic Games Stepped Back from the Brink of Extinction to Become the World's Best-known Brand – and a Multi-billion Dollar Global Franchise*, Twyford, Berks: London Business Press.

Phillips, B. (2007) *The 1948 Olympics: How London Rescued the Games*, Cheltenham: SportsBooks Ltd:.

Symson, V. and Jennings, A. (1992) *The Lords of the Rings: Power, Money and Drugs in the Modern Olympics*, London: Simon & Schuster.

Tomlinson, A. (2008) 'Olympic Values, Beijing's Olympic Games, and the Universal

Market', in M. E. Price and D. Dayan (eds) *Owning the Olympics: Narratives of the New China*, Ann Arbor: The University of Michigan Press.

ULI (2011) *Urban Investment Opportunities of Global Events*, London: ULI Europe.

Wallechinsky, D. and Loucky, J. (2008) *The Complete Book of the Olympics 2008 Edition*, London: Aurum Press.

Primary sources

IOC executive and sessional minutes and reports, the Olympic Museum, Lausanne.
Interviews with anonymous international sports reporter.

2

THE IDEALS OF THE FOUNDING FATHER

Mythologised, evolved or betrayed?

Lincoln Allison

> At Easter, in 1927, among the age-old ruins of Olympia, the Greek Minister of Public Instruction removed the sheeting that covered a monument commemorating the restoration of the Olympic Games. As he honoured me by recalling past events, my thoughts turned to Kingsley and Arnold, and to the chapel at Rugby where the great clergyman rests who was, as I see it, one of the founders of athletic chivalry.
>
> (De Coubertin 2000: 515)

Circus Maximus Modernus: a world professional Games

By the 1850s organised games as commercial entertainment were developing rapidly in the Anglophone world. There were vast attendances at English race meetings – occasions of 'vice and hideousness' as Matthew Arnold was to call them (Arnold 1993: 70). The stars of the All-England cricket XI were also attracting increasing numbers, particularly when they competed as individuals in single-wicket competition. Across the Atlantic, in New York, baseball was demonstrating similarly growing markets for games as commercial entertainment. A shrewd observer, noting the possibilities created by the steam railway, the telegraph and the mechanical lawnmower, might have easily concluded that both countries were on the brink of an era of gladiatorial entertainment. In particular, given the pace of globalisation in the 1850s, and given the relative ease with which the concept of organised games could cross borders, he or she might have envisaged the evolution of a World Games. It might be a festival held every year or every two years (four would be unattractive commercially) and would incorporate the world's most popular and spectacular games and physical feats. There would be all kinds of fighting, the racing of mechanical devices at high speeds, perhaps composite forms of football and of baseball/cricket, a series of tests to determine the world's

strongest man, *very* high diving, boomerang throwing and perhaps the reintro-
duction of the forms of aquatic fighting which so pleased Roman crowds. There
would be dancing girls and beauty contests and gambling on a suitably vast scale.

The development of a modernised Roman Circus was, of course, stymied and
its tendencies were limited, slowed and cast to the peripheries of cultural power,
at least until the invention of television. In the English case the phenomenon was
to persist well into the television age. D.J. Taylor, in his essay on the 'Corinthian
spirit', reports on his own contempt when his father took him to a professional
athletics meeting in the 1970s, and something similar was true of many people's
perceptions of rugby – including my own (Taylor 2006: 103–105). In its pomp, to
be 'amateur' was glamorous, prestigious, international; to be 'professional' on the
other hand was lowly and local. If there was a single reason why we reacted in this
way it was because the BBC had presented us with the assumption that gentleman
amateurs were the superior product. The perception of amateur superiority was
most dominant in England, but it affected many other societies to a lesser degree,
albeit the United States least of all.

From almost the outset modern games were to be dressed in the clothes of Greek
religiosity rather than those of Roman populism; for at least a century most sport
was to be subject to what I have called an 'amateur hegemony' (Allison 2001:
49–71). If there was a single year in which we can locate the triumph of these
tendencies it must be 1857. In that year the Indian 'mutiny' was defeated, leading
to the re-definition of the British Empire from a set of commercial networks to a
set of formal political institutions with an ethical mission. It was also the year in
which Thomas Hughes's *Tom Brown's Schooldays* was published, a vastly influential
novel the effects of which included a French aristocrat seventy years later thinking
about an English school while standing at a Greek historic site.

This chain of events, which gave us 'athletic chivalry' rather than gladiatorial
entertainment, is well documented, not least by Pierre de Coubertin, founder of
the Modern Olympics (De Coubertin 2000). Athletic chivalry can be defined by
its two component parts: the athletic is defined by de Coubertin's own expression of '*Citius, Altius, Fortius*', meaning 'faster, higher, stronger' and chivalry by
Arnold's conception of 'gentlemanly conduct', a phrase which has echoed down
the generations from the Doctor's sermons to the rulebook of FIFA in the twenty
first century. It has defined the real world games, which are in many respects as far
from being a world games based on the idea of entertainment as it is possible to
be. Most of what happens in the Modern Olympics has no real commercial
existence, nor much real commercial potential: which facts are fairly obvious if,
away from the Olympic context, you look at the market value of the television
rights in shooting, swimming, rowing, gymnastics and so forth. Even the core
Olympic sport, track and field athletics, is outside the top ten of sports commercially and would surely have to be radically reshaped if it were to have these
aspirations. Its 'blue riband' event – the 100 metres sprint – may be something that
most sports fans want to see, but lasting less than ten seconds it constitutes a tiny
sliver of entertainment. It is not punters yearning for entertainment which funds

the Modern Olympics, but governments and nations yearning for the prestige to be gained from activities which they consider to be much more significant than mere entertainment.

French leadership, English ideas, Greek dressing

In a typical passage, written in 1897, de Coubertin summarises the re-invention of athleticism in England and is worth quoting at length:

> The story of the physical renaissance in England is a curious tale to tell. Whatever the taste and zeal of the English in a former age for manly sports, there is no denying that the 18th century had made a clean sweep of it. The only places frequented by students were taverns and dives where they played cards. At Eton, some exercises did attract a few adepts, and Wellington was able to claim that the battle of Waterloo had been won 'on the playing fields of Eton'. But that was nothing more than an isolated incident. Besides, can one really compare these coarse amusements, marked by such brutality, with modern athleticism which is – you will forgive me for going, once more, against the grain of deep-rooted prejudices – a school of savoir-faire and social refinement? Look in Dr. Johnson's dictionary. Under the word *Athletic*, you will find a definition that shows that the very meaning of the culture of physical strength through exercise had been lost. Historians will put Canon Kingsley, and his group of 'Christian athletes' who professed and put into practice the adage *mens sana in corpore sano*, in the forefront of those who rediscovered this meaning. At the same time, the great Arnold appealed to athleticism, making it his most powerful ally at the restored Rugby. A few years later, the first athletic club was established at Exeter College, Oxford (1850). Five years after that, St. John's College, Cambridge, stepped to the fore in its own right. In 1857, Cambridge had an athletic federation, and its students organised competitions. In 1864, the first of the famous inter-scholastic meets took place, the results of which are now telegraphed from one end of the world to the other. The *Times* published just two scant lines on the results in a remote corner of the paper, which was otherwise filled with the somber details of the war between Denmark and Germany.
>
> How times have changed! 'From the furthest ends of the Australian pastures to the ranches of Texas, from the Pampas of South America to the plateaus of the Himalayas, around the Kraals of southern Africa and in the marketplaces of China and Japan, groups gather to hear the story of the battles of strength and endurance that take place on the Isis and the Cam . . .. (De Coubertin 2000: 282)

Elsewhere (p. 140) de Coubertin reports a conversation with W.E. Gladstone about the lack of athleticism at Eton in the early nineteenth century and expresses a scepticism about the authenticity (as opposed to the significance) of the famous Wellington quotation.

De Coubertin was often accused in France of 'Anglomania' and it is useful for him to be able to argue that the *athletisme* which he proposes so passionately is not typically or endemically English, despite the development of its modernised form taking place almost exclusively in England. It is the product of a reforming movement in society and education which has a reactionary dimension – in a good sense – insofar as it revives ideas of honour and chivalry which otherwise seem to have little place in a commercial society. Athleticism is about this potentially global movement and it has developed in England despite the coarse, 'John Bull', aspects of English culture; de Coubertin often asserts that the French will soon overtake the English in athletic matters.

All of this puts a good deal of historic work onto the shoulders of a handful of English educationalists and particularly Thomas Arnold. De Coubertin mentions Arnold on more than forty occasions in his published work, though some of these are reportage or the transcription of his editors, and in most of them he is *'le grand'*: the great Arnold, the great educationalist, the great headmaster. The references to Charles Kingsley (1819–75) are few and perfunctory by comparison. Yet it was Kingsley, Canon of Chester Cathedral and Regius Professor of Modern History at Cambridge as well as one of the most successful novelists of his age, who saw himself as training 'Christian athletes' and in reference to whom the term 'muscular Christianity' was coined (Vance 2004). De Coubertin had read *Tom Brown*, though, and visited Rugby; in any case, he could argue that Arnold was the true pioneer, a generation earlier than Kingsley.

De Coubertin's *'Jeux Arnoldiens'* became the Modern Olympics, but he makes it clear that the Hellenistic dressing, essential for dealing with the Greeks in respect of the 1896 games, is to be played down in the longer term. Of the meetings in 1897 he wrote:

> . . . the Hellenism that had permeated the atmosphere of the first Congress in 1894 started to fade before the influence of England . . . It was to Arnold that we turned, more or less consciously, for inspiration. (de Coubertin 2000: 372)

The most substantive element of this non-Hellenism was de Coubertin's insistence that the Games should move between host cities and not be held on a permanent Greek site. Thus one source of an understanding of the derivation of Olympic ideals would be the thoughts and milieu of Thomas Arnold. The difficulty arises that there are at least four Thomas Arnolds:

1. The real historical figure. Here I accept Herbert Butterfield's caution about the 'impossibility of history': we can never *know* historical figures because, even if they wrote a lot, we cannot know how much they dissembled, whether consciously or unconsciously (Butterfield 1924, 1931). Historians and biographers 'construct' their characters as novelists do, though according to different rules.

2. Thomas Hughes' construction of the Doctor in *Tom Brown's Schooldays*. The novel presents the unusual problem of an historical character who becomes far more famous in a work of fiction than he was or would have been otherwise.

Macbeth would be another example, except that Shakespeare makes no effort to be fair to the historical Macbeth whereas Hughes wants to write the Arnoldian gospel. So the differences between the historical and literary Arnolds are relatively slight. The important point is that Hughes himself was a far greater enthusiast for athleticism than was Arnold, even on Hughes's own account. Hughes's Christianity often sounds a good deal more muscular than Christian, as in his notorious defence of boys' fighting:

> . . . don't say 'No' because you fear a licking, and say or think it's because you fear God, for that's neither Christian nor honest. And if you do fight, fight it out; and don't give in while you can stand and see. (Hughes 1857/1999: 302)

Whereas the Doctor is hardly ever mentioned in the context of games; one of very few occasions is during Tom's first 'football' match: 'The Doctor and some of his family are there looking on, and seem as anxious as any boy for the success of the School-house' (Hughes 1857/1999: 107).

3. The prototype of an important movement for educational and social reform, the archetypal 'Victorian headmaster'. This is a version of Arnold even though most of Arnold's career was pre-Victorian. Other schools and later periods contained accounts of virtue which were markedly different in emphasis. De Coubertin visited most of the 'Clarendon' schools and both the ancient universities and admired aspects of all of them, but took Arnold as his personal symbol of the qualities he admired. There are, it must be noted, strong suggestions from some twentieth century social historians that his emphasis on Arnold was entirely misplaced. J.A. Mangan, for example, argues that:

> It must be made quite clear that the conviction that Arnold was responsible for the 'athletic sports system' of the public schools, although widely held, is, in the unmerciful expression of a recent commentator, a 'specific erroneous belief'. It does not accord with the evidence and should be firmly rejected. (Mangan 1981: 16)

Mangan gives much more attention the other Victorian headmasters such as C. J. Vaughan of Harrow (appointed in 1845) and Edward Thring of Uppingham (appointed in 1853); these two – and others – were far more enthusiastic about organised games than was Arnold and much more pro-active in ensuring their place in their schools. But the most obvious response to Mangan's argument is that the core ideas of modern organised games, as well as the antecedents of several different games, were developed by the *boys* at Rugby during Arnold's regime (which ended with his death in 1842). Rule books, white lines, captains, leather balls and many other features of modern games evolved in this period and it was 'the Doctor' who created the space for such evolution, both literally and metaphorically. And it was Arnold who insisted on the marriage of games with 'gentlemanly conduct'. Thus, I would argue that alumni of Rugby School such as Thomas Hughes, Richard Sykes and Thomas Wentworth Wills were both earlier and more important in their missionary work for games than were Mangan's headmasters. Hughes spread the word with his global bestseller, which is what brought Coubertin to Rugby. Sykes took the oval ball to the United States and Wills to Australia, where he re-invented rugby as the 'game of our own', Australian Rules[1].

4. The cipher for everything that de Coubertin believed and the symbolic inverse of everything that he believed to be wrong with French education and society. The greatest single *bête noire* for Coubertin was Félix-Antoine-Philibert Dupanloup (1802–78), Bishop of Orleans, Academician and author of *De L'Education* (1850). Dupanloup believed that education should teach a rigorous catholic faith and a narrow version of the classics. Above all, it should teach children the habits of obedience. In de Coubertin's mind nobody symbolised what was wrong with France and what was holding back French youth more than Dupanloup. Arnold therefore has a meaning and an attraction as the anti-Dupanloup.

Arnold, just as much as Christ or Marx, became the origin and exemplar of movements which were in many respects alien to his own beliefs. His disciple, Hughes, was the principal, if inadvertent, instrument of this transition. ('Disciple' is more than mere analogy here: in the later stages of *Tom Brown's Schooldays* there is a suggestion that the love of the headmaster is a proper stage on the journey to the love of Christ.) The Doctor was a Christian Whig; his disciple was a Christian Socialist. Arnold was an opponent of most of what constituted British imperialism in his own time, actively and especially of transportation to Australia and the plantation system in the West Indies. But the public schools, whose status he did more to enhance than any other single individual, became something like staff colleges of imperialism. He did much to revive the noble, ethical aspirations implicit in the word 'gentleman' in a capitalist society, but forty years after his death the Amateur Rowing Association was using that word to mean not-a-manual-worker.

Even the novel *Tom Brown's Schooldays* arguably experienced a twofold moral decay. It created a genre, the 'school story', but the thousands of imitators were, at best, imitators of only the second quarter of the book in which Tom establishes his place on the games field and vanquishes the bully Flashman. They did not imitate the second half of the book which features near-death experiences and spiritual transformations and in which the robust Tom learns the true meaning of Christian piety from the saintly and sickly George Arthur.

It is clear, and important to note, that for none of the Toms – Hughes, Arnold and Brown – was excellence at games of much importance or the results of games of any importance at all. Boys must play and they must try their best; they must stay within not only the rules, but also within the spirit of the game. But if they do those things it doesn't matter whether they win or not. 'Tom's Last Match' is a defeat. Our hero loses – and our author assumes that we will be not in the least bit perturbed by this. In every school story written since with which I am familiar the hero wins – and his winning can be taken to exemplify and reward his virtue.

But it would be wrong to think that the nature and value of games is presented unambiguously in those stories. There is debate and contest, as is exemplified in this example from when the genre was still at its peak, *Play Up, Buffs!*, written by a prolific and successful author of such stories, Herbert Hayens, and published in 1925:

> 'The kids are in high spirits,' observed Bruce, chatting with a group of seniors; 'I hope they won't be in the dumps at the end of the afternoon.'
>
> 'It's a pity they make such a fuss about it,' remarked Broadhurst quietly.
>
> 'Oh, come, old chap, naturally they want us to win; don't you?'
>
> 'Well, on the whole,' replied Broadhurst with a smile, 'I'd prefer that you knocked Barry and his merry men. All the same this sports rivalry is getting too serious, becoming a regular business instead of a pleasant game. We'll soon be as bad as the Americans.'
>
> 'Wish we were half as good,' Pierce chipped in; 'they're sweeping the board everywhere, breaking records like eggs.'
>
> 'That's just it – breaking records! I don't blame the pros.; it's their livelihood, and they have to make good the same as a prize-fighter or they won't draw the crowd. But what gets me is that we're egging on our amateurs to do just the same. It's getting to be a pure business stunt and very soon we'll have no sport left.' (Hayens 1925: 50–51)

Of course, the match is won – and Broadhurst himself turns out to be an excellent sportsman. The connection with the 1924 Paris Games and with the content of *Chariots of Fire* is irrefutable since it must have provided the prime experience that either the author or his characters would have had of American competitors.

Athleticism, chivalry and excess

In 1887 de Coubertin quoted Arnold as saying, 'I wish to form Christian gentlemen; my goal is to teach children to govern themselves which is far better than governing them myself' (de Coubertin 200: 107). Political theorists might well see this as an example of the second and third faces of power: you show you are truly self-governing by behaving as a Christian gentleman, which is, incidentally, what the headmaster wants you to be. English educational theory has been dominated ever since by the aspiration to maximise the autonomy of the educated individual, where autonomy tends to be measured according to the ability to choose prescribed courses of action. But in terms of organised games the autonomy was much more indubitable than this. At Rugby it was the boys, not the masters, who drew up and published books of rules for games; it was the boys who organised events; it was the boys, not the school, who paid for the 'Green' Pavilion in 1841 and who raised the money for various experimental rackets courts and this was the way funding worked until well after Arnold's death. So far as he was concerned this was a legitimate expression of their capacity for self-organisation and an outlet for their energies: he asked only that they behaved like gentlemen. But it was no more than that: physical activity was necessary, but it was not especially virtuous or valuable.

Coubertin, on the other hand, valued physical education and physical achievement *per se*. He understood the drive to win: he may have commented approvingly on the Bishop of Pennsylvania's suggestion that it was the taking part, not the winning, that mattered at the 1908 Games, but much of what he said elsewhere implied a very different emphasis. It was his insistence that the games were always about 'faster, higher, stronger' and he frequently defended practices which stern amateurs saw as 'excess'. In 1901 he wrote:

> Among those who do have (the spirit of sport), not all reach the limits of what they can achieve. Not all seek out fear in order to overcome it, fatigue to triumph over it, and difficulty to master it. Yet there seem to be more of these individuals than one might think at first glance. As a result, one can draw this conclusion: today, as in times past, the tendency of sport is towards excess. It aims at more speed, greater height, more strength . . . always more.
>
> That is its drawback, in terms of human balance, but so be it! That is also its nobility – and its poetry. (de Coubertin 2000: 148)

This is a pretty good statement of what our contemporary theorists would call 'the performance principle' (Hoberman 1992) – and I submit that de Coubertin's distinction between the 'spirit of sport' and the 'tendency of sport' is a useful analytical tool now as then. We know that he disapproved of the pedantries of disqualifying a great athlete like Jim Thorpe from the 1912 Games because he had been paid for playing baseball, and of the petty nationalism which led American journalists (in 1908 as in 2008) to print medals tables which showed the USA in first place even though nobody else's did. (In 1908 they did it by excluding 'less masculine' events like archery [Dobbs 1973: 159–164], in 2008 by simply totalling the number of medals irrespective of colour.) His disapproval of those who demonstrated an absence of magnanimity to fellow competitors, whether as winners or losers, was unswerving. It is not clear that he would have disapproved of 'drug cheats': provided the same rules applied to everybody, he left room, certainly, to see many forms of the enhancement of performance as legitimate excess, part of the tendency of sport.

De Coubertin had a freestanding belief in athleticism; irrespective of any other values he thought that physical activity and discipline made young males happier and freer. In the French case he saw it also as necessary to the 'toughening up' of the nation which was in turn necessary for a national revival. The argument that French education is excessively intellectual and insufficiently physical was an old one and it can be found, for example in one of Montaigne's most famous essays, 'De l'institution des enfants', written four centuries previously (Montaigne 1999: 62–106). Athleticism, in other words, was good with or without chivalry and de Coubertin might have found himself closer to Kingsley than to the revered and much-quoted Arnold. Kingsley's conception of the 'Christian athlete' prescribed physical fitness as a necessary condition of evangelism and as a supporter and confidant of Darwin Kingsley had a transcendent, if confused, sense of the value of 'fitness' (Vance 2004).

But if de Coubertin was a sportsman who valued the athletic and a French patriot who sought to foster national revival, he was also an aristocrat who believed in chivalry as a counter-value to the materialist values of commercialism and the grey egalitarianism of socialism. Thus he was delighted to find chivalry reborn – and in the most commercial of societies – under the names of 'sportsmanship' and 'gentlemanly conduct'. That much is clear: he invoked and praised chivalry all his life. What is much less clear is what he meant by it. *La chevalerie* in French has some of the ambiguities of 'gentleman' in English: it can suggest either moral worth or social status, though with perhaps an even greater nuance of ancient virtue. *Chevalier* is a word still used in the bestowing of honours in the modern French Republic. It is interesting, in this context, to recall Alexis De Tocqueville's remark that the word *gentilhomme* in French – the literal equivalent of 'gentleman' but with a heavier emphasis on social status – became risible and semi-obsolete after the Revolution (De Tocqueville 2000: 590–596). 'Chivalry' clearly suggests something 'higher' than mere commercialism or the pursuit of self-interest. It is an essential part of the appeal of sport that these 'higher' aspects should be part of it; this 'beyond', as we might call it, defines sportsmen as well as heroes. But what is it? And how would we know about it?

That de Coubertin is seeking a kind of beyondness in sport is evident in his insistent religiosity, including his constant assertions of the closeness between art and sport, and religion and sport; plus his insistence on the 'spiritual' dimensions of games exemplified by such gestures as the 'Hymn to Apollo' sung at the first IOC Congress. But 'chivalry', though exemplified, is never given ethical clarification. De Coubertin is not alone in this failing: the entire medievalism of the late Hanoverians and Victorians in art, literature and architecture suggests that we should look to the Middle Ages for something beyond commerce and self-interest, but is extremely reticent on the question of what the virtues are that go with the lances and pennants and armour. One of the earliest and most influential expressions of the medieval fashion was Sir Walter Scott's *Ivanhoe*. It is one of the most likely books for Thomas Hughes and his contemporaries to have read; and those boys, who drew up some of the first rulebooks in modern sport, must have known Scott's lengthy descriptions of medieval tourneys. But Scott is whimsical, mystical and ironic on the subject of the ethics of chivalry. When Rebecca of York asks Ivanhoe why he is risking his life when it seems irrational to do so, he replies:

> Rebecca . . . thou knowest not how impossible it is for one trained to actions of chivalry to remain passive as a priest, or a woman, when they are acting deeds of honour around him. The love of battle is the food upon which we live – the dust of the *mêlée* is the breath of our nostrils! We live not – we wish not to live – longer than while we are victorious and renowned. Such,

maiden, are the laws of chivalry to which we are sworn, and to which we offer all that we hold dear. (Scott 1997: 317)

The knight's answer seems to lie somewhere between 'There are some things a man has to do' and 'Girls wouldn't understand'. Victory and renown are the stuff of personal status, not of higher values. Most of what Ivanhoe is expressing is a preference for action over thought – much like de Coubertin's preference for physicality. Scott in fact offers us a kind of politically correct irony because the one person in the novel who is deeply spiritual and courageously steadfast to deontological ethics is Rebecca herself, who is female and Jewish.

There does not seem to be a coherent account of what 'chivalry' means ethically. But that does not make it meaningless: just as the minimal meaning of 'Arnold' for de Coubertin was 'anti-Dupanloup' the minimal meaning of 'chivalry' is 'anti-commerce' or 'anti-selfishness'. Or, as Tom Brown accepts it, when contemplating a future after Rugby, 'doing some real good. . .not mere money-making' (Hughes 1857/1999: 363).

The problem of amateurism

Superficially, de Coubertin's views on amateurism seem highly contradictory. In 1894, at the first Congress of the IOC, he argued that:

> We must uphold the noble and chivalrous character of athleticism, which has distinguished it in the past, so that it may continue to play the admirable role in the education of modern peoples that was attributed to it by the Greek masters. Human imperfection always tends to transform the Olympic athlete into a circus gladiator. A choice must be made between these two incompatible approaches to athletics. To defend us against the spirit of gain and professionalism that threatens to invade them, amateurs in most countries have established complex legislation that is replete with compromise and contradiction . . . The issues placed on the agenda of this Congress deal with the compromises and contradictions that persist in amateur regulations. (de Coubertin 2000: 299)

In his memoirs, in relation to the Paris Games of 1900, he said:

> Personally, convinced as I am that amateurism is one of the first conditions of the prosperity of sport, I have never ceased to work for it; and when in 1894 I proposed to revive the Olympic Games, it was with the idea that they would always be reserved for amateurs only. (de Coubertin 2000: 385)

And in 1901, in a letter to Charles Simon dealing with the question of an Olympic oath, he appeared to contradict himself within a sentence:

> Our reaction must be based on adopting a more intelligent, broader, and certainly narrower, definition of an amateur. (de Coubertin 2000: 599)

These three quotations – and many others – make him sound like a full supporter of the Anglophone elite version of what I have called the amateur hegemony.

But, taken as a whole, his position was far more complex and the issue was the bane of his life as he had to try to reconcile the very different practices and attitudes which were being applied in different countries and different sports. To this end the IOC constructed a number of surveys of its constituents on the details of amateurism, including an extensive one in 1914 (de Coubertin 2000: 653–657) which only confirmed how divided they were on the subject. He himself was strongly in favour of the training of professional physical educationalists – including degree level work at universities – which was anathema to the purists (and still has its opponents in the twenty first century). He was also keen to allow the military to parade such professional skills as riding, shooting and fencing at the Games, which must be the thin end of a logical wedge into the idea of amateurism. He regarded the disqualification of Jim Thorpe, 'the world's greatest athlete', from the 1912 Games for accepting payment for playing baseball as an embarrassment for the Olympic Movement. He was quoted in 1928 as saying that amateur regulations were a 'ludicrous obstacle' for the development of sport. And in his memoirs, looking back on the establishment of the Modern Games, he referred to:

> Amateurism, an admirable mummy that could be presented at the museum of Boulak as a specimen of the modern art of embalming! Half a century has gone by without it seeming to have suffered in any way from the unceasing manipulations to which it has been submitted. It seems intact. Not one of us expected it to have lasted so long. (de Coubertin 2000: 315)

All of which seem to place him at a good distance from the fanatically clear enthusiasm for amateurism in its technical sense which was to be demonstrated by Avery Brundage as President of the IOC from 1952 to 1972.

Part of the reconciliation of these apparent contradictions lies in de Coubertin's position as a forceful pragmatist who wanted to get his games on and had to pacify a wide variety of people, with very different opinions, in order to do so. But a more logical resolution is also possible, based on the complexity of the concept of amateurism. In an earlier book on the subject, I suggested that amateurism has at least three dimensions, which can be summarised as follows (Allison 2001: 3–16):

1. Spiritual/philosophical: doing things for the love of them (etymological) or as ends-in-themselves.
2. Social: the ability to afford sports and games, even intense ones, as leisure pursuits.
3. Financial: the absence of payment or other material reward.

De Coubertin strongly favoured amateurism in its spiritual dimension. He did not like the Anglophone insistence on an essentially social meaning for amateurism, not least because it offended against the universal aspirations of the Olympic movement. And he was exasperated by the constant arguments about the regulatory issues raised by financial definitions of amateurism. These included questions of expenses and 'broken time', the question of whether a professional could revert to amateur status, the issue of a professional in one sport being considered an amateur in another and so on. For de Coubertin, the wonderful spirit of chivalry does not reduce comfortably to a set of regulations about expenses claims!

However, there is another aspect of this issue which puts de Coubertin firmly in the amateur camp, at least in the spiritual sense. He may have been an exasperated moderate on the financial issues of professionalism when compared with the Rugby Football Union or the Amateur Rowing Association or Avery Brundage, but he was much less equivocal on the subject of commercialism, fearing all the implications of large crowds and gate-taking stadiums. Speaking in 1928, he said:

> Stadiums are being built unwisely all over the place. Those curious enough to leaf through the nine volumes of the *Revue Olympique* during the years when it was a monthly publication, the official publication of the International Olympic Committee, would find warnings against athletics as a show, and the eventual consequences of that approach – articles written eighteen, twenty and twenty two years ago. At the time I said that once seats for forty thousand spectators are built, you have to fill them, and that means drawing a crowd. To draw that crowd, you will need a publicity campaign, and to justify that publicity campaign you will have to draw sensational numbers . . . Yes, I said these things over and over again, but no one listened to me. Almost all the stadiums built in recent years are the result of local and, too often, commercial interests, not Olympic interests at all. (de Coubertin 2000: 184)

It should be noted that it is a journalist's summary of de Coubertin's statement and is more extreme in its language than most of his written work, but it does refer to a consistent position and is included in the official IOC version of his writings. As with the broader issue of amateurism in general, de Coubertin seems here to be a pragmatist unconcerned with logical contradictions as such. He wanted his games to be successful and to seem to be successful, which required large stadia. But, in general, he wanted young men, especially, to participate in sports and games rather than to watch them: the consequent issue of a large stadium which is very important for three weeks but not thereafter echoes down to our own times.

De Coubertin was not the only enthusiastic amateur who thought that the details of defining professionalism were not important. I have argued elsewhere that many unimpeachable amateurs and ethical enthusiasts for amateurism have expressed tolerance for the Jim Thorpe level of professionalism, but have regarded commercialism as the true antithesis of amateurism in its important sense (Allison 2001). That some people should make a living out of what for most is a leisure activity has proved more tolerable to amateurs than has the idea that sport should be redefined as commercial entertainment – and, in any case, some sports, notably cricket and racket games, entered modernity with a tolerance of professionalism and an idea of symbiosis between the amateur and the professional.

The origins and development of Olympic ideals

Both Thomas Arnold and Pierre de Coubertin defined their lives in terms of a number of projects, though these projects overlapped to a much lesser extent than one might assume given the number of occasions on which de Coubertin refers to Arnold and the reverential nature of most of those references. Arnold was an educationalist, evangelist and social reformer who approved of the games his pupils organised as an outlet for their energies, but also as a means by which they learned self-discipline and cooperation. De Coubertin was an aristocrat and sportsman who wanted to revive the physical in culture and, therefore, in education and who wanted to revive and 'toughen up' France. It is fair to speculate that if both had been able to foresee the triumph of competitive sport and organised games in the twentieth century de Coubertin would have been excited, but the Doctor would have been left cold. On the other hand both de Coubertin and Arnold's great interpreter, Thomas Hughes, saw sports and games as spiritual activities, with connections and analogies to religion. Sport as commercial entertainment was an abhorrent idea though, given the Doctor's death in 1842, it was left to his son Matthew to express that abhorrence. Games were justified by their uplifting of the human spirit and de Coubertin was always searching-out religious and artistic dressings and justifications for sport, perhaps most risibly in his own 'Ode to Sport' composed for the Stockholm Games in 1912 and entered successfully under a pseudonym for the poetry competition:

> O Sport, delight of the Gods, distillation of life!
> In the grey dingle of modern existence, restless with barren toil, you suddenly appeared like the shining messenger of vanished ages, those ages when humanity could smile. And to the mountain tops came dawn's first glimmer, and sunbeams dappled the forest's gloomy floor. (de Coubertin 2000: 629)

The remaining eight stanzas equate sport with Beauty . . . Justice . . . Daring . . . Honour . . . Joy . . . Fecundity . . . Progress . . . and Peace. In case anybody imagines that this was merely nineteenth century aristocratic fantasy, they should consider the 'Spirit of Sport' as it is defined by the World Anti-Doping Agency in the twenty first century in their justification of stringent regulations against performance-enhancing substances:

The spirit of sport is the celebration of the human spirit, body and mind
. . . . (It is characterised by) ethics, fair play and honesty; health; excellence
in performance; character and education; fun and joy; teamwork; dedication
and commitment; respect for rules and laws; respect for self and other
participants; community and solidarity. (Beamish and Ritchie 2006: 111)

A sceptical hypothesis might suggest that these *Coubertiniste* objectives remain in
twenty first century sport as a kind of empty ideological shell, like contemporary
Chinese Marxism. After all, much of what Avery Brundage, President of the IOC
from 1952 to 1972, had defined as the necessary regulatory implementation of
Olympic ethics disappeared in the 1980s. The 1984 'free enterprise games' in Los
Angeles which introduced full commercial sponsorship and broadcasting coincided
with the presidency of Juan Antonio Samaranch which allowed professional
athletes to compete at the games. The dynamic force behind these changes, which
had already had a major effect on the running of most sports, was television and
the image of billions of spectators passively watching hundreds of professional
athletes compete would have appalled almost anyone who could be considered to
be a founding father of modern sporting institutions. The spirit of the games had
also changed: a distinguished athlete who competed in three Olympiads told me
that, whereas in 1976 the Games still seemed to be about talented young people
for whom sport was a prolegomenon – however useful – to their careers, by 1984
the prevailing ethos was dominated by professional athletes for whom the Games
were a major event, but by no means the only major event (Allison 2001: 98–107).

But one could also argue that the essential spirit of sport *has* survived and that
the contradiction between commerce and sport assumed by French aristocrats or
English clergymen is an unreal contradiction (and less likely to be assumed by
Americans in any case). A yearning, at least, for 'chivalry' and 'gentlemanly
conduct' is evident wherever cheating or doping or the nature of sport are
discussed. Somewhere between these two possible accounts lies a complex set of
questions, laced with ambiguity, subjectivity and conceptual contest, about the
extent to which the Olympic Games can claim to embody the values they were
established to project. The claim is essentially unchanged in the current version
of the *Olympic Charter* (IOC 2007: 11). However difficult they are, they are the
most important questions which can be asked about the Games. I intend here to
break down the central question into a number of questions about discrete values:

1. *Gender.* Pierre de Coubertin's enthusiasm for games was conceived in terms
    of *boys*. He did not approve of women competing in the Olympic Games,
    though they did compete, to constantly varying degrees, during his lifetime.
    Since his death they have competed to increasing, though never equal,
    degrees and have taken part in some events, particularly those which test
    strength and stamina, which he consistently believed were inappropriate for
    women. However, most of the arguments for sport and games as essential
    components of human development can be applied to women as well as men

and it can be argued that de Coubertin failed to see this, but that his belief in the value of sport was couched at a far deeper level than his belief in its inappropriateness for women. Or it could be argued – as it has been argued in the case of religious and educational institutions – that the limitations on women were the interpretation of a fundamental principle in the light of a particular social context (which has now changed) rather than implications of the principle itself. In either case the growth of women's sport is the change most easily classifiable as an evolution of Olympic ideals rather than a betrayal.

2. *Amateurism*. The games remain amateur insofar as they do not award prize money, but all other stipulations defining amateur participants have been eroded. Most Olympic sport, however, remains largely non-commercial: the athletes are paid or otherwise supported by states or other sponsors looking for relatively cheap prestige in the global village event (relative, that is, to the sums of money required to produce champions in fully professional-commercial sports like Association Football or Formula One car racing or global-level horse racing). Compared with the hypothetical world games I discussed earlier the Olympics still consists mainly of sports whose competitors will not become wealthy from their sport: enthusiasts who have their moments of glamour and glory. I have argued elsewhere that such competitors often have a dedication and a love of their sport that is amateur in a spiritual sense and which distinguishes them sharply from career professional sportsmen in the major sports (Allison 2001).

   It is also important to realise that the idea that the Olympic Games are 'big business' is in its way just as much a fantasy as the idea that they are amateur. It relies on the confusion between 'business' in the sense of a financially significant activity which forms or creates the environment in which other organisations make profits (as charities and universities do) and 'business' in the classic sense of profit-maximising organisations capable of indefinite diversification. If the Games were business in this latter, primary sense, they would look like the *Circus Maximus Modernus* discussed earlier.

3. *Physicality*. For de Coubertin, if not for the English educationalists whom he admired, the culture of the body and the athlete was worthy of revival *per se*. There can be no doubt that the success of the Modern Olympics symbolises this revival more completely than any other event. The opponents of the new athleticism – high-minded intellectuals, Confucians, Marxists, feminists, nationalists et al. – have been routed by the universalism of the global festival of the athlete. De Coubertin would have relished London 2012 in ways that would have had the Arnolds groping between incomprehension and disapproval.

4. *The ideal of the all-rounder*. Common to all the ideological origins of modern organised games is the ideal of personal development. It is about body and mind together, character and leadership – all-round abilities. The 1981 movie *Chariots of Fire* emphasises Eric Liddell's achievements as a rugby player and a missionary and states Harold Abrahams' credentials as a lawyer and

broadcaster. The current *Olympic Charter* strongly emphasises this ideal in its brief statement of fundamental principles (IOC 2007: 11) when referring to sport as part of a 'balanced whole' of mind and body, to the 'harmonious development of man' and to the essential integration of sport with 'universal fundamental ethical principles'. However, a bleak model of the professional games player suggests a specialist who understands little beyond what earns him his living, who struggles for a purpose in life once he is too old to compete, and who is not allowed even to develop his sporting skills beyond his expertise. This is a research question rather than an answer, but haven't Olympic competitors become more narrowly gladiatorial as time has gone on? Is the figure of Olga Korbut, tyrannised into becoming a superb gymnast as a child and unable to find a life in any other field, to be contrasted with the likes of Liddell and Abrahams? Insofar as sporting competitors are ignoramuses, freaks or fanatics (as suggested, for example, in Mai Zetterling's gently subversive take on the 1972 weightlifting competition in the documentary film *Visions of Eight* which is discussed by Ian McDonald elsewhere in this volume) they fail to meet the ideal of the Olympian.

5. *Chivalry.* It has already been remarked how little clarification there is of the essential ethical concepts in sport in relation to the work they are required to do. This applies to 'sportsmanship' and 'gentlemanly conduct' as well as to their ancestor, 'chivalry'. Is there any nobility in sport? Whether there is or is not, it is entirely clear from journalistic critiques and official policies, not to mention public bar discussions, that we *want* there to be: the standard still exists and in that sense the Games are still a quest for athletic chivalry, even if it turns out to be as rare as good Christians in Christian societies. But as with Christianity – or socialism – there must come a point when reality falls so far short of the standard that the standard ceases to be relevant.

6. *The primacy of participation.* Perhaps the greatest single measure of agreement among the prophets of modern sport is that the benefits of the institution accrue almost entirely to participants. Nothing could more obviously fail to deliver these benefits than a tiny athletic elite, mostly separated from their peers from childhood, holding a crowd of a billion television viewers in thrall: a set of 'heroes' who excite our crude patriotism, but whom we make no attempt to emulate. A great deal of any judgement about whether the contemporary Olympic Games live up to their original ethical mission statement hangs on the question of whether they inspire broad sporting participation. It is certainly convenient for governments to believe that they do and ministers of sport are often all too ready with the anecdotal evidence about street football peaking after the cup final and tennis rackets emerging from the cupboard once Wimbledon is on the television. But I have argued elsewhere that macroscopic evidence very clearly suggests that it is possible to have a high degree of sporting culture without much Olympic success and be top of the medals table without any kind of grass roots culture of sporting participation. China and Argentina in respect of Beijing 2008 are the case in

point, being first and thirty fourth respectively in the medals table (Allison 2009). It is also clearly the case that the gladiatorial model naturally works to increase interest in the elite game while diminishing adult participation as a whole: American football since 1950 and English rugby since 1996 both demonstrate this. The more detailed evidence is difficult to assess. The complex assertion is that heroes (specifically national heroes) inspire participation, but there is much evidence both for and against this. The *Daily Telegraph*, wholeheartedly committed to the cause of London 2012, constantly suggests examples of such inspiration. The Tory Olympic spokesman on the London Assembly points out that participation in gymnastics, swimming and rowing is declining despite Olympic and other global success[2]. Perhaps it would have otherwise declined further? This is a subject which has not had the benefits of carefully designed research – perhaps because there is a studious lack of interest in the true answer. But the question remains of interest to most of the contributors to this volume and the general consensus would seem to be that though there is some anecdotal evidence for what we might call the 'inspiration effect' there is also broad circumstantial evidence for both the 'indifference effect' and the 'couch potato effect'.

Conclusion

The title of this chapter suggests there might be elements of myth, evolution and betrayal in the relationship between the development of the Modern Olympics and the ideals which inspired their foundation. I don't think there is much myth about the existence of such ideals: they are elusive and ambiguous and honoured in the breach from the start, but so it is with ideals. There has been evolution, certainly, in both our idea of physical culture and away from strict social and financial ideas of amateurism. The question of betrayal is more difficult to assess. It depends on whether one can still conclude that the Olympic Games continue to inspire sporting participation and whether they still offer us an ideal of chivalry. The sceptical answer to these questions is difficult to refute, but not proven.

Notes

1   I am most grateful to Rusty MacLean, the Chief Archivist of the Rugby School Museum, for access and information to the school, its premises, archives and artefacts.
2   Andrew Boff, quoted in "Falling numbers for Olympic sports", *Evening Standard*, November 3rd, 2009: 47.

References

Allison, L. (2001) *Amateurism in Sport: An Analysis and a Defence*, London: Frank Cass.
Allison, L. (2009) 'Towards a new playing field', *Standpoint* 12.
Arnold, M. (1993) *Culture and Anarchy*, Cambridge: Cambridge University Press. First published 1869.

Bale, J. and Christiansen, M. K. (eds) (2004) *Post-Olympism: Questioning Sport in the Twenty-First Century*, Oxford: Berg.

Beamish, R. and Ritchie, I. (2006) *Fastest, Highest, Strongest: A Critique of High-Performance Sport*, London: Routledge.

Butterfield, H. (1977) *The Historical Novel*, Richard West. First published 1924.

Butterfield, H. (1931) *The Whig Interpretation of History*, London: Bell.

De Coubertin, P. (2000) *Olympism*, Lausanne: Comité Internationale Olympique.

De Coubertin, P. (1996) *Mémoires Olympiques*, Paris: Editions Revue EPS. First published, 1931.

De Tocqueville, A. (2002) *Democracy in America*, Edited and translated by Harvey C. Mansfield and Delba Winthrop, Chicago: University of Chicago Press.

Dobbs, B. (1925) *Edwardians at Play, Sport 1890–1914*, London: Pelham.

Hayens, H. (1925) *'Play Up Buffs!'*, London: Collins.

Hoberman, J. (1992) *Mortal Engines: The Science of Performance and the Dehumanization of Sport*, New York: Free Press.

Hughes, T. (1999) *Tom Brown's Schooldays*, Oxford: Oxford University Press (facsimile of the 1857 edition).

International Olympic Committee (IOC) (2007)*The Olympic Charter*.

Macaloon, J. J. (ed.) (2007) *This Great Symbol: Pierre De Coubertin and the Origins of the Modern Olympic Games*, London: Routledge.

Montaigne, M. De (1998) *Essais*, Paris: Pockets Classiques.

Scott, Walter, (1997) *Ivanhoe* Penguin/BBC. First published 1819.

Tomlinson, A. and Whannel, G. (eds) (1985) *Five Ring Circus: Money, Power and Politics at the Olympic Games*, Ann Arbor: University of Michigan Press.

Taylor, D. J. (2006) *On the Corinthian Spirit: The Decline of Amateurism in Sport*, London: Yellow Jersey Press.

Vance, N. (2004) 'Kingsley, Charles (1819–1875)', *Oxford Dictionary of National Biography*, Oxford University Press.

Young, K. and Wamsley, K. B. (eds) (2005) *Global Olympics: Historical and Sociological Studies of the Modern Games*, Oxford: Elsevier.

3

THE PROMISE OF OLYMPISM

Graham McFee

Introduction

It is widely acknowledged that Baron Pierre de Coubertin's invention of the modern Olympic Games was fuelled by his belief in the value of sport: in particular, its educative value. And many governments have urged that sport has a value of this sort. Further, the promises of governments exhibit a fair degree of unanimity when 'advertising' the contribution of hosting the Olympic Games. But the values attributed and the improvements promised have not typically been those de Coubertin endorsed, at least once rhetorical claims are set aside. Does that suggest that the values de Coubertin urged for sport (and especially for the Olympics) are mere fictions, sheer idealism or a hopeless form of utopianism? At the least, these values cannot readily be discerned, after many years of the modern Olympic Games. Anyone seeking to defend a version of de Coubertin's position must meet such difficulties.

In effect, then, a defender of Olympism (that is, a defender of the possibilities inherent in the Olympic movement) must show why the lack of success in mani-festing the values de Coubertin urged is not, after all, an indictment of those values.

So I shall argue that de Coubertin urges the *intrinsic* value of sport, while governments have stressed *extrinsic* values; and that, once properly understood, de Coubertin's view is defensible. Further, I shall both explain and defend that view, by showing that there *is* an intrinsic value here (compare Culbertson, 2008; McFee, 2009); but one representing a possibility that often fails to be actualised – especially given the economic forces at work within the Olympic movement. So this view predicts the sorts of failures witnessed, without abandoning the commitment to the possibility of an Olympism as de Coubertin envisaged it: that is, an Olympism grounded in the intrinsic value of sport. My argument also offers (and explains briefly) a pessimism about the likelihood of this occurring. Yet even here many of the excesses of the Olympic movement can be explained away, as manifestations of human fallibility: hence, as not counting against the promise of Olympism.

The contrast, noted above, between *intrinsic* and *extrinsic* is very important throughout. Consider soap operas, which (for the purposes of the argument) are taken to have no intrinsic value. Clearly soap operas give pleasure and enjoyment to people; and, relatedly, they can offer a 'sophisticated and sensitive cultural lens' (Beckles 1995: 1) onto social relations – either in the Large or the Small of that cultural space. Similar extrinsic values could be claimed for sport; and rightly so. But, as this case shows, these values cannot depend on the topic being *sport* or *soap operas* at all, since exactly the same claims might be made for each. Thus, a theoretical structure explaining all there was to know about sport viewed from this extrinsic perspective would fail to explain the distinctiveness of sport.

The Baron, Olympism, and intrinsic value

Consider the following widely-quoted remark (Eyquem 1976: 138a; Eyquem 1966: 58; Tomlinson 1999: 214) about the project of Olympism:

> I shall burnish a flabby and cramped youth . . . *by sport*, its risks and even its excesses. I shall enlarge its vision and its hearing by showing it wide horizons . . . which, in engendering mutual respect, will bring about a ferment of international peace. (my emphasis)

In de Coubertin's plan to '. . . burnish . . . *by sport*', is the *sport* part important? Is there something special about the choice of sport here, rather than something else? Suppose a sixteen-day international music festival would command the same sort of attention from its audience and from the media (and from commercial sponsors, if this is relevant) – would that do just as well? Certainly, the sorts of infrastructural benefits ('it will give you a better train service', 'it will help with urban regeneration', or '. . . help with social inclusion') regularly cited as reasons for hosting the Olympic Games say nothing about sport, on the face of it.

But, for de Coubertin, it *was* important that the topic was *sport*: after all, the '. . . risks and excesses' to which he refers above are clearly those of sport. So, the force of its being sport here (from roughly de Coubertin's perspective) must depend on some feature of sport relevant to the project's explanation. That is, an *intrinsic* value to sport must be acknowledged. Moreover, de Coubertin made this move – perhaps that is just an *inference* from the passage above, but one to which we are entitled especially when seen in the light of what is about to be argued.

It is also important, for de Coubertin, that the aim of the Games (as of Olympism more generally) was broadly educational: that participation in sport *for its own sake* had a moral value (de Coubertin 2000: 588). Two aspects are noteworthy here, both traceable to de Coubertin's admiration for the culture of *athleticism* which he found in British Public Schools (no matter if it was actually there!). Thus, on more than twenty five occasions, de Coubertin (2000) attributes such views to Thomas Arnold, Headmaster of Rugby School (1828–1841), with Thomas Hughes's *Tom Brown's Schooldays* as a primary source of 'evidence' for this view. As Lincoln Allison highlights (elsewhere in this volume), there is good reason to suppose that Arnold himself did not hold such views. Peter McIntosh (1979: 27) provides an apt summary of key theses of such athleticism:

> . . . [a] that competitive sport . . . had an ethical basis, and . . . [b] that training in moral behaviour on the playing field was transferable to the world beyond. [my letters]

For de Coubertin, though, it was fundamental, first, that the benefit of sport is not limited to the playing field. Then if, in line with thesis [a] from McIntosh, at least some sport was potentially morally educative, that fact alone would not deliver de Coubertin's aims for Olympism; and hence the value he saw for sport. So athleticism's thesis [b] is needed, the one generalising beyond the sporting arena.

Then, second, the benefit here is for particular individuals: '. . . the individual view . . . [is] best and most desirable' (de Coubertin 2000: 543). Hence, it concerns *their* moral, educational development, in response to *their* motives, and such like.

So, for de Coubertin at least, justifying Olympism meant recognising some intrinsic value for sport; a value rooted in individual persons' learning and understanding, but with the possibility of moving at least beyond sports field or stadium. That is why he puts aside the *extrinsic*: sport was done, for instance, '. . . not in the interests of grammar or hygiene' (*ibid.*: 753). Yet how should this promise of Olympism be understood?

The extrinsic claims for sport

In answer, consider initially how governments have often understood this promise, noting that the protestations of typical governments about the value of sport amount either to repeated affirmations of sport's value – which, since they lack specific content, I shall term 'rhetoric'; or to a catalogue of *extrinsic* values of sport: that is to say, *uses* to which states might put sport.

Further, governments draw on these same resources when elaborating the value of hosting the Olympic Games. This mixture of rhetoric about sport's intrinsic value combined with a catalogue of extrinsic values is clearly visible in, say, the London bid for 2012 below. Taken together, these points show that governments typically regard Olympism's promise in extrinsic terms, despite claims to the contrary.

What are these extrinsic values? The sorts of specifically societal benefits claimed for sport might, more bluntly, be taken as uses to which the state might put sport. The list of uses of sport by the state in developing societies by Jim Riordan (1988) is offered here as typical: (a) Nation-building; (b) Integration; (c) Defence; (d) Hygiene and health; (e) Social policies (such as curbing prostitution); (f) International recognition.

In concerning specifically the state's *uses* of sport, the values or benefits on Riordan's list are explicitly *extrinsic*: although values of sport, they could also be arrived at without sport – in this sense, the selection of sport as one's tool is arbitrary. And infrastructural improvements could be added to the list. That helps us recognise these values as extrinsic.

The bid from London to host the Olympic Games of 2012 similarly mixes the rhetoric of intrinsic value with an elaboration of extrinsic benefits. Thus *Before, During and After: Making the Most of the London 2012 Games* (DCMS 2009) begins with the UK Government's Department of Culture, Media and Sport seeming to stress an intrinsic value, by claiming that it '. . . aims to improve the quality of life for all through cultural and sporting activities . . .', to involve '. . . more people taking up sport *simply for the love of sport*' (DCMS 2008: my emphasis).

But that intrinsic value (about 'the love of sport') is invisible in the 'headline ambitions' then elaborated:

- Inspiring young people through sport;
- Getting people more active;
- Elite achievement.

They suggest that 'improving the quality of life' might best be understood in, say, health terms only. (Why else is 'getting people more active' thought valuable?) The disappearance of the 'love of sport' from a summary of governmental promises (DCMS 2009), which all turn on potential extrinsic benefits to flow from hosting the Olympic Games, highlights that this was indeed mostly rhetorical flourish:

- To transform the heart of East London;
- To inspire a generation of young people;
- To make the Olympic Park a blueprint for sustainable living;
- To demonstrate the UK as a creative, inclusive and welcoming place to live in, visit, and for business.

Of course, governments are rightly concerned with infrastructural matters of just these sorts. And 'social benefit', identified along side the economic and infrastructural, seems to be cashed-out extrinsically; in terms of increased participation (see Girginov and Hills 2008), and then, derivatively, of health. Moreover, modern concerns with 'Legacy' clearly reflect that interest in the extrinsic (see MacAloon 2008).

Now, obviously sport can contribute to social welfare, and to the goals of the state more generally, in terms of these extrinsic issues; and doing so is valuable. But governments regularly make, and widely endorse, such claims to justify spending tax-cash on sport. That justification requires *proving* that sport indeed provides a route to those benefits. And part of such a proof must show that involvement of this kind with sport is the *best method* of achieving these extrinsic goals (or, anyway, a better method than some major alternatives) – say, that it costs less per unit of achievement (however that is determined). Because recognising these as extrinsic goals grants that they have no direct relation to sport. Hence they might have been achieved in other ways (recall the soap opera or the music festival). That, in turn, opens up a debate about which of these 'other ways' (if any) would be most effective. Once the intrinsic value of sport plays no part in that explanation of benefits, the role of *sport* here becomes a topic for discussion. Were sport selected just for its popularity (say), one might wonder whether some other activity might not be comparably popular . . . and so on.

The UK government, in respect of London 2012, and previous governments, both in the context of hosting the Olympic Games and outside it, have endorsed this kind of extrinsic justification of sport, once their rhetorical claims (which were never given substance) are stripped away. If the right account of the value of Olympism stresses *as well* (or *instead*) the development by the Olympic Games of sport's intrinsic values, the sorts of measure in place to determine success – which may (with luck) be appropriate to determine *extrinsic* success – may be beside the point.

Issues for intrinsic value

But what prospects has an account of the promise of Olympism recognising an intrinsic value of sport? Two or three immediate problems arise for any defender of (broadly) de Coubertin's picture.

1.   *Has sport an intrinsic value?* In effect, this asks whether sport (or anything else) is a candidate for intrinsic value – or, putting that another way, whether all value is extrinsic value. Drawing the contrast with extrinsic value involves recognising the possibility of intrinsic value; and denying it rejects the idea of intrinsic value across-the-board. So here we must grant the possibility of intrinsic value.

2.   The more specific question (*does **sport** have such intrinsic value?*) takes for granted that possibility. Then the debate for sport concerns the nature of such value ('what kind of value is it?'), or the nature of sport ('what kind of thing is sport?') – since, if such value is possible somewhere, why not here? And the issue addressed by referring to, say, the *nature* of sport is strictly relative to the context in which it arises (McFee 2010: 36–38; 177–193). That is, all talk of *natures* should be treated in a contextualised fashion, rather than an essentialist one. Thus, once the possibility of intrinsic value is acknowledged, such that (say) literature has it, and with the stress now clearly on sport, a better formulation might ask: *What is the nature (or explanation) of the value for sport?* Any answer to question 2 must bear in mind (and have a response for) the issue raised by question 3.

3.   *Why is the benefit not more obvious?* Or, to put that another way, how can there be so much violence and ear-biting, racism, and so on, among players and supporters if participation has this morally educative capacity? As a slogan: 'If sport is good, how come its people are so bad?'.

My response first answers question 2 above by presenting my account of sport's intrinsic value. In doing so, it shows why the potential for a morally educative outcome from sports participation is often not realised. That in turn allows a partial answer to question 3 above

In a previous book, *Sport Rules and Values* (McFee 2004), two explanations of the value of sport (broadly in line with Olympism) were offered. So, first, all sport has a moral possibility growing from its rule-following character. That I contract to play by the rules in their regulative uses and in accordance with the rules in their constitutive uses, and do so voluntarily, explains the moral obligation at the heart of sport. Thus, obligations to obey sport's rules are moral obligations both because sport's goal is its *lusory goal* (that is, its pre-lusory goal achieved by lusory means; basically, within the rules) – in contrast to various extrinsic goals, such as the desire for fame or for money – and because one's commitment to that goal is undertaken (relatively) voluntarily; one manifests the *lusory attitude*. Deploying in this way Bernard Suits's ideas about the nature of *games* highlights the sense of these as inevitable features of (typical) sports (Suits 1978: 41).

Since this explanation of sport's value is very weak, a second argument was introduced (McFee 2004: 129–148): that that moral character of some sport on some occasions functions as what I call a *moral laboratory*, providing an opportunity to 'practise' the use of key moral notions, such as *justice*, and moral metaphors, such as *fair-play* and *level playing field*, with less risked than, say, waiting for the attack of the mad axe-man before considering what behavioural obligations 'Thou shalt not kill' really sets in that context. In sport, at least typically, one's concern with how to apply one's principles, or what behaviour appropriately instantiates them, is never this urgent. Which is why *less* is risked – although, of course, less is precisely not nothing! So sport's *intrinsic* value resides in its capacity to function as a *moral laboratory* in exactly this sense, which draws on features of typical sports.

Rather than offering an extended treatment of the idea of *the intrinsic*, I focus primarily on the contrasting idea: *external* goods or goals are easily exemplified – the pursuit of money or fame are the most obvious – for they are clearly independent of the fact that this sport (or even sport) is being pursued. Typically, then, 'intrinsic' means little more than *not external*.

But does my account fail in practice? Doesn't that account suggest that sports players should be more morally aware than others? Yet a great many sports players manifestly are not morally aware; many do not recognise the force of moral considerations, to judge by their behaviour or pronouncements. Readers can probably supply enough examples of wife/girlfriend-beating, ear-biting, and racism to grant this point. Further, if Olympism has the force claimed, should there not be more evidence of a *globalising* moral concern? Again, that seems absent. What should be said?

To deal with this problem, I invoked two distinctions. The first contrasted two *explanations* of the reasons for one's action (although not, of course, two actual reasons): if asked why *I* did such-and-such, I offer my *motivating* reason. But, looking at the action in question, we often find a *good* reason – sometimes called a 'normative' reason – for that action. And, while neither of these strictly requires reference to my psychological processes, the reasons viewed as *motivating* are the ones I would mention if truthfully and accurately responding to the question of why I did that action. So, first, reasons viewed as motivating are distinguished from reasons viewed as normative. The second distinction, already mentioned, is between the reasons *external* to the activity, in that they would equally explain other activities, or *internal* to this one.

Then, for one to benefit from the moral value of sport, my account of that value requires that (a) one's *motivating* reasons (or one's reasons explained motivatingly) must be *good* (or 'normative') reasons; and further, (b) they must be *intrinsic* reasons. For moral benefits depend on how the activity is conceptualised: on what I take as the *intentional object* of my action – moral value requires appropriate intentional objects. It is as though I must be following a moral rule (if morality were a matter of rules) – so that behaviour which only *accords* with the rule will not count; one must be acting in that way *because of* the rule. Here, my succeeding in doing such-and-such is related to my trying to do *that thing* – the expression 'that thing' here picks out the intentional object of my action as I conceptualise it. And some other kinds of interests or benefits do not require reference to intentional objects. Thus, I acquire, say, the health-related benefits of sports participation however I regard that participation: that is, however I would characterise my participation – or, as we would say, whatever the intentional object of my participation. But that is not true if my actions are to be appraised morally. For an action with a different intentional object would not be *my* action.

This picture offers a way of dealing with counter-cases to the moral value of sport ('it obviously isn't working'). Suppose we ask, 'why are the sports players acting as they do?'. The structure of the position here shows through elements of our answers:

- Is the sports player's action for an *intrinsic* reason, or an extrinsic reason? If the reason is just extrinsic, clearly any benefit is not from sport as such. (It could as well have been realised from the soap opera or the music festival.)
- Is it for a *good* reason (or just a motivating reason)? If there is no good reason here, the participation is not really justified, but only explained. That is, we know why *this* person did it, but not why anyone else has a reason for similar action.
- But is it also the sportsperson's *motivating* reason? If there *is* a good reason, yet our sportsperson is not acting from it, it is not *that person's* reason (McFee 2004: 151–160). So whatever flows from that good reason cannot apply to our person.

My account, then, requires that the sportsperson's motivating reason also be a good reason, and an intrinsic reason: only then could sport's moral potential be realised. This offers three ways for that (complex) requirement to fail.

To capture the force of the conditions sketched above, note cases where they do not hold. First, suppose there is a *good* reason for behaving in such-and-such a way, but it is not my motivating reason. Then any benefit that accrues to acting on that good reason cannot accrue to me: my behaviour, although in accordance with that good reason, does not act *from* it. Similarly, if my reason for participation in sport is purely external to the sport (for instance, a prudential reason), any moral benefits from participation cannot accrue to me. For, in both cases, they are benefits only to those with appropriate intentional objects of their actions. One can participate in sport without meeting these conditions; so many apparent occasions for sport to be morally educative will fail – as we observe. Hence this picture explains why sport's intrinsically educative potential may well not be realised.

Of course, all this is an idealisation, designed to bring out the structure of my use of the *good reason* vs. *motivating reason* contrast. But at least it sketches a picture of moral concern as 'other-regarding': that is one explanation of why, to arrive at the moral case, my motivating reasons must be good reasons.

De Coubertin, values and for its own sake

Now, can de Coubertin's commitment to an intrinsic value for sport be connected to my account of that intrinsic value? Can my account of 'Olympic promise' plausibly be ascribed to de Coubertin?

Our 'yes' reply recognises the need for rational reconstruction from de Coubertin's writings. For this question is not simply about, say, what de Coubertin wrote or could have intended, although answers must start from de Coubertin's claims – such as the 'burnishing' quotation reproduced earlier. But attending solely to the letter of de Coubertin's writing may show nothing conclusive concerning the relation of his view to mine, since the issue is often what he meant, nor what he said.

Clearly, de Coubertin wrote about sport's intrinsic value: for instance, in commenting positively on '. . . those who love sports for sports' sake . . .' (de Coubertin 2000: 588); or in stressing '[t]he transposition from the muscular to the moral sphere . . .' (*ibid.*: 593). But, precisely what he meant by sports participation *for its own sake* is crucial. For de Coubertin's conception of the possibilities of sport was specifically educational. Thus, a passage above continues '. . . those who love sports for sports' sake, *for their educational value* . . .' (*ibid.*: 588 – my emphasis). And typical *extrinsic* concerns for sport, such as fame or financial reward, are regularly set aside. Hence de Coubertin criticises those who emphasise only winning, and thereby aim '. . . to make the Olympic Games into world championships' (*ibid.*: 557). Instead, what should be stressed is sports players developing '. . . enough moral strength in themselves to handle a deeply-felt defeat' (*ibid.*: 562). Here, then, an *intrinsic* value (or, at least, its possibility) is endorsed.

Those difficulties for human understanding at which de Coubertin aims sport are never completely resolved by economic or political changes alone: thus, he urges, sport does '. . . not now rest on political or economic foundations' (*ibid.*: 558). Of course, such factors cannot be ignored: as de Coubertin urges, '[s]ports have developed within a society whose love for money threatens to cause that society to rot right to the marrow' (*ibid.*: 557). Yet, since resolving economic and social inequalities cannot *alone* be sufficient, these economic or political foundations do not alone determine the moral condition of people.

But de Coubertin's view was not all idealisation: he realised that '[t]o ask people to love one another is merely a form of childishness' (*ibid.*: 580). To get beyond it, and generate people's respect for one another, '. . . they must first know each other' (*ibid.*: 583) – where this should reflect both knowing the person through his or her actions, and recognising that person's moral commitments (to justice, and the like). In Olympic competition, like other sports participation, competitors are permitted to 'try out' moral ideas with less risked than in society generally, so – in seeing others behaving with loyalty, justice and fairness – one may recognise '. . . the firm moral resolution which inspires them' (*ibid.*: 481).

Nevertheless, such rational reconstruction requires sensitivity. For instance, de Coubertin's own pronouncements sometimes reflect his historical or class position: that is, he writes simply as a *man* of his time. Then rational reconstruction should modernise his position in these respects, setting aside what he wrote. The most obvious case is his view of women's place – or lack of it – in the Games. Thus, famously, de Coubertin called for '. . . solemn and periodic exaltation of male athleticism . . . with the applause of women as a reward' (*ibid.*: 713). In 'The Philosophic Foundations of Modern Olympism' (*ibid.*: 583) he comments that, '[a]t the Olympic Games, . . . [women's] role should be above all to crown the victors, as was the case in the ancient tournaments.' Then his 'Forty Years of Olympism' (*ibid.*: 746) urges:

> I continue to think that association with women's athleticism is bad for . . . [the modern athlete] and that such athleticism should be excluded from the Olympic programme.

And his message to athletes of the IXth Olympiad (*ibid.*: 604) notes:

> As for the participation of women in the Games, I continue to oppose such a move. It is against my wishes that they have been admitted to an increasing number of events.

This is just 19th century thinking; and should be dismissed as such: our rational reconstruction is not obliged to include it, not least because it is detachable from other key aspects of his position. This offers a principled liberation from the *specifics* of Baron Pierre de Coubertin's ideas.

More on rational reconstruction: amateurism

Of greater importance for rational reconstruction, and looking *beyond* the agreements over specific Olympic ideals to the principles underlying them, is the contrast between what de Coubertin wanted, or believed in, and the form those ideas took in practice. For an account proclaiming loyalty to the *spirit* of de Coubertin's thinking must explain those re-draftings its elaboration requires. By far the most important ideas here concern the Olympic movement's allegiance to *amateurism*. In reality, de Coubertin's commitment to the intrinsic value of sport, and its place within Olympism, condenses around this topic.

Yet that is not the view usually taken. Many texts inform their readers that de Coubertin was committed to the Olympic Games being *amateur*: in this vein, IOC president Avery Brundage (1963: 30) urged that amateurism was '[t]he first and most important' of the rules of the Olympic movement. But many commentators miss that Brundage's view, reflecting that more usually ascribed to Olympism, contrasts revealingly with de Coubertin's own: and hence cannot rationally reconstruct de Coubertin's position. As Brundage (1963: 30) elaborated:

> [t]he first and most important of these rules, for good reason, was that the Games must be amateur. They are not a commercial enterprise and no-one, promoters, managers, coaches, participants, individuals or nations, is permitted to use them for profit.

Of course, de Coubertin was committed to opposing 'the evils of industrial civilisation' (MacAloon 1981: 188). Hence de Coubertin regularly used forms of words similar to those of other critics of commercialism in sport. But these comments do not, in fact, commit him to defending amateurism *as interpreted* by later versions of the Olympic movement. And views elaborating *amateurism* for the Olympics along Brundage-like lines continue to dominate. As Maraniss (2008: 331) records, after the Warsaw IOC session of 1937, Olympic Rule 26 read:

> An amateur is one who participates and always has participated in sport solely for pleasure and for the physical, mental, or social benefits he derives therefrom, and to whom participation in sport is nothing more than recreation without material gain of any kind, direct or indirect.

The term 'indirect' here was taken to mean that one could not benefit from one's sporting fame, even in contexts outside sport: hence, for instance, the one-year suspension for Lee Calhoun for getting married on the *Bride and Groom* television show (Maraniss 2008: 269–271), and the threats to Rafer Johnson's amateur status if he took a role in the film *Spartacus* (Maraniss 2008: 34–35). Further, Brundage took American sprinter Ray Norton's decision '. . . to sign a professional contract with the San Francisco 49ers football team when the Olympics were done . . . [to be] an affront to Brundage's strict standards of amateurism' (Maraniss 2008: 189).

De Coubertin rejected this picture of amateurism; in particular, it lacks his clear commitment to sport in the Olympic Games taking place *for its own sake* – since only then, he believed (and rightly), could participation be *educational*; and, in particular, morally educative.

Thus de Coubertin called for '. . . adopting a more intelligent, broader and certainly narrower definition of an amateur' (de Coubertin 2000: 599) than any current – especially any current within the Olympic movement as it then stood. For he feared '. . . that the terms 'amateur' and 'professional' are meaningless' (*ibid.*: 599) – or, at least, they would become so if trends then current continued. So, he urged, something must be done to preserve the Games:

> If we allow things to go on as they are, repugnant snobbery, the habit of lying, and the spirit of gain will soon invade our athletic associations. (*ibid.*: 599)

Here de Coubertin's worries concern both the inadequacy (and worse) of the accounts of amateurism then current, and the impact of a lack of appropriate regulation. What de Coubertin wanted, and what he objected to, are precisely in line with ascribing an intrinsic value to sport. So looking closely at *amateurism* highlights clearly both what he was opposed to in sport; and what he saw as sport's morally educative possibilities.

As Lincoln Allison (in his chapter in this volume; and in Allison 2001: 3–16) ably illustrates, de Coubertin accepts what Allison calls the 'spiritual/ philosophical' aspect of amateurism, while rejecting both the social and financial aspects. Below, I take these 'aspects' to reflect different understandings of what might, with justice, be called *amateurism*. And I motivate de Coubertin's principled rejection of two of those understandings in terms both of his commitment to an *intrinsic* value of sport, and of his frustration with those who kept re-asserting those understandings.

Clearly, de Coubertin used the term 'amateur' widely. Thus, in the invitation to the Sorbonne Congress of 1894, de Coubertin declares that:

> [t]o defend against the spirit of gain and professionalism that threatens to invade them, amateurs in most countries have established complex legislation that is replete with compromise and contradiction. (de Coubertin 2000: 299; see also MacAloon 1981: 166–167)

But, as he later wrote, '[t]he Programme for the Congress was drawn up in such a way as to disguise its main object, 'the revival of the Olympic Games': it merely put forward questions on sport in general' (de Coubertin: 310). And much of the rest of the Congress was devoted to discussions of amateurism, which de Coubertin dismissed as '. . . an admirable mummy' (*ibid.*: 315) – an apt image, capturing both age and desiccation, with the hint of preservation by embalming. Further, even that invitation to the Sorbonne Congress cites the corruption of sport by money ('gain'); hence, the issue raised was not directed at payment of athletes as such, but at the abuses that might follow.

De Coubertin fully understood the nature of the problem:

> Are athletes whose expenses are defrayed improperly and athletes who receive compensation for lost salary both amateurs, or is neither one an amateur? If only one of them is an amateur, which one is it? (*ibid.*: 652)

He is clear both that these questions admit no general answer, and that the search for a single reliable disambiguation of these accounts of the amateur presents Olympism with 'ludicrous obstacles' (*ibid.*: 194). And he recommends looking to 'cases' (*ibid.*: 653), as though acknowledging that no single reliable *general* formula here can ensure athletes' participation in sport *for its own sake*.

Of course, de Coubertin recognised the potential problems when the *focus* of one's participation was financial: that is, problems associated with commercialisation and with gambling. Commercialism, as one kind of extrinsic 'value' for sporting contests, represented a potential danger to de Coubertin's educative intents. So that, from the beginning (*ibid.*: 309):

> . . . a mercantile spirit threatened to invade sporting circles. Men did not race or fight *openly* for money, but nevertheless a tendency to a regrettable compromise had crept in.

And clearly one way to fail to participate in sport *for its own sake* would be to do it solely for money. So de Coubertin would agree with Brundage (1963: 30 above) that the Games '. . . are not a commercial enterprise'. But the 'solely' above is crucial here. The problem lies not in receiving money (say, to pay one's mortgage or feed one's family) but in participating for that reason *only*.

Of course, a related danger came from athletes whose livelihoods depended on sport, for then betting, or some such, might determine one's level of participation (see Hill 1992: 18). Thus de Coubertin (2000: 184) writes of '. . . unhealthy temptations' to fix matches and the like, and later calls explicitly for '[t]he suppression of Boxing Matches with purses' (*ibid.*: 237). For the educative is clearly precluded by, for instance, such kinds of match-fixing. Here, as de Coubertin (*ibid.*: 588) urged, '. . . "fair play" is in danger', the threat coming from '. . . the madness of gaming, the madness of the bet'. Yet this is the only one way among many to fail to participate in sport *for its own sake*. Put very crudely, then, de Coubertin saw that participation in sport performed solely for extrinsic reasons could not generate intrinsic values or benefits – which conclusion is, indeed, in line with our account. To grasp de Coubertin's position here, his commitment to sport done *for its own sake*, requires determining what his talk of 'amateurism' meant. And, in particular, what it did not mean.

In fact, de Coubertin confessed that '. . . the question [of amateurism] never really bothered me' (*ibid.*: 653): he saw that the *motivations* of athletes were of fundamental importance to whether or not their participation in sport was potentially educative, not '. . . whether an athlete had received a five franc coin' (*ibid.*: 654) – although this seems to be precisely what concerned, say, Brundage!

Certainly, de Coubertin tired of the issue: 'Here it was again – the same old question', he wrote in his *Olympic Memoirs* of 1932 (*ibid.*: 653). One can almost hear his exasperation. Thus, he lays out four 'competing' accounts of amateurism, which he took to be commonly used: an athlete ceased to be an amateur if he:

1. accepted a cash prize;
2. competed as a professional;
3. received a salary as a sports instructor or coach;
4. took part in 'open' events, i.e. open to all comers, including professionals. (*ibid.*: 654)

In commenting, de Coubertin highlights '. . . their great disparity' (*ibid.*: 654), stressing (a) that these were very different; so these were not four ways to make the *same* point; (b) that no single rule could satisfy them all, without requiring or generating exceptions; (c) that none had a plausible rationale.

By contrast, de Coubertin's position had a plausible rationale (as argued here): namely, that one's commitment to sport must leave one available to its morally educative possibility. For only then could sport benefit that *person* in the ways de Coubertin valued. Hence our 'guarantees' here, insofar as we have them, must derive from the motivations of athletes. So that, devoting a chapter to amateurism in the 1932 work just mentioned, de Coubertin maintained that, since it was the athlete's motivation that must be determined, the only *educationally* meaningful demonstration of participation in sport genuinely *for its own sake* was an athlete swearing the Olympic Oath, '. . . sworn on the athlete's national flag' (*ibid.*: 656). For there we see the athletes:

> . . . solemnly affirming that they have always been loyal and honourable in sport, and [that] it is in this spirit of loyalty and honour that they approach the Olympic contest. (*ibid.*: 545)

Such an oath was '. . . the only practical means to put an end to this intolerable state of affairs' (*ibid.*: 645). And worries about lying have no special purchase here, especially in the context of a knowledge of the athlete's past. But any athlete found to be lying would, in virtue of *lying* in this context, be clearly beyond the moral pale: his/her crime (of *lying on oath*) would be clear. Interestingly, de Coubertin's offered this comment while discussing Jim Thorpe: clearly, Thorpe would have passed this test for performing sport *for its own sake*. Thus de Coubertin's formulation (participation in sport *for its own sake*) comes to the same thing as mine: that one's motivating reasons be both good reasons and intrinsic reasons.

Were de Coubertin's position correct (as urged here), the Sorbonne conference of 1894 – from which the Modern Olympics originate – effectively hijacked this aspect of Olympism: de Coubertin's formulation ('participation in sport *for its own sake*') was read as an economic proscription, reflecting debates of the time: that athletes should not receive money from sport.

As we have seen, this was never de Coubertin's chief concern. Since his commitment was to participation *for its own sake*, rather than for some reward or other extrinsic benefit, de Coubertin was critical of those 'amateurs' who competed *just* for cups or glory – they fail to fit this bill of 'sport for its own sake' as badly as any who competed *just* for money. De Coubertin called these 'false amateurs' (*ibid.*: 650), commenting '. . . these amateurs are far less sporting than many a professional' (*ibid.*: 650). For de Coubertin's aim here was ensuring sportsmanship. And, often, the exclusions de Coubertin had in mind (or introduced) under the guise of defending *amateurism* had – as their motivation, at least – the avoidance of some specific advantage. So that it would be unfair for professional rowers (that is, people who earned their living by rowing) to compete against those who could not, in this way, practice the sport outside of sports-participation and training, since '[t]he man who can devote all his time to training is bound, nine times out of ten, to beat the man who lacks this opportunity' (*ibid.*: 642). Yet here the objection concerns fairness, not amateurism or its lack.

More importantly, de Coubertin might recognise the reciprocal point. For the aim here was to benefit humanity by producing moral individuals: the Olympic movement was not directed at producing or maintaining sport-absorbed monomaniacs. So the full-time athlete – the sailor who, because his wealthy father supports him, does nothing but sail his laser dinghy along the California coast – was as much de Coubertin's target as the professional (meaning *paid*) athlete, since here too '[t]he man who can devote all his time to training is bound . . . to beat the man who lacks this opportunity' (*ibid.*: 642). Both (full-time) professional and full-time 'amateur' have an advantage over the *amateur* in the literal sense of the word (the lover of sport) – so their competition with the real amateur is unfair. And neither participates in sport *for its own sake*, insofar as that involves keeping sport just one aspect of one's life, among others. Indeed, it is hard to imagine the full-time sportsplayer maintaining the balance needed to take what sport teaches into the outside world.

Olympism meets real life?

Initially, I asked whether commitment to Olympism was just idealism. My answer has been, 'no', although an explanation of the general failure to be morally educative of successive Olympic Games was offered. That explanation reaches only so far. For the history of Olympism includes another 'layer' of issues, not strictly failures of Olympism at all. For the corruption of the ideal should be contrasted with mere human fallibility: that is, failures of human beings in positions of power or authority to live up to the values or ideals of Olympism. Many of the excesses of the IOC, and NOCs, are (just) examples of human frailty: giving in to, say, the pressures provided by the economic situation of the Olympic Games. An ideal is not undermined *simply* by poor 'execution' of this kind.

Even then, some values here are sport-related. For some 'affronts' of Olympism impugn (say) the fairness – or the 'safety, in the legal sense – of the outcome, suggesting that athletes did not get 'their just deserts', while others do not. Consider three cases:

- Lots of Salt Lake City stories (see Jennings and Sambrook 2000) present, in effect, the bribery of IOC members undermining the fairness of the selection process for Salt Lake City as host city for the Winter Games of 2002. But this corruption did not significantly harm the events, since almost any first-world city could host the Games.
- At the boxing finals in Seoul, 1988, the acts of 'corrupt' officials meant that those who actually scored most did not win. Although this altered the outcome of athletic competitions, the problem was just practical, not conceptual – the sort of thing resolved by better selection and training of judges.
- In the Games in Seoul, 1988, some lists connecting 'A' and 'B' samples used in screening athletes for drug offences were accidentally shredded. As a result, the 'B' samples of many athletes could not be tested. Since this occurred near the end of competition, many of those athletes were in finals: hence one cannot be sure which late results were, in the legal jargon, *safe* (Jennings 1996: 241–243). The shredding order, from IOC member Alexandre de Merode, was attributed to an oversight, or to over-zealous employees. Again, this might be a failure of personnel, rather than of the ideal.

Although these cases operate differently, none indicates directly a failure of the promise of Olympism – all could be resolved by better selection, or better training, or better scrutiny of procedures: in short, by people behaving better. So these problems do not generate a critique of Olympism as such.

But, in recognising human frailty in our explanation of the corruption here, the market forces that may encourage it must be acknowledged. Such cases are difficult to adjudicate fairly, especially in the absence of all the facts. Perhaps, in the third case above, de Merode felt commercial pressures towards a lower number of positive drug tests for that Games (and I stress *felt*, even if not real). Certainly, an apparent conflict of interest could easily be imagined here. For he had reportedly announced that the 1980 Moscow Games were 'the most 'pure'', offering as '[p]roof of this the fact that not one case of doping was registered' (Jennings 1996: 237). Therefore a subconscious desire for fewer positive drug tests in Seoul might have compromised de Merode's judgement.

Further, the pressure of nationalism (say, on US sprinter Marion Jones) might be structural: that she felt obliged to cheat to meet the wishes of an admiring nation. So could this too be just *one* person's view of that pressure? That seems unlikely: the practices, and the pressure that fuels them, seem widespread. Hence anti-Olympic ideas may be inherent in nationalism, reflecting problems with the stress within Olympic rhetoric 'not on winning, but on taking part'. On just this basis, recall, de Coubertin (2000: 557) objected even to '. . . people who want to make the Olympic Games into world championship', since such a move towards an emphasis on winning potentially introduces what de Coubertin (*ibid.*: 562) called '. . . the semi-barbaric stench . . . [of] nationalism'. Certainly, these will all be reasons why the sorts of intrinsic values de Coubertin saw in sport fail to flourish.

Pessimism, and the 'real world'

So, suppose my claim that the *intrinsic* or *internal* value of sport is moral value remains justified. Perhaps my previous exposition manifested too much optimism, in the face of sport in the contemporary world. My new pessimism here derives partly from reflection on the degree to which the UK situation replicates the sad state of affairs in the USA described in Bill Morgan's book *Why Sports Morally Matter* (2006), especially as manifest in his students' attitudes. For instance, Morgan (2006: xiii) writes of students' '. . . unwillingness or incapacity to view sports from a moral vantage point', reporting their opinion that rules of sport should be '. . . viewed and treated as egoistic devices' (Morgan 2006: xiii). And these students might seem *more* likely to treat sport seriously: hence the depth of this concern.

Morgan's worry, then, is that the sportsperson's motivating reasons are rarely *good* reasons (since they are ego-centric reasons); and even less often (also) *intrinsic* reasons. For, in most cases, the good reasons for actions will be other-regarding reasons. But many *external* reasons are centrally self-regarding (again, our classic examples of the desire for money or for fame work well here); further, treating one's reasons as *motivating* reasons is always likely to bring out the self-regarding, and their contrast – with good reasons – is always with reasons either neutral or other-regarding.

At its heart, Morgan (2006: x) describes '. . . a noticeable coarsening of . . . [the students'] attitude regarding moral consideration in sports', such that '. . . moral examples . . . were falling on deaf ears' (Morgan 2006: xiii), resulting in a '. . . conflation of egoistic calculation and moral reflection' (Morgan 2006: xiii). Hence, that '. . . students' only apparent vocabulary for evaluating actions in sports was in terms of their positive (benefits) or negative (costs) effect on the aims and desires of the individuals who play them' (Morgan 2006: xiii). So they are all self-regarding, never other-regarding. Hence they can never benefit from sport's *intrinsic* value.

What has this to do with the real world? Morgan (2006: 26) rightly regards '. . . the unfettered role that market forces play in professional sports' in the USA as '. . . the main impetus . . . behind their excessive individualistic bent' (*ibid.*). Further, Morgan, in seeing how '. . . in professional sports, just about everybody is (or is encouraged to be) on the take' (*ibid.*), echoes de Coubertin (quoted earlier). Thus the failure (say, by Morgan's students) to grasp the moral considerations here may be traced to a self-regarding component within the 'Gordon Geko' of market forces.

However, Morgan rightly aims to locate the problem more centrally within sports (at least as practised). That is, the impact of the financial pressures should be recognised as a specific impact within the sporting practice as it is conducted, rather than just operating external to it. And perhaps such an explanation plays a key role in, say, the case of Marion Jones. So the problem is not, say, capitalism as such but *sport capitalism*. But this will not be internal to sport as such (nor to that particular sport), but only to that sport as currently understood or theorised.

Conclusion: the real promise of Olympism?

Initially, I implied that defending de Coubertin's position was not utopian: the qualifications required of that answer should now be clear – that any impact for the intrinsic value of sport will never be what, perhaps, de Coubertin hoped (especially given the unlikely combination of factors it requires). In part, the reason is apparent is his own exposition as I have reconstructed it: that the intrinsic value operates person-by-person, at the level of individuals. Hence that impact can never be as grand as some might hope. But that does not make it less real. And it explains why de Coubertin rightly assigned that role to *sport*, and not something else.

John MacAloon (1981: 89) claims, surely correctly, that de Coubertin never arrived at '. . . a satisfying philosophy of sport'. MacAloon explains this absence in terms of a '. . . compartmentalization in his thought and writing . . . [with] his political commentaries separate from his writings on sport, education and social reform' (*ibid.*). But a philosophy of sport satisfactory for de Coubertin as well as for us (more or less what the term 'satisfying' implies in MacAloon's use, above) would have been very difficult on the philosophical assumptions from de Coubertin's time: in particular, his account of the relation of human agency to its structural context (compare McFee 2002), and his explanation of the complexities of motivation. For instance, my own account – still short of 'satisfying', to judge by its critics – draws on philosophical theses both more recent and more contentious in just these areas. But I am urging that a modern version of de Coubertin's account of the promise of Olympism is ultimately defensible.

Critics of Olympism have regularly claimed that Pierre de Coubertin's aspirations were unrealistic, and therefore unrealisable. This is taken to explain the Olympic movement's failure to bring about social improvements of the kinds for which de Coubertin hoped; and to count against his conception of sport's intrinsic value.

But governments bidding to host Olympic Games ascribe to the Games values extrinsic to sport: the bid for London 2012 provided a clear example. So, in such criticisms, de Coubertin's position remains unaddressed. First, the criticism amounts to urging that de Coubertin's vision of the promise of Olympism does not meet the extrinsic goals that governments regularly ascribe to sport. Since de Coubertin was stressing an *intrinsic* value for sport, such extrinsic goals are beside the point. Second, there is good reason why such intrinsic value for sport remains a possibility often unrealised. Indeed, once the character of such value is understood, this is self-evident: the conditions for its realisation are complex. And, of course, as Tom Nagel (1979: xii) recognised:

> [w]hen powerful interests are involved, it is very difficult to change anything by arguments, however cogent, which appeal to decency, humanity, compassion, or fairness.

But this is a suitable ideal or aspiration here, which a more enlightened governmental conception of the potential of sport might join a more robust Olympic movement in pursuing.

References

Allison, L. (2001) *Amateurism in Sport: A Analysis and a Defence*, London: Frank Cass.

Beckles, H. McD. 'Introduction' to H. McD. Beckles and B. Stoddart (eds) *Liberation Cricket: West Indies Cricket Culture*, Manchester: Manchester University Press.

Brundage, A. (1963) 'The Olympic philosophy', *Proceedings of the International Olympic Academy*, 29–39.

Coubertin, P. de (2000) *Olympism: Selected Writings*, Lausanne: International Olympic Committee.

Culbertson, L. (2008) 'Does sport have intrinsic value?', *Sport, Ethics and Philosophy*, 2(3): 302–320.

Department of Culture, Media and Sport [DCMS] (2008) *Playing to Win: A New Era for Sport*, London: DCMS.

Department of Culture, Media and Sport [DCMS] (2009) *Before, During and After: Making the Most of the London 2012 Games*, London: DCMS.

Eyquem, M-T. (1966) *Pierre de Coubertin: L'épopée Olympique*, Paris: Calmann-Levy.

Eyquem, M-T. (1976) 'The founder of the modern Olympic games', in Lord Killanin and J. Rodda (eds) *The Olympic Games*. New York: Collier-Macmillan.

Girginov, V. and Hills, L. (2008) 'A sustainable sports legacy: creating a link between the London Olympics and sports participation', *International Journal of the History of Sport* 25(14): 2091–2117.

Hill, C. (1992) *Olympic Politics*, Manchester: Manchester University Press.

Jennings, A. (1996) *The New Lords of the Rings: Olympic Corruption and How to Buy Gold Medals*, London: Simon & Schuster.

Jennings, A. and Sambrook, C. (2000) *The Great Olympic Scandal: When the World Wanted Its Games Back*. London: Simon & Schuster.

MacAloon, J. (1981) *This Great Symbol: Pierre de Coubertin and the Origins of the Modern Olympic Games*, Chicago: University of Chicago Press.

MacAloon, J. (2008) '"Legacy" as managerial/magical discourse in contemporary Olympic affairs', *International Journal of the History of Sport* 25(14): 2060–2071.

Maraniss, D. (2008) *Rome 1960: The Olympics that Changed the World*, New York: Simon & Schuster.

McFee, G. (2002) 'It's not a game: the place of philosophy in the study of sport', in J. Sugden and A. Tomlinson (eds) *Power Games: A Critical Sociology of Sport*, London: Routledge.

McFee, G. (2004) *Sport, Rules and Values: Philosophical Investigations into the Nature of Sport*, London: Routledge.

McFee, G. (2009) 'The intrinsic value of sport: a reply to Culbertson', *Sport, Ethics and Philosophy* 3(1): 17–29.

McFee, G. (2010) *Ethics, Knowledge and Truth in Sports Research: An Epistemology of Sport,* London: Routledge.

McIntosh, P. (1979) *Fair Play,* London: Heinemann.

Morgan, W. J. (2006) *Why Sports Morally Matter,* London: Routledge.

Nagel, T. (1979) *Mortal Questions,* Cambridge: Cambridge University Press.

Riordan, J. (1988) 'State and sport in developing societies', in F. Broom, et al. (eds) *Comparative Physical Education and Sport* Volume 5, Champaign, IL: Human Kinetics.

Suits, B. (1978) *The Grasshopper: Games, Life and Utopia,* Edinburgh: Edinburgh University Press.

Tomlinson, A. (1999) *The Game's Up: Essays in the Cultural Analysis of Sport, Leisure and Popular Culture,* Aldershot: Arena.

4

THE OLYMPICS AS SOVEREIGN SUBJECT MAKER

Thomas F. Carter

This chapter offers a preliminary exploration of the basic premise of Olympic sovereignty over sport. The emergence of Olympic sovereignty is much more than the transformation of high performance sport that Beamish and Ritchie analyze (2006). Rather, the Olympic Games need to be understood as a specific project, unequivocally tied to particular political economic structures (Eichberg 1998) that promote themselves as being natural, unique, and universal despite, as I will argue, being none of those. The justifications of the Olympics are in no way self-evident, organic, or even necessary.

This exploration goes beyond the various historical and political analyses celebrating and criticising the Olympic Games (Bale and Christensen 2004; Barney *et al.* 2002; Guttmann 2002; Hill 1996; Lenskyj and Burstyn 2000; Payne 2006; Young and Wamsley 2005). All of these varied works examine the Olympics as a global institution and its political relations with other transnational and national institutions. A few look at the inner workings and internal politics of the IOC, usually from a more critical perspective (Jennings1996; Lloyd *et al.* 2008; Pound 2004; Senn 1999). Yet none actually question the International Olympic Committee's (IOC) claims of sovereignty over sport. The crucial question, then, is not on the internal political wrangling characteristic of the IOC, but on the world-wide governance of sport and, in particular, the IOC assertions that it alone determines how global sport shall be organised, experienced, and ruled. In short, at the heart of the IOC claims is the question of who decides how global sport shall be structured. Considering the complicated nature of this question, this chapter explores one particular facet of Olympic sovereignty: the ability to make its own subjects.

By claiming sovereignty over global sport, the IOC makes its own form of subjects, ones unbound by any state-based premise of citizenship, as global cosmopolitan 'citizens' who embody the ethos of the 'Olympic movement'. That ethos is not the dignity of humanity articulated in the IOC's charter nor is it the athletic credo of *citius, altius, fortius*, but has become, in the past twenty years, a neoliberal apparatus of subject making. The general argument laid out here, and I suggest that several of the chapters throughout this book [Caudwell, McDonald, Thorpe and Wheaton, Howe] exemplify the argument I put forth here, is that having the power to create sovereign subjects is an integral part of Olympism.

The nature of Olympic authorities' claims has evolved over the decades, but a specific shift during the last decades of the twentieth century has led to explicit assertions of Olympic sovereignty. This shift became initially visible at the 1992 Barcelona Games. These Games are considered to be a watershed Olympics for a number of reasons. The most commonly recognised of which is that this was the first Olympics in which professional athletes were eligible to compete in most events (boxing being one of the few exceptions). The US Men's Basketball team embodied this new ethos. The arrival of the Dream Team, twelve athletes, eleven of whom were world-renowned professionals at the height of their abilities, transformed the tournament into a spectacle of excess and exuberance, as well as dominating skills. The basketball tournament with the Dream Team was not an athletic competition. The outcome of who would win the gold medal was thought to be a predetermined conclusion. The question was not whether the Americans would win but by how much.

The 1992 Games also buttressed a significant shift within Olympism itself that began earlier in 1984. The 1984 Los Angeles Games were noted for the commodification of the Olympics themselves, transforming the Olympics from a celebration of human spirit into a money-making machine, a significant shift from the economic debacle that was the 1976 Montreal Games. The Dream Team also embodied this particular development. Conflicting contractual agreements between some individual athletes' corporate sponsor (Nike) and the official Olympic sponsor (Reebok) nearly resulted in the squad's absence from the medal ceremony. Only an eleventh hour compromise in which an American flag draped over the offending symbol on the protesting athletes' bodies allowed the ritual to commence per usual.[1] Beyond the commercialisation and commodification of the Olympic Games, a third, more subtle transformation occurred, one that passed virtually unnoticed but was most extensively manifest at the Barcelona Games. That transformation was the open assertion of Olympic sovereignty.

In the Men's 100m swimming final, Alexandr Popov outswam his seven rivals, touching the wall to earn the gold medal. Following Olympic protocol, Popov, dressed in his sanctioned warm-up track suit, waited for the medal ceremony to begin. The third place finisher stepped on the slightly raised platform on the left hand side of the dais and waved to the throng. The second place finisher stepped on the platform to the right hand side that was raised higher than the platform on the left had side and also waved to the crowd. Then Popov's turn came. He stepped onto the middle platform, the highest of the three, waved to the crowd and raised his hands together in celebratory triumph, grinning the whole while. Olympic officials approached the platform and in reverse order of their finishing, with due solemnity, each was presented his medal, bowing his head allowing the official to wreath the medal around his neck. After receiving their medals, they turned to face the crowd. Their national flags were raised and the national anthem of the gold medallist was played. Except the music played was not the Russian national anthem. Nor was it the Soviet anthem. Nor was the flag being raised in Popov's honour either Soviet or Russian. Instead, the beginning movement of the Olympic Hymn reverberated around the arena and the banner was the Olympic flag itself.

Popov was not merely a lone individual, but was a member of the Equipe Unifiée (Unified Team), also commonly named in English press coverage as the Commonwealth of Independent States (CIS), a nearly 500-strong contingent of athletes. The Unified Team was an 'exception' that demonstrates Olympic assertions of sovereignty. Conventionally, the sovereign exception marks out excludable subjects who are denied protections (Agamben 2005). The exception is an extraordinary departure in policy that can be deployed to include as well as exclude. The exception can also be a positive decision to include selected targets of calculated choices and value orientations (Ong 2006). Either way, it is the self-declared exception to the law that paradoxically legitimates the law's very application.

The athletes from the former USSR were not the only Olympians who participated in the 1992 Barcelona Games who did not fit within the legal strictures laid out by the IOC. Athletes from Republic of Macedonia and the Federal Republic of Yugoslavia (Serbia and Montenegro) also competed as Independent Olympic Participants. Macedonians had not formed a National Olympic Committee and were thus ineligible to compete under the Macedonian flag and Yugoslavian athletes were admitted despite United Nations sanctions prohibiting their participation at international events. Nor were these the only Games in which participants violated the very rules that the IOC created and enforce. Exceptions, albeit not on the scale found at the 1992 Summer and Winter Games, can be found in a surprising number of other Games, including the 2000 Sydney Games and the 1984 Sarajevo Winter Olympics, to just mention two.

An Olympic sovereignty

Olympic Festivals are spectacles of authority situated within nationalist discourses that simultaneously deploy multiple claims of sovereignty (Tomlinson and Young 2006). The opening and closing ceremonies of the Olympic Games are especially rife with these symbolic claims of authority that define specific kinds of relationships between the individual, states, and global sport (Tomlinson 2004, 2005). While the opening ceremony bequeaths Olympian status on all participants, the medal ceremony is the true demonstration of Olympic subject-making power. The Olympic medal ceremonies mimic the spectacle of the scaffold by physically and symbolically raising the subject of its power. Yet it is not the sovereign taking of life but the sovereign bestowing of life upon the subject that forms the heart of Olympic sovereignty.

Michel Foucault wrote extensively about the spectacle of the scaffold as a subject-making apparatus of sovereign power in which 'the tortured body is first inscribed in the legal ceremonial that must produce, open for all to see, the truth of the crime' (1977: 35). Public executions were much more than mere performances of judicial power; they were also rituals of political power. The crime in question constituted an attack on the sovereign since the law represents the will of the sovereign. The executed becomes *homo sacer*, he who can be killed with impunity (Agamben 1998). The public execution reconstitutes the sovereign by manifesting it in spectacular fashion. The aim, however, is not so much to re-establish a balance between subject and sovereign as to demonstrate the sovereign's ability to make the subject into the form it desires. Such ritual is necessary to make everyone aware, through the body of the subject individual, of the asymmetrical relations between the all-powerful sovereign and the individual who dares to challenge such claims. An execution's entire meticulous ritual apparatus inscribes the efficacy of sovereign power. It does not establish justice, rather it activates power. The ceremony of public torture and execution displays, for all to see, the power relations that make this force into law. Yet executions are not the only forms of spectacle that are performances of sovereign power.

Sovereignty has been historically grounded on the formal ideologies of rulership and legal jurisprudence and the Olympics have relied exclusively on legal jurisprudence formulations for its assertions. As a concept, however, it has oscillated from being a limited ontological manifestation of power expressed in legal form or in ideas of legitimacy to an emergent form of authority grounded in violence performed and designed to generate loyalty, fear, and legitimacy. At its base, sovereignty is the ability to kill, punish, and discipline with impunity and it is the body that is the site of this sovereign rule (Agamben 1998; Foucault 2003). In that base relation, then, specific kinds of subjects are made. The kinds of relations that sovereign power materialises force us to consider exactly what are the kinds of subjects being created.

A sovereign's ability to make subjects is dependent upon its ability to provide examples that etch themselves into the hearts of men through the inculcation of emotion (Foucault 1977: 49), whether that is the reduction of an individual to 'bare life' (Agamben 1998: 8–9) or the disciplinary power deployed to constitute new forms of social being (Foucault 1977: 135–140). For true sovereign power is not merely the taking of life but also the bestowing of life. This is the premise of sovereign power claimed throughout religiously ordained political institutions. It is not so much the concern with death that religions attempt to make subjects in their own image but their claims of being able to bestow specific kinds of life upon their subjects when they so choose. The promise of Heaven, of a life after death, is a means of claiming the power to bestow life upon whom the sovereign power chooses.

Sovereignty can exist in many overlapping and competing forms at many levels within the same territory and temporal frame. The Hobbesian idea of sovereignty – the capacity to make final and incontestable decisions about populations within a territory – must be seen as a tentative and never completed endeavor that constantly strives to halt its own fragmentation. It circulates uncertainly between populations and their embodied histories, constitutionally sanctioned authorities, and, where it exists, the written constitution that the authorities interpret (Connolly 2007: 33). An understanding of sovereignty as multiple, provisional, and always contested resonates meaningfully with the trajectory of imperial, post-colonial, and other global forms of governance. Pioneering explorations of the practices of global governance have concentrated mostly on the United Nations network of international institutions (Coles 2004; Merry 2006) and the everyday practices of the European Union's institutional governance via 'parliaments' in Brussels and Strasbourg (MacDonald 1996; Shore 2000). The Olympics are another network of international institutions that claims sovereign rule over sport yet the IOC network of global sport governance has yet to be fully considered in this light.[2]

Throughout much of the twentieth century the Olympics remained inextricably entangled in international politic conflicts. By the time of the 1936 Berlin Games, they had reached a truly spectacular proportion and were drawn into the centre of international political and economic dynamics (Hoberman 1986: 44). After World War II, the Olympic Games essentially served as a resonating platform of Cold War related nationalistic rhetoric in which medal winners became weapons to be ideologically deployed against the opposing camp (Wagg and Andrews 2007).

The collapse of the Soviet bloc shifted the international context of the Olympic Games. The Olympics were no longer the battleground of resolute opposing ideologies but an affirmation of another worldview. Prior to 1992 Olympic participants became Olympians first and then used that status to become celebrities, parlaying gold-medal status into other forms of capital. From 1992 onward a shift reversing that relationship has been occurring. This was apparent in the initial dilemma posed by the US Men's basketball team. The Dream Team were essentially already medalists before they set foot on court with the odds-on expectation being that they would win the gold. When they did, the issue over their corporate subjectivity came to the fore. Those Olympians were the site of a corporate conflict, asserting a different kind of sovereign claim to athletic bodies that had the potential to challenge IOC sovereign rule over sport. The symbolic conflict between Nike and Reebok heralded a shift in both the way the IOC understood the very subjects it created and the relationships between forms of being. That shift both threatened and reinforced the sovereign claims of the IOC, demonstrating the inherent fragility of sovereign power.

The fragility of Olympic sovereignty

The Olympic Charter is the evidentiary declaration of the sovereignty of the IOC and it has undergone significant revision in its existence. In its most current form, it is asserted that:

> The IOC is an international non-governmental not-for-profit organisation, of unlimited duration, in the form of an association with the status

of a legal person, recognised by the Swiss Federal Council in accordance with an agreement entered into on 1 November 2000. The decisions of the IOC are final. Any dispute relating to their application or interpretation may be resolved solely by the IOC Executive Board and, in certain cases, by arbitration before the Court of Arbitration for Sport (CAS). In order to fulfil its mission and carry out its role, the IOC may establish, acquire or otherwise control other legal entities such as foundations or corporations. . . . The IOC may recognise as IFs (International Federations) international non-governmental organisations administering one or several sports at world level and encompassing organisations administering such sports at national level. The statutes, practice and activities of the IFs within the Olympic Movement must be in conformity with the Olympic Charter, including the adoption and implementation of the World Anti-Doping Code. Subject to the foregoing, each IF maintains its independence and autonomy in the administration of its sport. (IOC 2010: 29, 57)

There are a number of assertions to sovereign rule within these statements that require further scrutiny. First of all, the IOC declares that its decisions are final, a clear declaration of sovereign rule. Secondly, the IOC claims sovereign domain over all International Federations; that is, the international governing bodies of various sports are only legitimate if they are recognised by the IOC and conform to the regulations set out by the IOC in this Charter. Third, the IOC claims that its Executive Board is the final arbiter in disputes related to sport, except in certain instances when the CAS may hear those disputes. Yet it was the IOC that created that august body and continues to insist on its primacy over the CAS. Other international federations have considered and even attempted to form their own versions of the CAS specific to their respective sport for resolving disputes. Ultimately, those efforts have failed as plaintiffs have turned to the CAS in instances when an IF's decision was not to the complainant's liking. Fourth, the IOC asserts a legal claim on the appropriation of other bodies, foundations or corporations, involved in the production and/or governance of global sport, thus asserting its primacy over potential rivals. In practice, this is limited to sovereign rule over international federations and National Olympic Committees (NOCs), but in theory this could also be extended over states' own ministries of sport, charitable organisations, international bodies, and transnational corporations like Nike or Adidas. Of course any such attempt to assert such authority over any other organisation(s) would result in a titanic struggle, as has occasionally occurred.[3]

These claims, however, are extremely fragile. Ironically, the basis for the entire legitimacy of the IOC as a sovereign global body is balanced upon the singular legal jurisprudence of the Swiss state. The IOC acknowledges as much in its first statement above, and then proceeds to gloss over that particular circumstance. Jean Chappelet and Brenda Kübler-Mabbot summarise those circumstances within the evolving legal relationship between the Swiss state and the IOC, noting that 'the IOC is not a "real" international organization but a non-governmental organization (NGO) with the legal form of an association under Swiss law pursuant to articles 60 to 79 of the Swiss Civil Code' (2008: 107). They further note that the agreement made on 1 November 2000 transforms the IOC into a specific "state of exception", a contradictory legal condition of being simultaneously within and outside the state (Agamben 2005), and it is this exceptional condition that allows the IOC to then claim sovereign power in its own right. In effect, both parties act as equals and either party can negotiate changes to or withdraw completely from the agreement if and when it chooses. In addition, a Swiss law passed in 2007 designed to regulate the relations between Switzerland and certain types of international organisations headquartered there provided the capability of establishing the extraterritoriality of IOC offices, juridical immunity, duty-free imports, and other rights normally only afforded to sovereign states (Chappelet and Kübler-Mabbot 2008: 109). These circumstances differ from the usual power relations between sovereign states and NGOs/INGOs and act as the juridical claims of sovereign status by the IOC.

The 2000 agreement also extended the IOC's existing privileges to its various foundations by granting quasi-diplomatic travel privileges for staff and employees, notably through the recognition of credentials issued by the IOC (Chappelet and Kübler-Mabbot 2008: 108). This sovereign right is asserted in the 2010 Charter in which the Olympic identity and accreditation card 'establishes the identity of its holder and confers upon the latter the right to take part in the Olympic Games' (IOC 2010: 102). Together with a passport or other official travel documents of the holder, this card authorises entry into the country of the host city despite whatever the policies and procedures might be in that sovereign state. So a passport and IOC card supersedes any visa requirements a state might require of citizens of certain states. For example, the US government requires all Cuban citizens to obtain a visa to enter the United States, but the IOC claims that its documentation overrides such state-based sovereign assertions. The IOC alone determines who is eligible to hold one of these cards.

Not only does the IOC determine who can and cannot travel under its jurisdiction but it determines the roles that any given individual may undertake while involved with the Olympics. In short, it determines the kind of Olympic subject an individual may become. For example, 'only those persons accredited as media may act as journalists, reporters or in any other media capacity. Under no circumstances, throughout the duration of the Olympic Games, may any athlete, coach, official, press attaché or any other accredited participant act as a journalist or in any other media capacity' (IOC 2010: 97).

Lastly, the IOC's ability to dictate to state governments how preparations for Olympic festivals shall be organised is another indication of Olympic sovereignty. Not only does the IOC claim sovereignty over the NOCs and the Organising Committees of Olympic Games (OCOGs), but the IOC can and does require states to alter their own legal jurisprudence to fit with IOC sovereign claims. The most recent example can be found in the lead-up to the 2012 London Games. The British parliament passed the London 2012 Act of 2006 designating the exceptional status of all things Olympic, brand, commodities, and rights of immanent domain over to land, public space, and transport in order to facilitate the production of the Olympic Games (OPSI 2006).[4] Normally the sole parvenu of sovereign states, the recognition of Olympic sovereignty, over and above British citizens' individual rights, is the recognition of Olympic sovereignty on a level of national states at the very least. In other words, the IOC is acknowledged to be the equal, at least in jurisprudential terms of political power and legitimacy, of the sovereign rulers of the United Kingdom. This symbiotic relationship in which Olympic authority is both negotiated and recognised by states sits at the centre of IOC claims to sovereignty. Olympic claims to sovereignty place the IOC on a level above that of state – both asserting and instantiating the Olympics' capacity to make subjects.

The subject-making apparatus of the Olympics

The ceremonial spectacle of Popov receiving his medal illustrates the sovereign power of the Olympics while simultaneously demonstrating that the Olympics are a subject-making apparatus. An apparatus is literally anything that has some capacity to capture, orient, determine, intercept, model, secure, or control the gestures, behaviours, opinions or discourses of living beings (Agamben 2009: 14). Therefore, it includes not only those vast disciplinary institutions that Foucault has analyzed, the prison, madhouse, hospital, schools, juridical courts and the like, but also incorporates literature, art, technologies (e.g., the pen, mobile phone, and the internet), and, of course, sport. Every apparatus implies a process of subject making and, on this basis, is first and foremost a machine that produces subjects. More than mere accidents of history in which humans are caught, apparatuses are rooted in the very processes of subject-making. A subject manifests in the relationship formed between being and apparatus. An individual being can be the site of multiple processes of subject-making: the user of technologies, the practitioner of art forms, the protester of policies, and so forth. In this sense, the Olympics are themselves an apparatus that captures individuals and makes them into specific kinds of subjects: Olympians.

Olympic subjects are beings caught in a bind. Allen Guttmann points out the contradiction between the Olympic Charter's statement that the Games 'are competitions between athletes in individual or team events and not between countries' (IOC 2010: 19) and the almost constant referral to the country the athlete represented in an event's results (Guttmann 2002: 2). Yet, the original conception of Olympians representing nations of the world was not tied to countries. 'A nation is not necessarily an independent State. There is an athletic geography that may differ at times from political geography' (Coubertin 2000a: 590). All too frequently this ideal is lost, as it was throughout most of the Cold War. Olympians are supposedly subjects who transcend other group affiliations. To be an Olympian is some quasi-utopian state of being that brings those individuals together in 'brotherhood', a kind of utopian collective on a world scale. Some even consider this contradictory projection of individualism and a utopian community as the key to the Olympics' widespread appeal and to its near hegemonic spread (Close, Askew and Xin 2007: 44).

The Olympics are simply 'good for humanity': as the IOC states, 'the goal of Olympism is to place sport at the service of the harmonious development of man, with a view to promoting a peaceful society concerned with the preservation of human dignity' (IOC 2010: 11). When 'Eddie the Eagle' barely flew above the frozen ground in Calgary in 1988 and 'Eric the Eel' thrashed his way across the pool in Sydney in 2000, they were celebrated not for being English or Ghanaian respectively, but for their 'Olympic spirit' – their indomitable humanity. Despite such celebratory platitudes, these Olympians also were and remain objects of derision for their 'audacity' at becoming Olympic subjects. Their existence contravenes the current ideals of Olympism because their efforts did not and cannot truly be appreciated.

Appreciation here not only refers to others placing an aesthetic value on a performance, but invokes the neoliberal notion of self-appreciation (Feher 2009). Neoliberal policies and discourses continuously encourage the (e)valuation of an individual by determining the 'bankability' of an actor, the 'employability' of a worker, and the 'marketability' of a person, skill, talent, or invention. A case in point are neoliberal athlete celebrities, such as David Beckham or Alex Rodriguez, in which it is not enough to simply play well but one must look good doing it to the point that looking good can supersede athletic success (e.g., glamourous tennis star Anna Kournikova). The main point of this form of neoliberal subject is to consistently (re)value one's self, that is, appreciate one's 'face' value.

This condition is the contemporary Olympic subject as evidenced by alpine athletes' appreciation *before* competing in the 2010 Vancouver Games.[5] In the lead-up to the 2010 Vancouver Games, four alpine athletes posed without many of the clothes necessary to compete in alpine events while wearing just enough to convey the alpine aspects of their athleticism in the annual *Sports Illustrated* swimsuit issue.[6] For these four, and many other athletes like them, they do not first become Olympians, hopefully winning a medal, and then garner increased celebrity from that condition of being, but approach becoming an Olympian from the other way around. Since the Dream Team of the Barcelona Games, many athletes regard becoming an Olympian as an opportunity to create greater appreciation and up their marketability rather than as the be-all and end-all of their athletic prowess. Instead of victory identifying new subjects, now medal 'hopefuls' are identified months prior to the Olympics and promenaded throughout various media as marketing mules for expectant corporations and nations.

Two years prior to the London 2012 Games saw these processes being played out in the United Kingdom. The BBC and other British media outlets were busy identifying 'medal hopefuls', showing their training sessions, providing biopics, and otherwise working in tandem with the athletes' themselves to increase their visibility (i.e., their 'face' value) and therefore, the individual capital of those subjects. Athletes, in general, now consciously produce their own subjectivities, appreciating individual capital prior to ever becoming an Olympian. Thus, the Olympians that grace our screens and dazzle us with their prowess during the 2012

London Games do so in order to be appreciated, and if that appreciation cannot be built upon as an Olympian, then other avenues of self-appreciation are pursued. Such a change of purpose is ultimately what distinguishes a neoliberal subject from its liberal predecessor.

Furthermore, beyond commercial opportunities, for a chosen few comes the chance of joining the ruling apparatus of the sovereign power by becoming an Olympic Statesman. Alexander Popov embodies this processes. After retiring from swimming, Popov became an IOC member in 1999 and is currently the Honorary Secretary of the IOC Athletes Commission, having served as a member of the Evaluation Commission for the 2016 Summer Olympics and representing athletes on the IOC Sport for All Commission. He thus parlayed his individual capital as Olympian into more lucrative work within the very institution that bestowed that form of subject life upon him.

Conclusion: Olympic sovereignty and the making of neoliberal Olympians

When Popov first stepped on the podium to receive his gold medal in 1992, that moment was when Olympic sovereignty became wholly visible. The raising of the Olympic flag and the playing of the Olympic Hymn during that medal ceremony explicity explicitly demonstrated the otherwise latent sovereignty of the Olympics. Both symbols only really appeared with the development of Olympic sovereignty. The flag was not used at Olympic Games until 1924 in Antwerp. The use of the Olympic Hymn, written by Kostis Palamas and Spyridon Samaras for the 1896 Athens Games, was not mandated by the IOC until the 1960 Games as a requirement.[7] It is the gradual assertion of the primacy of Olympic symbols that is evidence of the evolution and development of Olympic sovereignty.

Popov and the others of the Unified Team that had podium finishes were celebrated as Olympians; their nationality was not relevant. This condition rendering the nation irrelevant is normally masked when an Olympian wins an event. The Olympian in question, however, is not an individual of that nation but an individual representing that nation – a fine distinction admittedly, but an important one. This is the difference between the Olympic Games and all other global international sporting events, in those other events athletes are individuals *of* that country. There is no other condition of being in World Cups, World Championships, or other mega sports events. In the Olympics, athletes, coaches, and others are part of a contingent of Olympians that *represent* that country. When Olympians win their event, or medal in their event, they do so as Olympians representing a particular nationality. They do not cease to be Olympians with the raising of their national flag. The medal ceremony confirms that these medal winning individuals as Olympians and that is how they will be remembered.

When Coubertin first wrote, 'It is the duty and the essence of the athlete to know, to lead and to conquer himself' (Coubertin 2000b: 593), the only individuals that fit his ideal were the amateur athletes of gentlemanly persuasion.

They were the only ones that could approach sport purely as a means of self-improvement and possessed the requisite socioeconomic background to become future leaders. Some of this ethos still holds, but these values have evolved over time as well. In the early days, becoming an Olympian was intrinsically desirable; now becoming an Olympian is desirable for how it can add value have one's self, for its extrinsic worth. The ideals of Olympism compliment the current neoliberal assertions of the individual's role in society. Olympic sovereignty makes it possible to govern subjects seeking to increase the self-worth (i.e., their 'value', more precisely), to act on the way they govern themselves, by inciting them to adopt conduct deemed to valorise and to follow models for self-appreciation that modify their priorities and inflect their strategic choices.

Beginning in the late twentieth century, Olympic assertions of sovereign rule over sport accelerated. The assertion of IOC sovereignty was not a new item on the agenda. It has been a central tenet of the Olympics from their very formation. 'Olympism did not reappear within the context of modern civilization in order to play a local or temporary role. The mission entrusted to it is universal and timeless. It is ambitious. It requires all space and time' (Coubertin 2000c: 595). That universality, that timelessness, and that claim to all space and time are assertions of sovereign power. That power is deployed to (re)make the world in the Olympic image, as Olympic authorities wish it to be, not as the world actually is. The projection of Olympic sovereignty is not a totalitarian exclusive claim but a form of graduated sovereignty that has adapted to the changing circumstances of the global political economy.

The emergence of Olympic sovereignty has not been a static process nor does it remain static. It is constantly renewed, renegotiated, and reformed. The fragile, eroding and contested condition of sovereignty frequently results in the staging high-profile spectacles to make its power visible. In short, sovereignty needs to be performed and reiterated on a regular basis in order to be effective. The apparatuses of Olympic sovereignty make Olympians real and reproduce them through ritualised ceremonies. Yet the spectacle of subject making is insufficient to maintain sovereign power. Olympic sovereignty requires a vast array of apparatuses that assert primacy over competing actors, formal declarations of the primacy of its jurisprudence and recognition from other actors of its claim to juridical rule. As a claimant of sovereign rule over the governance of sport, it is somewhat ironic that the central claim to the IOC's legitimacy is predicated upon its recognition by a solitary sovereign state, the Swiss state, as a global institution. The neoliberal turn includes the abandonment of some aspects of state sovereignty (Harvey 2005: 64–88) and it is within that space that sovereignty over sport is being claimed by the IOC. Thus, Olympic sovereignty is a graduated form of sovereignty that acts in a dialectical relationship with the global Westphalian state system. It is a mutually confirming yet entirely precarious existence in which the IOC recognises states yet only exists because states recognise its own, independent, sovereign authority.

Notes

1 While it was only two of the twelve who took issue with the corporate symbols on the Olympic sanctioned clothing, the symbolic conflict threatened the entire ritual since the others refused to take part unless the entire squad were all on the dais.

2 For a more detailed discussion of sovereign subject making in global sport, see Carter 2011.

3 The struggles between UNESCO and the IOC over the governance of world sport in the 1970s makes this clear (Chappelet and Kübler-Mabbott 2008: 113–114).

4 The London 2012 Games are by no means unique in this regard. Similar assertions of eminent domain were made in the build-up to the 2010 Vancouver Games (O'Bonsawin 2010) and the 2000 Sydney Games (Lenskyj 2002; Morgan 2003) among other Olympic venues.

5 The Olympics are not unique in this regard. The US Men's football team visited the White House prior to competing in the FIFA 2010 World Cup in South Africa. Historically, sports teams and athletes only make presidential visits after winning a championship, not before they even accomplish anything.

6 They were Lindsey Vonn and Lacy Schnoor (alpine skiers) and Hannah Teter and Clair Bidez (snowboarders), all of whom were members of the US alpine team (see http://sportsillustrated.cnn.com/2010_swimsuit/winter/). Further elaboration of this shift is provided in Wheaton and Thorpe's chapter on the incorporation of snowboarding into the Olympic orbit.

7 Prior to 1960, each host country normally commissioned a local (i.e., national) composer to compose an official hymn for those specific Games. Since then, the music and lyrics of the Olympic Hymn have been used for the parade during the Opening Ceremonies (although the lyrics are often changed to the national language of the host nation) and it is a stipulation of the IOC that the Olympic Hymn is performed during both the opening and closing ceremonies (on occasion, the host has negotiated its use solely at either opening or closing ceremonies, but again, this is unusual).

References

Agamben, G. (2009) 'What is an apparatus?', in *What is an Apparatus? and Other Essays* (D. Kishik and S. Pedatella, transl.), Stanford: Stanford University Press.

Agamben, G. (2005) *State of Exception* (K. Attell, transl.), Chicago: University of Chicago Press.

Agamben, G. (1998) *Homo Sacer: Sovereign Power and Bare Life* (D. Heller-Roazen, transl.), Stanford: Stanford University Press.

Bale, J. and Christensen, M. K. (eds) (2004) *Post-Olympism? Questioning Sport in the Twenty-first Century*, Oxford: Berg.

Barney, R., Wren, S., and Martyn, S. (2002) *Selling the Five Rings: The IOC and the Rise of Olympic Commercialism*, Odgen: University of Utah Press.

Beamish, R., and Ritchie, I. (2006) *Fastest, Highest, Strongest: A Critique of High-Performance Sport*, London: Routledge.

Carter, T. F. (2011) *In Foreign Fields: The Politics and Experiences of Transnational Sport Migration*, London: Pluto Press.

Chappelet, J.-L., and Kübler-Mabbot, B. (2008) *The International Olympic Committee and the Olympic System: The Governance of World Sport*, London: Routledge.

Close, P., Askew, A., and Xin, X (2007) *The Beijing Olympiad: The Political Economy of a Sporting Mega-Event*, London: Routledge.

Coles, K. (2004) 'Election day: the cultural constructions of democracy through technique', *Cultural Anthropology* 19(4): 551–580.

Connolly, W. E. (2007) 'The complexities of sovereignty', in M. Calarco and S. DeCaroli (eds) *Giorgio Agamben: Sovereignty and Life*, Stanford: Stanford University Press.

Coubertin, P. de (2000a) Letter to Victor Silberer, editor *Allgemeine Spotzeitung* (Vienna) April 1911, in N. Müller (ed.) *Olympism: Selected Writings*, Lausanne: Comité Internacional Olympique.

Coubertin, P. de (2000b) 'New mottoes', in N. Müller (ed.) *Olympism: Selected Writings*, Lausanne: Comité Internacional Olympique.

Coubertin, P. de (2000c) 'The emblem and the flag of 1914', in N. Müller (ed.) *Olympism: Selected Writings*, Lausanne: Comité Internacional Olympique.

Eichberg, H. (1998) 'Olympic sport: neo-colonialism and alternatives', in H. Eichberg. J. Bale and C. Philo (eds) *Body Cultures: Essays on Sport, Space and Identity*, London: Routledge.

Feher, M. (2009) 'Self-appreciation; or, the aspirations of human capital', *Public Culture* 21(1): 21–41.

Foucault, M. (2003) *Society Must be Defended* (D. Macey, transl.), London: Penguin.

Foucault, M. (1977) *Discipline and Punish: The Birth of the Prison* (A. Sheridan, transl.), New York: Vintage.

Guttmann, A. (2002) *The Olympics: A History of the Modern Games*, Chicago: University of Illinois Press.

Harvey, D. (2005) *A Brief History of Neoliberalism*, Oxford: Oxford University Press.

Hill, C. (1996) *Olympic Politics*, Manchester: Manchester University Press.

Hoberman, J. (1986) *The Olympic Crisis: Sport, Politics and the Moral Order*, New Rochelle, NY: Aristide D. Caratzas.

IOC (2010) Olympic Charter (February 11). Lausanne: IOC available at www.olympic. org/Documents/Olympic%20Charter/Charter_en_2010.pdf [accessed 23 May 2010].

Jennings, A. (1996) *The New Lords of the Rings: Olympic Corruption and How to Buy Gold Medals*, London: Pocket Books.

Lenskyj, H. J. (2002) *The Best Olympics Ever? Social Impacts of Sydney 2000*, Albany: SUNY Press.

Lenskyj, H., and Burstyn, V. (2000) *Inside the Olympic Industry: Power, Politics, and Activism*, Albany: SUNY Press.

Lloyd, R., Warren, S., and Hammer, M. (2008) *2008 Global Accountability Report*, London: One World Trust.

MacDonald, M. (1996) 'Unity in diversity: some tensions in the construction of Europe', *Social Anthropology* 4: 47–60.

Merry, S. E. (2006) *Human Rights and Gender Violence: Translating International Law into Local Justice*, Chicago: University of Chicago Press.

Morgan, G. (2003) 'Aboriginal protest and the Sydney Olympic games', *Olympika: The International Journal of Olympic Studies* 7: 23–38.

O'Bonsawin, C. M. (2010) '"No Olympics on stolen native land": contesting Olympic narratives and asserting indigenous rights within the discourse of the 2010 Vancouver games', *Sport in Society* 13(1): 143–156.

Ong, A. (2006) *Neoliberalism as Exception: Mutations in Citizenship and Sovereignty*, Durham: Duke University Press.

OPSI (Office of Public Sector Information) (2006) London Olympic Games and Paralympic Games Act of 2006. http://www.opsi.gov.uk/acts/acts2006/ukpga20060012_en_1 [accessed 24 May 2010]

Payne, M. (2006) *Olympic Turnaround: How the Olympic Games Stepped Back from the Brink of Extinction to Become the World's Best Known Brand*, London: Praeger.

Pound, R. (2004) *Inside the Olympics: A Behind-the-Scenes Look at the Politics, the Scandals, and the Glory of the Olympics*, London: Wiley-Blackwell.

Senn, A. (1999) *Power, Politics, and the Olympic Games*, Champaign, IL.: Human Kinetics.

Shore, C. (2000) *Building Europe: The Cultural Politics of European Integration*, London: Routledge.

Tomlinson, A. and Young, C. (eds) (2006) *National Identity and Global Sports Events: Culture, Politics and Spectacle in the Olympics and the Football World Cup*, Albany: SUNY Press.

Tomlinson, A. (2005) 'Picturing the Winter Olympics: the opening ceremonies of Nagano (Japan) 1998 and Salt Lake City (USA) 2002', *Tourism, Culture and Communication* 5(2): 83–92.

Tomlinson, A. (2004) 'The disneyfication of the Olympics? Theme parks and freak-shows of the body', in J. Bale and M. K. Christensen (eds) *Post-Olympism? Questioning Sport in the Twenty-first Century*, Oxford: Berg.

Wagg, S. and Andrews, D. L. (eds) (2007) *East Plays West: Sport and the Cold War*, London: Routledge.

Young, K., and Wamsley, K. B. (eds) (2005) *Global Olympics: Historical and Sociological Studies of the Modern Games*, Amsterdam: Elsevier.

5

THE TECHNICOLOR OLYMPICS?

Race, representation and the 2012 London Games

Daniel Burdsey

September 2008 – London calling

With the last speeches and fireworks of the closing ceremony signifying the end of the Beijing Olympiad, the focus immediately shifted to the UK as London took up the mantle for the succeeding Games to be held in 2012. On a bright, late summer's afternoon in London, the handover party was in full swing, centred on the city's iconic Buckingham Palace and Mall. This was a public party in every sense, with a large crowd of flag-waving Londoners in attendance and millions more people watching the BBC's live television broadcast of the event. On screen, co-presenters Matt Baker and Claudia Winkleman – two of the corporation's suitably 'safe', white faces of Middle Englishness – eagerly sought out sound-bites from British Olympians and the general public alike, with those appearing on camera offering entirely positive endorsements of the impact the Olympics/ Paralympics might have on the city and its residents.

On the temporary stages, crowds and viewers were treated to live performances by Will Young, James Morrison, Scouting for Girls, The Feeling and McFly – nice, identikit, white boys, playing nondescript white pop music.[1] Before sport had even been taken into consideration, this spectacle presented a portrait of London far-removed from that found a few miles east in the city's five official Olympic boroughs, and one seemingly out-of-sync with the much-lauded ethnic and cultural diversity that was emphasised in the successful bid to host the Games. Residents of east London are a community that, according to Lord Coe, 'will be touched by the Games' (quoted in Lee 2006: 177), but how might they be affected? What had been promised and how was this to be squared with reality once the Olympic bulldozers moved into the neighbourhood?

The winning bid: rhetoric and representation

Much has been made of the significance of the London bid committee's decision to centralise the city's ethnic and cultural diversity in their attempt to win the Games and the prominence of this emphasis in the promotional rhetoric espoused by local and national government in the lead-up to the Games. In particular, the involvement of a multiethnic group of London schoolchildren and a promotional video that included 'a black boy runner from Nigeria; an Asian girl gymnast; a white Western female swimmer; and a male cyclist' (Tomlinson 2008: 74) are widely cited as major 'selling points' that tipped the balance towards London when the final decision was made in Singapore in July 2005 (Lee 2006). At the time, the then Prime Minister, Tony Blair, stated that 'London is an open, multi-racial, multi-religious, multicultural city and rather proud of it. People of all races and nationalities mix in with each other and mix in with each other well' (quoted in *Guardian* 2005b). Similarly, Nelson Mandela, who provided official support for the bid, argued that 'there is no city like London. It is a wonderfully diverse and open city providing a home to hundreds of different nationalities. I can't think of a better place to hold an event that unites the world' (quoted in *Guardian* 2005a).

It is easy to criticise what, on the surface at least, appears to be an opportunistic (even tokenistic), focus on London's diversity. Yet for the committee to have alternatively ignored minority ethnic communities altogether would have drawn similar condemnation for its misrepresentative portrait of the city. Nonetheless, Newman's (2007: 263) description – drawing on Beck (2006) – of the strategy as a form of 'banal cosmopolitanism' is an apposite description for another example of British sport's contrived approach to celebrating ethnic and cultural diversity. The main concern of this chapter is to evaluate the evidence on which these claims of diversity are based and to discuss the extent to which they are likely to be reflected in the Games – both in their organisation and in the competition itself. In other words, centralising notions of power and representation, it analyses the potential disjuncture between the content of the bid and the ways in which diversity might actually be embraced in, and through, the 2012 Games.

In their attempts to win the Games, bidding cities respond to both the IOC's current interests and its traditional philosophy of Olympism, and in doing so try to demonstrate the application of these tenets to their own municipal contexts (Rustin 2009; Smith 2008). There is a particular Olympic discourse that cities are expected to endorse and replicate, and consequently the bidding process arguably amounts to little more than 'going through the motions'. Particular boxes need to be ticked, traditionally around commitment to urban regeneration and economic growth, although a focus on environmentalism and communities has emerged over the last two decades. As Poynter (2008: 135) points out, 'since 1992, "Legacy" has assumed a considerable significance to the IOC – as its evaluation process has incorporated environmental and other social dimensions – and is now firmly focused upon non-sport-related outcomes as a source of legitimation for hosting the Games'. However, 'a bid is an attempt to win something, whereas in practice, there are different and sometimes unforeseeable ways in which outcomes are mediated' (Smith 2008: 11, see also Horne and Manzenreiter 2006). As such, whilst it has been argued that 'it is, in fact, ultimately impossible to make any such clear distinction between "rhetoric" and "reality" or "language" and "practice"' (Pitcher 2009: 18), many of the avowals made during bid processes often transpire to be aspirations at best and empty promises at worst.

Critics such as Saunders (2007) and Alibhai-Brown (2009) have questioned the sincerity of sections of the bid and organising committees in employing the language of diversity, suggesting that it represents a valuable, but disingenuous, form of bidding capital. Taking this into account, this chapter asks the following broad question: could London 2012 be a case of Olympic diversity or will it simply be an Olympics in a diverse city? A response to this is formed via addressing three further, specific lines of enquiry: who is organising the Games? Who will be competing at the Games? Who will be watching the Games? Before this, the chapter first provides some crucial socio-political and demographic context for the area in which the Games will take place.

Racialised politics in/of East London and the context for the Games

The geographical focus for the 2012 Olympic Games is Stratford, the 'town centre' of the London Borough of Newham. It is the site for the Olympic Park which comprises the Olympic Stadium, Aquatics Centre, Hockey Centre, Basketball Arena, Handball Arena, London Velopark and Olympic Village. Stratford is not technically part of the *traditional* East End of London – an area that is usually viewed as coterminous with the borough of Tower Hamlets, situated longitudinally between the borough of Hackney and the river Thames, and latitudinally between the City of London and the river Lea (Farrar 2008). Yet if a broader interpretation of east London is employed (see Keith 2008), then Stratford sits right in the middle of this quarter of the city. This more expansive reading is pertinent to the present analysis for three reasons. First, although the Olympic Games centre on Newham, there are a further four official Olympic boroughs: Greenwich (the only one located south of the Thames), Hackney, Tower Hamlets and Waltham Forest. Second, London's post-war eastward urban sprawl means that locations that were once distinct entities, such as Barking, have now been subsumed within the wider metropolis, bridging the gap between the city and the Essex hinterland. Third, in order to try to understand the area's *racial* politics – both historically and contemporarily – it is imperative to look beyond the traditional boundaries of the East End.

This chapter cannot do justice to the complexity that characterises the ethnic and racial demographics of the area, but some noteworthy episodes provide a degree of context for the arguments raised here. The East End is popularly understood through a history of dockland industry, the Blitz, the emergence of the Labour Party, and the trade union activity of Will Thorne and Keir Hardie, and is characterised as possessing an unparalleled community spirit and sense of unity through adversity. This is embodied by the notion of the cheerful, chirpy Cockney and the East End 'family' which extends beyond its usual genealogical meaning. However, despite the existence of forms of contingent 'neighbourhood nationalism' (Back 1996), for many residents, the Cockney identity has always been inexorably underpinned by manifestations of working-class (British) whiteness – a relationship that, at its extreme, has underpinned exclusionary practices and support for racist politics in the post-war era (Wemyss 2006). The most notable academic accounts of this community have been Young and Wilmott's (1957) classic study of Bethnal Green and Dench et al.'s (2006) controversial follow-up in which they attribute racial conflict in the area to the marginalisation of white working-class groups through social and housing policy (see Moore 2008 for a critique). Yet, to focus simply on the area's white, British working-classes belies its heterogeneity. Its once thriving docks, plus large post-war immigration from the New Commonwealth, means that African, Caribbean and South Asian groups combine to comprise a substantial minority ethnic presence. The 'white' population contains 'established' Greek, Irish, Maltese, Polish, Turkish and Greek Cypriot, and Jewish communities, as well as more recent migrants from EU Accession countries. Since the 1980s development of the docklands and the construction of Canary Wharf, certain districts have also undergone rapid gentrification and become home to white, middle-class professionals.

East London has a darker history though, which goes far beyond the characterisations often espoused by popular cultural representation and the sanitised consumption of ethnic 'Otherness' that occurs within the area's rapidly increasing gentrified districts (Banerjea 2000). As Farrar (2008: para. 1.2) points out, 'conflict and contestation also characterise the broader historical sociology of the area', whilst Wemyss (2006) highlights that, although a discourse of openness and tolerance has traditionally existed amongst residents of the East End area, in practice it has simultaneously operated alongside the exact opposite, manifest in racist violence and electoral support for Far Right parties. East London is enshrined as both a site of (neo-)fascism and anti-racism, having witnessed the Battle of Cable Street, British Asians defending Brick Lane from the National Front, and the Rock Against Racism carnival in Hackney's Victoria Park. The area has seen a number of high-profile racist murders, most notably that of Stephen Lawrence in Greenwich in 1993, but also Rolan Adams and Rohit Duggal in the same borough (Hewitt 2005), and previously Altab Ali in Tower Hamlets in 1978. Furthermore, it was in Tower Hamlets that Derek Beackon of the British National Party (BNP) became the nation's first fascist councillor in 1993.

A contemporary analysis of what Sinha (2008: para. 1.4) labels 'the changing local racialised politics of East London' highlights that the BNP has extended its menacing influence beyond inner London, and that 'outer East London is the new front line in the battle against the British National Party' (Joseph Rowntree Reform Trust 2005: 5; see also Lowles 2009). In the 2006 local elections, the party won nearly every seat it contested in the borough of Barking and Dagenham (Keith

2008). Whilst the overwhelming defeat of BNP leader Nick Griffin in the 2010 general election suggests that the party's influence may have been stemmed for the time being, the area is a key focus for the emergent English Defence League (Collins 2010).

Taking the previous discussion into account, some statistics on the ethnic composition of London and, in particular, the five Olympic official host boroughs are also necessary. All minority ethnic groups (as distinguished by UK census categories) are over-represented in London compared to the UK as a whole, whilst the host boroughs have an even larger proportion of minority ethnic communities than the rest of London: whites comprise 92.1 per cent of the British population, 71.2 per cent of London and 58 per cent of the five official host boroughs; the Asian/Asian British population represents 4 per cent of the UK, 12.1 per cent of London and 20 per cent of the host boroughs; the Black/Black British population represents 2 per cent of the UK, 10.9 per cent of London and 16.1 per cent of the host boroughs; 'mixed' groups represent 1.2 per cent of the British population, 3.2 per cent of London and 3.3 per cent of the host boroughs; Chinese or 'other' groups represent 0.8 per cent of the British population, 2.7 per cent of London and 2.7 per cent of the host boroughs. In terms of religious faith, 19 per cent of the population of the five host boroughs are Muslim, 3 per cent are Hindu, 1.5 per cent are Sikh, 1.5 per cent are Jewish and 1 per cent are Buddhist (Olympic Delivery Authority 2007: 7–8).

From 'multiculturalism' to 'diversity': the language of London 2012

London is certainly not the first Olympic Games to focus on issues of multicultural diversity. From the 2000 Sydney Summer Games to the Winter Games in Vancouver in 2010, organising committees have been highly adept at the contrived, superficial appropriation of 'ethnic' imagery – whilst at the same time marginalising, displacing and, in some instances, even propagating or supporting the harassment of, minority ethnic and/or aboriginal peoples (Lenskyj 2000). At the same time, 'through the effectiveness of image making and "imagineering" [they have] made invisible the political and ethnic fissures which characterise host populations' (Hylton and Morpeth 2009: 223). Few other organising committees have, however, made these themes such a primary and enduring part of their promotional rhetoric. Furthermore, in contrast to the appropriation of imagery related to specific indigenous groups, such as Aboriginal Australians or First Nation groups in Canada, the London bid focused on diversity *per se*.

In the introduction to the Olympic Delivery Authority's 'Race Equality Scheme', Sir Roy McNulty states that:

> Diversity was central to the bid for London to host the Games. We recognise the diversity of the population of the UK, of London and of the five Host Boroughs. We are committed to realising the full advantages of

this diversity in delivering our programme. (quoted in Olympic Delivery Authority 2007: 1)

Similarly, Tony Blair described his 2005 Singapore speech as 'a story of a city that was comfortable with the future, open, actually believed its diversity was a source of richness and strength, and was kind of confident and unafraid' (quoted in Newman 2007: 263).

The use of a discourse of 'diversity' in the period since London was awarded the 2012 Games is highly significant, for its selection represents much more than pure semantics. Fundamentally, it enables issues around ethnicity and culture to be emphasised, but without necessitating the adoption of a particular ideological position. In this regard, it reflects a broader shift whereby 'diversity' has replaced 'multiculturalism' as the preferred language of politicians and associated agencies.

As Vertovec and Wessendorf (2010) illustrate, over the last decade there has been a widespread backlash against notions of multiculturalism in Western Europe. Whilst Pitcher (2009: 22) argues that multiculturalism can be 'politically agnostic' and 'does not necessarily signify anything beyond a basic recognition of the facticity of social and cultural diversity', in the UK it is increasingly situated as being at odds with a shared notion of Britishness and the adoption of certain core values. This backlash is primarily directed at Muslim communities, influenced by the urban unrest involving young British Muslim men in northern England during the summer of 2001 and the London transport bombings in 2005. Specifically, opposition is directed towards the religious and cultural practices of some sections – although, in the dominant imagination, it is often erroneously assumed to be *all* members – of these groups, such as living in separate districts, support for *Sharia* law, the *niqab* or *burka* and 'honour killings'. It is widely perceived that local authorities have been reluctant to challenge these practices because of the culturally relativist policies of municipal governance and, accordingly, multi-culturalism is to blame for a lack of 'community cohesion' (Cantle 2008) between these and other groups.

However, whilst the Labour government – and associated agencies such as the Equality and Human Rights Commission – rapidly withdrew from multiculturalism as an ideology and state practice during the latter years of its most recent tenure, celebrating cultural difference at an abstract level was, and remains, central to the London bid and organising committees' public statements. This is where the shift in nomenclature is crucial. As Vertovec and Wessendorf (2010: 18) point out, 'while "multicultural" has mostly disappeared from political rhetoric and "integration" has plainly appeared, continuing support for immigrant and minor-ity cultural difference is evident in the growing use of notions of "diversity"'. Accordingly, this latter term has become embedded, at the expense of overt references to multiculturalism, in the publicity and documentation around the London Games. For example, in LOCOG's (2008) diversity and inclusion strategy, whilst the word 'multicultural' is used just one, 'diverse' or 'diversity' are mentioned nearly 200 times. In sum, this move enables a continuing, politically-expedient and sufficiently nebulous focus on the multitude of communities in London, without having to engage with a contentious and increasingly redundant political concept. The chapter now turns to what this diversity does – or, rather, does not – look like in practice.

Diversity in practice? Organising, competing at and watching the Games

Who is organising the Games?

As is the case with much of the governance and management of elite sport in the West, London's diverse and sizeable minority ethnic populations are poorly represented in the agencies organising the London Olympics. According to the organisations' official websites, only one of the thirteen members of the Olympic Delivery Authority (ODA) board, one of the eighteen members of the London Organising Committee of the Olympic Games and Paralympic Games (LOCOG) board, and two of the seventeen members of the LOCOG Senior Team are from minority ethnic backgrounds.[2] All thirteen members of the British Olympic Association (BOA) board are white. As of 2007, the ODA had a workforce of 171 people. This included full-time employees, those seconded from other organisations and temporary agency staff. Just over thirteen per cent of the total workforce were from minority ethnic backgrounds (Olympic Delivery Authority 2007: 17), signifying considerable under-representation in relation to the overall composition of the host boroughs' populations.

A more detailed breakdown shows that minority ethnic employees are less likely to be full-time employees of the ODA (ten per cent of total staff), but more likely to be seconded (nineteen per cent) or agency staff (sixteen per cent) (*ibid.*: 30–31). Stratifying this data in terms of pay bands, minority ethnic groups comprise ten per cent of administrative support positions, twenty-two per cent of professionals, eight per cent of managers and eleven per cent of heads of function. Crucially, as of 2007, there were no minority ethnic directors (*ibid.*: 17). It is this last statistic that is most alarming, mirroring concerns raised elsewhere regarding the notion of a 'glass ceiling' in the hierarchies of many Western sport clubs and institutions, which prevents progression from the playing field into positions of power, influence and control. For appointments made through the ODA's recruitment strategies, white people make up sixty-seven per cent of applicants, yet represent eighty-nine per cent of appointments. Conversely, whilst almost one-quarter of applicants are from minority ethnic backgrounds, they obtain only ten per cent of positions (*ibid.*: 32).[3] By March 2009, only thirteen per cent of the 250 personnel directly employed by LOCOG were from a minority ethnic background. This percentage was matched with the 4,101 workers employed by contractors at the Olympic Park (London 2012 Equality and Diversity Forum 2009: 19).[4]

Demonstrating what appears to be a limited commitment to accountability and showing little evidence of tangible plans to overcome under-representation, the ODA's (2007: 19) official response to this state of affairs is that it is:

concerned at the drop of BAME [black, Asian and minority ethnic] representation between application and appointment. Detailed analysis of the cause of this is not possible, due to the lack of detailed information on each stage of the assessment process. As a result arrangements for a programme of recruitment training have been put in place.

However, in 2009, the Equality and Human Rights Commission was so concerned about LOCOG's failure to engender diversity and equality in its workforce that it threatened them with legal action – to which LOCOG' s response was that, as a private company, it was not obliged to meet the commission's stipulations on such representation (Doward 2009).

In terms of volunteers, 70,000 are to be recruited to work at the Games and a pre-volunteering programme has been implemented that 'will target disadvantaged groups and deprived communities' (HM Government 2006: 42). However, even LOCOG recognise the potential difficulties in this strategy with Chief Executive, Paul Deighton, admitting that 'a Bangladeshi housewife is not naturally going to sign up' (quoted in McRae 2010). Furthermore, whilst volunteering potentially represents a means of increasing minority ethnic representation at the Games, as has been pointed out in relation to other Olympics, volunteering schemes are actually a means of exploiting human capital and generating free labour (Seifart 1984). Consequently, the high percentage of minority ethnic volunteers simultaneously reinforces the racialised relations of late-modern capitalism and sustains the white hegemony of the organising committee (and the Olympic Movement more generally).[5]

Who will be competing in the Games?

According to LOCOG (2008: 4), 'delivering this vision [of diversity] can't just be about recruiting a diverse workforce, it has to be about partners, suppliers, competitors, officials and spectators; in fact everyone connected with the Games'. In terms of competitors, whilst the global scope of participants will give the London Games (just like any other Summer Games) a truly multinational and multiethnic flavour, how does the composition of Team GB – the 'home' state – fit into this aspiration?

At the Beijing Olympics, Team GB won 19 gold, 13 silver and 15 bronze medals. If the total number of medals awarded is counted (i.e. including every member who contributed to a team medal, such as four medals for Team Pursuit Track Cycling; and double-counting multiple winners), the haul consists of 31 golds, 25 silvers and 21 bronzes. Of this total of 77 medals, 52 were won in just three sports: rowing (23), cycling (19) and sailing (10). The vast majority of participants in these sports continue to come from privileged backgrounds, and have benefited from the support structures of public school and/or university systems. As such, they remain almost exclusively 'white sports' and there were no minority ethnic British medallists in these pursuits in 2008. In other events, only six British medallists in Beijing were from minority ethnic backgrounds.

That this percentage is broadly representative of the minority ethnic population of the UK itself cannot be disputed. However, in terms of the claims made about legacy, role models and inspiring participation amongst young people in London, it is certainly not a symbol of ethnic diversity, nor reflective of either the city or the wider British sporting landscape. With UK Sport continuing to prioritise funding those sports in which athletes have a track record of success and/or the potential for future podium achievements – rowing, cycling and sailing, together with athletics and swimming will all receive over 22 million pounds during the London Olympiad of 2009–13 (UK Sport 2010) – British medal successes in London will, again, most likely come from white, middle-class athletes.

Who will be watching the Games?

Perhaps, then, it will be left to the spectators to provide the diversity aspired to by the organisers. The ODA (2007: 5), for instance, states that 'our goal is to create an Olympic Park, venues and facilities, both for the Games and for future use which are inclusive for women and men of all races, cultures, faiths and ages'. Of course, an Olympic Games provides an unprecedented level of sporting attractions over a fortnight, appealing to a range of sporting tastes, from the large stadium experience of track and field to the intense atmosphere of the dojo. Packed venues, replete with Union flag-waving minority ethnic Britons would certainly provide an overt, public corroboration of the organisers' claims.

The London Games certainly appear to have received substantial support from the city's residents (Newman 2007), especially, for instance, in comparison to Chicago's unsuccessful bid for the 2016 Games. However, as Lenskyj (2004: 152) states, 'the Olympic industry has the power to suppress local dissent and to promote the illusion of unequivocal support on the part of host cities and countries'. Positive endorsements of the London Games and its potential repercussions are certainly not as widespread as is perhaps assumed, with certain members of the local east London population refusing to support claims about the putative social and economic benefits (BBC Radio 2010, Slavin 2010). Sinclair (2008), for example, details a plethora of groups and communities marginalised by the Games and (likely to be) affected by broken promises and misinformation, from amateur footballers on Hackney Marshes to the Traveller community at Clays Lane. Furthermore, support for (or non-opposition to) an event in terms of its wider repercussions (e.g. claims around regeneration and legacy) and actually participating in it, by way of being a paying spectator, are an entirely different matter.

More specifically, the assumption that large numbers of the local minority ethnic population will flood into Olympic venues is myopic to say the least. A brief glance around the area's professional football stadia – Upton Park, the New Den, Brisbane Road, the Valley and Victoria Road – will illustrate that nearly all the fans are white, with these patterns mirrored in other elite sporting events. The exclusion of minority ethnic spectators from live sporting events remains manifest throughout the whole of the UK, not just in East London, and remains one of the most unaddressed issues in both anti-racist policy and academic scholarship around race and sport. As such, there is little insight into the reasons for this state of affairs, although racism and the overwhelming whiteness of professional sporting institutions are certainly contributing factors. Economic factors, particularly the nexus between ethnicity and social class might also play a significant role. According to the Economic Deprivation Index, host boroughs Newham and Tower Hamlets, along with nearby Barking and Dagenham, all made the top ten of most deprived local authority areas annually between 1999 and 2005 (Fawbert, 2011). The cost of Olympic tickets has not (at the time of writing) been announced, but there is a danger that admission costs will price a large number of local residents out of the market – and that is for the events that are even available to the public, with Paul Deighton already admitting that 'people with privileged access' will dominate the crowd at the men's 100m athletics final (quoted in McRae 2010).

Let us think hypothetically for a moment, though, that east London's minority ethnic communities do possess the desire, means and opportunity to watch live events at the Games. As Newman (2007) points out, it is naive to assume that their allegiances would be directed towards British athletes. The sporting affiliations of young diasporic citizens are multiple, with interest and support simultaneously directed towards nations of residence and those of ancestry. Indeed, research on minority ethnic Britons shows that sport is an important arena for the reproduction and contestation of ethnic and national identities, and that these patterns are complex, nuanced and influenced by a wide range of factors (Back et al. 2001; Burdsey 2006). Whilst there would undoubtedly be widespread support for Team GB, this could easily operate alongside – and in some cases be surmounted by – that for Jamaican sprinter Usain Bolt, the Nigerian football team or the Pakistan hockey squad.

Concluding remarks

Back (2005: 20) points out that 'the fact that London is a multicultural and cosmopolitan city is now beyond question but this brings no guarantees'. This applies as much to the Olympic Games as it does to parliamentary politics or the everyday lives of London's residents. Returning to Sir Roy McNulty's avowal that 'we are committed to realising the full advantages of this diversity in delivering our programme' (quoted in Olympic Delivery Authority 2007: 1), the current analysis has demonstrated the flimsy evidence on which this and related claims are made. Specifically, it has established that, at present, neither the Games workforce nor Team GB appear to embody this espoused diversity, whilst predictions regarding the number of minority ethnic spectators attending the Games may be over-estimated.

As this chapter has highlighted, many of the claims made around the London Games and diversity are couched within the discourse of legacy. Arguably, then, the most important question to ask, going forward, is: do local communities in east London have the power and capacity – or, indeed, the inclination – to make this legacy work? The challenge for LOCOG and the ODA, as well as local and national government, is to ensure that the infrastructure and capacity-building for this to be possible is in place. If not, by the time that the Olympic juggernaut rolls out of town towards Rio, the likelihood is that this will simply be another case of the Olympics in a diverse city, rather than the London Olympics promoting and achieving meaningful, sustainable diversity.

Notes

1   Leona Lewis, Hackney's dual-heritage singing superstar, was performing in Beijing, belting out a version of 'Whole Lotta Love' with Led Zeppelin's Jimmy Page, atop a red London *Routemaster* bus.
2   I am grateful to Oliver Miller for discussion on this issue.
3   The ethnic background of ten per cent of applicants is unknown (Olympic Delivery Authority 2007: 32).
4   As of March 2010, there were just 150 construction apprentices working on the Olympic site. Only one of them came from Hackney (*Hackney Citizen* 2010).
5   One potentially positive development is the Official Sports bursary-training programme, which aims to facilitate new groups to become technical officials before the Games. As of March 2009, 70 per cent of the 102 bursaries had gone to minority ethnic recipients (London 2012 Equality and Diversity Forum 2009: 56).

References

Alibhai-Brown, Y. (2009) 'The London Olympics are failing their racial promises', *Independent*, 21 December.

Back, L. (1996) *New Ethnicities and Urban Culture: Racism and Multiculture in Young Lives*, London: London University Press.

—— (2005) '"Home from home": youth, belonging and place', in C. Alexander and C. Knowles (eds) *Making Race Matter: Bodies, Space and Identity*, Basingstoke: Palgrave.

Back, L., Crabbe, T. and Solomos, J. (2001) '"Lions and black skins": race, nation and local patriotism in football', in B. Carrington and I. McDonald (eds) *'Race', Sport and British Society*, London: Routledge.

Banerjea, K. (2000) 'Sounds of whose underground? The fine tuning of diaspora in an age of mechanical reproduction', *Theory, Culture and Society* 17(3): 64–79.

BBC Radio (2010) 'Great expectations: part one', BBC World Service, 23 February.

Beck, U. (2006) *Cosmopolitan Vision*, Cambridge: Polity Press.

Burdsey, D. (2006) '"If I ever play football Dad, can I play for England or India?": British Asians, sport and diasporic national identities', *Sociology* 40(1): 11–28.

Cantle, T. (2008) *Community Cohesion: a New Framework for Race and Diversity* (Revised and Updated Edition), Basingstoke: Palgrave.

Collins, M. (2010) 'Barking mad', *Searchlight* 421, July.

Dench, G., Gavron, K. and Young, M. (2006) *The New East End: Kinship, Race and Conflict*, London: Profile Books.

Doward, J. (2009) 'Sebastian Coe's London Olympics team in row with equality watchdog', *Observer*, 20 December.

Farrar, M. (2008) 'Analysing London's "New East End": how can social science make a difference?', *Sociological Research Online*, 13, 5. http://www.socresonline.org.uk/13/5/7.html. Accessed 2 December 2009.

Fawbert, J. (2011) '"Wot, no Asians?": West Ham United fandom, the cockney diaspora and the new East Enders', in D. Burdsey (ed.) *Race, Ethnicity and Football: Persisting Debates and Emergent Issues*, Abingdon: Routledge.

Guardian (2005a) 'A famous victory', 7 July.

—— (2005b) 'London celebrates Olympics decision', 6 July.

Hackney Citizen (2010), 'Only one Hackney apprentice on Olympic site', 10 March.

Hewitt, R. (2005) *White Backlash and the Politics of Multiculturalism*, Cambridge: Cambridge University Press.

HM Government (2006) *Building on Success: London's Challenge for 2012*, London: Government Office for London.

Horne, J. and Manzenreiter, W. (2006) 'An introduction to the sociology of sports mega-events', in J. Horne, and W. Manzenreiter (eds) *Sports Mega-Events: Social Scientific Analyses of a Global Phenomenon*, Oxford: Blackwell.

Hylton, K. and Morpeth, N. (2009) '"Race", sport and East London', in G. Poynter and I. MacRury (eds) *Olympic Cities: 2012 and the Remaking of London*, Farnham: Ashgate.

Joseph Rowntree Reform Trust (2005) *The Far Right in London: a Challenge for Local Democracy?*, York: Joseph Rowntree Reform Trust.

Keith, M. (2008) 'Between being and becoming? Rights, responsibilities and the politics of multiculture in the New East End', *Sociological Research Online* 13(5). http://www.socresonline.org.uk/13/5/7.html. Accessed 2 December 2009.

Lee, M. (2006) *The Race for the 2012 Olympics: The Inside Story of How London Won the Bid*, London: Virgin Books.

Lenskyj, H. (2000) *Inside the Olympic Industry: Power, Politics and Activism*, Albany: SUNY Press.

—— (2004) 'Making the world safe for global capital: the Sydney 2000 Olympics and beyond' in J. Bale and M.K. Christensen, (eds) *Post-Olympism? Questioning Sport in the Twenty-first Century*, Oxford: Berg.

London Organising Committee of the Olympic Games and Paralympic Games (2008) 'The world in a city: diversity and inclusion strategy', London: LOCOG.

London 2012 Equality and Diversity Forum (2009) 'Working towards an inclusive Games: the first Annual Report of the London 2012 Equality and Diversity Forum', London: Greater London Authority.

Lowles, N. (2009) 'Battlefield Barking and Dagenham', *Searchlight* 414, December.

McRae, D. (2010) 'My constant worry is that we get 70% right, but not all of it', *Guardian*, 20 July.

Moore, R. (2008) '"Careless talk": a critique of Dench, Gavron and Young's *The New East End*', *Critical Social Policy* 28(3): 349–60.

Newman, P. (2007) '"Back the bid": the 2012 Summer Olympics and the governance of London', *Journal of Urban Affairs* 29(3): 255–67.

Olympic Delivery Authority (2007) 'Race equality scheme', London: ODA.

Pitcher, B. (2009) *The Politics of Multiculturalism: Race and Racism in Contemporary Britain*, Basingstoke: Palgrave.

Poynter, G. (2008) 'The 2012 Olympic Games and the reshaping of East London', in R. Imrie, L. Lees, and M. Raco (eds) *Regenerating London: Governance, Sustainability and Community in a Global City*, Abingdon: Routledge.

Rustin, M. (2009) 'Sport, spectacle and society: understanding the Olympics' in G. Poynter and I. MacRury (eds) *Olympic Cities: 2012 and the Remaking of London*, Farnham: Ashgate.

Saunders, M. (2007) 'The regeneration games', *Mute: Culture and Politics After the Net* 2(6): 106–25.

Seifart, H. (1984) 'Sport and economy: the commercialisation of Olympic sport by the media', *International Review for the Sociology of Sport* 19(3/4): 305–15.

Sinclair, I. (2008) 'The Olympics scam', *London Review of Books* 30(12): 17–23.

Sinha, S. (2008) 'Seeking sanctuary: exploring the changing postcolonial and racialised politics of belonging in East London', *Sociological Research Online* 13(5). http://www.socresonline.org.uk/13/5/7.html. Accessed on 2 December 2009.

Slavin, M. (2010) 'A Bangladeshi view of the Olympics', http://www.gamesmonitor.org.uk/node/955. Accessed on 28 May 2010.

Smith, M. (2008) 'When the Games come to town: host cities and the local impacts of the Olympics', London East Research Institute Working Papers, University of East London.

Tomlinson, A. (2008) 'Olympic values, Beijing's Olympic Games, and the universal market', in M. Price and D. Dayan (eds) *Owning the Olympics: Narratives of the New China*, Ann Arbor: University of Michigan Press.

UK Sport (2010) [List of sport funding] http://www.uksport.gov.uk/pages/summer_olympic_sports_home/. Accessed 12 January 2010.

Vertovec, S. and Wessendorf, S. (2010) 'Introduction: assessing the backlash against multiculturalism in Europe', in S. Vertovec and S. Wessendorf (eds) *The Multiculturalism Backlash: European Discourses, Policies and Practices*, Abingdon: Routledge.

Wemyss, G. (2006) 'The power to tolerate: contests over Britishness and belonging in East London', *Patterns of Prejudice* 40 (3): 215–36.

Young, M. and Wilmott, P. (1957) *Family and Kinship in East London*, London: Routledge and Kegan Paul.

6

YOUTH SPORT AND LONDON'S 2012 OLYMPIC LEGACY

Marc Keech

The arrival of a red double-decker London bus in the Bird's Nest stadium at the end of the Beijing Olympics signified the beginning of the most important four years in contemporary British sport. Whilst the Olympic Delivery Agency (ODA), responsible for the building of facilities, and the London Organising Committee for the Olympic Games (LOCOG) are on target to present the 2012 Olympic and Paralympic Games appropriately, it is the Government's responsibility, as underwriters to the Games, to ensure that policies for sport have been developed to deliver the legacy of the Games in the UK and to enact the promise to use the Games to inspire the country to become more physically active. With a featured aspect of the London 2012 bid emphasising how the Games would promote and develop sporting participation across the UK (DCMS 2007), it is impossible to overstate the ambition that the UK has set itself.

The 2012 Games mark a significant development for a host country: the first time that a host country's domestic sport policy has been so blatantly enshrined in Olympic legacy ambitions. The International Olympic Committee (IOC) specifically requires host cities to evaluate legacy indicators within *post*-event reports. From those, participation levels have emerged as a key indicator as the IOC seeks to justify its claims about the impact of the Games in host countries and worldwide. The Olympic Games Global Impact (OGGI) initiative, requiring organising committees to collect annually data from the time of the successful bid until two years after the event, includes obtaining data on participation rates in sport. It remains to be seen how effective that initiative will be in providing the appropriate data (Toohey and Veal 2007: 74). More often than not, host countries/ cities have benefited from economic and tourism legacies. Barcelona is widely seen to have transformed itself as both a business and a tourist destination on the basis of hosting the 1992 Summer Games (Kennett and Moragas 2006). Some (such as Sydney) have facilities that have remained at the forefront of sport in that country but others (notably Athens) have facilities which are not only 'white elephants' but which have now fallen into states of terminal disrepair.

In the UK, there are five main commitments identified in the Labour Government's Legacy Action Plan (LAP) (DCMS 2008: 6–7):

- To make the UK a world-class sporting nation, in terms of elite success, mass participation and school sport.
- To transform the heart of East London.
- To inspire a new generation of young people to take part in local volunteering, cultural and physical activity.
- To make the Olympic Park a blueprint for sustainable living.
- To demonstrate that the UK is a creative, inclusive and welcoming place to live in, to visit and for business.

Security threats notwithstanding, we can anticipate that London 2012 will be a well-managed and organised event. But when considering the challenges facing the Games, developing increased participation and achieving a legacy for young people is an objective more difficult to achieve than the other four commitments combined. Using a six-week, time-limited mega-event to inspire young people to participate for a lifetime and ensure that adults return to, or increase, participation in sport and physical activity is an immense undertaking. In order to lever increased participation levels through the London 2012 Olympic Games, the structure of, and investment in, Physical Education and School Sport (PE) has to be maintained. However, at the time of writing this chapter the portents boded ill, as not long after taking up office in May 2010 the Conservative-Liberal Democrat Coalition Government instituted a programme of drastic public spending cuts within which youth sport and school-based physical education were major targets. A partial reprieve of funding did little to lift the gloom of the long-term picture.

This chapter provides a longer-term analysis of ways through which rhetorical commitments made towards youth sport during the bidding process to host the 2012 Olympics have since been acted upon (or not), and an evaluation of the capacity of relevant institutions to fulfil legacy plans.

Methods of problem identification and structuring often precede and take priority over methods of problem solving in policy analysis, but the developmental nature of acquired public policies, such as delivering legacy, are complex and multifaceted processes that involve interaction between a wide variety of state and non-state actors from supra-national level to particular individuals and interest groups. Often, politicians fall into the trap of seizing on claims for short-term political gain, but in open and democratic societies, policy is not merely imposed: instead it is progressed via open debate, consultation and negotiation. It is through these processes that new orthodoxies emerge, consensus evolves, and directions and meanings are decided. As policy emerges from speculative proposal into legislative action, the openness of debate is transcended and accepted and transmitted meanings become more fixed and closed. Policy which once was openly debated then assumes a momentum of its own, claiming a consensual 'voice' (Tomlinson 1993: 85). The scrutiny of policy is necessarily analytical and descriptive in various measures, but in the case of sports policy for young people and the associated legacy of London 2012, the size of the ambition requires careful examination, especially after the formation of the aforementioned Coalition Government in May 2010.

The sustainability of participation legacy – a step too far?

From the early 1990s a commitment to sustainable sports legacies emerged as an element of the Olympic Movement's mission and was, by 2007, firmly located within the Olympic Charter and as a function of the Olympic Games. Legacy refers to the level of economic, social, environmental and cultural development of a host city that takes place after the show has left town. Its evaluation is, as Girginov and Hills (2009) note, much broader than a 'snapshot' study of the economic 'impact' of the event. A legacy is a long-lasting effect of an event or process. It can be positive or negative, intended or unintended, hard, soft, tangible or intangible, but generally accrues over time. Mangan (2008: 1869) observes that legacy issues include:

> commonly recognised aspects (urban planning, sport infrastructure) to less recognised intangible legacies such as urban revival, enhanced international reputation, increased tourism, improved public welfare, additional employment, more local business opportunities, better corporate relocation, chances for city marketing, renewed community spirit, better inter-regional cooperation, production of ideas, production of cultural values, (affectionate) popular memory, education, experience and additional know-how. These positive legacies stand in contrast to negative legacies such as debts from construction, high opportunity costs, infrastructure that is not needed after the event, temporary crowding out, loss of tourists that would have visited the host city if the event was not taking place, property rental increases, and socially unjust displacement and redistributions.

What is missing from this list is the promise that the London 2012 bid made: inspiration and the associated benefits of increased participation. The London 2012 bid was built on the promise that the Games would be used to inspire the country to become more physically active and to tackle wider social and economic issues such as exclusion, obesity and unemployment; it will be the first time that the Olympics/Paralympics and legacy planning has worked hand in hand. Any legacy research, as Girginov and Hills (2009: 163) note, is therefore inherently political, and as such open to scepticism. The 'soft' legacy of London 2012, social capital, inspiration and the emphasis on youth contributes to what MacAloon (2008: 2065) noted as the growth in:

legacy talk all around the IOC . . . the apparent simplicity of the concept is the first thing to note in accounting for its attraction and ready diffusion among Olympic neophytes. The 'legacy now' concept and expression have spread very quickly through younger Olympic bodies, such as the 2016 applicant cities. This is an exceptionally important development . . . because it encourages communities not to focus so exclusively on longer-term bricks and mortar projects and cost/benefit projections that they lose sight of the real pay-off in new social and political capital that can be created in early stages of a bid, as normally segregated urban status segments and class fractions are very nearly forced into communication with one another.

In contrast to the speculative rhetoric in the Olympic movement about the potential impact on participation, Toohey (2008) discussed the speed with which satisfaction at the Sydney Olympics quickly turned to criticism when the overall legacy of the Games, especially concerning participation, was examined. It became evident that despite short 'spikes' in participation in some sports, overall levels of participation gradually declined and it was impossible for any study to conclude that that the population had become more active, echoing previous caution regarding trickle-down effects from previous games (Oldenhove, cited in Toohey 2008: 1960). The 2009 publication of the Crawford report, *The Future of Sport in Australia,* unequivocally recommended a re-emphasis of Australian sports policy to address downwardly spiralling levels of health and sport participation. The report was not well-received by the Australian Institute of Sport. Nevertheless, the Australian Government responded by publishing its first national sports policy, in May 2010. Two firm commitments, in response to Crawford's recommendations, were the establishment of:

> measurable national objectives and priorities for public funding, includ-ing success for high performance and participation with domestic and/ or international significance, and capacity to contribute to the Australian Government's objectives for social inclusion and preventative health, and; financial and non-financial strategies to achieve those objectives, including strategies that provide for greater participation.
>
> (Commonwealth of Australia 2010: 11)

In many respects, the impact of hosting the Olympics in Australia, with regard to participation, has been to force Government and sports organisations to reconsider their policy objectives to ensure that the impact of investment in sport and physical activity, domestically or through hosting international events, has been worthwhile. Governments, the IOC and domestic sports organisations, not to mention host cities, are compelled to commit to the notion that increased participation will be a legacy of hosting the games. Veal and Frawley (2009) contend that such commitments are part of campaigns to muster public support for hosting the Games and, invariably, to justify expenditure of public funds for the purpose. Like any public policy, the claim should be exposed to rigorous testing as part of public accountability processes, and this process can only be enacted by ensuring that measures of grassroots sport participation are available for the host city, region and nation on a comparable basis before and after hosting the Games. The UK might just be the first country to follow such a method, although there are variations in how participation is measured in the four countries that comprise the UK – England, Scotland, Northern Ireland and Wales – as responsibility for developing and measuring participation is devolved to each nation.

Writing before the London 2012 bid, Coalter (2004) questioned the extent to which potential models of the behavioural change required to demonstrate the impact of the Olympics and Paralympics on participation could be demonstrated. First, sporting role models could be seen to develop widespread participation, although asking people generally to name Britain's recent Olympic medallists often elicits only a few key names who already receive widespread coverage. Second, the media could lead the growth of participation through coverage of the event but the majority of people in the country will experience the Olympics and Paralympics through their television or alternative media sources, thus leading to inactivity as they become passive spectators rather than active participants. Third, coverage of specific sports could increase participation in that sport, but the sports in which Britain is traditionally successful are technically difficult and dependent upon expensive technical equipment and scarce specialist facilities (rowing, canoeing, cycling, sailing, three day eventing and so forth). It is evident that if participation is to increase, a large number of people will have to demonstrate significant behavioural change in terms of lifestyle: either from non/lapsed-participant to regular participant; or from regular participant to even more frequent participation. For young people, the situation is varied and different (Collins 2010).

There is also the consideration of the infrastructure required for increased participation in sport. The Local Government Association (LGA-2010: 3.1) contested that local authorities are, along with sports clubs, the principal deliverers of sport in England investing £1.5 billion per year in sport (including capital spend). The LGA claimed that government, non-departmental public bodies and NGBs will not deliver increased grass roots participation on the back of the 2012 Games – a claim reinforced by, first, the abolition of the national 'Free Swimming' scheme by the Coalition Government and an act which undermined the potential of local authorities to provide strategic leadership and delivery in one area of legacy planning; and, second, by evidence from the Active People survey for 2009, which demonstrated no statistically significant participant change overall, no changes in membership for 22 of the sports funded for 2009–13, increases for five (bowling, cycling, rowing, taekwondo, and volleyball) and decreases for squash and canoeing (Collins 2010). The LGA (2010: 3.6) argued that:

> The answer to the question of how we can best use the Games to encourage
> people to be more active must be much deeper than national programmes
> and national legacy boards to co-ordinate legacy. The day-to-day reality of

delivering a thriving sporting offer is councils' bread and butter. We think government could be making more use of us in meeting our shared sporting legacy ambitions and what councils are already proactively doing.

School facilities also present similar problems. Despite unprecedented investment in facilities since 2003, many schools have to travel to facilities, especially in inner city areas, whilst other schools still have only small indoor facilities. By 2012, it is forecasted that 32% of men and 31% of females will be obese (Collins 2010). Around three in ten boys and girls aged two to fifteen are either overweight or obese (31% and 29% respectively – NHS 2010: 19). In their 2009–2013 Whole Sport Plans a number of NGBs targeted participation rises from 16.5% to 25% in four years; twelve promised participation growth over 20% and four over 50% (Collins 2010). Schools face a shortage of adequately trained teachers, particularly at primary level, and for many teenagers, especially girls, school sport amounts to aversion therapy, the experience effectively quashing any inclination they might otherwise have had to participate in sport.

What is clear is that, first, there has been a lack of historical evaluation of legacy (Cashman 2006); and second, there is a lack of rigorous research regarding claims made about the relationship between legacy and participation. SPEAR's (2009) overview of the available evidence of the effects of previous Games upon sport participation is unequivocal; the Games have not increased participation. Nevertheless, hosting the Games continues to be seen as a potential driver of increased participation. More importantly, no previous Games employed strategies aimed at raising physical activity or sport participation. As such, the use of an Olympic Games to raise physical activity and sport participation has not been attempted in any real sense. Furthermore, and as if to reinforce the scale of the challenge facing sports policy in the UK, there seems to be little evidence about the impact of the Olympics and Paralympics specifically and directly on young people's participation. The 2012 Games is thought likely to be most effective at raising participation frequency in sport and the most formal physical activities among current or lapsed participants who are already positively engaged with sport (SPEAR 2009: 10), but for young people the picture is less clear. Despite this major caveat, politicians continue to espouse the intended 'legacy' of London 2012. London won the right to host the 2012 Olympic Games because it would offer a 'legacy' for the youth of the world and young people in Britain. But it is not clear that the Government, regardless which political parties are in charge, can deliver on its promises.

The Olympification of sports policy for young people under 'New' Labour – 2008–2010

The attendance of former Prime Minister Tony Blair at the Singapore Olympic Congress, where London was awarded the 2012 Games, was seen by many as crucial to the bid. Blair added political gravity to the bid, and his video message during the final presentation to IOC members endorsed the claims of Lord Coe, the Chair of LOCOG, about the London 2012 Olympic and Paralympic Games inspiring the youth of the world. Consideration of how to leave a legacy of participation did not begin quickly enough, however, whilst the Labour Government monitored the establishment of the ODA and the LOCOG. In its LAP, the Labour Government (DCMS 2008) made a number of commitments to legacy including the headline ambition of inspiring young people through sport and increasing the profile of sport in the school curriculum, whilst also acknowledging the intent that participation be an intended outcome of the London 2012.

In the 2010 UK General Election, all three main political parties made commitments to successfully hosting the Olympics and Paralympics, but it was only the outgoing Labour Party who provided further detail, in a sports manifesto, justifying the Games and their associated costs (£9.35 billion) in the face of the recession, through many intended legacy benefits (Labour Party 2010). Former Prime Minister, Gordon Brown, acknowledged that no host country has achieved a legacy of participation but also asserted that Britain will achieve a legacy. Furthermore, the Labour Party championed the further renaissance of sport in schools, acknowledging that whilst sport in schools had not ever been a main element of any political party's manifesto, hosting the Olympics has made it one that was seen as essential. Griffiths and Armour (2010) noted that whilst it was too late to establish anything new, embedding legacy ambitions within existing PE and school sport structures offered the most likely chance to obtain a legacy for young people.

Labour's LAP (DCMS 2008) set out a cross-Government target to get two million more adults active through sport and physical activity by 2012. The LAP target applied to adults aged over 16 and was based on individuals achieving three sessions of at least 30 minutes of at least moderate intensity activity per week. The DCMS and Sport England were to lead on getting one million more people doing more sport. A range of other Government departments were to deliver programmes that would increase wider physical activity and attempt to increase participation by a further one million more people. Many of the programmes were outlined in the Department of Health's (DoH) physical activity plan, *Be Active, Be Healthy* (DoH 2009), a plan not recognised by the new coalition government. Sport England's Active People survey, the largest survey of participation in sport in any one country, was to be the measure for the two million target. The LAP, however, made no mention of targets for young people, despite the claims made during the bidding process.

The key element regarding sports policy for young people in the creation of the LAP was the Physical Education, School Sport and Young People (PESSYP) strategy. Overseen by the Youth Sport Trust (YST), a registered charity and, in effect, the Government's main delivery partner, the strategy saw considerable growth, impact and development in PE and School Sport opportunities. By 2008, 90% of 5—16 year-olds received two hours of PE and school sport a week, up from 25% in 2003 (DCSF 2008). Gordon Brown, in one of his first policy announcements as Prime Minister, pledged in July 2007 to increase the target to five hours a week. In February 2008 he backed this by pledging £775m over the next three years, of which £100m would be spent on promoting competition. The 2008–2011 strategy sought to extend the amount of opportunity through what became known as the 'five hour offer'. In addition to at least two hours per week of high quality PE and Sport in school for all 5–16 year-olds, all children and young people aged 5–19 would be offered opportunities to participate in a further three hours per week of sporting activities provided through schools, Further Education Colleges, clubs and community providers. The intention was to create a sustainable legacy both in terms of future elite success and grass roots sport. The scale of recent investment in PE and school sport under Labour had been unprecedented and the importance of school/youth sport to developing lifelong participation in sport and physical activity was fully recognised. The role of Sport England included increasing regular participation in sport by one million by 2012/13 and working with the YST to enable young people to access at least five hours of sport a week and sustaining current participation in sport by ensuring that participants have a high quality experience and working to reduce the 'drop-off' in sports participation between the ages of 16 and 18 (Sport England 2008: 6). Speaking in early 2008, Lord Coe shared the caution of many in education who believed there were not enough specialists, especially in primary schools, to deliver a legacy through PE and School Sport. Coe was adamant that London 2012 will provide the inspiration, but less certain that the state school system is ready to nurture it (Kelso 2008).

> We shouldn't kid ourselves, we are coming from a long way back. This is not something that has crept up on us for the last five years. It is not enough to say, We've got the games, everything else is going to fall into place. We've really got to grab this territory back quickly, and I will take a lot of convincing that it doesn't start in schools.

Childhood and adult obesity in England and the UK has never been higher and levels of physical inactivity have never been lower, despite the findings from the annual PESSYP survey. For boys, on weekdays, the proportion who spent four or more hours doing sedentary activities was 35% of those who were not overweight or obese, 44% of those classed as overweight and 47% of those classed as obese. For girls, a comparable pattern was found: 37%, 43% and 51% respectively. (NHS Information Centre 2010: 20). Nevertheless, the 2009–2010 PE and School Sport survey reported (Quick et. al 2010: 4–6) that:

> Across Years 1–13, 55% of pupils participated in at least three hours of high quality PE and out of hours school sport during the 2009/10 academic year . . . an encouraging increase of five percentage points in terms of the proportion of pupils in Years 1–13 taking part in three hours of PE and out of hours school sport. Participation levels are highest in Years 4–6, and also reasonably high in Years 1–3 and Years 7–8. They are at their lowest in Years

12 and 13. The 2009/10 survey found a very large increase in the proportion of pupils participating in intra-school competitive activities during the academic year–up from 69% (of Years 1–11) in 2008/09 to 78% in 2009/10. Like participation in intra-school competition in general, regular participation has also increased substantially over the last year – up from 28% of Years 3–13 in 2008/09 to 39% in 2009/10.

The coalition's PE and sports policy: creating an Olympic legacy or destroying its foundations?

With the election of a new government and the winds of austerity howling following the Comprehensive Spending Review in October 2010, there are dire warnings in the UK of the scale of the challenge about building a participation legacy for young people if the investment of the into PE and School Sport is not sustained. The 'Building Schools for the Future' programme, established by Labour and utilised by many schools to rebuild sports facilities, was immediately cut in the emergency 50 day budget in June 2010. NGBs, responsible for the majority of raising participation levels have, whilst supporting in varied measures the elements of school competition, continued to exclude or marginalise the school system from whole sport plans and paid only lip service to including junior squads within the school sport systems and structures. The comparatively sophisticated nature of the evaluation of UK/English sports policy means that there are systematic data measures in place to record increases or decreases in participation, after the Games. But whether increases can be directly attributed to holding the events as a result of hosting the London 2012 Olympics and Paralympics is doubtful.

The Coalition Government put deficit reduction at the heart of its economic policy, arguing that the poor state of the UK's public finances posed a greater threat to economic recovery than cuts in spending. Parents are perplexed as to how the Olympics can inspire primary aged young people (aged 5–11) when the curriculum and the majority of after-school clubs focus not on the development of sport *per se*, but on development of physical activity and skill-related activities. The 2012 Games will not automatically help to raise participation in sport. If, instead, the Games are levered into current political thinking, policy planning and implementation there is a chance, but only a chance, that as part of wider physical activity and sport policy/participation initiatives the 2012 Games might be able to contribute to increasing the frequency of participation in sport of existing participants, or to rekindling interest in lapsed sport participants, through a demonstration effect (SPEAR 2009). Giving evidence to the DCMS Select Committee (Parliament UK 2010), former IOC Communications Manager, Mark Dolley, noted the following:

> The Olympic movement understands the demonstration effect, which is the ability of Olympic athletes to inspire. That said, there is also perhaps a need

for a second effect which has been identified which is that we could possibly be creating a festival effect around London 2012, explicitly linked to it, in order to encourage people who have become disconnected from sport to reconnect. It is this notion that if you have become disconnected from sport you are probably not going to be that directly inspired just by the sight of Olympians and you probably need to be drawn back into sport by something that transcends sport. Is there the opportunity to do something in that particular field? Yes, I believe so.

Since the formation of the Coalition Government, there have been changes to policy and to the structures which implement policy that focus on the development of increased competition. The DCMS have stated that the Games offer a 'fantastic opportunity to improve the lives of young people. They allow us to: promote the Olympic ideals of striving for excellence, doing your best, fair play and cultural understanding encourage positive views of disability improve diversity and community get children and young people involved in sport, and to help them to make healthy living choices engage underachieving and disaffected young people improve the nation's language learning make young people more aware of other countries' (DCMS 2010). The following programmes will deliver this vision: *Get Set* is a web-based resource for young people aged 3–19 and their teachers; *International Inspiration* uses sport to engage and inspire young people across the world; and the *2012 Young Ambassadors Programme*. No mention is made of participation or competition and it not evident that the Coalition Government recognises Labour's LAP.

The PESSYP Strategy has since been dismantled by the Coalition. School Sport Partnerships, the networks that organised out of school hours activities and competition, will disappear in August 2011 and it will be up to schools locally to decide on their priorities. It is certain that there will be no PE and School Sport Survey in the future, thus possibly disintegrating the research base from which to measure the intended legacy of participation. The Coalition Government has nailed its colours firmly to the mast. Increased levels of competition will be at the heart of the legacy for young people. There will be a new Olympic and Paralympic-style sports competition for young people across England and it will be a key part of the Government's plans to generate a lasting sporting legacy. The focus will be on recognised Olympic/Paralympic sports but, as noted above, few schools will be able to support some of the sports that Britain is most successful in, notably cycling, sailing, rowing and three-day eventing. Every school, including mainstream and special schools, will be given the opportunity to get involved. The national finals are to be held in the run-up to the London Olympic and Paralympic Games in 2012 and there is stated ambition for the competition to continue after 2012. Schools will also be encouraged to host in-house Olympic-style sports days so that children of all abilities have the opportunity to compete. Schools now have their own autonomy and priorities, receiving a lump sum and it is up to them to decide how much they invest into elements of the curriculum. It's possible that schools will drop certain subjects, and the question to be asked is whether schools will be committed to PE and school sport when alternatives are available.

Although there has been no overt acknowledgement, the Coalition's priorities seem heavily influenced by a report which suggested that failure of central funding to increase participation indicates that a more effective alternative would be to disburse all central funds directly to schools, which should be free to use this money as they see fit on sporting activities for their pupils (Burkard and Cleverly 2010: 24). The scrapping of the £160 million annual funding to the Youth Sport Trust, in the CSR on October 20th 2010, signalled the dismantling of a network which may have provided the legacy promised. In a personal email, seen by the author, Burkard responded to an impassioned plea from a Partnership Development Manager (Parliament UK 2010):

> In principle, we are opposed to centrally-funded initiatives which create winners and losers, and which rob schools of the right to choose what is best for their pupils. Personally, I would rather see the growth of something akin to American sports programmes, where basketball and American football matches between schools draw large gates and are covered by local radio – the revenues they generate support whole-school sports activities both in and after school. The strong emphasis on competition creates keen interest in sport, which obviates the need for bureaucratic structures designed to encourage participation.

Burkard's reply seems based on a system which is not at all sustainable in publicly-funded UK models of education provision. Evidently, the emerging issue is a greater governmental concern about competitive sport in schools. It was part of Labour's agenda but it seems an even stronger reflex for the Coalition. In September 2010, the YST announced the greater variety of provision (Quick et al. 2010: 6):

> Schools provided on average 19.0 different sports from a pre-specified list. This is a small increase over the average number of sports provided in 2008/ 09 (18.6). Schools had links to an average of 9.1 listed clubs. When compared to the 2008/09 survey, this represents an increase from 8.2, continuing the upwards trend. Football, cricket, dance, rugby union, swimming, athletics and tennis are the most widespread clubs.

The Children's Minister, Tim Loughton, was not satisfied (Vasager 2010: 3):

> Young people's involvement in competitive sport remains disappointingly low. We aim to spark a competitive sport revolution by giving thousands of young people the chance to compete at the Olympic and Paralympic-style school sport competitions in 2012.

That prompts some immediate questions about how more competition relates to Physical Education, and to issues of health and obesity, and to whether competition is likely to be inclusive and what effect these competitions will have on existing school resources and programmes. Another underlying theme, perhaps based more on instinct than ideology, is the Conservative preference/prejudice for competition. Other than pointing to the 'legacy' of those who have had a public school education, there seems to be no underlying rationale for this preference/ prejudice in favour of competitive team sports and no explanation of how competitions relate to participation and Olympic legacy for the vast majority of young people. Only by changing a system that in the past has focused too closely on the able and the willing, can the government's ambitions be met. But, surely, competition does not increase participation per se; rather, it is regular participation that engenders entering the competitive arena.

Time's run out – the wasted opportunity for a legacy of participation

The concept and policy of 'legacy' should be subject to acute scrutiny under the Coalition government. For the IOC, in Athens (2004) and Beijing (2008) once these Games were over, the issue of legacy was quietly dampened. Neither Olympic Games proved to be a conduit for increased participation in sport within either host country and often no great efforts seem to have been made to do much to remedy this. In 2004, it became evident that the IOC did not think much about legacy, being more concerned that the facilities were finished on time. In Beijing, legacy was promised and the venues were declared as the best ever seen as the international audience marvelled at the iconic Bird's Nest stadium and the Water Cube, a superlative tribute to Chinese engineering standards. But, information regarding the participation in sport of the world's largest population since the Olympics does not seem to be available.

As a result of the Olympics, sport has never been higher on the UK political agenda and regular claims have been made by politicians of all parties about its potential to inspire. While there's little doubt that the London 2012 Olympic and Paralympic Games will be outstanding events, making significant contributions to the regeneration of East London, there is, as noted above, no compelling evidence that the time-limited spectacle of the Games has ever sustainably promoted improved levels of participation, or levels of health and fitness, or increased competition. As Kelso (2008) noted, faced with incontrovertible evidence of a health and fitness disaster, 'New' Labour's [established] identifiable policy and funding commitments, set in train a wholesale restructuring of how school sport was delivered. In the five years to 2008, £1.5 billion of exchequer and lottery funding was been diverted to school sport, with a further £775m promised to 2011. Through the Coalition's austerity measures, fuelled by consistent accusatory announcements about Labour's mismanagement of the economy, significant questions now exist concerning about what will be left of the established structures through which Olympic inspiration could be leveraged into behavioural patterns of young people outside of the school curriculum. With Sport England and NGBs identified as being mainly responsible for legacy[1], the question is 'what and who will be left for them to work with?'. With schools being given the option to structure curriculum and invest in subjects as they see fit, will PE and school sport remain priority areas? It is hard to imagine that they will.

Conclusion

Legacy is both an irresistible term for policy makers and also a fallacious, illusionary concept which cannot be enacted through rhetorical public policy statements alone. Under Labour's administration in the build-up to London 2012, the opposition's criticism of the Government focused on the way in which existing sport policies were aggregated into one overarching programme to demonstrate the legacy potential of increased participation. Once in power, following its free-market philosophy, the Coalition has been busy dismantling Labour's 'legacy' in the dubious belief that increased amounts of competition will stimulate widespread grassroot recruitment into sport.

In order to be successful, Olympic/Paralympic bids are required to state the host's intention to leave a legacy from hosting the event. But London's aspirations of leaving a legacy of participation domestically, and of providing inspiration for the youth of the world, promised more in this regard than any previous Olympic bid. Furthermore, that undertaking was propelled swiftly into formal policy statements from the DCMS, often to justify a final budget four times more than originally stated. London 2012 marks the first opportunity for any host country to use existing research evidence to demonstrate the patterns of participation within an Olympic host country but the extent to which the Games' long term impact on participation will remain elusive.

At the end of the day, post-Olympic participation or legacy is not anything to do with LOCOG, the ODA nor the IOC. The buck stops with the Coalition Government, now responsible for fulfilling the legacy claims, but which – less than two years before the Games – seems intent on dismantling the structures established by Labour and stamping its own imprint on what legacy for young people will look like. With far less resources, an emphasis on competition, and with more changes to sport policy and associated structures still to come, it seems highly unlikely that London 2012 will come close to keeping its legacy promises. No amount of political blame and counter-blame will shield the fact that for young people, sadly, London 2012 looks likely to be a missed opportunity. And once the Circus has left town, who will be there to clean up the mess left by the elephants?

Note

1   Letter from Jeremy Hunt, Secretary of State for the Department of Culture, Media and Sport to Richard Lewis, Chair of Sport England, October 20th 2010.

References

Burkhard, T. and Clelford, T. (2010) *Cutting the Children's Plan: a £5 billion experiment gone astray*, London, Centre for Policy Studies available via http://www.cps.org.uk/cps_catalog/Cutting%20the%20Children.pdf [accessed August 4, 2010]

Cashman, R. (2006) *The Bitter-Sweet Awakening: The Legacy of the Sydney 2000 Olympic Games*, Sydney: Walla Wall Press.

Coalter, F. (2004) 'Stuck in the blocks? A sustainable sporting legacy', in A. Vigor, M. Mean and C. Tims (eds) *After the Gold Rush: A Sustainable Olympics for London*, London: Institute for Public Policy Research/DEMOS.

Commonwealth of Australia (2009) *The Future of Sport in Australia*, Australia: Barton ACT.

Commonwealth of Australia (2010) *Australian Sport: The Pathway to Success*, Australia: Barton, ACT.

Collins, M. (2010) 'From "sport for good" to "sport for sport's sake" – not a good move for sports development in England?', *The International Journal of Sport Policy and Politics* 2(3): 367–379.

DCMS (2007) *Our Promise for 2012: How the UK Will Benefit from the Olympic and Paralympic Games*, London: DCMS.

DCMS (2008) *Before, During and After: Making the Most of the London 2012 Games*, London, DCMS.

DoH (2009) *Be Active, Be Healthy*, London: Department of Health.

Girginov, V. and Hills, L. (2009) 'The political process of constructing a sustainable London Olympics sports development legacy', *International Journal of Sport Policy and Politics* 1(2): 161–181.

Griffiths, M. and Armour, K. (2010) 'Physical education and youth sport in England: conceptual and practical foundations for an Olympic legacy?', Paper presented to the one day conference: Fit for London, 2012? An Assessment of UK Sport Policy in Comparative Contexts, University of Birmingham, July 19th, 2010.

Kelso, P. (2008) 'Faster, higher, stronger: the Olympian challenge facing school sports', *The Guardian*, February, 2, available via http://www.guardian.co.uk/politics/2008/feb/02/uk.olympics2012 [accessed 22 February 2008].

Kennett, C. and de Moragas, M. (2006) 'Barcelona 1992: evaluating the Olympic legacy', in A. Tomlinson and C. Young (eds) *National Identity and Global Sports Events: Culture, Politics, and Spectacle in the Olympics and the Football World Cup*, Albany: State University of New York Press.

[The] Labour Party (2010) *The Labour Party Manifesto 2010: A Future Fair for All*. London: The Labour Party.

Local Government Association (2010) *Written evidence on the 2012 Olympic legacy*, submitted to the Culture, Media and Sport Committee, January, available via http://www.publications.parliament.uk/pa/cm200910/cmselect/cmcumeds/memo/olympics/ucm2302.htm [accessed May 17, 2010].

Mangan, J.A. (2008) 'Guarantees of global goodwill: post-Olympic legacies – too many limping white elephants?', *International Journal of the History of Sport* 25(14): 1869–1883.

MacAloon, J. (2008) ' "Legacy" as a managerial/magical discourse in contemporary Olympic affairs', *International Journal of the History of Sport* 25(14): 2060–2071.

NHS Information Centre (2010), *Statistics on Obesity, Physical Activity and Diet: England, 2010*, London: Health and Social Care Information Centre.

Parliament UK (2010) Examination of Witnesses (Questions 1–19) Mr Mark Dolley and Ms Tessa Sanderson CBE. *DCMS Select Committee Inquiry to the Legacy of the Olympic and Paralympic Games*, available via http://www.publications.parliament.uk/pa/cm2009

10/cmselect/cmcumeds/416/10030302.htm [accessed May 10, 2010].

Quick, S., Simon, A. and Thornton, A. (2010) *PE and Sport Survey*, London: Department for Education, Research Report DFE-RR302.

SPEAR(Centre for Sport, Physical Education and Activity Research) (2009) *A Systematic Review of the Evidence Base for Developing a Physical Activity and Health Legacy from the London 2012 Olympic and Paralympic Games*. London: Department of Health.

Tomlinson, A. (1993) 'Interrogating the policy text', in A. Tomlinson and G. McFee (eds), *Education, Sport and Leisure: Connections and Controversies*, Eastbourne: Chelsea School Research Centre.

Toohey, K. (2008) 'The Sydney Olympics: striving for legacies – Overcoming short-term disappointments and long-term deficiencies', *International Journal of the History of Sport* 25 (14): 1953–1971.

Toohey, K. and Veal, A.J (2007) *The Olympic Games: A Social Science Perspective (2ⁿᵈ edn.)* Wallingford: CABI Publishing.

Vasager, J. (2010) 'School sport is growing but not fast enough, say Ministers', *The Guardian*, 24 September, p. 3.

Veal, A.J. and Frawley, S. (2009) *Working Paper No 6: 'Sport for All' and Major Sporting Events: Trends in Sport Participation and the Sydney 2000 Olympic Games, the 2003 Rugby World Cup and the Melbourne 2006 Commonwealth Games*, Sydney: School of Leisure and Tourism Studies, University of Technology, Sydney.

7

DOPING AND THE OLYMPICS

Rights, responsibilities and account-abilities (watching the athletes)

Barrie Houlihan

The context of the International Olympic Committee's involvement in anti-doping

In the 1980s and early 1990s there were two statements that were routinely made by the then President of the IOC, Juan Antonio Samaranch, at the conclusion of the Olympic Games. The first was to congratulate the hosts on organising the 'best games ever' or some such similar phrase and the second was to comment on the continuing success in the 'fight against doping'. Although the first statement was designed in part to flatter the hosts there was usually some substance to the assessment as 1980 marks the date from which hosting the Olympic Games became a competitive event in its own right with each set of bidding cities and subsequent hosts feeling compelled to out do the excesses of their predecessors. The second statement was much more difficult to verify and indeed was always delivered in a tone which suggested either wishful thinking or a wilful disdain for the evidence.

Today the IOC's role as the putative leader in the 'fight against doping' has been assumed by the World Anti-Doping Agency (WADA), but for many years the IOC was the acknowledged global lead organisation and much of the current anti-doping framework was initiated by the Committee. While it is easy to criticise the IOC for 'not doing more', given its rapid increase in income from 1980 and its undeniable status as the world's most prestigious sport organisation it is important to bear in mind the precise nature of the organisation and, more specifically, its relationship with athletes. In particular, it should be remembered that the IOC is an event organising body and has no direct contractual links with athletes outside the various Olympic competitions: it is the international federations with whom the athlete has a contractual relationship. Nevertheless, the IOC has been at the heart of the international response to doping since the mid 1960s and a review of the way in which the IOC's role emerged and evolved provides a sharp insight into the global politics of anti-doping policy.

The 1980s was the decade when doping in Olympic sport was recognised to be extensive and in some countries and events endemic. It was also the period when the limitations of the Olympic movement to respond effectively to the problem became sharply apparent. Each of the three Games – Moscow in 1980, Los Angeles in 1984 and Seoul in 1988 – highlighted particular deficiencies in the capacity of the IOC and, more specifically, that of its Medical Commission. The 1980 Games, at which responsibility for doping control rested with the Moscow Organising Committee (MGOC), put the fox in charge of the henhouse. Victor Rogazhin, chair of the MGOC, understandably was keen to trumpet the quality of its laboratory: less understandable was the endorsement of the Moscow testing regime by the United States Olympic Committee physician, Daniel Hanley, who commented that 'the capacity of the labs in Moscow seems to be perfectly adequate, and the testing will be carefully overseen by the Medical Commission [of the IOC]' (quoted in Hunt 2008). Similar naively optimistic comments were made by a series of high level sports administrators in the early 1980s which tended to drown out the more sceptical voices of people such as Dr Arnold Beckett and Dr Manfred Donike (both members of the IOC Medical Commission). The Moscow laboratory conducted over 6,000 sample analyses and found not a single breach of the anti-doping regulations. Although there was widespread suspicion of the factors underpinning the success of Soviet athletes (and that of its allies, especially the German Democratic Republic) the problem of the inadequacy of the IOC anti-doping regime was not confined to communist countries as the winter Olympic Games, held at Lake Placid, USA, also failed to produce one positive laboratory analysis from almost 800 urine samples.

Although a substantial part of the problem of doping (and of the ineffectiveness of the IOC response) was due to the role of powerful governments, such as those of the Soviet Union and the GDR, in promoting state-orchestrated doping, part also lay in the inadequacy of IOC resources (or at least investment) to ensure that analytical techniques kept pace with the development of new doping practices and substances. For example, just at the time when a reliable test had been developed for anabolic steroids athletes moved on to the use of testosterone for which no reliable test then existed. However, what was also becoming increasingly apparent to those concerned to tackle the issue of doping more robustly was the jurisdictional confusion between international federations and the IOC and between international federations and their domestic affiliates. In addition, it was also becoming clear that many international federations had poorly drafted anti-doping regulations which even moderately astute lawyers were able to exploit.

Following the Moscow Games the IOC, through its Medical Commission, made some attempt to reform its anti-doping policy and practices, but the achievements were modest. In particular, the Medical Commission began to consider how drug testing might be organised between Olympic Games. However, the Commission was also acutely aware that extending its remit beyond the Games would requires the agreement and cooperation of the international federations many of who were deeply suspicious of the expansionist ambitions of the IOC and were inclined to resist any attempt to expand the Committee's jurisdiction in the area of doping for fear that this would lead to greater influence over International Federation (IF) events. Progress consequently tended to be limited to bi-lateral agreements with a small number of individual IFs over matters such as laboratory recognition and agreement on sanctions for athletes committing doping violations. The new President of the IOC, Juan Antonio Samaranch, added little momentum to the admittedly modest anti-doping efforts of the Medical Commission prompting Richard Pound to comment that Samaranch 'always thought the IOC Medical Commission was dangerous' (quoted in Hunt 2008: 16). He later commented that 'to him [Samaranch] the fight against doping was more of a nuisance than a gut issue' (Pound 2006: 91). The extent of Samaranch's hypocrisy towards the issue was illustrated by his response to the 1998 Tour de France doping scandal when he commented that the list of prohibited substances was too long and should be restricted to those that damage an athlete's health.

Matters had certainly not improved by the time of the 1984 Olympic Games held in Los Angeles and it is arguable that the American organisers were just as cynical in their attitude towards doping as their Soviet counterparts and also that the IOC was just as ineffective in 1984 as it had been in 1980. Following rumours of extensive doping at the IAAF World Championships in Helsinki in 1983 the United States Olympic Committee (USOC) introduced pre-competition testing for steroids in the run-up to the Los Angeles Olympics. However, the testing regime was not used to identify and exclude drug users. As Hunt (2008: 16) reports:

> Dr Voy [USOC Medical Officer] later learned that many athletes were allowed to compete despite affirmative indications of doping. In a self-incriminating report that was withheld until after the conclusion of the 1984 Games, USOC President F. Don Miller admitted that eighty-six athletes, including ten at the Olympic Trials, tested positive for banned substances before competition in Los Angeles.

The strenuous opposition of the Los Angeles Games organiser, Peter Ueberroth, to a drug testing regime that might jeopardise the profitability of the Games received a sympathetic response from IOC President Juan Antonio Samaranch. Although twelve athletes tested positive at the Games none was American. It was clear that throughout the 1980s and 1990s the primary concern of the IOC President and many local Games organisers was to protect the public image of the Games from the taint of doping scandal even if that meant ignoring the mounting evidence of extensive and systematic doping.

Up to the late 1990s the IOC was at best equivocal about the issue of doping in sport and also about its own role in the fight against doping. There was a lack of consistency and clarity about the organisation's motives for tackling the problem with a concern for the image of the Games being the most evident justification. However, while the IOC continued to prevaricate the problem of doping and the sporting, scientific and political environment in which it was located was evolving in ways which would result in a significant marginalisation of the Committee. When the crisis that enveloped the 1998 Tour de France erupted the IOC looked like an organisation that was politically out of its depth and one which lacked the leadership acumen and diplomatic skills and resources to be much more than a bystander as other policy actors made anti-doping policy decisions around the IOC rather than with it.

The major change within the sporting environment was the rapid increase in the 1980s of the number of international sports events – world championships and grand prix events – prompted by the abandonment of amateurism. The increase in athlete mobility due to the development of international competition circuits and the popularity of (and financial capacity to enable) training in warm climates meant that many athletes spent little time in their home country and within the jurisdiction of their home federation. In addition, the IOC was increasingly aware of the weaknesses of an anti-doping regime that relied on in-competition testing when the most common use of drugs was as training aids. However, the introduction of out-of-competition testing involved a level of transnational co-operation and an expenditure of resources that few federations or governments had anticipated and that the IOC was clearly incapable of engineering.

A further change to the sporting environment was the increased litigiousness of elite athletes who were able to use their newfound wealth to challenge positive doping results and involve their IFs in court cases which were costly even if the federation was successful. Well-documented cases involving elite athletes such as the German Katrin Krabbe and the Australian Martin Vinnicombe drew the attention of the federations to the potential cost of defending their decisions in court and also made them aware of just how vulnerable many of their decisions were, due to the poor drafting of regulations and the failure to ensure compatibility of domestic regulations with those of the international federation and with the domestic federations in other countries.

The scientific environment had also changed dramatically in the 1980s. Not only was the extent of experimentation by athletes increasing, but so too was the pace at which new drugs were entering the elite athlete market. Although the use of steroids was to remain the central concern of anti-doping authorities new techniques and drugs (the manipulation of testosterone levels and the use of human growth hormone) meant that the cost of devising reliable tests and the cost of maintaining the laboratories and staff to conduct sample analysis was growing at a rapid rate and fast outstripping the financial capacity of federations and the IOC.

Finally, the political environment had changed substantially. The state-orchestrated doping evident in many Central and Eastern European countries had ended with the collapse of communism in 1989 and the United States government was, at long last, beginning to acknowledge the need for action on doping in Olympic sport. The long term commitment of the Council of Europe to the promotion of anti-doping within its member states was also starting to show signs of impact. Finally, and perhaps most importantly, there was a growing recognition among the countries of the economically developed world that mega-sports events, of which the Olympic Games was the most significant, were a valuable political prize. Mega-sports events were increasing seen as possessing the potential to deliver a wide range of non-sports benefits with the economic and the diplomatic being the most important. If the potential of these events was to be fully realised then the risk of embarrassment due to doping violations needed to be minimised.

As is frequently the case, government agendas are often set by exogenous events such as crises. For Canada and Australia it was a serious doping crisis that led the governments of both countries to adopt a much more supportive and active role in relation to doping. The Dubin Inquiry in Canada following the Ben Johnson's positive test result at the Seoul Olympics in 1988 and the Australian Senate Committee's investigation of allegations of doping at the Australian Institute of Sport left a lasting legacy of international activism (Australian Government, 1989; Dubin, 1990). The state enquiries in Canada and Australia prompted a radical change in attitude and led both countries to establish state-supported anti-doping agencies which are currently among the most respected.

By the mid to late 1990s it was clear that global anti-doping policy was at a turning point, but it was unclear which direction policy would take. There was a much sharper recognition of the scale and complexity of the problem, there were certainly more active policy actors (both sporting and governmental), there was increasing scepticism regarding the determination and capacity of the IOC to lead on the issue, and some of the substantial structural barriers to closer global co-operation had been removed, most significantly the end of the Cold War. An optimistic assessment of the prospects for the development of a more effective anti-doping policy would refer to *inter alia* to: the vastly improved international political climate; the increasing number of countries that had established anti-doping agencies; the increase in the number of countries involved in multilateral agreements, such as the International Anti-Doping Arrangement between a small group of countries, including Australia, Canada, The Netherlands and Sweden, which enabled the diffusion of good practice in testing and education and also acted as a lobby within the wider global political and sports community; and the number of forums available for the exchange of information among sports organisations and between sports and governmental organisations had increased significantly. A less optimistic assessment of the state of anti-doping policy in the mid-1990s would point not only to the poor record of doping violation detection (for example Ben Johnson had been tested over 15 times while using steroids before he tested positive in 1988), but also to the daunting nature of the challenge of engineering global agreement across non-governmental sports organisations and governments.

The history of anti-doping policy development is substantially one where policy change is prompted by crisis. The death of the Danish cyclist, Knud Jensen, at the Rome Olympics in 1960 led the IOC to establish a Medical Commission, the death of the British cyclist Tom Simpson in 1967 was a catalyst for the entry of the Council of Europe into the anti-doping policy arena, and the positive drug test for Ben Johnson resulted in a major change of policy towards doping by the Canadian government and by the IOC. Not surprisingly it was another scandal, the extensive doping uncovered at the 1998 Tour de France, which cut through the policy inertia in the late 1990s and eventually led to the establishment of the World Anti-Doping Agency in 1999.

The World Anti-Doping Agency and the changing role of the IOC

The establishment of WADA was not only a rare, if not unique, collaboration between governments and non-governmental organisations, but also marked the loss of policy leadership by the IOC and the need for the Committee to adapt to a new role in relation to anti-doping. In the years since the establishment of WADA anti-doping policy has steadily moved beyond the reach of sports organisations and is now firmly entrenched as an element of public policy. While at the formal level sport organisations have equal authority with governments within WADA and over the global fight against doping in reality sports organisations in general, and the IOC in particular, play an increasingly peripheral supporting role.

In terms of governance WADA, through its 38 member Foundation Board, is accountable both to the Olympic movement (IOC and the Olympic international federations) and to governments with the funding of the Agency coming equally from the two sets of organisations. The close formal relationship between the Olympic movement and WADA is reinforced by a number of informal links. In the early years of the Agency Richard Pound, who was an IOC member and had held a number of senior positions within the organisation including that of Vice-President, was appointed as the inaugural WADA President. Although he has now relinquished the WADA Presidency he remains a member of the Foundation Board and is also still a member of the IOC. Of equal importance is the role of Arne Ljungqvist who is the WADA vice-president and also President of the IOC's Medical Commission.

The close relationship between WADA and both governments and the Olympic movement was crucial in its early years as it sought to produce a World Anti-Doping Code which would generate support from the major sports federations and also from the thirty or so leading 'sports powers'. The Code, which came in to force in 2004, rapidly established itself as the global reference document for all major international sports events, all major international federations and the activities of public sector national anti-doping organisations (NADOs). The authority of the Code was reinforced in 2005 by the publication of the International Convention Against Doping in Sport[1] which entered into force in February 2007 and which, by late 2010, had been approved by 149 countries. The UNESCO Convention gave legal weight to the Code and imposed legal obligations on UN member states to support the implementation of the Code. Without going into detail the 2004 Code was, not surprisingly, focused on the use of drugs and the detection of doping violations through laboratory analysis. The impact of WADA and of the Code was substantial and rapid. Within six years of its establishment the Agency had: produced a Code (in a commendably transparent manner) which was quickly accepted as the global standard; negotiated with UNESCO the preparation of an anti-doping Convention which would bind governments to the Code; had put the organisation on a secure financial footing; had begun to fund research on testing techniques; and had helped to establish the Court of Arbitration for Sport as a widely respected independent court of appeal in doping cases.

Almost as soon as the Code came into force discussions were taking place about its revision. Some of the pressure for revision arose from the need to address a number of very specific issues overlooked in the initial version, such as the status of retired athletes who decide to return to competition, but some was the result of a radical reappraisal of the role of WADA and NADOs which would have significant implications for the rights and responsibilities of athletes and their support staff and would move the centre of gravity in policy-making further from the Olympic movement. Two aspects of the revised Code, which came into force in January 2009, have particular significance for the pattern of rights, responsibilities and accountabilities in relation to anti-doping and also illustrate the scale of change namely, the decision to 'move upstream' and the whereabouts requirements.

Moving 'upstream' refers to the decision to widen the focus of anti-doping activities from the important, but narrow, focus on the use of prohibited substances to the manufacture, supply and trafficking of performance enhancing drugs. Table 1 summarises the range of anti-doping rule violations covered by the 2009 Code and, in the right-hand column, indicates the process by which evidence of a violation will be obtained. The 2009 Code also gave greater emphasis to address-ing violations by an athlete's support staff. The shift in emphasis from a policy primarily dependent on laboratory analysis to one which sought to augment evidence from the laboratory with evidence from customs and excise and police departments represents a major change in the network of organisations involved in anti-doping. The anti-doping network in which the central members were sports organisations (domestic and international federations), accredited laboratories, national anti-doping organisations and, on occasion, the Court of Arbitration for Sport was being widened through the introduction of some very powerful agencies for whom elite sport doping is a relatively minor concern. However, if the manu-facture and supply of prohibited substances was to be tackled then the involvement of the police and customs services was a necessary condition, but one which is also giving additional momentum to the move away from treating doping as a matter to be addressed by sports organisations to one that is increasingly reliant on the law, police and criminal courts.

WADA, supported by UNESCO, is clearly supportive of the introduction by governments of specific legislation to outlaw the supply and trafficking in per-formance enhancing drugs and to date around twenty countries have introduced such legislation. Moreover, the move is supported by the IOC which viewed the uncovering, through a series of police raids, of blood doping organised by members of the Austrian ski team at the Turin Winter Olympics as evidence of the effectiveness of, and necessity for, wider investigative powers. The IOC and

TABLE 1.1 Types of Anti-Doping Rule Violation

Anti-doping rule violation	Sanction for first violation	Athlete/Athlete support staff	Action/source of evidence (test and/or investigation)
Presence	2 years	A	Test
Use	2 years	A	Investigation
Refuse sample	2 years	A	Test and Investigation
Whereabouts failure	2 years	A	Test and/or Investigation
Tampering	2 years	A/AS	Investigation
Possession	2 years	A/AS	Investigation
Trafficking	4 yrs – lifetime	A/AS	Investigation
Administration of Prohibited Substance	4 yrs – lifetime	A/AS	Investigation

Source: Adapted from the 2009 World Anti-Doping Code

WADA both note that the doping would not have been uncovered if the anti-doping authorities had had to rely solely on the Code and if Italy had not had specific legislation in place giving the police search powers in relation to performance enhancing drugs. In the wake of the raids the Austrian Olympic Committee banned six athletes and 14 officials (from the cross country and biathlon teams including coaches and some medical staff) for life from the Games and accepted the resignation of vice president of the Austrian Ski Federation.

Fuelled by the effectiveness of the Italian investigation the IOC is putting pressure on the UK to introduce similar legislation in time for the 2012 Games arguing that the UK is out of step with other leading anti-doping countries in Europe such as France, Italy and Sweden. According to Arne Ljungqvist, World Anti-Doping Agency board member 'I think legislation is very important that criminalises certain offences as detailed in the WADA code because it allows public authorities to intervene where we cannot. We as sports authorities have our limited possibilities regulated by our code. We can do testing but we cannot do searches' (quoted in the *Daily Telegraph* 8th November 2008).[2] The IOC view is reinforced by the British Olympic Association, whose President, Lord Moynihan, introduced a bill into the House of Lords in 2010 which would give police greater search powers. So far UK Anti-Doping, the UK's NADOs, is resisting IOC and BOA pressure arguing that existing laws are sufficient. Irrespective of the decision regarding the extension of police powers in the UK it is clear that, arguably of necessity, the policy network for anti-doping has widened to incorporate some very powerful policy actors and whose long term impact on the direction of policy is at best uncertain.

A second controversial element of the revised Code is the extension of the requirements for athletes to notify their NADO of their whereabouts. Under the 2009 Code all athletes within the registered testing pool of either their international federation or their NADO must provide, on a quarterly basis, details of their whereabouts including an address where they can guarantee to be for one hour each day for the purposes of sample collection. The new requirements have raised both practical and ethical concerns. As regards the practical considerations Hanstad and Loland (2008) studied 32 NADOs and found that fewer than three-quarters had a registered testing pool of athletes and only half of those had a system in place for collecting whereabouts data. Of greater concern was the variation in the response and attitude of NADOs to a missed test. According to the 2009 Code if an athlete is not at the address that he or she specified or gives inaccurate information about their location on three occasions within an eighteen month period they are liable to be charged with a doping violation. Hanstad and Loland (2008) found considerable variation in response to a missed test with about one-fifth of their sample reporting that they had no procedures in place should an athlete not be at the specified address and one-third reporting that they would try to contact them by phone thus effectively undermining the rationale for unannounced testing. The practical problems of implementing the whereabouts system was reinforced in the report from the WADA observation team at the Beijing Olympics which stated that 'Nearly half of the National Olympic Committees present in Beijing did not provide whereabouts information for their athletes to enable the most effective pre-Games and Out of Competition testing programme' (WADA 2008: 4). Apart from the practical problems of implementing the whereabouts system concern has also been expressed regarding whether the system infringes the right to privacy of athletes (see Schneider and Butcher 2001; Kayser et al. 2007). Concerns about the intrusive nature of the whereabouts system has prompted a legal challenge under European Union law by a group of 65 athletes.

Conclusion

For an organisation that had been able to exercise tight control over anti-doping policy and management at its own events and was the clear policy leader within the global sports community the loss of influence was abrupt. If the 1998 Tour de France had not been the catalyst then some other crisis would have provoked change. In many ways the IOC's loss of leadership on doping was a consequence of the growing salience of the Olympic Games and especially hosting the Games to governments. If the main motivation for President Samaranch to tolerate anti-doping activity was his concern with preserving the image of the Games this was certainly a concern shared by potential host cities and governments. The preference of governments in the 1980s to ignore the issue was far less sustainable from the 1990s and the alternative was to tackle the problem more directly. As a result the nature of the problem simply outgrew the administrative, legal and political capacity of the Olympic movement. The current involvement of the United Nations, the clear preference for legislation to combat the use of performance enhancing drugs and the desire to 'move upstream' provide further evidence of the scale of change that has taken place in the anti-doping policy network.

However, while the role of the IOC has undoubtedly changed it still makes an important contribution beyond its financial support to WADA. It is still the IOC that has the strongest links with the national Olympic committee in the country that hosts an Olympic Games and it is the NOC that is responsible for co-ordinating the pre-Games and in-competition testing. Since 2000 the standard and extent of testing has been much greater than at previous Games. Moreover, the strength of the IOC's commitment to ensuring the probity of the Olympic Games is reflected in its decision to retest over 900 blood samples from the Beijing Olympics which resulted in six athletes testing positive for the blood-boosting agent CERA. Further evidence of the IOC's continued commitment to supporting the work of WADA is the decision to drop baseball from the Olympic programme. Although the main reason was the limited global scope of the sport especially in Europe, the continued lack of enthusiasm exhibited by Major League Baseball in the United States towards the serious doping problem in the sport was considered to have contributed to its exclusion in 2005 (Pound 2006: 131). Finally, the distance between the two organisations that marred the early years of WADA, due to some extent to the antipathy that Samaranch felt toward Richard Pound, has been replaced by a more positive relationship although as will be argued below there is still much more that the IOC could do to support the Agency.

WADA has successfully managed the first phase in the development of the international policy regime tackling doping, but there must be some concern about the organisation's ability to deal with the next phase of development which primarily involves the consolidation of the gains made since 1999. The Agency and the global effort to combat doping faces four issues associated with complexity, capacity, commitment and compliance. Complexity refers to the tendency for international legal and quasi-legal agreements to become more complex over time as policy-makers seeks to close loopholes, satisfy legitimate sectional interests/ special cases, respond to change in the external environment etc. The best codes and conventions are those that retain the clarity that is the product of parsimony: complexity confuses implementers and those that the code is designed to protect.

Capacity is more significant issue, but less so for WADA and more for the organisations on which it relies for policy implementation i.e. NADOs, international federations and NOCs. Mention has already been made of the limited capacity of many NOCs and NADOs in relation to the implementation of a fundamental element of the Code – the whereabouts system. Ensuring that the weaker IFs, NOCs and NADOs have the minimum necessary resources (administrative capacity, expertise, finance and legal support) to implement the Code is crucial. UNESCO has provided some modest support for capacity building within NADOs in relation to its Convention, but this would appear to be an opportunity for the IOC to provide greater support not only for NOCs, but also for the smaller international federations, possibly through its Olympic Solidarity Commission or through some new fund.

Commitment refers to the potentially difficult task of maintaining enthusiasm for anti-doping not only because there are competing pressures within governments and federations for anti-doping resources, but also because demonstrating unequivocally both progress and value for money is extremely difficult if not simply impossible. Over the last forty years or so anti-doping activists have had to be alert to those windows of opportunity when policy can be advanced. Most of those opportunities have arisen as a result of scandal and crisis which is a fragile basis on which to build and deepen commitment to a policy: after a period of time what was once considered scandalous is considered routine.

The final challenge concerns demonstrating compliance. The WADA Code and the UNESCO Convention both need to be monitored in order to ensure that signatories 'follow through' on their acceptance of the documents. At present compliance is monitored mainly by means of self-completion questionnaires which have to be seen as a weak form of monitoring. Alternative or supplementary forms of monitoring, such as inspection visits as conducted at one time by the Council of Europe in connection with its anti-doping convention, would be expensive. While beyond the resources of both WADA and UNESCO the funding of independent monitoring visits by the IOC would be an important way for the Committee to provide a high profile endorsement of the work of the two organisations and ensure public recognition of its continuing support for anti-doping.

Notes

1   http://portal.unesco.org/en/ev.php-URL_ID=31037&URL_DO=DO_TOPIC&URL_SECTION=201.html (accessed 13th November 2010).
2   http://www.telegraph.co.uk/sport/othersports/olympics/london2012/3405340/IOC-pressure-Great-Britain-to-change-doping-laws-ahead-of-London-Olympics-2012.html (accessed 13th November 2010).

References

Australian Government (1989) *Drugs in Sport*. Interim report of the Senate Standing Committee on the Environment, Recreation and the Arts, Canberra: Australian Government Publishing Service.

Dubin, C.L. (1990) *Commission of Inquiry into the Use of Drugs and Banned Practices Intended to Increase Athletic Performance*, Ottawa: Canadian Government Publishing Centre.

Hanstad, D-V. and Loland, S. (2008) 'Athletes' whereabouts: similarities and differences in interpretation and implementation within NADOs', paper presented at the 10th ANADO workshop, Lausanne, Switzerland, 31 March.

Hunt, T.M. (2008) 'The lessons of crisis: Olympic doping regulation during the 1980s', *Iron Game History*, April/May, 12–25.

Kayser, B., Mauron, A. and Miah, A. (2007) 'Current anti-doping policy: A critical appraisal', *BMC Medical Ethics* (8.2). Available from http://www.biomedcentral.com/content/pdf/1472–6939–8-2.pdf

Pound, R. (2006) *Inside Dope*, Mississauga, Ontario, Canada: Wiley.

Schneider, A. and Butcher, R. (2001) 'An ethical analysis of drug testing', in W. Wilson and E. Derse (eds) *Doping in Elite Sport*, Champaign, Ill: Human Kinetics.

WADA (2008) *Report of the Independent Observers: XXIX Olympic Games, Beijing 2008*, Montreal: WADA.

WADA (2009) *World Anti-Doping Code*, Montreal: WADA.

8

THE OLYMPIC DOCUMENTARY AND THE 'SPIRIT OF OLYMPISM'

Ian McDonald

Introduction

Towards the end of *Sixteen Days of Glory*, the official documentary on the 1984 Olympic Games, hundreds of joyous athletes are shown pouring into the packed Los Angeles Memorial Coliseum stadium during the closing ceremony. As they do, the dulcet yet stentorian narrator declares:

> And so it was on the evening of August 12th, the sixteen days of glory came to their close. And the young men and women who gave us this daily celebration join together for the last time to say their final farewells. They had entered the arena, made the attempt, and competed with honour. And all of them will go back to their homes the better for it and for these moments there was beauty on this earth. It was left for one poet to write, we have seen the best that is within us. A tribute to all the hope and dreams of our youth. A hymn to the highest form of the human spirit, a hymn to the nations.

This is as good an articulation of the so-called 'spirit of Olympism' as will be found anywhere. It is also hyperbolic nonsensical sentimental rhetoric. And what is more, most viewers would probably agree that it is. It is doubtful that Peter Ueberroth, the entrepreneurial President of these first privately financed Games, or Juan Antonio Samaranch, the erstwhile Francoist and then President of the IOC, really believe that the Games reveal 'the best within us'. But the veracity of the voice-over is not at issue. Such rhetorical flourishes are essentially performative, not intended to reflect truth, but to meet a range of needs: an emotional yearning among people for the Olympics to stand for noble ideals; for the sponsoring corporations to profit as Whannel (2008: 122) put it 'by the presence of ideals'; for the IOC to maintain its global sporting hegemony. Without the wrapping of the quasi-religious 'spirit of Olympism', these different types of investment in the Olympic Games would yield few returns. So 'we' all go along with it even though 'we' know it is hyperbolic nonsensical sentimental rhetoric because without that we fear there would be an ideological void, reduced profits and limited political gain, and that these sixteen days of glory would simply, prosaically, become sixteen days of (largely minor) sports competition. The articulation of the 'spirit of Olympism' is simultaneously its own instantiation in an otherwise ideologically ambiguous sporting event. So does this mean that the role of the official Olympic documentary is simply to help reinforce the key ideological pillar of the Olympic Movement? If that is the case, might we be justified in denouncing the official Olympic documentary as IOC propaganda? This chapter attempts to provide some answers to these questions.

I begin by providing an overview of the emergence of the Olympic documentary, followed by some reflections on the relationship between Olympism, the Olympic documentary and the documentary as a filmic practice. Then I examine three key Olympic documentaries, each revealing a different understanding of the relationship between the Olympic documentary and the spirit of Olympism. These films are Kon Ichikawa's poetic *Tokyo Olympiad* on the 1964 Games; David L. Wolper's experimental *Visions of Eight* on the 1972 Games; and Bud Greenspan's 'ode to sporting endeavour' in *Sixteen Days of Glory* on the 1984 Games[1].

The emergence of the Olympic documentary

Although the first projected motion picture films were being made in 1896, the inaugural Games of the modern era, held in that year in Athens, were not filmed. No filming was done of the Games in Paris in 1900 or at the St. Louis Games in 1904. The first Olympics to be filmed were the 1908 Games in London, where Pathé recorded around 60 minutes worth of competition inside the White City Stadium. A small amount of filming was done at the subsequent Games in Stockholm in 1912 and at the Games in Antwerp in 1920. But the first Olympic feature film, as opposed to newsreels of the events, was made on the 1924 Summer and Winter Olympic Games in Paris, with *Les Jeux Olympiques Paris 1924*. Two Olympic feature films followed it in 1928, on the Winter Games in St. Moritz, *Das Weisse Stadion*, and on the Summer Games in Amsterdam, *De Olympische Spelen*. However, none of these feature films gained much exposure and remain obscure though highly significant artefacts of Olympic history (McKeever 2011).

The first significant Olympic film, in terms of cinematic merit as well as exposure is *Olympia*, Leni Riefenstahl's epic account of the landmark 1936 Olympic Games in Berlin. *Olympia* has become the most analysed, debated and notorious of all the Olympic films, widely acknowledged as a pioneering and technically brilliant film, but also accused of serving the propaganda machinery of the Nazi regime. In this chapter, I will NOT be examining Riefenstahl's *Olympia*. That has been done many times before (for example, Downing 1992, Hinton 2000, MacKenzie 2003, McFee and Tomlinson 1999, Rodriguez 2003) and I do not have much to add except to say that *Olympia* is significant not simply as a film text in its own right, but also because it is both the 'significant' and 'operational Other' of all subsequent Olympic films. That is to say that all Olympic films are compelled to speak to or against the treatment of Olympism in *Olympia* (Vaughan 1999). Thus in the shadow of the controversy stoked by Riefenstahl's film as it were, I will explore how the spirit of Olympism gets expressed in three key official Olympic documentaries, and how each speaks to or against the form and aesthetics of *Olympia*. Before turning to each of these films, I will make some preliminary comments about the relationship between Olympism, the Olympic Games and the documentary as filmic practice.

The dialectics of the Official Olympic Documentary: oxymoron or opportunity?

John Grierson, widely considered the 'father' of the documentary movement that emerged in the inter-war period, defined the documentary as the 'creative treatment of actuality'. In similar vein, the contemporary documentary theorist, John Corner (2008), referred to it as the art of record: both reveal the same challenge facing the documentary filmmaker – how to deal with and understand something that is attempting to represent reality by using specific aesthetic devices. Following Paul Ward, a fundamental feature of documentary is that it 'makes assertions or truth claims about the real world or real people in that world' (2005: 8). What then are aesthetic devices that have been used in the official Olympic documentaries to make 'assertions or truth claims' about the Olympic Games? Importantly, what are we to make of any such truth claims given the official status of the documentary? Does the prefix 'official' negate the documentary value of the film? It not only identifies the commissioning body – the IOC and the respective Olympic Organising Committees (OOC) of the Games – but might it also signal that the fidelity of the 'assertions or truth claims' being made are to the national OOC and the IOC, who as official bodies are in possession of the 'correct' meaning and interpretation of Olympism and the Olympic Games?

Undoubtedly, the notion of an official documentary would be oxymoronic to many documentarians – fidelity, they argue, must be with the subject (or to values) not the sponsoring body. However, at the same time, the official documentary provides an opportunity that would otherwise not likely exist for filmmaker's to turn their gaze on sporting competition as an expression/reflection/distortion of humanity, and therefore of Olympism.

As the official ideology of the Olympic Movement, Olympism is an oft-debated term. Olympism reflects a synthesis of de Coubertin's interpretation of classical Greek and English public school conceptions of sport: its basis is a belief in the progressive educational value of sport, generalised from the individual to the sphere of international politics (de Coubertin 1966). Thus, Olympism places sport at the centre of a universal campaign for peace and international understanding, drawing on the mythology of the truce and the symbol of peace associated with the Games in Antiquity. Of course, many critics have dismissed Olympism as a dominant ideology that conceals the true imperialistic, nationalistic and capitalistic nature of the Games (for example, Brohm 1978, Lenskyj 2000, Tomlinson and Whannel 1984). Others have argued that while the philosophy of Olympism seems to have little bearing on the reality of the Olympic Games, they are ideals that are worth preserving and act as a measure against which the Olympics has departed form these ideals (for example, Lucas 1992, MacAloon 1981, Morgan 2006)

So what are the parameters of the official Olympic documentary? Historically speaking, the 'brief' for the official Olympic documentary is firstly to provide a record of the Games: to capture a representative range of events, the winners and losers, heroic feats and records broken, all inflected through the patriotic prism of the host nation of course. Secondly, the aim is to promote the spirit of Olympism. However, in the era of the televised Games with instantaneous coverage of the action, the portrayal of the Games takes on a commemorative rather than an informational function. And with a diminished news-value role, the second aim of propagating/interpreting Olympism takes on a heightened role. In other words, the imperative to do something different from that which has already been covered on television forces the filmmaker to address more explicitly questions of meaning and interpretation such as the spirit of Olympism. In this sense, the official Olympic documentary in the age of instantaneous coverage is returning to an emphasis on ritual over record, an interesting reversal of the trend noted by McKeever (2011) in his analysis of the emergence of the first Olympic films in the 1920s.

There is also a structural challenge facing the filmmaker. The subject of the official Olympic documentary is not actually the Olympic Games but, more narrowly, Olympic competition. The official Olympic documentary does not engage with historical and political contexts to any serious extent nor in interrogating issues surrounding the run-up and staging of the Olympic Games. The coordinates of the official Olympic documentary are limited to the sporting competition and issues and events directly associated with them. Contextual factors are incorporated only in so far as they illuminate the sporting competition, such as the back-stories on athletes, or the responses of spectators for example. Thus in *Sixteen Days of Glory*, the USSR-led boycott is mentioned a few times, but only insofar as it prevented athletes from pursuing their dream in 1980.

However, sometimes this imperative to keep the camera lens focused on the sporting action can produce more imaginative and even compelling ways to reveal the political dimensions of the Games. This was the case with the British director John Schlesinger, who wanted his contribution to the compilation film *Visions of Eight* to be on the Israeli hostage crisis. The producer, Wolper, told him that it was beyond the remit of the official documentary! Schlesinger ingeniously managed to circumvent this injunction on his documentary duty by telling the story of the hostage crisis through the experience of Ron Hill, the British marathon runner. In response to a question about how the ongoing hostage crisis is affecting him, Hill responds by saying that it has definitely affected him. However, even before we have the opportunity to hope that he is referring to the tragic circumstances of the hostage crisis, Hill asserts that it has affected him because it has disturbed his meticulous preparations for the marathon! So compelling filmmakers to engage with sporting events as sporting events, with athletes as athletes, need not necessarily result in depoliticised stories. Indeed, such constraint can sometimes produce unexpected opportunities to gain insightful perspectives. There is something neatly dialectical about the official Olympic documentary itself providing the catalyst for some of the most interesting and even radical filmic representations of Olympism.

Tokyo, 1964. Tokyo Olympiad and problematising Olympism

When the Japanese Organising Committee of the Olympic Games approached Kon Ichikawa to direct the official documentary of the 1964 Games in Tokyo, they gave him the standard instructions: a) to produce a documentary record of the Games emphasising the successes of the host nation and b) to capture the true spirit of the Olympic Games. Ichikawa did not take too much notice of the first objective – he was not a sports fan, was not interested in the results and reasoned that anyway most of the Games would have already been broadcast, in this the first mass television Games, before his documentary was released. But as an acclaimed filmmaker who married artistic technique with a humanistic spirit, he was very keen to explore and try to capture the philosophy of Olympism. In an interview in 1992 (which appears as an extra on the DVD of *Tokyo Olympiad*), Ichikawa explained that he knew little about sport and had never seen the Olympics, and so he repeatedly watched Riefenstahl's *Olympia*, referring to it as a 'great textbook'. In a neat display of wit and tact (after all, Riefenstahl was still alive in 1992) he said that such was his admiration of *Olympia,* that he felt he could not emulate it. He decided 'to do the opposite . . . so in my film, rather than focusing on physical beauty and strength, I wanted to explore the internal dimensions of the athletes. I wanted my film to be sort of the antithesis of Riefenstahl's *Olympia*'. Instead of recording the results, celebrating the winners, wallowing in the flag-raising medal ceremonies, Ichikawa set himself the cinematic task of capturing a different dimension of the Olympics: that of a spectacle that both reflects the ordinariness of the people that make the Games, but also offer glimpses of the transcendent possibilities of sport.

With a sincerity not yet soured by the subsequent commercialism and cynicism associated with later Olympic Games, in the same 1992 interview Ichikawa reflected on on how, in *Tokyo Olympiad,* he had sought out what he interpreted as the humanistic core of Olympism: 'I wanted to infuse my imaginations into the images and capture the essence or true nature of the Olympic Games. Every four years, people come together from all over the world . . . expressing peace and harmony between people of different races . . . that's the spirit of the Olympic Games'. But in the process of turning his filmic gaze on sport, Ichikawa underwent his own journey that led ultimately to his problematising the nature of elite of sport and the so-called spirit of Olympism:

> While filming the Tokyo Games, I learned a great deal from these competi-
> tions. I was touched by their pure humanity. . . . their sense of purpose. . .that
> thought had not occurred to me before . . . it was not just the athletes'
> physical magnificence, or how fast they are, or their excellence, but simply
> them as human beings with a sense of purpose. . . . I got more and more
> attached to the idea and wanted to explore it.

It is this attraction to the seemingly autotelic aspect of athletic competition rather
than any anti-nationalism or elitism that may have drawn Ichikawa to focus his
cameras on the competitive act itself rather than the result of the act or even the
identity of the athlete. What is usually edited out of television coverage becomes
the focus of Ichikawa's gaze. For example, in filming the shot-put, Ichikawa prefers
to linger, in close-up, on the repetitive rituals performed by over-sized bodies as
they prepare to put the shot rather than on the throw itself.

The coverage of the final of the Women's 80 meters hurdles is typical of another
aspect of Ichikawa's distinctive gaze. Here, a fascination with the repetitive rituals
performed by athletes is combined with an appreciation of the visual and aural
distinctiveness of the hurdling event to produce a challenging documentary
aesthetic. The race is first captured in slow motion from the side of the track,
focusing on the contorted facial gestures as the athletes stride the hurdles. It is
impossible to identify the winner, or indeed whether the race has concluded, before
it cuts to a long shot of the empty track from the point of view of the finishing line
with the athletes warming up in the distance before the starting line. Here we see
athletes making their preparations. Ichikawa chooses to focus on the Japanese
athlete Ikuyo Yoda as she warms up. Unbeknown to her, the distant camera zooms
in and follows her walking, exercising, then sweeping the track with a broom,
casually whistling, doing backward rolls, then cartwheeling, loosening her neck,
more walking, before the film cuts to all of the athletes at starting blocks. Yoda has
placed a lemon near her starting block. Then a long pause as the athletes wait for
the starter gun. All that can be heard are the sounds of flags fluttering, and then
the starting gun fires, and the camera cuts back to the finishing line for a wide pan
of the athletes. The sound is muted, rendering the event in an eerie silence, broken
only by the clatter of a hurdle knocked over. The race is shown again, not in real
time, as might be expected, but also in slow motion. The viewer feels disturbed,
unsettled, and anxious. Only when the first athletes cross the finishing line does
the sportscaster announce; 'Yoda of Japan loses. The Rising Sun flag will not fly
but she ran and jumped her best'. Thus, the race is portrayed through a 40 second
slow motion of the race (which was actually run in 10 seconds) from the side,
followed by 4 minutes focusing on the preparation of the athletes, and then
another 40 seconds slow motion of the same race but from a different angle.

Ichikawa's much vaunted preoccupation with the 'little man' and 'the outsider'
is best captured in the profile, indeed the only profile in the film, of Ahamed Isa,
a twenty-two year-old 800-metre runner from Chad, a story of 'a stranger in a
strange land'. Isa is just one of two athletes representing the former French colony

that only secured independence in 1960. 'He's much older than his country', remarks the narrator, 'His father, a chief, died of small pox' and 'He speaks one of the many dialects of Arabic'. But Isa is never seen talking to another athlete, his solitude highlighted by the team spirit and camaraderie of other competitors in the Olympic Village. After Isa fails to qualify for the final of the 800 metres, he is captured tucking into his dinner in the communal dining room in the athletes village, as the narrator observes, 'He's always alone. He must be lonely. But for now he is calm and content'. The radical aspect of Ichikawa's coverage of the 800 metres event lies in an omission. This is the official film of the Olympic Games, yet it profiles an unknown competitor of mediocre ability from a country that few people have heard of, who does not even make the final, while almost completely ignoring Peter Snell from New Zealand, who broke his own Olympic record to win what was to be his third gold medal, thus confirming his status as one of the greatest middle distance runners of the 20th century.

Ichikawa's explorations take him beyond a platitudinous rendering of Olympism with its rhetoric about universal peace, friendship and equality, to elicit the beauty, tragedy, heroism, idiocy, and joy of the human condition as it is expressed and suppressed in the playing, watching and officiating of sport. In capturing the psychological quirks of the athletes, the joyful innocence of the spectators, the fussy conscientiousness of the officials, the dramatic spectacle of competition whether in the stadium, in the countryside or on water, Ichikawa keeps us empathically attached to the people (athletes, officials and spectators). Equality is evidenced in the sense of importance that all spectators (whether Emperors or 'ordinary people'), athletes (winners and losers) and officials (the starters or helpers) are presented.

Audie Bock described *Tokyo Olympiad* as 'Beautifully humanistic . . . a near revolution in sport documentaries' (Bock 1985: 219). However, the Japanese Olympic Committee did not agree: there were not enough scenes of Japanese athletes, the national flag, the imperial family, the new arenas, and the new Tokyo. Ichikawa was accused of indulging in making art instead of producing a true documentary record of the Olympic Games. The Olympics Minister, Ichiro Kono, commented, 'I saw the preview of the film made to leave a record of the Tokyo Olympics. It overemphasises artistic aspects and I do not believe it is a proper record of the event' (quoted in Quandt 2001: 337).

However, the power and the radicalism of *Tokyo Olympiad* is that it is an official Olympic film that captures the humanity of sport while not reinforcing the ideology of the Olympic Movement. It beautifully peels away the rhetorical skin of Olympism while maintaining an empathetic connection to those who desire it to be true. By the end of the film we can still admire the athletes, connect with the spectators and recognise the individuality of the officials, but the idealism that we are encouraged to feel at the beginning of the film for Olympism and its rhetoric of universal peace and the transcendent power of sport has been revealed as hollow (McDonald 2008).

Munich, 1972: Visions of Eight as the 'anti-official' official Olympic Documentary

When the American film producer David L. Wolper pitched his idea for the official film of the XX Olympiad in Munich to Willi Daume, the president of the West German Olympic Committee, he was met with some skepticism. The idea of a compilation film with eight short documentaries by eight international *feature* film directors *was* different. The concept certainly did not play well with a few of his committeemen who were upset at the idea of the film being awarded to a non-German. It is customary that the host country provides the filmmaker for the official Olympic documentary. However, Daume threw his support behind Wolper. He argued that different was good – after all, the official film needed to stand apart from the daily television coverage to compete for attention. And it would also be very different from *that* previous official Olympic film made in Germany. So *Visions of Eight* was commissioned. The contributing directors were Milos Forman from Czechoslovakia, Kon Ichikawa from Japan, Claude Lelouch from France, Juri Ozerov from the Soviet Union, Arthur Penn from the U.S.A., John Schlesinger from England, Mai Zetterling from Sweden and Michael Pfleghar from Germany.

Perhaps inevitably, *Visions of Eight* is an uneven film. The contributions range from the formulaic and banal: i.e. 'The Beginning' by Yuri Ozerov, (who incidentally went on to direct the official documentary of the 1980 Games in Moscow), to the comic and bizarre: i.e. 'The Decathlon' by Milos Foreman, to the aesthetically innovatory, i.e.: 'The Highest' by Arthur Penn. The two most interesting pieces are 'The Strongest' by the only female director, Mai Zetterling, and 'The Longest' by John Schlesinger. Both of these films radically disrupt the dominant narrative of Olympism and the construction of the Olympian heroic athlete. In introducing her film on weightlifting, Zetterling signals her detachment from sport:

> I chose weight-lifting because I know nothing about it. And I supposed one thing that really fascinated me was that these men work in total isolation and they are obsessed. They don't seem to have any life apart from lifting. I am not interested in sports but I am interested in obsessions.

In this compelling portrayal of weightlifters, Zetterling opens with a close-up shot of a flyweight lifter practising lifts. As the camera pulls back, the lifter is actually alone in a deserted Olympic Village. He soon becomes a spec in a panoramic view of the Village and the city in the background. The themes of isolation, loneliness and obsession are efficiently established. The next scene takes us into the vast exercise hall where the weight lifters are going through their daily calisthenics and warm-ups—each athlete apparently oblivious of the other. A sense of purpose, to recall Ichikawa's phrase, is apparent, as is the isolation – the athletes rarely talk to each other and certainly not to the camera. In his contemporaneous review of the film for *Sports Illustrated* George Plimpton likened the movement of the weight-lifters in the hall to a set of 'mechanical toys wound up and set loose on the carpet'

(1973). In competition, without commentary or music the camera focuses on the shapes of the weightlifters' bodies, their puffing cheeks as they crouch before the weights. There is little that is glamorous, heroic or inspirational here. By contrast, the closing shot of the film seems to acknowledge the humanity of the lifters. With training complete and the competition over, two British weightlifters are leaving the exercise room carrying their kit bags. One of them is Terry Purdue (1.82m /144KG) a super heavyweight, massive, moving away from the camera in a slow, regal waddle; walking beside him is the same diminutive flyweight lifter seen at the beginning of the film, Precious McKenzie (1.45m / 53KG), tiny anyway but especially by comparison. They chat with each other as they walk out of the frame. Coming after the bleakness of training and competition, Plimpton finds humanity in this unlikely pairing '. . . perhaps they are going off to have a beer somewhere. One hopes so' (1973).

In 'The Longest', John Schlesinger, director of the critically acclaimed *Marathon Man* starring Laurence Olivier and Dustin Hoffman, features another marathon man – Ron Hill from Great Britain. As mentioned above, Schlesinger uses this particular marathon runner to cover the Israeli hostage crisis. However, he not only manages to include the biggest story of the Games in the official documentary but also provides a disturbing insight into the single-minded mentality of the Olympian that has little affinity with the 'spirit of Olympism'. Schlesinger juxtaposes images of the hostage crisis with shots of Hill on training runs in his native Lancastrian countryside. Then in response to an unheard question about how the hostage crisis and the subsequent deaths have affected him, Hill replies:

> It's affected me in that it has put my race a day later. Really I have had to stay right out of it and try not to think about it at all. I don't want to think about what happened because I presume I would get emotional about it. I just want to stay right away from it. I'm here for one thing and that is to run a marathon. And anything that distracts me from that I just don't want to know about it.

Hill's response might be seen as utterly professional, as the expected and correct response of a high performance athlete about to run the most important race of his life. But by juxtaposing images of the dead athletes with Hill's frank response, and then likening him to a robotic, ethically detached, scientific machine, methodically logging his runs and meticulously planning the race ahead, Schlesinger is presumably inviting us to condemn Hill. But I think to do so would be a mistake – it would be a moralistic response based on ignorance about the demands of high-performance sport. A more interesting sociological response would be to reflect on the disjuncture between the spirit of Olympism and the demands of Olympic competition, and ask why it is that high performance sport, Olympian sport, necessitates such amorality.

The radicalism of *Visions of Eight* is as much in its form as its content. The cultural and ideological power of the Olympic Games is dependent on its coherence as an event, part of a Movement located within a history. It does not lie in the individual sporting competitions, which, with the possible exception of some of the track athletic events, are to most people in the world obscure and minor sports . The official Olympic documentary tends to reflect and reinforce this holistic aspect through the ideology of Olympism. *Visions of Eight*, intentionally or otherwise, effectively disaggregates the Olympic Games, strips it back to a range of isolated and frankly esoteric minor sport competitions, with largely dysfunctional or obsessive character types. Free from the sentimentality of Olympism, the focus on sport reveals an alternative 'truth-claim' that is decidedly anti-official. This is why *Visions of Eight* can be considered the anti-official official Olympic Documentary. Needless to say, that experiment has not been repeated in subsequent Games.

Los Angeles, 1984: Sixteen Days of Glory and the propagation of Olympism

In 1982 the Los Angeles Olympic Organising Committee and the International Olympic Committee awarded the rights to film the 1984 Games to Bud Greenspan. Greenspan was already a veteran sport documentarian: in 1976 he won an Emmy for a 22 hour-long series on *The Olympiad*. 'Our approach to the film was clear' said Greenspan, 'We knew that ABC would handle the daily events coverage well, but we had to do something different. . .What we've captured on film are the personal stories of individual performers, athletes in various sports striving for their part in the glory of the Games' (Greenspan, 1985: 702). *Sixteen Days of Glory* adopts the expository mode of documentary practice. As the documentary theorist Nichols states, 'The expository text addresses the viewer directly, with titles or voices that advance an argument about the historical world' (1991: 34). The key aesthetic device used in *Sixteen Days of Glory* is the powerful voice-over that didactically addresses the audience so as to leave little doubt about the inspirational, epic and mythological status of the Olympic Games.

For Greenspan, the Olympic Games are indeed a vindication and celebration of the spirit of Olympism. In fact what Greenspan offers us through the character-led stories is a series non-fiction parables of Olympism. For example, Greenspan tells the personal story behind the British athlete David Moorcroft, who as the world record holder, went into the 5000 metres as one of the favourites but ended up coming last. Initially intending to focus on the famous New Zealand miler, John Walker, Greenspan, noticing Moorcroft's discomfort at the starting line-up, was alerted to a more evocative story. The doubts about whether Moorcroft had fully recovered from a range of different ailments and injuries grew in Greenspan's mind. As Moorcroft, clearly in pain, begins to drop off from the back of the pack, Greenspan instructs his cameramen to shift from Walker, who was anonymous in the middle of a chasing pack, to Moorcroft. Shots of Moorcroft dragging himself round the track in last place are cut with interviews with Moorcroft and his wife, Linda, recalling the physical and mental agony of the race. But there is no room in *Sixteen Days of Glory* for losers. Moorcroft may have come last but he is recast a heroic and inspirational athlete running for pride and honour, a concrete manifestation of the Olympic ethos about participation counting more than winning. Through steely endurance and driven by a love for his wife anxiously watching in the stadium, Moorcroft not only completes the race but just avoids the humiliation of being lapped by the eventual winner, Said Aouita from Morocco. Moorcroft's story is a 'triumph of the will'. And there is redemption: as the narrator points out at the end of the race, the gold medallist Aouita failed to break the world record set by David Moorcroft in Oslo two years previously.

The stories in *Sixteen Days of Glory* are used either to extol the spirit of Olympism or reinforce 'American' values; for example, the commitment to the Olympic ethos of amateurism by the Judo gold medallist Yasu-Hiro Yamashita or the celebration of the family in the story of Ed Moses, his wife and his recently deceased father. The womens' marathon, run for the first time in Olympic history, is used as an opportunity to celebrate gender equality and to reinforce the 'epic, mystical and mythological' nature of this quintessential Olympic event. Greenspan's portrayal contrasts sharply with the marathons in *Tokyo Olympiad* and *Visions of Eight*. In Greenspan's film, the ending of the race is purely celebratory, dominated by jubilant faces and shows of female camaraderie. In *Tokyo Olympiad*, for example, athletes are cheered by spectators as they cross the finishing line followed by distressed and exhausted also-rans, stumbling and collapsing into the arms of waiting officials. We see close-ups of battered feet, gaunt faces, and the finishing area scattered with barely moving prone and supine bodies. Of course the narrator in *Tokyo Olympiad* salutes the achievement of the marathon runners, but the images allow a more ambivalent response to be formed by the viewer in a way that simply is not possible in Greenspan's sanitised and celebratory portrayal.

Apart from the parables of Olympism told through the sporting events, Greenspan glorifies the pomp and pageantry of the Opening and Closing ceremonies while obsequiously saluting the organisers of the Games. For example, as the LA OOC President begins to address the stadium in the Open Ceremony proceedings, the narrator cuts in: 'For Peter Ueberroth, it is a day of special celebration . . . As he speaks, one reporter types the lead to his story. It reads: the athletic competitions are still a day away, but the first gold medal has already been won. It goes to Peter Ueberroth'. The closing ceremony in particular is an unrelenting tribute to the winners and to American nationalism. The final shots of the film are of the closing ceremony cut with a montage of beaming and emotional athletes receiving gold medals and of the raising of different national flags. It is accompanied by the chorus to the 'Hymn to the Nations' adapted to incorporate some of the national anthems of the respective gold medallists. But this apparent nod towards a putative community of nations is tempered by the closing shots in the film: a rousing rendition of the US national anthem set against fireworks exploding in the night sky over the Olympic stadium. cut with clips of the many US athletes standing proudly, emotionally, on the medal podium.

Andrews and Wagg argue that sport during the Cold War was a form of culture that served as 'an abundant and emotive landscape upon which claims for moral and ideological superiority were aggressively advanced' (2006: 3). The early 1980s were a particularly confrontational phase of the Cold War under the Presidential office of Ronald Reagan, and the 1984 Olympic Games proved that the so-called Western democracies could equal anything offered up by the Eastern communist-bloc in the realm of sport. Thus, Greenspan's rendering of the 1984 Games may appear as an innocent filmic 'love-letter' to Olympism – but would it not be more aptly interpreted as a piece of Cold War propaganda? With its nationalist glorification of sacrifice and heroism, an appropriate if provocative subtitle to *Sixteen Days of Glory* could have been 'Triumph of the Athletic Will'. The bracketing of *Olympia* and *16 Days of Glory* suggests a historiography that challenges the tendency to single-out Riefenstahl's *Olympia* as the only real propaganda film of the Olympics.

Conclusion: the heterogeneity of the Olympic documentary

Clearly more cases need to be considered before any firm assessments can be made about the official Olympic documentary as a genre. Eight Summer Olympic Games have passed since 1984 and *Sixteen Days of Glory*. It would be interesting to see if such disruptive and subversive forms of documentary filmmaking such as *Tokyo Olympiad* and *Visions of Eight* are specific to their time and place, or whether the increased professionalisation of the Olympics heralded by the 1984 Games has closed down the space for more experimental and contemplative documentaries. And I have not even mentioned the official documentaries of the Winter Olympics. Then there is London 2012. . . . What can we expect? If the image-management control evidenced hitherto within LOCOG and the ODA is any indication, then one can expect that the creative reins will be held tight on the production of the official documentary of London 2012. The 2012 documentary is more likely to be in the tradition of Bud Greenspan than Kon Ichikawa.

At the outset of this chapter, I posed two questions: is the role of the Official Olympic Documentary simply to help reinforce the key ideological pillar of the Olympic Movement? If that is the case, might we be justified in denouncing the official Olympic documentary as IOC propaganda? What I hope has come through forcibly is that the tradition of official Olympic documentaries is not monolithic. The three documentaries examined here reveal a range of different aesthetics: from the didactic and expository in *Sixteen Days of Glory* to the poetic and experimental in *Tokyo Olympiad* and *Visions of Eight* respectively. They also raise a range of perspectives: from the zealous propagation of Olympism, to a problematising of Olympism, even at certain points to a puncturing of the mythical bubble of Olympism. The official Olympic documentary reveals that it is yet another space for the ongoing debates about the construction of Olympism and the meaning of the modern Olympic Games.

Film details

Tokyo Olympiad (1965, 170 minutes, Japan). Directed by Kon Ichikawa. Produced by Suketaro Taguchi.

Visions of Eight (1973, 110 minutes, USA/West Germany). Directed by Milos Forman (The Decathlon), Kon Ichikawa (The Fastest), Claude Lelouch (The Losers), Yuri Ozerov (The Beginning), Arthur Penn (The Highest), Michael Pfleghar (The Women), John Schlesinger (The Longest), Mai Zetterling (The Strongest). Produced by David L. Wolper.

Sixteen Days of Glory (1986, 145 minutes, USA). Directed by Bud Greenspan. Produced by Cappy Productions.

Notes

1   The Directors of all three films have died: Kon Ichikawa on February 13th, 2008 aged 92; David L. Wolper on August 10th, 2010 aged 82; and Bud Greenspan on December 25[th,] 2010 aged 84.

References

Andrews, D. and Wagg, S. (Eds) (2006) *East Plays West: Sport and the Cold War*, London: Routledge.

Bock, A. (1985) *Japanese Film Directors*, Tokyo: Kodansha International.

Corner, J. (2008) 'Documentary studies: dimensions of transition and continuity', in T. Austin and W. de Jong (eds) *Rethinking Documentary: New Perspectives, New Practices*, Berkshire: Open University Press.

De Coubertin, P. (1966) *The Olympic Idea: Discourse and Essays*, Germany: Carl-Diem-Institut.

Downing, T. (1992) *Olympia*, London: BFI.

Ellis, J. (2000). *John Grierson: Life, Contributions, Influences*, Edwardsville: Southern Illinois University Press.

Greenspan, B. (1985) 'Sixteen Days of Glory', *The Runner*, September: 54–58.

Hinton, D. (2000) *The Films of Leni Riefenstahl*, London: The Scarecrow Press.

Lenskyj, H. (2000) *Inside the Olympic Industry: Power, Politics and Activism*, Suny Press: USA.

Lucas, J. (1992) *Future of the Olympic Games*, Illinois: Human Kinetics.

MacAloon, J. (1981) *This Great Symbol: Pierre de Coubertin and the Origins of the Modern Olympics*, Chicago: University of Chicago Press.

Mackenzie, M. (2003) 'From Athens to Berlin: The 1936 Olympics and Leni Riefenstahl's *Olympia*', *Critical Inquiry* 29(2): 302–36.

McDonald, I. (2008) 'Critiquing the Olympic documentary: Kon Ichikawa's Tokyo Olympiad', *Sport in Society* 11(2): 298–310.

McFee, G. and Tomlinson, A. (1999) 'Riefenstahl's *Olympia*: ideology and aesthetics in the shaping of the Aryan athletic body', *The International Journal of the History of Sport* 16(2): 86–106.

McKeever, L. (forthcoming, 2011) 'Rituals and records: the films of the 1924 and 1928 Olympic Games', *European Review*.

Morgan, W. (2006) *Why Sports Morally Matter*, London: Routledge.

Nichols, B. (1991) *Representing Reality*, Bloomington, IN: Indiana UP.

Plimpton, G. (1973) 'Olympic Visions of Eight', *Sports Illustrated* http://sportsillustrated.cnn. com/vault?article/magazine/MAG1087706/index.htm.

Quandt, J. (ed.) (2001) *Kon Ichikawa*, Ontario: Cinematheque.

Rodriguez , M. (2003) 'Behind Leni's outlook: a perspective on the film *Olympia* (1938)', *International Review for the Sociology of Sport* 38: 109–116.

Segrave, J. and Chu, D. (eds) (1981) *Olympism*, Champaign, Illinois: Human Kinetics.

Tomlinson, A. (1984) 'De Coubertin and the Modern Olympics', in A. Tomlinson and G. Whannel (eds), *Five Ring Circus: Money, Power and Politics at the Olympic Games*, London: Pluto Press.

Vaughan, D. (1999) 'Berlin versus Tokyo', in *For Documentary: Twelve Essays*. Berkeley: University of California Press.

Ward, P. (2005) *Documentary: The Margins of Reality*, London: Wallflower.

Whannel. G. (2008) *Culture, Politics and Sport: Blowing the Whistle, Revisited*, London: Routledge.

9

TORCHLIGHT TEMPTATIONS

Hosting the Olympics and the global gaze

David Rowe and Jim McKay

Introduction: relaying messages to the world

The Olympic Games is much more than the festival of sport that runs in a chosen location for a few weeks every four years. Of wider significance is the festival of national representation that runs through the bidding process to the announcement of the successful host, the seven years until the Games are actually held, and the immediate and long-term assessment of the Games' successes, failures and overall legacy. This Olympic cycle has at its heart the politics of representation and, in particular, contestation over the power to project the enduring image and to write the orthodox history of each Olympiad. Therefore, hosting the Olympic and Paralympic Games is always a delicate and risky exercise for the local organising committee, because it must satisfy the competing demands of three main audiences: the International Olympic Committee (IOC), foreign visitors and TV audiences, and the local population.

It is particularly important to convince locals that the massive resources involved are on balance beneficial for the host city and nation, not least by stimulating positive external impressions that will deliver tangible benefits. The justification for bidding, and the complexion of anticipated benefits for hosts and visitors, is highly variable. The successful case advanced to secure the 2012 Games for London emphasised recognition of 'Diversity [as] a key reason why London, one of the most multicultural cities in the world, was chosen to host the Games in the bidding process' (London 2012, 2010a). This Olympic city 'brand' (as it is called by the London Organising Committee of the Olympic and Paralympic Games (LOCOG)) is substantially different to that presented in support of Beijing 2008 by its organising committee (BOCOG). In foregrounding the opening up of a formerly closed society to the world under the slogan 'One World One Dream', BOCOG 'conveys the lofty ideal of the people in Beijing as well as in China to share the global community and civilization and to create a bright future hand in hand with the people from the rest of the world' (Beijing 2008a).

Having used the media to secure the hosting rights, every local organising committee must then continue to manage its image favourably under the gaze of both local and global audiences. Although the Opening Ceremony of the Summer Games, the world's most-watched television broadcast (Neilsen 2008), is a pivotal mediated moment, many other events from the day that the bid is secured until the 'sacred' Olympic flame is extinguished at the Closing Ceremony significantly affect the historical resonance of the Games. The IOC's decisions about which countries are 'fit' to host the Olympics have been fraught with controversy, given the immense economic, political and cultural stakes involved. Thus, it was unsurprising that awarding the 2008 Olympics to Beijing in 2001 immediately precipitated myriad calls for protests and boycotts over human rights abuses and environmental degradation in China. In this chapter we will focus on the controversial Torch Relay that preceded the 2008 Beijing Olympics, critically analysing the ways in which it became a vigorous and, at times, violent contest over the legitimacy of China's role in the Games and, by extension, of the moral status of the nation itself. In the light of this case study, and with regard to London 2012 and its successors, we seek to lay bare the paradoxical cultural politics of the quest by Olympic cities and nations to harness the global gaze to their advantage while risking widespread disapproval – and even disgrace.

Tracking torch trajectories

> *Sporting chivalrous contest helps knit the bonds of peace between nations. Therefore may the Olympic flame never expire.* (Adolf Hitler, shortly before the 1936 Berlin Olympics; cited in Bowlby 2008)

Contrary to conventional wisdom, the Olympic Torch Relay ceremony did not originate in ancient Greece. Like the modern Olympics, the ritual is an 'invented tradition' which first appeared at the 1936 'Nazi Olympics' that were, in turn, embedded in the wider glorification of Aryan ideals (MacAloon 2011; Mandell 1987; Whannel 2008; Young 2008). The Torch Relay was commercialised at the 1984 Los Angeles Olympics when the IOC abandoned its formal commitment to amateurism (Tomlinson 2005), became embroiled in charges of nepotism by IOC officials at Sydney 2000 (McKay, Hutchins and Mikosza 2000), and emerged as a global commodity-spectacle at the 2004 Athens Olympics. The passing of the torch from hand to hand between Greece and the home nation, and within the host country itself, created the opportunity for host nations to showcase their 'national character' to a global audience well before the Games, and for various Olympic sponsors to display their own brands in routine news coverage of the passage of the torch (Tomlinson and Young 2006). China anticipated being able to announce itself on the world stage through the longest Torch Relay in history, with 22,000 torch-bearers covering 137,000 km (85,000 miles) in 20 countries on all continents over 130 days. This 'Journey of Harmony' claimed, in conventional Olympic rhetoric, to be beyond politics while being irrevocably tied to the political. Their 'remarkable visibility' meant that the 'Olympics are obviously the best time to show off the new China and its people' (Xu 2008: 249). This anticipated recognition of the concept of the 'new China' weighed heavily on Chinese expectations of the Games (see several contributions to Price and Dayan 2008), thereby exacerbating the disappointment – indeed, outrage – experienced, both at the level of the Chinese Communist Party and among much of the citizenry, when the Relay functioned as an almost unprecedented media catalyst (challenged in recent times only by the Tiananmen Square massacre in 1989) for extensive world condemnation of China.

Like all host countries, China faced the complex and contradictory circumstances of inviting world attention while also attempting to manage scrutiny and criticism both inside and outside the sporting arena. This task, as we will demonstrate, constituted a severe test to a regime used to controlling dissent within its own borders, but much less practised in semiotic 'wars of position' organised around 24-hour global news cycles (Luo and Richeri 2009). As Susan Brownell (2008: 163) has observed, 'the Chinese side has little understanding of how to use the media to promote a positive image', both in terms of respect for sporting and societal achievements (as measured, respectively, by higher medal counts and lower proportions of the population living in poverty). The unpreparedness of the Chinese elites to manage negative publicity suggests a certain naivety borne out of, in part, acceptance of Olympian myths that are treated with widespread scepticism, if not contempt, by many journalists and members of the general public outside the brief periods of competition within its sporting 'Temple of Heaven'.

There were forewarnings that the Relay would be a target for protests. A year before the Beijing Games commenced, Korporaal (2007) observed that 'The Torch Relay for the Beijing 2008 Olympic Games will be the longest ever, exposing it to potential anti-Chinese demonstrators including supporters from Falun Gong and the Free Tibet movement'. More significantly, in February 2008 human rights groups indicated that they would demonstrate in several countries because of China's support for Sudan in the crisis in Darfur (*The Australian* 2008). But it was not anticipated that the first protest would occur live before a global audience at the flame-lighting ceremony in Olympia in March, when representatives of *Reporters Sans Frontières* (Reporters without Borders), which had earlier called for a boycott of the Opening Ceremony in Beijing, displayed a black flag depicting the Olympic rings made from handcuffs during a speech by Liu Qi, President of BOCOG (an event that was blacked-out in telecasts to Greece and China [Hersh 2008]). Then, as the lit torch departed the mountain, TV cameras caught further protests by pro-Tibet activists, so setting the tone and rhythm of a formidable public relations challenge for China that would last until the torch passed into China-controlled audio-visual space (Rowe, Gilmour and Petzold 2010).

At such moments, the promotional advantages of hosting the Games are inverted – the very 'meditational' mechanisms that were intended to draw positive interest becoming the global equivalent of a commission of inquiry into the state of the nation. This process is by no means unprecedented – all Olympic hosts, having attracted a massive media contingent for several weeks around the time of the Games, and considerable attention beforehand (such as during the bidding process and its aftermath), are subject to inspections that, alongside 'soft' touristic appraisals and 'colour' pieces, can involve quite penetrating external assessments of the 'fitness' of the nation (see, for example, Lenskyj 2008). During the Sydney 2000 Olympics, for example, there was considerable interest in Australia's progress – or, more appropriately, lack thereof – in achieving reconciliation with its Indigenous people (Bruce and Hallinan 2001; Rowe and Stevenson 2006).

The 2008 Torch Relay, therefore, mutated from a routine 'feel good' news snippet into a dramatic global media event, its journey enabling a predictable set of appointments in time and space for protestors and news media alike, although there were rapid changes to security arrangements and to the path of the Relay itself, and the additional 'variable' of counter-protests (both organised and spontaneous). In such media-rich environments as Canberra, Paris, London, San Francisco and New Delhi, the torch passed through spaces that subjected China to intense, wide-ranging criticism, and which invited popular dramatisations of dissent that rendered the long history of, in particular, China-Tibet relations, in concentrated form. Thus, the dynamic created by the passage of the torch through turbulent public spaces, and the quasi-militaristic protection of it via strategic occupation by local police and, crucially, uniformed Chinese guards, symbolically paralleled the Chinese state's oppression of Tibetans and of their own people. What might under other circumstances have been regarded as routine, approved protection by a foreign power of their 'precious assets' (for example, the large Secret Service contingent that always accompanies the US President and other senior politicians when abroad) was here commonly represented as an aggressive and illegitimate assertion of control. Given the crucial role of the protests in London for both the rest of the Relay and the lead-up to London 2012, we concentrate mainly on how events there were represented and interpreted by Western and Chinese media. There is also an element of symmetry to this analysis in that the torch that caused so much controversy in transit between London and Beijing must return to London as the succeeding host city.

'A flaming mess at Downing Street' and a round-the-world trip

In London 80 torch-bearers were scheduled to carry the flame on a celebratory 31-mile journey from Wembley Stadium to the O2 Arena in Greenwich, accompanied by the Chinese flame attendants and about 2,000 Metropolitan Police officers. Just before the Relay commenced, Lord Colin Moynihan, former Sports Minister and chairman of the British Olympic Association, addressed the crowd and optimistically declared that, 'The power of this Olympic torch will shine a light on the recesses of the host city and China's record' (Anthony 2008). However, within five minutes of quintuple Olympic champion Sir Steven

Redgrave beginning proceedings, a protestor attempted to seize the torch from the second torch-bearer, a teenage schoolgirl, as she boarded an iconic red London bus (ironically, a cultural object heavily featured in the London 'Handover' at the Closing Ceremony of Beijing 2008). The event then degenerated into a day-long mêlée in which torch-bearers were constantly harassed and scuffles broke out among police, anti-Chinese protestors, pro-Chinese nationals, and flame attendants. On police advice the Chinese ambassador abandoned the official route and took the torch through central London's Chinatown with a substantial police escort. At Whitehall a large crowd demonstrated under heavy security:

> [Police] were there in every known guise: helicopter police, mounted police, motorcycle police, bicycling police, Ford Transit van police, standing police, wrestle-you-to-the-ground police in black Andy Pandy suits, and even jogging police. (Hamilton 2008)

By evening nearly 40 people had been arrested and the affair had morphed into a(nother) sensational global media event. The mainstream British media strongly denounced what occurred in various ways: 'farce' (O'Connor 2008a), 'military-style operation' (Edwards and Thomas 2008), 'chaos' (Kelso 2008a), 'flaming mess at Downing Street' (Hamilton 2008), and 'fiasco [that] beamed around the world on TV, made Britain a laughing stock on the international stage' (Daily Mail 2008). Editors, journalists, cartoonists, writers of letters to editors, and bloggers decried several parties: the police for being incompetent, heavy-handed, and complicit with Chinese authorities; the Labour government for cowardice, and like the police, being both inept and complicit with the Chinese regime; and the torch-bearers, LOCOG and IOC for supporting an oppressive totalitarian system (Lawson 2008; The Independent 2008a). Even former Sports Minister and sitting Labour MP Kate Hoey (2008) stated that Olympic ideals were a 'grotesque charade' and that she was 'angry that the Prime Minister seemed to have caved in to Chinese pressure to participate'. Comparisons were also drawn between the repressive Chinese government and the 1936 'Nazi Olympics' (Bennett 2008). The most vitriolic comments were directed at the Chinese flame attendants, who were described as 'vile', 'horrible', 'robotic', 'mysterious', and 'retarded' (O'Neill 2008), a 'paramilitary police from a force spun off from the country's army' (Macartney and Ford 2008), and 'goons intimidating people who tried to protest against wicked injustice' (Wheatcroft 2008).

Virtually all of the above motifs were condensed in a feature article by Greenhill, Rees and Allen (2008) in the *Daily Mail* (ironically, a right-wing tabloid usually given to condemn such disruptive demonstrations). The story's headline 'Olympic torch fiasco: Lord Coe blasts "horrible Chinese thugs" who barged their way through London' signified both the disastrous nature of the Relay and the brutish behaviour of the Chinese guards. The conduct of the guards was further condemned by the comments of Sebastian Coe, a renowned former double Olympic champion and world-record holder, past MP, and chairman of LOCOG: 'They tried to push me out of the way three times. They are horrible. They did not speak English. They were thugs'.

Coe, who was unaware that his comments were being recorded by a reporter, also stated that, 'One thing in Paris is to get rid of those guys', in reference to the flame attendants, who were now in France on the next leg of the Relay. The story also noted the reaction of former *Blue Peter* presenter and torchbearer Konnie Huq, who was jostled during her leg of the Relay and also criticised the attendants. There was both speculation about the backgrounds of the attendants and criticism of British police and politicians for failing to control them, and conjecture about doing away with the Relay for London 2012. Revelations of the private fury of police at being embarrassed by having to protect the torchbearers by jogging next to them were presented alongside accounts of the 'mayhem' and 'farce' surrounding the Relay in Paris, where police abandoned it due to continual protests, and looming disruptions during the next stage in San Francisco. The article was also accompanied by dramatic images: Huq encircled by attendants as a protester tried to seize the torch; three pictures from Paris (one of police on roller blades and firemen in tracksuits surrounding the torch in a bus, and two of harried torch-bearers); and two photos of huge pro-Tibet banners flying from the Golden Gate Bridge in San Francisco.

There were few deviations from the above codes, a notable exception being on the independent online site *spike*, in which the above reactions were cast as 'hysterical' reprises of the 'Yellow Peril' (O'Neill 2008). It is important, though, not to take newspaper commentaries entirely at face value, given their attunement to domestic politics. Thus, as noted, right-wing 'law'n'order' newspapers like *The Daily Mail*, *The Daily Telegraph* and *The Times* were unusually sympathetic towards pro-Tibet protests that tried to block the passage of the torch, while left-leaning papers like *The Guardian* were especially critical of what they saw as British government capitulation to a rising geo-political power. In both cases, although for different reasons and from divergent political positions, the target was the British Labour Government as much as the Chinese regime. Here, the politics of representation 'enlisted' the current as well as the following hosts.

Instead of a 'Journey of Harmony', the London phase of the Relay became a global spectacle of conflict that both reinforced perceptions of Chinese tyranny and encouraged further protests in subsequent stages of the Relay, thus presenting Chinese officials with a daunting PR challenge in the four-month lead-up to the Opening Ceremony. It is not possible here to detail the events surrounding the Torch Relay as it passed through Paris (France), San Francisco (USA), Buenos Aires (Argentina), Dar es Salaam (Tanzania), Muscat (Oman), Islamabad (Pakistan), New Delhi (India), Bangkok (Thailand), Kuala Lumpur (Malaysia), and Jakarta (Indonesia) before reaching Canberra (Australia). At most sites there were political tensions of various kinds (sometimes leading to large-scale protests and often withdrawals by well-known torchbearers), frequent adjustments to the Relay (usually involving shortening the passage and placement in more easily secured areas), although levels of political freedom in individual countries were also highly variable (Luo and Richeri 2009). By the time the Torch reached

Australia, pro-China forces had regrouped, producing a large and vigorous counter-demonstration. Thousands of Chinese foreign nationals, mainly students, and Chinese-Australians, travelled by bus to Canberra to support China and the 'Sacred Flame', amid accusations that their actions were orchestrated by Chinese authorities under the guise of defending the Chinese nation, and resulting in some angry confrontations with pro-Tibet demonstrators and some arrests (Rowe, Gilmour, and Petzold 2010).

After Canberra the Torch passed through Nagano (Japan), Seoul (South Korea), Pyongyang (North Korea), and Ho Chi Minh City (Vietnam). Political disagreements between China and Taiwan linked to the former's claiming of Taiwan as Chinese territory, and the latter's assertion of its national sovereignty, had already led to the cancellation of a Taiwan leg of the Relay. The Torch then arrived at another 'disputed' though now incorporated Chinese territory, Hong Kong, before its transportation through Macau onto the Chinese mainland, where security arrangements and crowd and news media control were much easier for the Chinese authorities. The long domestic leg included Tibet, but was cut short to one day (from three) for security reasons, although by this time the devastating May 12 Sichuan earthquake had overshadowed the Torch Relay and, indeed, generated much more sympathetic coverage of China than at any time prior to the launch of the Relay in Greece (Rowe, Gilmour, and Petzold 2010). By the time the torch reached the Olympic Stadium in Beijing on the 8 August it had covered more ground and seen more 'action' than at any previous Olympics. As the London Games approach, it is important to divine the socio-political implications of an exercise that went badly wrong, and yet generated competing readings and disputed consequences.

Paradoxes of protest

The world and its events are represented very differently in the creation of histories, and in this regard the 2008 Torch Relay was no different from any other mediated spectacle (Horne and Whannel 2010). BOCOG, for example, gave a radically different account of the turbulent events in London:

> There have been attempts made to disturb and sabotage the Torch Relay by a small number of 'pro-Tibet independence' activists. Local people in London strongly opposed the attempt to sabotage the Torch Relay. And the behavior of 'pro-Tibet independence' activists has aroused resentment and received condemnation in London. We strongly condemn the actions of the few pro-Tibet independence activists who have attempted to sabotage the Olympic Torch Relay. The Olympic flame belongs to the world and these actions are a serious violation of the Olympic spirit. They are bound to fail and will surely arouse the resentment of peace-loving people who support the Olympic Games. (Beijing 2008b)

So, in this account the crowds of protestors became a small, marginal group of malcontents. Lord Coe, noted above as having been jostled by 'horrible Chinese thugs', was quoted in this BOCOG press release as saying that, 'It's exciting to see people come out to celebrate sports and the Olympic value. I went to Oxford Street Relay today and found people understand what's Olympics is about [sic]' (Beijing 2008c).

These statements typify an official strategy of playing down dissent and condemning criticism and protests while pronouncing 'textbook' Olympic rhetoric about international peace and understanding. However, there is no doubt that both Chinese elites and many citizens were angry about Western coverage of both the riots in Tibet and the protests against the Torch Relay, and there was an 'explosion of nationalist sentiment' both in China and amongst some elements of expatriate populations in other countries (Kurlantzick 2008) that cannot be entirely attributed to official manipulation. Here it is necessary to acknowledge the resurgence of Chinese nationalism in the 21st century, widespread privileging among its population of material advancement and national security before formal political rights, and the postcolonial legacy of Western expansionism (Brownell 2008).

The IOC, which had chosen China to host the Games and justified the decision on the grounds that it would advance human rights within that country, sent contradictory messages about the protests. On one hand, IOC President Jacques Rogge was clearly rattled, acknowledging that the disruptions had placed the Games in crisis following the IOC's choice of China as host: 'It is very easy with hindsight to criticize the decision. It's easy to say now that this was not a wise and sound decision' (Jennings 2008). On the other hand, he ostensibly supported China's intolerance of pro-Tibet protests by declaring that under IOC 'anti-propaganda' rules, athletes who displayed Tibetan flags at Olympic venues – including at the opening and closing ceremonies, on the medal podia and in their own rooms at the Athletes' Village in Beijing – could be expelled (O'Connor 2008b). In an in-depth interview Rogge stated that Western expectations about China quickly redressing human rights issues were 'unrealistic', given that 'It took us 200 years to evolve from the French Revolution . . . Let's be a little bit more modest . . . we owe China to give them time' (Blitz 2008).

The credibility of the IOC was damaged a week before the Opening Ceremony, though, when one of its Vice Presidents, Kevan Gosper, who also chaired the IOC's press commission, emotionally claimed that that he had been betrayed and humiliated by IOC executive members who'd struck a secret deal with Chinese authorities to censor the international media during the Games (Evans and Korporaal 2008). Just four days before the Games began, Rogge reiterated that athletes who violated the anti-propaganda rules would be punished (Hutchins and Mikosza 2010), and criticised protestors for contradicting the request of the Dalai Lama, 'not to disrupt the Torch Relay and not to use violence'. He also expressed optimism that once the Games began people would 'forget about the smog and the rows over censorship and human rights and focus on the sport' (Bond 2008).

Yet, as noted above, the Torch Relay provides a perfect opportunity to prosecute 'rows over censorship and human rights' before there is any opportunity to 'focus on the sport'. As the Relay began in China, the influential Dick Pound, a former IOC Vice-President, was quoted as stating that:

> . . . the Chinese organisers had been warned against holding an international leg because of the geo-political sensitivities . . . The risks were obvious and should have been assessed more closely. The result was that there was a crisis . . . There should be a resolution to do away with the international portion of the Torch Relay. (O'Connor 2008c)

The IOC later abolished the international leg for subsequent Olympics and also restricted the ceremony to the host country after the flame was lit in Greece. Thus it would be easy to see why some observers concluded that the Torch Relay was a 'public relations disaster for the hosts' (*USA Today* 2008). However, the Relay must be viewed in the wider context of both Chinese nationalism and other aspects of the Games. In conjunction with other developments, the protests served both to bolster nationalism in China and perhaps even to embolden China's ruling elites. For instance, it can be argued that the protests enhanced the legitimacy of China's rulers by fuelling nationalistic and anti-Western sentiments in China (Callick 2008). Indeed, according to Manzenreiter (2010:42), 'the efforts and attention of the Chinese government were overwhelmingly addressing domestic concerns and the need of educating the Chinese for the challenges of globalization and immediate encounters with the West'. However, domestic priorities are always already international concerns under circumstances where local populations are being 'primed' for global engagement through (as also in the case of the 2010 Shanghai Expo) a mega event designed, simultaneously, to look and to project inwards and outwards.

Even on the day of the Opening Ceremony, the front-page of *The Independent* carried a story with an image of a solitary Chinese soldier watching fireworks explode over the Bird's Nest during the Opening Ceremony with the headline, 'A nation poised on the brink of historic change, but will China see the light?'. However, the accompanying feature article ('The greatest show the world has ever seen') intimated that China would both weather the controversy surrounding the Relay Ceremony and proceed to earn kudos for its management of subsequent events:

> It was all that was promised here in the fabulous chameleon of the stadium . . . It then spread like the magic fire of some great forest across the vast and, for so long, hidden land. This, it was hard if not impossible to dispute, was the greatest show the world had ever seen and it brought joy that became delirium in 1.3 billion people. The launch of the 29th Olympics was so stunningly choreographed, so meticulous planned . . . and went so far back into China's ancient history you suspected that Confucius himself might have been pleased. (Lawton 2008)

Logistically, China ran the Olympics efficiently and effectively, albeit rather humourlessly (Hyde 2008), and nationalistic pride soared as Chinese athletes won the largest number of gold medals and finished second overall in medals to the USA. The Closing Ceremony was another pyrotechnical triumph and Rogge praised China for hosting a 'truly exceptional Games' (*The Independent* 2008b) – though, significantly, withholding the 'best Games ever' endorsement strategically used by his predecessor, Juan Antonio Samaranch. Some British journalists were so bedazzled by how China managed the 16-day program that they urged LOCOG officials not to try to match Beijing's 'extravaganza', and were told that this was not their intention (Engel 2008 Grose 2010; Kelso 2008b; Steel 2008; White 2008a 2008b). Shortly after the Handover Ceremony, London Mayor Boris Johnson said that he had not raised China's human rights record at a meeting with his Beijing counterpart because 'I don't think you will necessarily achieve what you want in this context by showboating and grandstanding' (Branigan and Scott 2008). While according to one British journalist, it was Chinese power that had spoken loudest:

> The protests that blighted the start of the torch's journey in London and Paris, heroic though they were in the eyes of Tibetan freedom fighters, were obliterated by the audacity of the coming power. China; no longer the sick man of Asia. (Garside 2008)

China's hosting of the Olympics and the Torch Relay protests, it is clear, did not effect substantial political change, although expectations of significant reforms by means of the Games were, it might be argued, more IOC rationalisation than realistic calculation. China has perpetuated its lamentable world leadership in capital punishment; myriad dissenters continue to be harassed and imprisoned; and the celebration of the 60th anniversary of the founding of the PRC in 2009 was reminiscent of the nationalism that surrounded both the Opening and Closing Ceremonies. Chinese leaders might even have acquired greater confidence in, for example, their dealings with US President Barack Obama, negotiations at the conference on climate change in Copenhagen, disputes over internet censorship with Google; and protests in various countries at the screening of a film about the Uighurs, and meetings between political leaders and the exiled Uighur leader Rebiya Kadeer and, familiarly, the Dalai Lama.

The leading Chinese artist Ai Weiwei, a design consultant for the Bird's Nest Olympic Stadium (work that he has now disowned), has argued forcibly that:

> There has never been such a police state. The Olympics clearly showed how this state is a dictatorship: nobody can ask any questions; there is no place for discussion. They don't care if anybody is happy or not happy about this; they don't give you clear-cut sheets on the cost of the Games, what they spent. Did we make anything from it? There is no discussion; no space in the newspapers – only how many gold medals we got. (quoted in Ryan 2010)

Despite such assessments, there have also been some signs of an uneven improvement in media freedom that can be linked directly to hosting the Games, such as the permanent Olympics-inspired freedom of foreign correspondents to interview Chinese citizens without official permission (although subsequently restricting the activities of their Chinese news assistants – Human Rights Watch 2009), and indirectly in the form of some Chinese magazines more openly criticising authorities and officials without immediate, direct reprisal. Protests against the Relay had contradictory and uneven impacts that are difficult to ascertain. Majumdar and Mehta (2010), for example, argue that the protests through the Torch Relay created diplomatic pressure leading to talks between China and envoys of the Dalai Lama, but that these made little subsequent progress. In general terms it can be safely argued that there has been little advancement of the cause of Tibetan independence or autonomy. It is also now established that, for London 2012, the Torch will see much less of the world.

Conclusion: lessons relayed to London

Given the above scenario, it is difficult to make predictions about the experience and outcome of the Torch Relay for London 2012. It is, though, known that it will be a much more manageable intra-country event:

> Lit in Olympia, the Torch will travel throughout the UK. Carried by Torch bearers selected through a ballot process, the Olympic Flame will pass through communities, with entertainment, shows and concerts marking its arrival. There will be educational programmes for young people and the chance to take part as a volunteer. (London 2012 2010b).

In part this arrangement could be read as consistent with London's decision (as much by necessity as choice) to eschew competition with Beijing for 'monumentalism' or 'gigantism'. More important, though, is that no opportunity will be given between Greece and the UK for the Torch Relay to operate as a vehicle for mass political protest. The organisers of London 2012 had already decided not to 'go international' with the Relay, so reducing the time and space available for Olympic protestors. However, this is no guarantee that the Relay will be exempt from demonstrations. Having now lost its 'sacred' aura, the ceremony might be too great a temptation for numerous protest movements to ignore.

The experience of Beijing, from the moment of the first transfer of the flame on Mount Olympus and the media conflagration that followed it, has commended to London a 'small target strategy'. The concentrated attention paid to the Olympics and Paralympics for a short period of competition only occurs after a long period of anticipation. Before the sport commences, the hosts seek to extract maximum financial and image value from the long lead-up to the Opening Ceremony. We have seen how the 2008 Torch Relay, as it proceeded from Mount Olympus to the Tibetan plateau to the Olympic Stadium, dramatised contestation over China's place in the world. For the most part, the view that emerged was not flattering to the host nation (to say the least), and there is little doubt that it and the IOC would, in retrospect, never have delivered such a convenient vehicle for furious political protest. In the specific case of London 2012, the precise route for the torch was not publicly announced until 2011. What has been public knowledge for much longer is that security will be unprecedented at the Lighting Ceremony in Greece, and that the grandiose global vision of the 2008 Torch Relay will be reduced to a defensively local and decidedly 'down home' view.

The lesson of the 2008 Torch Relay is, then, instructive both for London 2012 and, in broader theoretical terms, for the analytical understanding of mega media sports events like the Olympics. Regarding the London Games, the rhetorical device that is the transportation of the flame is part of a risk calculation that embraces such diverse elements as reputational damage and the prevention of terrorism. For the Olympic Games as mega event, the temptation to engage in such expansive gestures reveals the limits of power over representation that can be exercised by even the most assiduous of planners. For those – all aspiring and successful Games hosts – seeking to use the role to give a good account of their country, they are working with an entity (the nation) that 'has become something of a free-floating signifier relatively detached from the "state" within the swirling contours of the new global order' (Urry 2003: 87). Among the 'swirling contours' of a voracious global media complex and a range of 'media savvy' pressure groups and claims makers, the temptation to harness 'the Olympic spirit' can lead with disconcerting speed to the unromantic necessity of damage control.

References

Anthony, S. (2008) 'Police forced to call in reinforcements as protesters disrupt Olympic torch relay', *The Guardian*, 6 April, http://www.guardian.co.uk/sport/2008/apr/06/1 (last accessed 6 March, 2010).

Beijing (2008a) 'One world one dream', http://en.beijing2008.cn/spirit/beijing2008/graphic/n214068253.shtml (last accessed 5 March, 2010).

Beijing (2008b) 'Press release on the worldwide Beijing Olympic torch relay', http://torchRelay.beijing2008.cn/en/news/headlines/n214296388.shtml (last accessed 5 March, 2010).

Beijing (2008c) 'Press release on the worldwide Beijing Olympic torch relay', http://torch relay.beijing2008.cn/en/news/headlines/buzz/ (last accessed 21 March, 2010).

Bennett, C. (2008) 'At least the torch tour shone a light on Olympic hypocrisy', *The Observer*, 13 April, http://www.guardian.co.uk/commentisfree/2008/apr/13/olympic games2008.china (last accessed 6 March, 2010).

Blitz, R. (2008) 'IOC's Rogge asks for more time for China', *The Financial Times*, 26 April, http://www.ft.com/cms/s/0/ac69a7b2–1325–11dd-8d91–0000779fd2ac.html (last accessed 6 March, 2010).

Bond, D. (2008) 'Jacques Rogge: don't wreck the spirit of the Olympic Games', *The Telegraph*, 4 August, http://www.telegraph.co.uk/sport/othersports/olympics/2495720/Jacques-Rogge-Dont-wreck-the-spirit-of-the-Olympics-Games—-Olympics.html (last accessed 6 March, 2010).

Bowlby, C. (2008) 'The Olympic torch's shadowy past', *BBC News*, 5 April, http://news.bbc.co.uk/1/hi/world/europe/7330949.stm (last accessed 13 February, 2010).

Branigan, T and Scott, M. (2008) 'Beijing won't beat London, says Johnson', *The Guardian*, 22 August, http://www.guardian.co.uk/sport/2008/aug/22/olympics2008.boris (last accessed 5 March, 2010).

Brownell, S. (2008) *Beijing's Games: What the Olympics Mean to China*, Lanham, MD: Rowman and Littlefield.

Bruce, T. and Hallinan, C. (2001) 'Cathy Freeman and the quest for Australian identity', in D. L. Andrews and S. J. Jackson (eds), *Sport Stars: The Cultural Politics of Sporting Celebrity*, New York: Routledge, pp. 257–70.

Callick, R. (2008) 'Inflamed passions', *The Australian*, 26 April, http://www.theaustralian.news.com.au/story/0,25197,23599515–28737,00.html (last accessed 5 March, 2010).

Daily Mail (2008) 'Olympic farce: former Blue Peter presenter Konnie Huq lashes out at "robotic" Chinese torch minders', 7 April. http://www.dailymail.co.uk/news/article-557886/Olympic-farce-Former-Blue-Peter-presenter-Konnie-Huq-lashes-robotic-Chinese-torch-minders.html (last accessed 6 March, 2010).

Edwards, R. and Thomas, D. (2008) 'Olympic torch relay nearly abandoned', *The Telegraph*, 7 April, http://www.telegraph.co.uk/news/main.jhtml?xml=/news/2008/04/07/ntorch 107.xml (last accessed 6 March, 2010).

Engel, M. (2008) 'Opening ceremony takes gold', *The Financial Times*, 8 August, http://www.ft.com/cms/s/0/3bcd284e-6573–11dd-a352–0000779fd18c,dwp_uuid=723ba 534–41c2–11dc-8328–0000779fd2ac.html (last accessed 5 March, 2010).

Evans, L. and Korporaal, G. (2008) 'IOC lies on web access have hurt my reputation: Kevan Gosper', *The Australian*, 1 August, http://www.theaustralian.com.au/news/ioc-lies-have-hurt-my-standing-gosper/story-e6frg7mo-1111117075735 (last accessed 5 March, 2010).

Garside, K. (2008) 'Light fantastic: China's opening ceremony thrills the watching world', *The Telegraph*, 9 August, http://www.telegraph.co.uk/sport/othersports/olympics/2525 453/Light-fantastic-Chinas-opening-ceremony-thrills-the-watching-world-Olympics.html (last accessed 5 March, 2010).

Greenhill, S., Rees, G. and Allen, P. (2008) 'Olympic torch fiasco: Lord Coe blasts "horrible Chinese thugs" who barged their way through London', *Daily Mail*, 8 April, http://www.dailymail.co.uk/pages/live/articles/news/news.html?in_article_id=557941&in_page_id= 1770 (last accessed 6 March, 2010).

Grose, T. K. (2010) 'London admits it can't top lavish Beijing Olympics when it hosts 2012 Games', *U.S.News & World Report*, 14 March, http://www.usnews.com/news/world/articles/2008/08/22/london-admits-it-cant-top-lavish-beijing-olympics-when-it-hosts-2012-games.html (last accessed 5 March, 2010).

Hamilton, A. (2008) 'A flaming mess at Downing Street', *The Times*, 7 April, http://www.timesonline.co.uk/tol/news/article3695058.ece (last accessed 6 March, 2010).

Hersh, P. (2008) 'When silence isn't gold(en) for the Olympics', *Chicago Tribune*, 25 March, http://newsblogs.chicagotribune.com/sports_globetrotting/2008/03/when-silence-is.html (last accessed 13 February, 2010).

Hoey, K. (2008) 'Olympic ideals? It's a grotesque charade', *The Telegraph*, 8 April, http://www.telegraph.co.uk/opinion/main.jhtml?xml=/opinion/2008/04/08/do0803.xml (last accessed 6 March, 2010).

Horne, J. and Whannel, G. (2010) 'The "caged torch procession": celebrities, protesters and the 2008 Olympic torch relay in London, Paris and San Francisco', *Sport in Society* Special Issue 'Documenting the Beijing Olympics' (edited by D.P. Martinez) 13(5): 760–70.

Human Rights Watch (2009) 'China: new restrictions target media. Government curbs local news assistants, threatens "blacklist"', http://www.hrw.org/en/news/2009/03/18/china-new-restrictions-target-media (last accessed 20 March, 2010).

Hutchins, B. and Mikosza, J. (2010) 'The Web 2.0 Olympics: athlete blogging, social networking and policy contradictions at the 2008 Beijing Games', *Convergence* 16(3): 279–97.

Hyde, M. (2008) 'London can take heart from these spectacularly humourless Games', *The Guardian*, 23 August, http://blogs.guardian.co.uk/sport/2008/08/23/london_can_take_heart_from_the.html (last accessed 5 March, 2010).

Jennings, A. (2008) 'Fallen ideals: investigating political conflict and corruption in the IOC and FIFA', Chelsea School Lecture, University of Brighton, 17 April, http://74.125.155.132/search?q=cache:uiyQXRtMPdwJ:www.transparencyinsport.org/chelsea_school_lecture+Jacques+Rogge,+now+trying+to+pretend+that,+%22with+hindsight%22,&cd=2&hl=en&ct=clnk&gl=au&client=firefox-a (last accessed 5 March, 2010).

Kelso, P. (2008a) 'Arrests, fights, jeering: Olympic spirit flickers amid the chaos', *The Guardian*, 7 April, http://www.guardian.co.uk/world/2008/apr/07/olympicgames2008.china3 (last accessed 6 March, 2010).

Kelso, P. (2008b) 'London looks on in awe at the ultimate celebration', *The Guardian*, 9 August, http://www.guardian.co.uk/sport/2008/aug/09/olympics2008.olympics2012 (last accessed 5 March, 2010).

Korporaal, G. (2007) 'Beijing torch relay a new heigh', *The Australian*, 4 August, http://www.theaustralian.com.au/news/sport/beijing-torch-Relay-a-new-heigh/story-e6frg7mf-1111114104357 (last accessed 5 March, 2010).

Kurlantzick, J. (2008) 'China's next-generation nationalists', *The Los Angeles Times*, 6 May, *http://www.carnegieendowment.org/publications/?fa=view&id=20095* (last accessed 5 March, 2010).

Lawson, D. (2008) 'Beijing is the right place for the Olympics', *The Independent*, 8 April, http://www.independent.co.uk/opinion/commentators/dominic-lawson/dominic-lawson-beijing-is-the-right-place-for-the-olympics-805771.html (last accessed 6 March, 2010).

Lawton, J. (2008) 'The greatest show the world has ever seen', *The Independent*, 9 August, http://www.independent.co.uk/sport/olympics/the-greatest-show-the-world-has-ever-seen-889262.html (last accessed 5 March, 2010).

Lenskyj, H. (2008) *Olympic Industry Resistance: Challenging Olympic Power and Propaganda*, Albany, NY: State University of New York Press.

London 2012 Olympic and Paralympic Games (2010a) 'Diversity and inclusion', http://www.london2012.com/get-involved/jobs/working-for-locog/diversity-and-inclusion.php (last accessed 5 March, 2010).

London 2012 Olympic and Paralympic Games (2010b) 'Ceremonies', http://www.london2012.com/games/ceremonies/index.php (last accessed 6 March, 2010).

Luo Q. and Richeri, G. (eds) (2009) *Encoding the Olympics: Comparative Analysis on International Reporting of Beijing 2008: A Communication Perspective.* Lausanne: International Olympic Committee, http://doc.rero.ch/record/12568?ln=en (last accessed 5 March, 2010).

MacAloon, J. J. (ed.) (2011) *The Flame Relay and the Olympic Movement*, London: Routledge.

Macartney, J. and Ford, R. (2008) 'Unmasked: Chinese guardians of Olympic torch', *The Times*, 9 April, http://www.timesonline.co.uk/tol/news/world/asia/article3671368.ece (last accessed 6 March, 2010).

Majumdar, B. and Mehta, N. (2010) 'It's not just sport: Delhi and the Olympic torch relay', *Sport in Society* 13(1): 92–106.

Mandell, R.D. (1987) *The Nazi Olympics*, Champaign, IL: University of Illinois Press.

Manzenreiter, W. (2010) 'The Beijing Games in the Western imagination of China: the weak power of soft power', *Journal of Sport and Social Issues* 34: 29–48.

McKay, J., Hutchins, B. and Mikosza, J. (2000) 'Shame and scandal in the family: Australian media narratives of the IOC/SOCOG scandal spiral', *Olympika: The International Journal of Olympic Studies* IX: 25–48.

Neilsen (2008) 'Beijing Olympics draw largest ever global TV audience', 5 September, http://blog.nielsen.com/nielsenwire/media_entertainment/beijing-olympics-draw-largest-ever-global-tv-audience/ (last accessed 13 February, 2010).

O'Connor, A. (2008a) 'Hopes swiftly extinguished by violence and farce', *The Times*, 7 April, http://www.timesonline.co.uk/tol/news/world/asia/article3695050.ece (last accessed 6 March, 2010).

O'Connor, A. (2008b) 'Athletes who take Tibet stand face Olympic cut', *The Times*, 11 April, http://www.timesonline.co.uk/tol/sport/olympics/article3724308.ece (last accessed 6 March, 2010).

O'Connor, A. (2008c) 'No Olympic torch relay for London 2012', *The Times*, 6 August, http://www.timesonline.co.uk/tol/sport/olympics/article4465672.ece (last accessed 6 March, 2010).

O'Neill, B. (2008) 'The invasion of the robotic thugs', *spiked*, 9 April, http://www.spiked-online.com/index.php/site/article/4963/ (last accessed 6 March, 2010).

Price, M.E. and Dayan, D. (eds) (2008) *Owning the Olympics: Narratives of the New China*, Ann Arbor, MI: The University of Michigan Press.

Rowe, D. and Stevenson, D. (2006) 'Sydney 2000: sociality and spatiality in global media events', in A. Tomlinson and C. Young (eds) *National Identity and Global Sports Events: Culture, Politics, and Spectacle in the Olympics and the Football World Cup*, New York: State University of New York Press, 197–214.

Rowe, D., Gilmour, C. and Petzold, T. (2010) 'Australia: mediated representation of global politics', *The International Journal of the History of Sport*, Special Issue, 'Encoding the Olympics – The Beijing Olympic Games and the communication impact worldwide' (edited by L. Qing and G. Richeri), 27: (9/10), 1510–33.

Ryan, C. (2010) 'Easy does it', *The Australian Financial Review Magazine*, March, 2010: 36–39.

Steel, M. (2008) 'Let's make a virtue of being useless', *The Independent*, 13 August, http://www.independent.co.uk/opinion/commentators/mark-steel/mark-steel-lets-make-a-virtue-of-being-useless-892821.html (last accessed 5 March, 2010).

The Australian (2008) 'Protests to disrupt Olympics torch run', 16 February, http://www.theaustralian.news.com.au/story/0,25197,23220762–2703,00.html (last accessed 5 March, 2010).

The Independent (2008a) 'There are no winners in this farcical event', 8 April, http://www.independent.co.uk/opinion/leading-articles/leading-article-there-are-no-winners-in-this-farcical-event-805767.html (last accessed 6 March, 2010).

The Independent (2008b) 'Spotlight turns to London as Beijing Games end', *The Independent* 24 August, http://www.independent.co.uk/sport/olympics/spotlight-turns-to-london-as-beijing-games-end-907545.html (last accessed 5 March, 2010).

Tomlinson, A. (2005) 'Olympic survivals: the Olympic Games as a global phenomenon', in L. Allison (ed.) *The Global Politics of Sport: The Role of Global Institutions in Sport*, London: Routledge.

Tomlinson, A. and Young, C. (eds) (2006) *National Identity and Global Sports Events: Culture, Politics, and Spectacle in the Olympics and the Football World Cup*, New York: State University of New York Press

Urry, J. (2003) *Global Complexity*, Cambridge, UK: Polity.

USA Today (2008) 'Vietnamese cheer torch, last int'l stop', *USA Today*, 29 April, http://www.usatoday.com/news/world/2008-04-29-torch-vietnam_N.htm (last accessed 5 March, 2010).

Whannel, G. (2008) 'Pass the torch and follow the money', *Red Pepper*, 4 August: http://www.redpepper.org.uk/Pass-the-torch-and-follow-the (last accessed 20 March, 2010).

Wheatcroft, G. (2008) 'After this shaming farce, we should put out the Olympic flame for good', 8 April, http://www.dailymail.co.uk/pages/live/articles/news/news.html?in_article_id=557963&in_page_id=1770 (last accessed 6 March, 2010).

White, J. (2008a) 'China raises the bar with a jaw-dropping Olympic opening ceremony', *The Telegraph*, 9 August, http://www.telegraph.co.uk/sport/othersports/olympics/2525845/China-raises-the-bar-with-a-jaw-dropping-Olympic-opening-ceremony—-Olympics.html (last accessed 5 March, 2010).

White, J. (2008b) 'London 2012 will be the "fun Olympics"', *The Telegraph*, 26 August, http://www.telegraph.co.uk/sport/othersports/olympics/2563858/Seb-Coe-interview-London-2012-will-be-the-fun-Olympics.html (last accessed 5 March, 2010).

Young, C. (2008) 'Olympic boycotts: always tricky', *Dissent Magazine*, Summer, http://www.dissentmagazine.org/article/?article=1233 (last accessed 13 February, 2010).

Xu, Guoqi (2008) *Olympic Dreams: China and Sports, 1895–2008*, Cambridge, MA and London, UK: Harvard University Press.

10

TASTE, AMBIGUITY AND THE CULTURAL OLYMPIAD

Shane Collins and Catherine Palmer

Introduction

The 1948 London Olympics embodied Pierre de Coubertin's ideal of bringing 'sport' and 'culture' together in the one event. Arts and cultural competitions were held alongside sporting events, with Great Britain winning gold in the oils and watercolour painting competition. This was the last time that cultural events were held as part of the Olympic Games. In 1952, a programme of cultural events was launched that was intended to complement the sporting action of the Games. For the first time, arts events were effectively competing with sporting events for funding and public and political support, whilst embedded within an overarching Olympic framework. This 'Cultural Olympiad' as it became known, comprises a four-year programme of arts, music, literature, dance and performance that variously showcases the cultural pursuits of the artistic community within host cities, regions and nations, as well as highlighting aesthetic aspects of sporting competition, regional attributes and perceptions of national character and culture. The events that comprise the Cultural Olympiad are funded and conceptualised as entirely separate from the sporting Olympiad, while nonetheless intended to resonate with much of the key imagery and iconography of the Games. This separation of the sporting Olympiad from the Cultural Olympiad – of sport from culture – poses a number of questions that dominate current policy debates. Shifting policy agendas and competing tensions around the funding of the Olympics raise a number of concerns about 'taste', culture, values and political priorities. It is these issues that this chapter takes as its point of departure.

The relative obscurity of the Cultural Olympiad – it is estimated that only two percent of the United Kingdom's adult population have heard of it (Thorpe 2010) – provides a point of contrast with the Olympic Games. Unlike the Olympic Games, the planning of the Cultural Olympiad is not subject to the same degree of public accountability. Unlike the Olympic Games, where athlete preparations, urban regeneration schemes and improvements to transport and other infrastructure have all been scrutinised in the lead up to the event, the 'backstage' preparations for the Cultural Olympiad have scarcely registered on the public's radar. This public ambivalence is important, for it will be the spectacle itself of the Cultural Olympiad; the artworks, the entertainment, the music, the street performances and the installations, among other things, that will bring into sharp relief many of the concerns that are focused upon the Games more broadly. Issues of legacy, impact and value for money, while barely registering in public and political discourse around the Cultural Olympiad pre-2012, will be topics of considerable public and political debate during and post-2012. It is for this reason that an analysis of a Cultural Olympiad that is largely overshadowed by the sporting Olympics makes an important and original contribution to studies of politics, power and representation in relation to sporting (and other) mega-events.

The chapter begins by tracing the historical development of the Cultural Olympiad before turning to some of the issues and challenges for London 2012, particularly the ambiguous and contested nature that underpins the process of embedding a cultural festival within a sporting one. Drawing on an analysis of the mercurial definition of 'culture', public and political debate over the relative value of funding of sport and art, as well as the shifting nature of the Cultural Olympiad itself, the chapter is particularly concerned to explore the implications for cultural policy that emerge from the tensions and synergies between the sporting Olympiad and the Cultural Olympiad. Informed by the theoretical framework of Pierre Bourdieu, particularly his notion that aesthetic judgment is both subjective and social at one and the same time, the chapter offers some reflections on 'taste', 'culture' and public and political bias in the nature and purpose of art and sport.

History of the Cultural Olympiad

The emergence of the modern Olympics Games established the world's premier sporting mega-event. Held every four years in different geographic locations, the summer Olympic Games provides a spectacle of sporting excellence across 26 sports. Founded in 1896 by Baron Pierre de Coubertin , the modern Olympics sought to integrate both sport and art. Coubertin's motives for establishing the Games were based upon the belief that organised sport could be a means for both physical and cultural renewal (Essex and Chalkley 1998). From their inception the Olympic Games were intended to be more than purely a sporting event; an integral part of the celebrations was the cultural programme (Gold and Gold 2007). For de Coubertin, it was the combination of sporting and cultural events that was to 'symbolize the universality and diversity of human culture' (Fensham 1994: 177). In his efforts to establish the Games, Coubertin also used the inclusion of the arts as a persuasive mechanism to garner public and political support; they were a central strategy in gaining support for his proposed revival of the Olympics Games (Stevenson 1997). In particular, the visual arts and music were used to influence the 'prominent educators and public figures' (Guttman 1992: 14) to support Coubertin's vision of a modern Olympic Games.

Since 1896, every Olympics Games has held displays of art and culture, however the extent and level of support for its inclusion as an element of the sporting Olympiad has been erratic. It was not until the 1912 Olympic Games in Stockholm that the first official Art competition was held (Hampton 2008). As with sporting events, medals were allocated for various traditional artistic disciplines including architecture, painting, sculpture, literature and music. As with the sporting events, these were awarded to individuals representing the various nations competing in the Games. Starting slowly, the number of entrants in the art competition gradually increased. At the Stockholm Games only 35 pieces of work were submitted to the five categories. By the Amsterdam Games in 1928 however, over 1,100 pieces of work were exhibited (Hampton 2007). Despite the growing number of entrants, opposition to the Arts within the Olympic festival emerged although the grounds for this are unclear. Prior to London 1948, the International Olympic Committee (IOC) discussed abandoning the arts event. This proposal was however rejected with the Secretary of the British Olympic Association, Evan Hunter, writing 'To suggest the exclusion of Art would be regarded by the most cultural and influential people in the international Olympic spheres as a retrograde step. There would be more resistance to the removal of Art than for many of the non-Universal Activities' (Hampton 2007: 188). Competition in the Arts therefore remained for the 1948 London Olympics, however the standard of the entries was considered so poor that in 'six of the fourteen classes only Honourable Mentions were awarded' (Hampton 2008: 189). While all countries that attended the 1948 Games were invited to submit original pieces of work inspired by sport, there was difficulty in recruiting entries. Rules surrounding the time period in which entries were completed (works must have been carried out since January 1944) and, in this post-war period, a shortage of material all contributed to the poor quality of entries (Hampton 2008).

After the London Games the structure of the Art competition changed dramatically. Art at the Olympic Games was to be exhibited without the formal recognition or honour of competition. Host cities were to now hold arts festivals: in other words, art at the Olympics was no longer to be prioritised alongside competitive sporting events. It remains unclear what was the catalyst for this sudden change, however a number of reasons have been suggested including 'organizational problems, the poor quality of entries, and fundamental conceptual opposition' (Gold and Revill 2007: 69). Since 1948, and the removal of structured competition, host countries have staged art exhibitions that demonstrate the art and culture of that country or displays of international art (Girginov and Parry 2005). Further changes occurred in 1954 when modifications to the Olympic Charter resulted in Organising Committees having greater flexibility with regard to the type of entries that could be received and displayed. No longer was there a requirement for art to have a specific sport connection, rather, host cities could use the Olympic Arts Festivals to showcase the host city and nation (Gold and

Revill 2007: 71). This shift also opened a new role for the arts within the Olympiad by allowing the Olympic Arts festivals to contribute to both regional and national agendas.

From 1956 to 1988, the structure, organisation and content of the Olympic Arts Festivals displayed considerable variation. The duration of events ranged from one week to a year, and the content and focus of events varied depending upon the agenda and interests of the host nation. National artistic displays were the focus of several host cities such as Melbourne 1956, Tokyo 1964 and Montreal 1976, while for others such as Mexico City 1968 and Seoul 1988, a more international display of art was the focal point (Gold and Revill 2007). A consistent trend however was the growing interest in the cultural festivals that were held alongside the sporting activities; by the 1988 Seoul Olympics not only was the sporting festival attracting large audiences but the cultural festival was also attracting audience numbers in their millions.

The changing format of the cultural displays continued toward the latter party of the twentieth century. In 1992 the organisers of the Barcelona Olympic Games introduced the four-year Cultural Olympiad[1] which involved a celebration of art over a four-year period that would culminate in an Olympic Art Festival. While the sporting festival is limited to 16 days under the Olympic Charter no such restrictions are placed upon the cultural festival (IOC 2007). While the establishment of the Cultural Olympiad indicates yet another shift in the structure and focus of the cultural programme it has also introduced a challenge for host cities. With a requirement to start the Cultural Olympiad only three years after the awarding of the Olympic Games, limited time is available in which to develop such an extensive programme of cultural and artistic activities, most of which require a considerable lead time, as well as significant human and financial resources. This has been compounded in more recent times by funding issues. Cultural programmes at Barcelona 1992, Atlanta 1996 and Sydney 2000 suffered budget cuts due to the need for Organising Committees to retrench, highlighting a constant challenge that cultural programmes face in competing for funding against the more high profile sporting events of the Olympic Games.

It was against this backdrop that London developed its successful bid for the hosting of the 2012 Olympic Games and Paralympics. Central to the winning bid for London 2012 was the promise to create a sporting and cultural legacy: as Lord Coe stated, 'We want the Cultural Olympiad to bring art and sport together, inspiring and unlocking creativity and talent all round the country' (London 2012, 2010c). The emphasis of the London 2012 Cultural Olympiad is on promoting national displays and activities that celebrate Britishness, inspire and involve young people and generate a positive legacy. Five ambitious promises which include sporting, cultural, environmental and economic goals have been developed against which the success of the 2012 Games will be measured (refer DCMS 2008b). It is through the Cultural Olympiad that the London Organising Committee of the Olympic and Paralympic Games (LOCOG) promises to inspire a generation of young people through opportunities to learn new skills and take part in new activities. Other key programmes that will contribute to achieving this promise will be the London 2012 Education Programme and the International Inspiration programme.

Four headline ambitions cascade from the promise to inspire youth. Of particular relevance to the Cultural Olympiad is the promise to develop 'New Cultural Activities [which will offer the opportunity for] tens of thousands of young people to participate in cultural activities as a result of the London 2012 Games' (DCMS 2008b: 43). Consistent with previous Cultural Olympiads, the themes of the cultural programme are broad and incorporate a range of cultural and artistic activities. The themes of the programmes are to encourage audience participation; make public spaces exciting; raise environmental sustainability, health and well-being issues through culture and sport; honour and share the values of the Olympic and Paralympic Games; create unique collaborations and innovations between communities and cultural sectors; and support the learning, skills and personal development of young people through links to our education programme (London 2012, 2010a).

This brief review highlights the constantly changing role and structure of culture and arts within the modern Olympic Games. Despite Coubertin's wishes to stage an event that incorporates and celebrates both sporting and cultural events in an effort to promote Olympism, this aim is one that has been under-exploited (Girginov and Parry 2005). There appears to have been a separation of art from culture (despite claims to the contrary) and an increasing vagueness and ambiguity as to the purpose of culture within the Olympiad. Placing culture as an integral part of the successful bid for the Olympic Games raises a number of questions as to how the Cultural Olympiad of 2012 will be presented and delivered.

Definitions of 'culture'

The opening historical tour raises a number of issues for London 2012: in particular, the way in which the host nation determines the objectives of the Cultural Olympiad and how 'culture' itself is defined. As highlighted above, the 2012 Cultural Olympiad will offer a range of cultural activities, calling into question the way in which cultural activities are selected and how culture will be defined. Outside of the mandatory formal cultural ceremonies, such as the Opening and Closing Ceremonies and torch relay, are nine major projects that form the backbone of the London Cultural Olympiad (London 2012, 2010b). The nine projects focus upon a range of activities with the underlying objective of showcasing Britain's cultural diversity and high standard of national art. There remains considerable ambiguity however as to how this will be defined for the Cultural Olympiad.

In stark contrast to the sporting events that are clearly identified and defined, there is a lack of conceptual clarity surrounding the term 'culture' within the planning and promotion of the Cultural Olympiad. Planning documents have signalled that a broad meaning is to be adopted: 'Culture covers not only pursuits such as visiting galleries, museums and theatres but also activities as diverse as carnival and street theatre, fashion, gaming, photography, heritage and the natural environment, and many more' (DCMS 2008b: 45). While it is a point developed further in the discussion, it is worth noting here that such 'definitions' of culture are not definitions at all, but a list of things to do. Alongside this, the Cultural Olympiad is also to appeal to understandings of 'Britishness', a task that immediately alludes to a more anthropological understanding of culture as a human experience by which people make meaning through their engagement with the world around them. It is this slippage – or lack of conceptual clarity – as to how the term culture is to be used and interpreted in this unique sporting and artistic context that is already undermining public support for the nature and purpose of the Cultural Olympiad. Anish Kapoor, an artist, supports this observation when asked to comment on what the Cultural Olympiad means: 'The Cultural Olympiad is complicated because it's rather nebulous' (London 2012, 2010d). The question 'What is the Cultural Olympiad?' has been raised by popular media, the public and members of the arts community alike (Higgins 2009). This supports the findings of research conducted in 2007 which found the public considered the Cultural Olympiad to be the public's lowest prioritised legacy promise (DCMS 2008b: 9–10).

Despite the Cultural Olympiad being launched in September 2008 as part of the handover from the Beijing Olympiad, it is only recently that the lack of definition has spilled into the public domain. With just over 900 days until the opening of the Olympics Games the term Cultural Olympiad has now been abandoned. In explanation Tony Hall (Chair of the London 2012 Cultural Olympiad Board) argued that the public may not know the words 'culture' and 'Olympiad' and that the event would be a 'festival of festivals' (Collins 2010). As a result of this ambiguity, in 2010 the Artistic Director, Ruth Mackenzie, was tasked with developing a term and definition that the public will understand (Tait 2010). With only two years until the opening ceremony this poses a number of questions surrounding the marketing and promotion of the Cultural Olympiad and the ability of the London Olympic Organising Committee (LOCOG) to achieve its ambitious legacy goals. While this ambiguity allows and indeed encourages a wide-ranging selection of cultural and artistic activities, it can also lead to 'remarkable discontinuities' particularly in regard to LOCOG's commitment to achieving its ambitious cultural bid proposal, particularly when budget and resource allocation is already debated and contested (Garcia 2002).

Funding priorities

Indeed, it is funding of the Cultural Olympiad that highlights concerns regarding political priorities. The claim that 2012 would link culture and sport in an effort to revive the spirit of the Olympic Games is a bold one. As the LOCOG Chair of Culture claimed, 'By putting culture into the story of the Olympics, we will change the way the Games are seen for ever' (Higgins 2009). How strongly this commitment rests with the broader planning of the Olympic Games remains unanswered, particularly in relation to the level of resourcing allocated to the Cultural Olympiad. With an overall budget of £9.325 billion (and rising), the London Olympics Games claims it will leave a long-term cultural and sporting legacy for the whole nation (DCMS 2008a). How funding is structured and allocated provides a somewhat different perspective.

The overall funding package mentioned above is funded by three key sources, The National Lottery, Central Government and London City for the Olympic and Paralympic Games (DCMS 2008a). Only the mandatory ceremonial events (which include the Opening and Closing Ceremonies, medal ceremonies, torch relay and the welcome of Athletes to the Village) make up the part of the Cultural Olympiad that is included in this official funding package. Cultural Olympiad activities, such as the Major Projects and the UK-wide Cultural Festival will instead receive funding from a range of public and private partners (DCMS 2008a). Indeed, it is estimated that revenue raised through corporate sponsorship with partners such as BP, EDF Energy and BT is in the order of £750 million. The absence of a clear structure for funding, along with an absence of an assured revenue stream, indicates the priority given to the sport over culture.

This disparity is reinforced in the overall budget allocations provided for the sporting and cultural Olympiads. In contrast to the stated £9.325 billion budget for the Olympic Games the total budget for the Cultural Olympiad has been far more difficult to ascertain. It is estimated that between £55 and £80 million has been allocated for delivering the Cultural Olympiad (outside of the mandatory cultural events). While not an insignificant amount, this makes up less than 2 per cent of the funding package for the Olympic and Paralympic Games. An additional consequence of this funding structure is the implication of uncertain revenue streams which may lead to difficulties in planning and delivery. Given that London 2012 is thought to have won the battle to host the Games in part due to its promise to hold a vibrant artistic festival calls in to question the ongoing political commitment to support the Cultural Olympiad. Furthermore, there is concern amongst the arts community that funding for the cultural Olympiad will impact upon arts organisations that are already bracing themselves for cuts in revenue (Lister 2009; Higgins 2009). Concern within the arts community has stressed that not only is investment in the Cultural Olympiad required but ongoing investment at a sustainable and consistent level in the arts sector is also required if London is to hold a successful Cultural Olympiad (Calvi 2007).

These funding issues raise questions as to the extent to which the Cultural Olympiad is included as an integral part of the planning for the Games more broadly. Despite claims by LOCOG's Chair of Culture, Jude Kelly, that 'By putting culture into the story of the Olympics we will change the way the Games are seen for ever' (Higgins 2009), it would appear that the rhetorical commitment has outweighed that of actual resource allocation. The lack of a coordinated resource package also signals a lack of integration between the art and culture, and sporting activities. As argued by Garcia if art events are not well integrated into a sporting events management and promotion, 'the potential for the impact is diminished' (2001: 201).

Taste, values and political priorities

The issues surrounding the difficulties in defining the Cultural Olympiad raises further questions as to taste and values, – or, in other words, where and what should tax payers' money actually be spent on? As highlighted above, Olympic cultural programmes have differed on a number of factors, not least has been the variation between popular events as opposed to elite displays of what may considered 'high art or culture' (Garcia 2002). The values and themes of the 2012 Cultural Olympiad have been developed after consultation with the arts and culture sectors within the UK. As Bourdieu (1984) recognises, taste is defined by those in power. This has resulted in a range of cultural and artistic activities that are diverse and indicate a shift towards popular events that will encourage participation. The central plank of the Cultural Olympiad comprises nine major projects which include Disability Art and Culture, A Collection of World Stories, World Shakespeare Festival, Film, Discovering Places, Somewhereto (empowering young people to use space), Outdoor Arts, Sounds, and Artists Taking the Lead.

In Artists Taking the Lead, 12 public arts projects, commissioned to a total value of £5.4 million, bring the debate of taste and values into sharp relief, and make their inclusion in the Cultural Olympiad open to critical scything (Spero 2009). For example, the 'Lionheart' project takes inspiration from Richard the Lionheart and the local textile industry in Nottingham, producing three 30ft hand crocheted lions which will be displayed in city centre. The 'Forest Pitch' project will see the part destruction of a forest for the development of a football pitch. After hosting two football matches made up of amateurs, the forest will return to nature and be able to reclaim its space. Finally, the Flow project involves a floating watermill which will power itself and other musical instruments. The diversity of these projects calls into question not only 'taste' but also the existence of a clear vision for the Cultural Olympiad. Since the commissioning of the 12 public arts projects the Chair of the Cultural Olympiad Board has stated that he now wants more emphasis on the Summer Games themselves.

The inclusion of particular artistic choices in the programmes, and the anticipated public backlash as to some of these choices, alerts us to the social patterning of 'taste' and values that underpins the theoretical framework of the French sociologist Pierre Bourdieu (1984). Divisions between the centre and the periphery – or London and the regions – between public, participatory art and the display of art works in the more exclusive spaces of galleries and the office foyers of principal sponsors such as BP and BT, between notions of instrumental and intrinsic value, and frustrations from within the arts sector as to the perceived funnelling of funding away from the arts towards sport, or indeed, the lack of funding for mainstream arts, other than through the period of the Cultural Olympiad, all serve to highlight the particular judgments of taste and privilege that underpin the discourse of the Cultural Olympiad.

Indeed, changes to the Cultural Olympic Board have highlighted concerns regarding the progress of the Cultural Olympiad as well as the type of art and activities that will be prioritised. Senior and respected members of the arts community have been selected which are able to combine 'high' and 'low' art, while also addressing aesthetic concerns. As Tony Hall (Chair of the Cultural Olympiad Board) proclaimed, the Cultural Olympiad has 'a chance to change the way this country looks at art and culture by making a statement that this [the Cultural Olympiad] is as important as sport' (Tait 2010). What remains unclear is who decided what will be considered as art or culture that is significant enough to be included amongst the programmes. The Cultural Olympiad has been presented as an integral part of the Olympic spirit, however the connections between the cultural activities and its legacy have also been questioned. Cultural observers argue that it is important to think about how to create something absolutely wonderful first and then let the public and history decide whether a legacy has been created; it is 'ruinously stupid to think about creative legacy as a starting point' (Thorpe 2010). Of course what is 'absolutely wonderful' remains unclear.

The political prioritisation of the Olympiad from the Cultural Olympiad has been further illustrated in the planning and execution of the cultural activities for 2012. Traditionally, there has been a considerable gap between the activities and eagerness of the host city to propose cultural activities at the bid stage and the commitment and readiness of the Olympic organising committee to deliver upon these promises (Garcia 2002). After the euphoria of winning the right to host the 2012 Olympics, the ability to meet some very ambitious cultural bid proposals appears to have waned. The Director of the Tate Museum, for example, observed 'the original bid projects were put together by committee, some have legs and frankly some don't' (Higgins 2009). An example of this has been the quiet dropping of the Culture Ship that would set sail and collect artefacts from around the world (Lister 2009). This gap, between proposed cultural activities at the bid stage and the readiness of LOCOG to implement them, may be further amplified by the ambiguous direction of the IOC on what constitutes the cultural programmes. Within the IOC Charter specific reference is made for the host city to stage 'a programme of cultural events which must cover at least the entire period during which the Olympics Village is Open' (IOC 2007: 80) – no further direction is provided.

The gap between the bid and implementation stage is in stark contrast to the funding, organisational structures and promotion that have been implemented for the Olympiad. While the rhetoric of LOCOG and the politicians reinforces the desire for culture and sport to be placed side by side in celebration this appears to be where any juxtaposition stops. The aspiration of the Olympics Minister Tessa Jowell that 'The cultural festival and the cultural legacy are integral to the Olympics and just as with sport, we must ensure a sustainable legacy, not just in

London but throughout the UK' (London Development Agency 2010) remains uncertain.

Discussion of the Cultural Olympiad raises a number of questions for policy and practice debates in relation to the planning and execution of an artistic event of this nature and for London 2012 more broadly. Central to these is an absence of a definition of 'culture' in organisational understandings of the Cultural Olympiad. As indicated previously, the broad sweep of activities included within the proposed programme of events spans visits to galleries, museums and theatres as well as public works such as street theatre, fashion and photography exhibits. Certainly, the Cultural Olympiad, in keeping with the broader Olympic agenda of increasing participation, should include a range of artistic pursuits for the public to engage with, however the point here is that these activities appear more as a list of things to do, rather than a programme that has been developed within a grounded understanding of 'culture' as a process and product of human experience. That is, it appears the fundamental question of what culture means for the Cultural Olympiad has not been adequately addressed in thinking through the nature and purpose of the events on offer. Without conceptual clarity as to how the term culture is to be used and interpreted in the context of the Cultural Olympiad, it is already proving difficult for organisers to schedule a programme of activities that will have a definitional coherence throughout, and that will appease public disquiet as to the 'value' of the event. We see this most clearly in the decision to abandon the term 'the Cultural Olympiad' on the basis that the public may not understand the words 'culture' and 'Olympiad (Collins 2010). In many ways, it is less important that the public understands these terms – their role in the event is to appreciate and attend the artistic works on offer – than for the organisers to have an internal coherence in how they are understanding the terms, and their symbolic import, when planning and implementing an event of this scale. Such ambiguity also raises questions as to how (and when) the Cultural Olympiad will be evaluated. The lack of political prioritisation and delays in planning make any robust evaluation difficult. Lessons may well be drawn from Liverpool, the 2008 European City of Culture, where a five-year research project was commissioned to assess the extent to which the five key outcomes were achieved (Garcia *et al.* 2010). The ability to measure the impact of a Cultural Olympiad would undoubtedly have great benefits not only for London 2012 but for future host cities.

Following on from this, debates about definitions of 'culture' inevitably stray into the territory of 'taste' and 'values'. These are already proving pivotal to the discursive construction of the unfolding narrative of the Cultural Olympiad (or 'Festival of Festivals'). The Cultural Olympiad will exemplify the Boudieuian maxim that 'taste is defined by those in power' (1984) – to which we would add, 'and contested by those without'. Not withstanding the appeal to regional ownership of such exhibits, the prospect of three 30 ft, hand crocheted lions gracing the streets of Nottingham will provide a focus for an anticipated public and media backlash as to the costs of mounting such public works in the broader context of the rising costs of the Olympic Game and Paralympics during a global economic downturn that has already come under considerable public and political scrutiny. Questions about whether such efforts constitute 'art' or indeed 'money well spent' will also be raised. Experience of previous Games, however, suggests that such public outrage melts in the dazzle of the spectacle once the Games commence and the medals are won. The extent to which this is the case for the London Games and Cultural Olympiad will be interesting to monitor.

Equally, the extent to which the Cultural Olympiad adds value to the programme of sporting events will be closely followed. In her analysis of the cultural and arts programmes offered at the Sydney Olympics in 2000, Garcia (2001) makes a strong case for what she calls 'event augmentation' in which the staging of artistic and cultural events helps to foster appeal for the sporting event among audience segments who would not otherwise be reached by (or interested in) the sporting action. Given the ambiguities of definition of culture, a highly contentious political climate and considerable attention already focussed on measures and outcomes of 'legacy' more broadly, these indicators of impact will be particularly pertinent for the London 2012 Cultural Olympiad and its relationship to the Olympic Games and Paralympics.

Debates about value and privilege also circulate more broadly with the re-allocation of government spending from the arts. There is already considerable disquiet from within the arts community, with the Arts Council of England losing more than £100 million of its funding over the next four years to help pay for the spiralling costs of the Olympic and Paralympic Games (Olympic Lottery Distributor, 2010). Implicit here is a valuing of sport over culture – a reductionist separation that the Cultural Olympiad is meant to overcome through its appeal to other audiences not necessarily interested in the jingoistic competition of the sports events on offer.

This is particularly the case for young people who are central to many of the narratives and imperatives that surround the Olympics more broadly. The capacity of the Cultural Olympiad to inspire youth to participate in cultural activities that can then be sustained in any kind of meaningful way is an issue that, like participation in sport and physical activity, invites cynicism, given the devolution of funding and, ultimately, the subordination of the Cultural Olympiad to the sporting action of the Olympic Games themselves.

Conclusion

This chapter has been concerned to trace out some of the issues and challenges for the London 2012 Cultural Olympiad. It has been particularly interested to explore some of the ambiguities and tensions that surround the process of embedding a cultural festival within a sporting one.

Underpinning much of the controversy surrounding this event is a debate about the intrinsic or instrumental value of the Cultural Olympiad (Gibson 2008). Two of the key aims of the programme – to raise environmental sustainability health and well-being issues through culture and sport and to support the learning, skills and personal development of young people – link to other policy agendas in ways that have instrumental benefits for these policy sectors, while other programme themes such as honouring and sharing the values of the Olympic and Paralympic Games have intrinsic 'value' in and of themselves, rather than necessarily connecting to a broader social policy agenda. Such distinctions are important for a wider consideration of culture and cultural policy in the UK, for the politics of production that underpin the planning and implementation of events like the Cultural Olympiad are far more nuanced and complex than such distinctions typically allow for. More sophisticated understandings of notions of culture, taste and value are important to consider in this particular policy context so as to better engage with the specific realities of the arts and sector when mounting multi-year, multi-sited cultural programmes on the scale of the Cultural Olympiad. Indeed, the Cultural Olympiad of the London 2012 Olympic Games and Paralympics offers a timely opportunity for reflecting on some of the key questions of taste, value and culture that have long been a part of commentary and debate within the social sciences.

Notes

1   The term 'Olympiad' refers to the four-year period that is opened and celebrated by the Games. The Cultural Olympiad for the 2012 Olympic Games will begin in September 2008 and end in September 2012.

References

Bourdieu, P. (1984) *Distinction: A Social Critique of the Judgement of Taste*, London: Routledge.

Calvi, N. (2007, May 15) 'Olympiad gains £28 million for cultural projects', *The Stage*. http://www.thestage.co.uk/news/newsstory.php/16856/olympiad-gains-28-million-for-cultural (accessed 2 February, 2010).

Collins, N. (2010, January 30) '2012 Cultural Olympiad "too hard to understand"', *Telegraph*. http://www.telegraph.co.uk/sport/othersports/olympics/london2012/7105123/2012-Cultural-Olympiad-too-hard-to-understand.html (accessed 15 February, 2010).

DCMS (2008a) *London 2012 Olympic and Paralympic Games: Annual Report January 2008*, Author: London.

DCMS (2008b) *Before, During and After: Making the Most of the London 2012 Games*. Author: London

DCMS (2010) *London 2012 Olympic and Paralympics Games: Annual Report February 2010*. Author: London

Essex, S. and Chalkley, B. (1998) 'Olympic Games: Catalyst for Change', *Leisure Studies* 17(3): 187–206.

Fensham, R. (1994) 'Prime time hyperspace: The Olympic City as Spectacle', in K. Gibson and S. Watson (eds) *Metropolis Now: Planning and the Urban in Contemporary Australia*. Leichhardt: Pluto Press.

Garcia, B. (2001) 'Enhancing Sport Marketing through Cultural and Arts Programs: Lessons from the Sydney 2000 Olympic Arts Festivals', *Sport Management Review* 4(2):193–219.

Garcia, B. (2002) *The Concept of Olympic Cultural Programme: Origins, evolution and projection*. Paper presented at Centre d'Estudis Olimpics, Barcelona.

Garcia, B., Melville, R. and Cox, T. (2010) *Impacts 08; European Capital of Culture Research Programme*, University of Liverpool.

Gibson, L. (2008) 'In defence of instrumentality', *Cultural Trends* 17(4): 247–257.

Gibson, L. (2009) 'Cultural landscapes and identity', in L. Gibson and J. Pendlebury (eds) *Valuing Historic Environments*, London: Ashgate.

Girginov, V, and Parry, J. (2005) *The Olympic Games Explained: A Student Guide to the Evolution of the Modern Olympics*, Abingdon: Routledge.

Gold, J. R. and Gold, M. M. (2007) 'Introduction', in J. R. Gold and M. Gold (eds), *Olympic Cities: City Agendas, Planning, and the Worlds Games, 1896–2012*, Abingdon: Routledge.

Guttman, A. (1992) *The Olympics: A History of the Modern Games*. Urbana: University of Illinois Press.

Hampton, J. (2008) *The Austerity Olympics: When the Games came to London in 1948*, London: Aurum Press.

Higgins, C. (2009, March 25) 'Is the Cultural Olympiad a runner?', *The Guardian*. http://www.guardian.co.uk/uk/2009/mar/25/cultural-olympiad (accessed 15 February, 2010).

IOC (2007) *Olympic Charter*, Lausanne: International Olympic Committee.

Lister, D. (2009, March 21) 'David Lister: We don't need a cultural olympiad', *The Independent*, http://www.independent.co.uk/opinion/columnists/david-lister/david-lister-we-dont-need-a-cultural-olympiad-1650629.html (accessed 16 February, 1010).

London 2012 (2010a) *About the Cultural Olympiad*. http://www.london2012.com/get-involved/cultural-olympiad/index.php (accessed 21 February 2010).

London 2012 (2010b) *Major Projects*. http://www.london2012.com/get-involved/cultural-olympiad/major-projects/index.php (accessed 27 February, 2010).

London 2012 (2010c) *Cloud sculptures and imaginary worlds feature on major arts project shortlist*. http://www.london2012.com/news/2009/08/cloud-sculptures-and-imaginary-worlds-feature-on-major-a.php (accessed 27 February 2010).

London 2012 (2010d) *Cultural Olympiad*. http://www.london2012.com/videotranscripts/cultural-olympiad.php (accessed 7 March, 2010).

London Development Agency (2010) *London 2012 Appoints culture, ceremonies and Education Director for Olympic Games and Paralympic Games*. http://www.london2012.com/press/media-releases/2006/06/london-2012-appoints-culture-ceremonies-and-education-di.php (accessed 5 March, 2010).

Olympic Lottery Distributor (2010) *Our Funding Decisions*. http://www.olympiclotterydistributor.org.uk/docs/text.php?id=2:2:4:0 (accessed 15 January, 2010).

Spero, J. (2009) 'A gold medal for the Cultural Olympiad', *The Arts Desk*, http://images.theartsdesk.com/index.php?option=com_k2&view=item&id=424:a-gold-medal-for-the-cultural-olypiad&Itemid=29 (accessed 23 February, 2010).

Tait, S. (2010, February 6) 'Is it too late to save the Cultural Olympiad?', *The Art Desk*. http://www.theartsdesk.com/index.php?option=com_k2&view=item&id=930:opinion-cultural-olympiad&Itemid=29 (accessed 8 March, 2010).

Thorpe, V. (2010, July 8) 'What can Sotheby's teach the 2012 Olympics?', *The Guardian*, http://www.guardian.co.uk/culture/charlottehigginsblog/2010/jul/08/art-sothebys-cultural-olympiad (accessed 27 July, 2010).

Thorpe, V. (2010, January 10) 'Power Tussle threatens Arts Olympics', *The Guardian*, http://www.guardian.co.uk/culture/2010/jan/10/power-tussle-2012-arts-olympics (accessed 17 February, 2010).

Tomlinson, A. and Whannel, G. (1984) 'Introduction', in A. Tomlinson and G. Whannel (eds) *Five-Ring Circus: Money, power and politics at the Olympic Games*, Pluto Press: London.

11

SEX WATCH

Surveying women's sexed and gendered bodies at the Olympics

Jayne Caudwell

> The only thing about sex and gender that the Olympic committee know for sure is this: the only women who are undeniably 100% women are royalty, as Princess Anne was the only female athlete who didn't have to submit a sex test at the 1976 Olympics in Montreal. And of course it had nothing to do with the fact that she was the daughter of Canada's Head of State, Queen Elizabeth II.
>
> What makes a 'real woman'? Is it chromosomes, testosterone levels, sex organs, or a love of the colour pink? I don't know, and actually I don't care. But what I do know is that I sure as hell don't want to be told what it is to be a woman by a group of self-appointed experts from the Olympic Committee. (Shaw 2008, www.thefword.org.uk)

Introduction

After the 1964 Olympics in Tokyo, and for the past four decades since, the International Olympics Committee (IOC) has performed a series of testing in their endeavours to define and categorise the sex and gender of athletes: more specifically, women athletes. This testing regime was actually initiated by the International Amateur Athletic Federation (IAAF) in the mid 1960s. Women athletes taking part in the 1966 European Track and Field Championships (Budapest, Hungary) and Commonwealth Games (Kingston, Jamaica), and 1967 European Track and Field Championships (Kiev, USSR) and Pan American Games (Winnipeg, Canada) were required to appear naked in front of a panel of officials who visually confirmed and certified their sex and gender (Puffer 1996; Shy 2007). These early tests have been described by many as 'nude parades' (Wackwitz 1996) and were challenged on various levels, including – rather ironically – their 'scientific' validity.

Although procedures adopted by the International Association of Athletics Federations (IAAF) and IOC are not directly linked, during this era – the 1960s – both turned to medicine and science to help verify the legitimacy of athletic bodies (Wrynn 2004). In the case of drug testing, they tested all athletes' bodies; in the case of sex testing, they tested only women's bodies. Following World War II, in the shadow of the Cold War (cf., Ritchie 2003), and with this new scientific turn (cf., Wrynn 2004), the IOC developed its own approach to sex-testing women athletes, and the first IOC-devised sex test became mandatory at the 1968 Winter Games in Grenoble (France) and the 1968 Summer Games in Mexico City.

Prince Alexandre de Merode, a member of the all-male IOC[1] from 1964 (until his death in 2002) and in charge of setting up the IOC Medical Commission in 1967, claimed that the IOC Medical Commission's sex/gender tests were devised to prevent cheating (Fastiff 1991–1992; Teezel 2006; Wackwitz 1996, 2003). The type of cheating the IOC suspected was that of men masquerading as women: more specifically, and in the aftermath of the 1936 Berlin Olympics (Ritchie, Reynard and Lewis 2008), men from Soviet-bloc countries masquerading as women.[2] From 1968 onwards, the sex test was compulsory for all women wishing to participate in the Olympics. However, eight years after the test was made mandatory, one woman was exempt: Princess Anne of England. One can only assume that Princess Anne did not receive her '"Olympic certificate" verifying her gender' (Wrynn 2004: 222) or wear her badge of femininity – 'femininity card' – when in the Olympic Village (Davison and Frank 2006).

Sex testing at the 1968 – and subsequent – Olympics (1970s–1980s) has proved problematic and dubious. Sex tests were often conducted inadequately, and the aim to verify women's sex premised on the presence of an XX chromosome pattern has been shown to be flawed (McArdle 2008; Puffer 1996; Shy 2007; Tucker and Collins 2005). Wackwitz (1996, 2003) argues that this testing regime – late 1960s through to the late 1980s – reflects a form of social control by the IOC. For the period, the ever-increasing numbers of women athletes in an increasing number of Olympic events were, in effect, forced to *prove* they were women. Womanhood for many within the IOC meant displaying visibly desirable heterosexual femininity (cf., Wamsley 2008) as well as passing a standard test of chromosomal make-up (Cole 2000b).

With mounting opposition to the sex test from within the scientific community as well as those challenging its integrity on grounds of human rights, ethics and legality, the IOC devised and announced their next model of testing. Gender verification tests, which involve assessment of genetic coding, were conducted at the 1992 Winter Olympics in Albertville (France) and Summer Olympics in Barcelona (Spain). The 1992 version, known as the PCR (polymerase chain reaction) test, examined the individual's DNA from buccal cells for the presence of the SRY gene (a testis-determining gene) (Pilgrim, Martin and Binder 2002–3; Puffer 1996). If a woman athlete's sex was called into question by the presence of a Y chromosome or a testis-determining gene, she underwent further genetic, visual and gynaecological examination. In this way, the revised tests, relying on the 'latest' science, aimed to *prove* women athletes were not men (Wackwitz 1996, 2003).

As with sex testing, the gender verification test and the regime of compulsory testing remained controversial.[3] As late as 1999, some 30 years after its initial attempts to 'authenticate' women's athletic/sporting bodies, the male-dominated IOC conceded, and 'quietly. . . suspended' (Cole 2000a: 331) mandatory testing. The Olympics in 2000 (Sydney), 2004 (Athens), and 2008 (Beijing)[4] were *officially* sex and gender test-free. However, the IOC continues to have the authority to test individuals on a suspicion- and case-by-case-based basis. Moreover, and within their most recent policy on transsexual athletes, they still have the power '. . .to take all appropriate measures for the determination of the gender of a competitor' (www.olympics.org). It is almost certain that this power will be mobilised at the next Olympics (London 2012) and not only in relation to transsexual athletes, but more specifically, in the aftermath of the recent (2009/10) banning and subsequent reinstating of 'Caster' Semenya by the IAAF.

In 2003, the IOC Medical Commission directed its scientific-testing attention to the emerging issues surrounding transsexual athletes. On October 28th, 2003, *The Statement of the Stockholm Consensus on Sex Reassignment in Sports* (Stockholm Consensus) appeared in time for Athens 2004. Additionally, in mid January 2010, according to Kolata (2010), the IOC turned its medical and scientific spotlight on intersex women athletes. More specifically, how the IOC Medical Commission will 'diagnose' and 'treat' intersex athletes. Within these most recent discussions, the IOC Medical Commission frames intersex as a 'disorder' (www.intersexualite. org). I return to this point below.

In this chapter, I consider the IOC's fetish with and continuing surveillance of the sexes and genders of athletes' bodies. I further explore the issues surrounding sex testing, gender verification, intersex bodies and the recent policy on transsexual athletes, to demonstrate the regulatory nature of these checks and the IOC's unrelenting endeavours to control women's bodies. I briefly consider the recent incidents involving the IAAF and Mokgadi 'Caster' Semenya to help highlight the intricacies and ambiguities of sex, gender and human bodies. Finally, I discuss transsexual athletes and the Olympics. Throughout, I aim to demonstrate the messiness of sex and gender identification and the futility of seeking out sexed and gendered bodies that are 'pure' and unambiguous – especially in the name of 'fair' competition. In all, the discussion seeks to highlight the political and social power of the IOC and how its dominant position within elite competitive sport affects women athletes.

Genetics, genitals, gender and [no]guarantee

> . . . the properly gendered body has been a means of shoring up Olympic ideals and maintaining the Olympic brand . . . .. (Cole 2000a: 332)

Critical thinkers within sport and gender studies, science and medicine, and law and legal studies have long questioned the intent and validity of the IOC's tests to classify and corroborate a binary sex system. Critics of the IOC's mandatory testing regime (1968–1999) attack the practice and the procedures from a range of contextual points of view. I briefly focus on just three: the testing of women's sexed bodies, but not men's; the difficulties in advocating just two bifurcated categories for what constitutes 'true' sex; and the beliefs surrounding what determines a 'fair' playing field in elite competitive sport.

Testing only women athletes for eligibility for Olympic competition is discriminatory, degrading, demeaning and humiliating. Furthermore, it is an attempt to control women's bodies and their femininity/masculinity. For the last five decades, women athletes have participated under the officiously-tight surveillance of the IOC Medical Commission and its definition of what it means to be a 'woman'. As a system of governance and an established sporting institution, the IOC is imperialistic, patriarchal, sexist, misogynist, and heterosexist (cf., Jennings 1992; Lenskji 2000; Wamsley 2008). Its surveillance of women's sexed bodies creates an atmosphere – for women – of fear and shame. For these athletes, the fear of being 'tested' and judged, and the fear involved in anticipating 'test results' as well as the potential public shame that might ensue, are strong regulatory practices. In their work on gender and sexuality, both Probyn (2005) and Warner (1999) demonstrate the social and cultural power of public – and institutional – discourses of fear and shame. There are many cases cited[5] in which women were either falsely accused or publically exposed – on the global stage – as not complying with the IOC Medical Commission's mandate on genetic, chromosomal and genital configurations.

The advocacy that there are only two 'true' sexes that constitute 'real' men and 'real' women has also been criticised for attempting to anchor socially-constructed concepts such as 'sex' and 'gender' to a range of diverse bodies. This attempt to shore up, naturalise and normalise sex, gender and the body has been criticised by some feminist and queer scholars. These critics challenge the foundational premise that a sex-gender identity is fixed and stable, identifiable and absolute. Instead, they argue that both sex and gender should be understood as socio-culturally produced and ascribed. As constructs, 'sex' and 'gender' are viewed as ideas and ideals that serve to inform, reinforce and endorse normative categories. These normative categories operate – menacingly – to exclude and make unliveable non-normative versions of sex-gender-desire (Butler 1993 2004). For many feminists and queer theorists it is the processes that produce, regulate and constrain sex and gender that are the topic of critical interrogation. In this vein, critics have uncovered the ways religious beliefs and attitudes (Wackwitz 2003), scientific and medical intervention (Cavanagh and Sykes 2006; Fastiff 1991–92; Sykes 2006; Wrynn 2004), the law and legal system (Fastiff 1991–1992; Shy 2007; McArdle 2008) and competitive sporting discourses of fairness and equity (Jonsson 2010; Sykes 2006; Teetzel 2006; Wamsley 2008) influence the IOC Medical Commission's desire to uphold a two-sex system and fix 'true' sex to genes, chromosomes and genitals.

It is often assumed and taken for granted that elite competitive sport provides a level playing field for all athletes. The main reasons frequently given by the IOC for sex testing, gender verification and their current statement on sex reassignment are to prevent cheating and '. . . to make sure all female athletes compete under identical anatomical conditions' (cited in Cole 2000b: 136). The testing of only women and the seemingly developing attention to male-to-female transsexual athletes (Cavanagh and Sykes 2006) and intersex women operates from the premise that fairness is reliant upon the separation of men – as superior physical beings – from women.

As commentators have pointed out, sporting competition is predominantly and inherently unfair. In fact, unfair physical advantage is endemic to sport. For instance, the recent achievements of Usain Bolt and Michael Phelps highlight the ways that some men's bodies, because of their size, shape and length ('anatomical conditions'), are more able to succeed in certain physical endeavours than other men's bodies. As an Editorial (following the Semenya incident) in the *New Scientist* (28th August, 2009) iterates: 'We don't stop athletes competing with each other on the basis of inborn biological differences such as height or their proportion of fast and slow muscle fibres, nor as a result of medical history' (p. 5).

Additionally, athletes from advanced-capitalist countries are more privileged than athletes from poor countries in relation to seemingly limitless access to information, knowledge, facilities and equipment. These privileged, usually Western, athletes gain invaluable cultural capital for successful participation in elite competitive sport.

To test only women athletes, to insinuate that there is a 'true' sex within a two-sexed system, and to assume fair competition can be guaranteed through the surveillance of women's sexed and gendered bodies: each of these positions is problematic. Men's athletic bodies have not been systemically tested (over an almost 50 year period) for 'true' sex, and we know very little about their (inevitable) sexed and gendered variations and ambiguities. In fact, there is an implicit assumption to this dominant but silent discourse that all men's bodies are homogeneous, 'pure' and 'natural' and, therefore, men's Olympic competition, in relation to embodied sex and gender, is presented as, without any doubt, 'fair'. On the other hand, we do know that not all women's bodies conform to the rigid norms laid down by the IOC.

Ritchie *et al.* (2008) claim that gender verification tests at the 1992 (Barcelona, Spain) and 1996 (Atlanta, USA) Olympics identified respectively 15 and 8 women participants with sexual ambiguity. But they conclude:

> Notably, gender testing in athletics has never identified an individual deliberately misrepresenting [her or his] gender. Testing has, however, created controversy and embarrassment for a significant number of female athletes competing, often unknowingly, with some form of intersex disorder [sic]. Indeed, there is no evidence that female athletes with DSDs [Disorders of Sexual Development] have displayed any sports relevant physical attributes which have not been seen in biologically normal [sic] female athletes. (p. 398)[6]

Mokgadi 'Caster' Semenya and ambiguous athletic bodies

After winning the 800m final in Berlin at the 12th World Championships in Athletics on 19th August 2009, 18-year-old Caster Semenya was pounced on as the lead story by a voracious global sports media. In his eloquently-written academic article on the incident, Nyong'o (2010) argues: 'World-class female athletes have long made people anxious, particularly gorgeously muscle-bound black ones' (p. 96). Soon after the race, the IAAF – reacting to a media-provoked frenzy of accusation and seemingly mass alarm over Semenya's ambiguously-sexed and -gendered body – initiated their *modus operandi* for gender verification testing. (The IAAF has the same procedures as the IOC: testing on a suspicion- and case-by-case-basis). The tests were completed, as with previous gender verification protocols, without humanitarian consideration for the woman athlete. As Hart (2010) makes the point, Semenya's 'most intimate medical details [were] picked over by the World's media' (Telegraph.co.uk).

Semenya was subjected to a series of scientific trials intended to ascertain her 'true' sex (cf. Levy 2009). In the end, she lived through deeply dehumanising, extremely public and, at times, ferocious debates over her newly-pathologised body. Some writers (Levy 2009; Nyong'o 2010) have likened the ways white-Western nations engaged with Semenya's black athletic body to the gruesome treatment of Saartjie Baartman[7] (the so-called 'Hottentot Venus', also from South Africa).

Indian runner Santhi Soundarajan and 800m silver medallist at the 2006 Asian Games (Doha, Qatar) spoke out against the treatment – by the IAAF and global media – of Semenya. Soundarajan had similarly experienced public shaming when the IAAF, post-event, verified her sexed and gendered body as not legitimate to compete and divested her of her medal. The peoples of South Africa also strongly opposed the actions of IAAF. Levy (2009) suggests that the South African response might reflect a larger protest against the classification, reclassification and taxonomies of human beings imposed by white peoples on South Africans post 1950 (as one example, the practices culminating from the Population Registration Act of 1950 required visually different [i.e. black] individuals to carry identification cards to prove their right to be in certain places). During an interview on the matter Soundarajan encouraged Semenya to fight the IAAF and stated that she had been unable to appeal her own case because of her impoverished circumstances (www.time.com). Soundarajan and Semenya share very similar socio-economic backgrounds, however Semenya does have lawyers who contested her banning by Athletics South Africa (ASA). On July 7th, 2010, after almost a year waiting for her 'test' results, Semenya was 'cleared' by 'medical experts' to compete as a 'woman' (Reuters, *The Jakarta Post* and *The New Zealand Herald*).

Semenya's case raises many issues worthy of further critical discussion, particularly the intersectionalities of 'race', ethnicity, class and gender in elite sporting contexts, the IOC and the Olympic Games. Discourses of sexism and racism are evident within the Olympic Movement (Nadalin 2000; Wamsley

2008). However, how these discourses impact on women's bodies that do not fit into the genetic, chromosomal and gynaecological classification parameters set out by the IOC's Medical Commission are yet to be fully explored; discussions to date tend to focus on white-European women athletes (cf. Ritchie, Reynard and Lewis (2008) on Stella Walsh, Irina and Tamara Press).

There are many terms that seek to describe sex and gender non-normativity. Such terms depict the genetic, chromosomal, gonadal and hormonal complexities evident in the human race. Expressions about intersex individuals range in their inferences; for instance, reference to 'hermaphrodites' in the worlds of art and literature, and, 'disorders of sexual development' (DSDs) in the medical sciences. Notably, the Organisation Intersex International (OII) strongly opposes current scientific terminology such as 'disorders of sexual development', arguing that it is reductionist and imperialist (www.intersexualite.org). In a refreshingly positive definition, the UK Intersex Association (ukia) describes intersex peoples as: 'individuals born with anatomy or physiology which differs from contemporary ideals of what constitutes 'normal' male and female' (www.ukia.co.uk).

Importantly, the UK Intersex Association allude to the point that so-called 'normality' is not fixed, and their definition highlights that there will always be shifting but contemporary versions of 'normal'. In this vein, Ritchie *et al.* (2008) argue that the '[c]lassification of intersex is challenging and controversial' and that there is a 'myriad of conditions featuring varying types of sexual ambiguity' (p. 395). However, despite the variations, complexities and uncertainties apparent in humans' embodiment of sex and gender, the International Intersex Consensus Conference, in 2006, agreed and established a classification model. If nothing else, their newly-formed taxonomy registers the currently-known embodied variations and complexities of sex and gender. Unfortunately, it also sets these variations as stable and fixed categories.

The IOC have previously dealt with, albeit inconsistently, women's ambiguous athletic bodies. There are now-infamous cases from the past, which are relatively easy to find, and include Stella Walsh and Helen Stephens, Ewa Klobukowska (cf. Cole 2000b), and Maria Jose Martinez Patino (cf. Nelson 1996). However, given the sensitive and very personal nature of sex test/gender verification 'results', and, the justified criticisms of IOC disclosures, more recent incidents involving the IOC remain silenced. The treatments by the IAAF of Soundarajan and Semenya provide our most contemporary exemplars of how sport governing bodies regard women athletes' ambiguous bodies. Soundarajan remains a 'disqualified' woman and Semenya has recently 're-qualified' as a woman athlete. To date, the IOC does not have official *policy* on intersex woman athletes. It does, however, have an invaluable historic record of cases of intersex women athletes, as well as a politics of pathologising and medicalising these women athletes' bodies.

Unfortunately (and highly probable for London 2012) the IOC intend to produce official policy on intersex. In an attempt to address existing and potential practice by the IOC on intersex issues, the Organisation Intersex International (OII) has posted a petition on its website (www.intersexualite.org):

We, the undersigned, support the members of the Organisation Intersex International, in their demands that:

1. The International Olympic Committee (IOC) reject demands that female athletes with intersex variations have their variations diagnosed and treated.
2. The IOC allow the above mentioned athletes, known as intersex women, to compete as females without having to undergo diagnosis or 'treatment.'
3. The IOC, its press, and medical practitioners refer to females with intersex variations as 'women with intersex variations' and not 'women with disorders of sex development.'

Despite such protests, it is likely that the IOC will stick with its existing conservative, medicalised and scientific models to define intersex persons. Such classifications intentionally seek to nullify uncertainty and eradicate ambiguity, and, they aim to established patterns of 'logic' that are based on an assumed 'norm'. Such medicalised logics of normalcy are already apparent in the taxonomies that govern participation by athletes with disabilities in the Paralympics. As McArdle (2008) points out, the system of labeling athletes with disabilities developed in spite of a general shift 'away from the medical model of disability' (p. 41). For Olympic athletes with a disability, their bodies *are* judged through a medical lens–the IOC's. This regulatory regime, which categorises these athletes, can be described using McRuer's notions of 'compulsory able-bodiedness' (2006) because classification is ruled by a so-called 'norm' of able-bodiedness.

The IOC's adoption of *The Statement of the Stockholm Consensus on Sex Reassignment in Sports* similarly draws from medical and scientific discourses and ideologies on 'normal' sex and 'normal' gender in order to govern transsexual participation at the Olympic Games.

The Olympics and transsexual athletes

The IOC and the IOC Medical Commission have been relatively quick (compared with other sport governing bodies) to declare their interest in the rights of transsexual[8] people by 'allowing "a person who has changed sex" to compete' (www.olympics.org). The IOC Medical Commission's conditions for transsexual athletes' inclusion (established via The Stockholm Consensus 2003) were accepted by the IOC Executive Board on 17th May, 2004. Many sport governing bodies have not been so keen to recognise the human and legal rights of transsexual athletes and some of these organisations have sought exemption from anti-discriminatory legislation. Initially, this was the case in the UK and UK Sport (Cavanagh and Sykes 2006; McArdle 2008; Shy 2007; Sykes 2006).

However, after being found in breach of the European Convention on Human Rights, the UK Parliament passed the Gender Recognition Act – also in 2004. It is Section 19 (s.19) of the Act that prompted the release of the document 'Transsexual People and Sport: Guidance for Sporting Bodies' by the Department for Culture, Media and Sport in May, 2005. Since this date, and following an initial reluctance, UK Sport adopts this anti-discriminatory policy.

The UK Gender Recognition Act, 2004, enables transsexual people to gain full legal status in their 'acquired gender'. This legal recognition is issued by a Gender Recognition Panel, which provides a Gender Recognition Certificate. There are certain conditions and the Panel must be satisfied that the applicant:

- has, or has had, gender dysphoria,
- has lived in the acquired gender throughout the preceding two years, and
- intends to continue to live in the acquired gender until death. (www.opsi. gov.uk)

Such legal recognition is crucial for athletes wishing to participate in the Olympics (London 2012) because the IOC's Stockholm Consensus on Sex Reassignment after puberty is dependent on three criteria, which include the following: '[l]egal recognition of their assigned sex has been conferred by the appropriate official authorities'. Athletes who transition before puberty are accepted as 'legitimate' participants by the IOC. However, athletes who transition after puberty must not only be 'legal' members of their 'acquired gender', they must have completed 'surgical anatomical changes' and 'hormonal therapy appropriate for the assigned sex [must have] been administered in a verifiable manner and for a sufficient length of time to minimise gender-related advantages in sport competitions' (www. olympics.org). If surgery involves a gonadectomy, then the athlete must wait for a two-year period before participating in competitive sport.

At this juncture, it is worth noting that criteria for a recognised transsexual identity/subjectivity as set down by the IOC (and UK Gender Recognition Act) are 'very narrow' and 'exclude a large segment of the international transsexual community' (Cavanagh and Sykes 2006: 78). The conditions required to gain a Gender Recognition Certificate (e.g. 'until death') and compete in the Olympics (e.g. 'surgical anatomical changes') are obdurate and absolute. They are problematic because, for instance, gaining legal recognition remains impossible in many countries, including parts of America and Europe. Additionally the terminology and language of some cultures do not adhere to dominant (and fixed) Western versions of 'transsexuality': for example a 'third gender' is formally recognised on identification cards in Nepal; passport application forms in India have three gender options – 'female', 'male' and 'other'; and the Bugis people of Makassar, Indonesia, acknowledge five types of gender: female, male, *calalai*, *calabai* and *bissu*.

To date, popular and scholarly commentaries on both the UK Gender Recognition Act and the IOC's Stockholm Consensus tend to be wholly preoccupied with what Cavanagh and Sykes (2006) refer to as 'unfair competitive advantage' (p. 76). This discourse surrounds the inclusion of male-to-female transsexual athletes. The popular press and sport media have displayed intense ridicule and transphobia towards transsexual athletes (usually male-to-female) in sport and in the Olympics (Cavanagh and Sykes 2006; Charlish 2005). And, within academia, scholars have focused on the 'fairness' debate from scientific, legal and philosophical perspectives (cf., Charlish 2005; Coggan, Hammond and Holm 2008; Gooren 2006; Ljungqvist and Genel 2005; Teetzel 2006).

The discourses of fairness and elite competitive sport are so deeply engrained that it is often forgotten that sport performances, sporting competition, fairness, the Olympics Games as well as sex and gender are all socially, culturally and historically constructed. They have been produced over time in ways that privilege, valorise, and glorify certain bodies. The disregard for female-to-male transsexual athletes (Cavanagh and Sykes 2006, Wamsley 2008) demonstrates some of the existing and persisting hierarchies implicit to these productions. Here, the assumption is that being born a woman, regardless of body transitions (female to male), does not present a threat to 'natural' male superiority.

The IOC's policy on transsexual athletes repeats many of the gendered ideologies apparent within previous sex test and gender verification regimes. These ideologies produce, through 'positivist and biologistic logic' (Nyong'o 2010: 98), normative sex and gender within a supposedly 'perfect' two-sex system. In their insightful article on the issue, Cavanagh and Sykes (2006) state:

> . . . we argue that the IOC policy . . . is a new disciplinary technique to manage binary gender designations . . . we contend that the almost obsessive attempt to manage gender and to cast a definitive mould on the sex of bodies examined, in Olympic sporting competition, is indicative of a refusal to accept the changeability of bodies . . .. (p. 77)

Conclusion

It is evident that the IOC and the IOC Medical Commission have been, and remain, preoccupied with sex and gender, more specifically the multiple ways women athletes embody sex and gender. Their dogged surveillance of women's Olympic bodies reflects processes of Western hetero-patriarchy and the institutional control of normative (and compulsory) sex-gender identities/subjectivities. This surveillance (including official surveillance of male-to-female transsexual athletes and the possible future official surveillance of intersex women) represents systemic regulatory and medicalised-scientific practices that span five decades. There is a distinct lack of comparative surveillance and concomitant medicalised-scientific sport discourse on men's sexed and gendered bodies which are presumed to be homogeneous and 'natural', and therefore, exempt from the same officious scrutiny and gendered Olympic discourses of 'unfair competitive advantage'. This is all the more remarkable given the little that currently is known about the ambiguities and nuances within men's genetic, chromosomal, gonadal and hormonal make-up.

One of the consequences, on men's sporting bodies, of this lack of overtly public knowledge is that elite male competitors/rivals (and the media) do not devalue the successes of individual men gold medallists. In fact, superhuman feats by men athletes are greatly applauded. Their achievements are not measured in relation to individual men's sex and gendered bodies and characteristics such as 'unnatural' levels of 'natural' testosterone and/or 'identical anatomical conditions'. In contrast, women who achieve superhuman feats are evaluated in terms of their sex and gender. For example, the recent headline 'Semenya's coach hits out as rival rails "we are running against a man"' (Roberts 2010) is a prime example and represents a longstanding discourse which other elite sportswomen have endured.

Men Olympians have escaped surveillance of their sexed and gendered bodies. Women have not, and this has left a legacy of suspicion and shame which besieges women's participation in the Olympics. For women elite athletes, such as Semenya, there are certain ironies that surround their successes. As Nyong'o (2010: 98) argues:

> . . . instead of insisting upon the naturalness of her gender, how about turning the question around and denaturalizing the world of gender segregated, performance-obsessed, commercially-driven sports, a world that can neither seem to do with or without excessive bodies like Semenya's and their virtuosic performances?

The Olympics showcase and spectacularise unusual and 'abnormal' bodies. These bodies are greatly admired for their breathtaking and brilliant performances. The Olympics encourages excessive bodies and extreme accomplishments. However, the Olympic bodies and Olympic achievements which are accepted, encouraged and legitimised, are those that match the IOC's narrowly constructed sex and gender rhetorics. For women, the IOC's definitions, terms and doctrines are conservative, highly specialised and deeply medicalised. Jonsson (2010: 249), in his philosophical piece on '. . . the birth of a new kind of athlete: (non-gendered) cyborg athletes', explicates how existing sporting policies and practices premised on liberal notions of fairness and the assumed 'naturalness' of bodies are in fact flawed.

IOC policy and practice on sex testing/gender verification, intersex and trans-sexual people epitomises this emphatic emphasis on 'fairness' and 'naturalness'. Consequently, it means, as argued by Jonsson (2010: 255), that some '. . . athletes are not allowed to be as good as they can be'. This is the nub of the issue. The IOC watches over Olympic bodies, especially women's bodies, and it polices the excesses and extremes of these bodies in order to adhere to socially and culturally specific constructions of sex and gender.

Notes

1   Women were not admitted on to the IOC until 1981. For 87 years the IOC was exclusively all-male.
2   In 1957, Dora Ratjen, a high jumper in the 1936 Berlin Olympics, confessed that he was a man and that 'Nazi officials had persuaded him to masquerade as a woman to bring

glory to the Reich' (Editorial, *New Scientist*, 2009: 5). In the women's high jump 'Dora' (Hermann Ratjen) came 4th.

3   Of interest, in 1996 the Norwegian parliament passed a law making genetic testing for the purposes of gender verification in sport illegal in Norway (Macaulay, Hamidi, and Treurnicht-Naylor 2010: 26).

4   However, it was reported widely that the 2008 Olympics were very well prepared to test women athletes: 'For more than a year, officials in Beijing have been designing a special laboratory to determine the sex of any athletes taking part in this year's Olympic games' (Saner 2008).

5   'Linsey Schmidt' (pseudonym) in 1968 was fearful of sex testing and the shame that she might be a man – she trained with men and disguised herself as a man so she could compete in marathons. Influenced by the new wave of IOC testing, she thought that because she was such a good runner she might in fact be a man. The Russian sisters – the Press sisters – after many successes in the 1950s and early 1960s disappeared from international competition, probably as a result of impending compulsory sex testing. There are several women who found out through Olympic participation they had chromosome patterns that did not match the desired XX advocated by the IOC. For example, Ewa Klobukowska had 'one chromosome too many': she had an XXY pattern; and Maria Jose Martinez Patino, despite looking like a typically feminine woman, had an XY pattern. Other women such as Kirsten Wengler were publicly humiliated only to find out they had been tested incorrectly. And Susan Natrass was tested needlessly: she took part in trap shooting, an event open to both men and women in which contestants competed against each other regardless of their sex and gender.

6   For me, the use of the terms 'disorder' and 'normal' are inappropriate because they position intersex as pathological. The Organisation Intersex International (OII), since 2006, has been campaigning against the term 'disorders of sexual development' (DSDs).

7   According to Hobson (2006), 'Saartjie Baartman, the first in a line of South African women exhibited, was brought to London in 1810. It is quite possible that other South African women followed in this trajectory, since Hottentot Venus exhibitions continued well after Baartman's death in 1816 (Gilman 1985, 88; Edwards and Walvin 1983, 181–82). Baartman was put on display, first by Dutch exhibitor Hendrik Cezar, as a mythical and "strange"-shaped "Hottentot," a display framed by a history of colonial domination' (Hobson 2006: 89–90).

8   'Transsexual' tends to be used by the medical and scientific communities. 'Transgender' is often preferred by those people living within trans communities. 'Transgender' encapsulates the diversity of trans bodies, whereas 'transsexual' tends to indicate surgery, which not all trans people can afford or want.

Bibliography

Bhowmick, N. and Thottem, J. (2009) 'Gender and athletics: India's own Caster Semenya', http://www.time.com/time/world/article/0,8599,1919562,00.html.

Boylan, J. F. (2008) 'The XY Games', *The New York Times*. 3rd August, 2008.

Butler, J. (1993) *Bodies that Matter. On the Discursive Limits of Sex*, London: Routledge.

Butler, J. (2004) *Undoing Gender*, London: Routledge.

Cavanagh, S. L. and Sykes, H. (2006) 'Transsexual bodies at the Olympics: The International Olympic Committee's policy on transsexual athletes at the 2004 Athens Summer Games', *Body & Society* 12(3): 75–102.

Charlish, P. (2005) 'Gender Recognition Act 2004: transsexuals in sport: a level playing field?', *International Sports Law Review* 5(2): 38–42.

Coggon, J. Hammond, N. and Holm, S. (2008) 'Transsexuals in sport – fairness and freedom, regulation and law', *Sport, Ethics and Philosophy* 2(1): 4–17.

Cole, C. L. (2000a) 'Testing for sex or drugs', *Journal of Sport and Social Issues* 24(4): 331–333.

Cole, C. L. (2000b) 'One chromosome too many?', in K. Schaffer and S. Smith (eds) *The Olympics at the Millennium: Power, Politics and the Games,* New Jersey: Rutgers UP, pp. 128–146.

Davison, K., and Frank, B. (2006) 'Sexualities, genders, bodies and sport: Changing practices of inequity', in K. Young and P. White (eds) *Sport and Gender in Canada,* Second Edition, Toronto: Oxford University Press.

Editorial (2009) 'Gender bending the rules for Caster Semenya', *New Scientist* 203 (2723): 5.

Editorial (2010) 'Caster Semenya's lawyers threaten to sue ASA to allow her to compete', *http://www.guardian.co.uk/sport/2010/apr/01/caster-semenya-lawyers-asa.*

Fastiff, P. B. (1991–1992) 'Gender verification testing: balancing the rights of female athletes with a scandal-free Olympic Games', *Hastings Constitutional Law Quarterly* 19: 937–961.

Gooren, L. J. (2008) 'Olympic sports and transsexuals', *Asian Journal of Andrology* 10(3): 427–432.

Hart, S. (2010) 'Caster Semenya back on track to resume promising career', *The Telegraph.* 14th July, 2010.

Hobson, J. (2003) 'The "Batty" politic: toward an aesthetic of the Black female body', *Hypatia* 18(4): 87–105.

Jonsson, K. (2010) 'Sport beyond gender and the emergence of cyborg athletes', *Sport in Society* 13(2): 249–259.

Kolata, G. (2010) 'IOC Panel calls for treatment in sex ambiguity cases', *The New York Times,* January 20th, 2010.

Lenskyj, H. J. (2000) *Inside the Olympic Industry: Power, Politics and Activism,* Albany: SUNY.

Levy, A. (2009) 'Either/or. Sports, sex, and the case of Caster Semenya,' *The New Yorker,* November 30, 2009: 46–59.

Lewis, P. (2009) 'Gender tests get shake-up', *Herald on Sunday,* August 23, 2009: 68.

Ljungqvist, A. and Genel, M. (2005) 'Transsexual athletes – when is competition fair?', *The Lancet* 366(1): 42–43.

Macaulay, C. M., Hamidi, M. and Treurnicht-Naylor, K. (2010) 'Gender verification testing: necessary for the integrity of international athletics, or inexcusable breach of personal privacy?', *University of Western Ontario Medical Journal* 79(1): 25–27.

McArdle, D. (2008) 'Swallows and Amazons, or the sporting exception to the Gender Recognition Act', *Social & Legal Studies* 17(1): 39–57.

Nadalin, C. (2000) 'The Olympics in retrospect: winners, losers, racism, and the Olympic ideal', in K. Schaffer and S. Smith (eds) *The Olympics at the Millennium: Power, Politics and the Games,* New Jersey: RUP.

Nelson, M. B. (1996) *The Stronger Women Get, The More Men Love Football: Sexism and the American Culture of Sports,* Ohio: Avon.

Nyong'o, T. (2010) 'The unforgiveable transgression of being Caster Semenya', *Women and Performance: A Journal of Feminist Theory* 20(1): 95–100.

Pilgrim, J., Martin, D. and Binder, W. (2002–2003) 'Far from the finish line. Transsexualism and athletic competition', *Fordham Property Media Entertainment Law Journal* 13: 495–549.

Probyn, E. (2005) *Blush: Faces of Shame,* Minneapolis: University of Minnesota Press.

Puffer, J. (1996) 'Gender verification: a concept whose time has come to pass?', *British Journal of Sports Medicine* 30(4): 278.

Reuters (2010) 'Semenya misses out on African C'ship selection', *The Jakarta Post*, July 13th, 2010.

Reuters (2010) 'Semenya gets all clear to compete as a woman', *The New Zealand Herald*, July 8th, 2010.

Ritchie, I. (2003) 'Sex tested, gender verified: controlling female sexuality in the age of containment', *Sport History Review* 34(1): 80–98.

Ritchie, R., Reynard, J. and Lewis, T. (2008) 'Intersex and the Olympic Games', *Journal of the Royal Society of Medicine* 101: 395–399.

Roberts, B (2010) 'Semenya's coach hits out as rival rails "we are running against a man"', *The Independent*, August 24th, 2010.

Saner, E. (2008) 'The gendertrap', *The Guardian*, 30th July, 2008.

Shaw, M. (2008) 'Gender-testing for 'suspicious-looking' female Olympic athletes in Beijing', 29 July, www.thefword.org.uk.

Shy, Y. L. E. (2007) '"Like any other girl": male-to-female transsexuals and professional sports', *Sports Law Journal* 14: 95–110.

Simson, V. and Jennings, A. (1992) *The Lords of the Rings: Power, Money and Drugs in the Modern Olympics*, London: Simon and Schuster.

Sykes, H. (2006) 'Transsexual and transgender policies in sport', *Women in Sport and Physical Activity Journal* 15(1): 3–13.

Teetzel, S. (2006) 'On transgendered athletes, fairness and doping: an international challenge', *Sport in Society* 9(2): 227–251.

Tucker, R. and Collins, M. (2005) 'The science and management of sex verification in sport', *South African Journal of Sports Medicine* 21(4): 147–150.

Wackwitz, L. A. (2003) 'Verifying the myth: Olympic sex testing and the category "women"', *Women's Studies International Forum* 26(6): 553–560.

Wackwitz, L.A. (1996) 'Sex testing in international women's athletics. A history of silence', *Women in Sport and Physical Activity Journal* 5(1): 51–68.

Wamsley, K. B. (2008) 'Social science literature on sport and transitioning/transitioned athletes', Paper prepared for the *Promising Practices: Working with Transitioning/ Transitioned Athletes in Sport Project*, The University of Western Ontario.

Warner, M. (1999) *The Trouble with Normal*, Harvard: HUP.

Wrynn, A. (2004) 'The human factor: Science, Medicine and the International Olympic Committee 1900–70', *Sport in Society* 7(2): 211–231.

12

CHILDREN OF A LESSER GOD

Paralympics and high-performance sport

P. David Howe

Introduction

On October 23, 2009 during a live stand up routine in Manchester, British comedian Jimmy Carr, known for his edgy humour, made the following joke:

> Say what you like about those servicemen amputees from Iraq and Afghanistan, but we're going to have a fucking good Paralympic team in 2012.

Perhaps not surprisingly there was a degree of public outcry regarding this line in the days that followed (see Moss 2009). Working as an anthropologist with a personal interest in Paralympic sport, in part because of my own participation as an athlete and administrator, I found the joke funny but the public outcry troublesome on a number of fronts. First of all British soldiers, while no doubt more physically fit than the general public, are not necessarily fit by the standards of Paralympians. The assumption that they would get a place on the Paralympic team shows a lack of awareness on the part of Carr and the public alike. Traditionally there is a close link between the military and Paralympic sport in Britain. There is a contemporary link with a Paralympic Military Program called *Battle Back*[1] that has been run by the ministry of defence in the United Kingdom since the spring of 2008. However, only a few of these injured ex-service personnel might be fast-tracked into the high performance training programme and have the possibility of gaining selection to the British 2012 Paralympic team. The hidden irony in the Carr joke is delicious. July 29th 1948 was the opening ceremony of the fourteenth Olympic Games, held at Wembley, London, and it was the also the day of the first archery competition between two teams of war-wounded paraplegics held at Stoke Mandeville Hospital in Aylesbury just north of London. The teams competing were from the Garter Home for War Veterans from Richmond in the county of

Surrey and the Pensions Hospital in Stoke Mandeville. As an event it was a very small affair but it is considered to be the beginning of the Paralympic Movement (Bailey 2008; Britten 2009). It is this small event over 60 years ago that makes the joke by Carr far from tasteless and rather appropriate.

The 2012 Paralympic Games in returning to Britain are truly coming home. Should some of the participants be veterans of contemporary global conflict it would be rather fitting to the legacy and vision of the Paralympics' founding father, neurosurgeon Sir Ludwig Guttmann (Bailey 2008). Today even though the Paralympic Games are presented as part of the Olympic Festival, and are formally part of the Olympic Movement, the International Paralympic Committee (IPC) still has a very uneasy relationship with its able-bodied relative. This uneasy relationship can be explored using the concept of human rights to unpack whether there is equitable treatment of able and disabled athletes within high performance sport. In so doing, this chapter examines the concept of human rights as the often associated by-product of legislation for social justice (Rawls 1971) in order to establish a framework to determine whether integration within high performance sport can be seen to have been successful.

Over the last twenty years the IPC and its network of national affiliates have placed integration of the disabled firmly on the sporting agenda (Labanowich 1988; Steadward 1996; Vanlandewijck and Chappel 1996). To date this process of integration has been widely accepted as a positive step but there has been little critical reflection upon the process. Integration can be seen as central to discussions of human rights. By drawing on both the United Nations' (UN) *Vienna Declaration* of 1993 and the more recent *Convention on the Rights of Persons with Disabilities* of 2006 this chapter explores the literature surrounding issues of integration. In doing so it offers a culturally driven, philosophical interpretation of human rights and their value in understanding elite sporting provision, focusing upon issues related to social justice in a context wherein Paralympic athletes are often seen as 'less than able'. Beginning with a brief outline of the organisation of Paralympic sport before turning its attention to the relationship between disability sport and human rights, this chapter uses this material to ground a discussion about integration before finally exploring the close symmetry between the ethos surrounding the Olympic and Paralympic Movements.

The organisation of Paralympic sport

Before the establishment of the IPC, sport for the disabled was organised internationally by a number of sporting federations. Each of these federations had a responsibility to a constituent body of member nations and structured a sporting calendar for impairment specific groups, from grassroots to international level (DePauw and Gavron 1995). The federations, namely the Cerebral Palsy International Sport and Recreation Association (CP-ISRA), International Blind Sport Association (IBSA), International Sports Federation for Persons with Intellectual Disability (INAS-FID), and, the International Wheelchair and

Amputee Sport Association (IWAS)[2], were established with the explicit intention of creating opportunities for people with disabilities and using sport as a vehicle for their empowerment. Collectively these federations are known as the International Organisations for Sport for the Disabled (IOSDs). It was the IOSDs and their predecessors that helped to organise the Paralympic Games from 1960 to 1988. Early Games were organised and run on a much smaller scale than those now under the influence of the IPC. The rapid growth of the IPC in the last few years has enabled it to establish an extensive network of 167 national affiliates that in some cases replicate or replace the national governing bodies of the federations.

The IPC currently organises and administers both the Paralympic Games and the quadrennial World Championships for individual Paralympic sports, such as swimming and athletics. Using the resources of the four federations listed above (including athletes, volunteer administrators, and classification systems) the IPC has arguably turned the Paralympic Games into the most recognisable and possibly most influential vehicle for the promotion of sport for the disabled. Like many other modern sporting spectacles, the Paralympics is well-organised with a relatively high profile that attracts significant media coverage and commercial sponsorship. Almost 4,000 athletes from 146 nations competed in the 2008 Paralympic Games in Beijing, making the Paralympic Games unquestionably the main international sporting forum for athletes with various degrees of impairment.

Since the establishment of the IPC in 1989 those involved with this institution have worked tirelessly to heighten the public profile of elite sports for the disabled. A year prior to the establishment of the IPC the Paralympic Games began a pattern in the sporting calendar of following directly on from the Olympic Games, making use of the same venues and state-of-the-art facilities. In many respects this has helped to legitimate elite sport for the disabled. The IPC first became the international partner of the local Paralympic Games organising committee in 1992. As a result the IPC has been able to strongly influence the direction and organisation of all subsequent Paralympic Games. Under the supervision of the IPC there has been a move toward the commercialisation of sport for the disabled that has been managed in partnership with increased media coverage of flagship events (Schantz and Gilbert 2001; Schell and Rodriguez 2001; Smith and Thomas 2005).

Internationally the IPC and the International Olympic Committee (IOC) signed an agreement in 2001 which benefited the IPC by providing it with long-term financial support, access to high quality facilities in which to hold the Paralympics, and countless other commercial opportunities. For the IOC the positive publicity and public praise for the charitable activities of the IPC were particularly welcome as this came at a time when the organisation's core values were being publicly scrutinised in light of scandals associated with the 2002 Salt Lake City Winter Olympic Games. In 2003 this agreement was amended to transfer 'broadcasting and marketing responsibilities of the 2008, 2010, and 2012 Paralympic Games to the Organizing Committee of these Olympic and Paralympic Games' (IPC 2003: 1). While agreements such as this will ease financial concerns for the IPC, they may force a restructuring of sport for the disabled. The IOC demands that the Paralympic Games are restricted in size to 4,000 athletes. Limiting the size of future Paralympic Games, in the eyes of the IOC, makes it a more manageable product to market. The marketing of the Olympics and Paralympics as a single entity has undermined the IPC's autonomy to use the Paralympic Games to educate the public about athletes with a disability. The erosion of this educational imperative is problematic because one of the IPC's explicit aims is the effective and efficient promotion of elite sport for the disabled. Moreover, the IPC's dictum 'empower, inspire and achieve'[3] suggests the Paralympic movement is concerned with empowering its athletes in hope that their performances will inspire others to great achievements. It is these tenets that form the foundation of the ideological movement of Paralympism. As a result anything that negatively impacts upon their successful achievement is likely to have a detrimental influence upon the Paralympic Movement.

Classification is a contested terrain in Paralympic sport and another element of the organisational structure within sport for the disabled that contributes to its distinctive habitus (Howe and Jones 2006). Classification is simply a structure for competition similar to the systems used in the sport of judo where competitors perform in distinctive weight categories. A cumbersome and complex classification system, central to the Paralympic Movement, is the result of the historical development of sport for the disabled (DePauw and Gavron 1995; Steadward 1996; Vanlandewijck and Chappel 1996). As far as the IOC and IPC are concerned this system detracts from the Paralympic Games as a sporting spectacle because it confuses spectators (Smith and Thomas 2005). Sports such as swimming have established an integrated functional classification system with a limited degree of success (Richter et al. 1992; Richter 1994; Daly and Vanlandewijck 1999). There has also been some preliminary discussion related to an integrated system in athletics (Tweedy 2002) but to date only a disability-specific classification system has been used. The IPC is attempting to modify the classification system to suit aims and objectives that appear to be at odds with the ethos of the Paralympic Movement.

Within sport for the disabled, competitors are classified by their body's degree of function and therefore it is important that the classification process achieves equity in the Paralympic sporting practice and enables athletes to compete on a 'level playing field' (Sherrill 1999). It is this – the pursuit of equity not only within the world of Paralympic sport but also between the Paralympics and the mainstream – that gives me cause to turn toward the concept of human rights.

Disability, human rights and sport

Human rights are principles that are regularly used to highlight the wrong being done to an individual on the basis of an infringement of a basic need that is considered inherently 'natural'. The concept of 'natural rights' that should govern humanity comes originally from the work of philosopher John Locke in the seventeenth century (Locke [1689] 1970) and while human rights are not seen to be 'natural' today there is a sense in the discourse surrounding discussions of rights that there is something in all human societies that leads us to believe in inherent basic rights (Donnelly 1985; Freeman 2002). However, philosophers remind us that a 'right' can only be achieved as the end result of a moral argument and not as a premise for the discussion in the first place. Following Harris:

> when it is said that someone has a right to something, that just means that in all circumstances of the case she should not be hindered in or prevented from doing or achieving something. And if it is asked why she should not be hindered, the answer is *not* 'because she possesses something called a right which has been independently established or "discovered"', but simply because there are good moral reasons why it is wrong to hinder her. (1985: xvi)

In other words, for the purpose of this chapter rights should not be seen as objects or things an individual possesses but as entitlements that are the result of a moral or legal argument. As a result the *Universal Declarations of Human Rights* of the UN was designed to highlight that all people should be treated with respect. This statute should not be seen as an answer to human rights violations but rather as a marker that they have and do occur. After all, the UN is not a utopian body but a political one and since its Declaration was written there have been hundreds of examples of the existence of gaps between the ideology associated with the establishment of universal human rights and the lived reality. As Freeman suggests, 'It is *politically* important that human rights have been codified in international and national law, but it is a mistake to believe that the legalization of human rights takes the concept of politics out' (2002: 10).

United Nations human rights legislation is *not* intended to impose a legal obligation upon nation states but as a set of guidelines that are seen as identifying universally good behaviour. In other words the *Universal Declaration of Human Rights* outlined what the UN felt were 'moral and political principles that could make a *prima facie* plausible claim to universality' (Freeman 2002: 36). The claims for universality are laid out in *Article 2* which states that we are all entitled to freedoms 'without distinction of any kind, such as race, colour, sex, language, religion, political or other opinion, national or social origin, property, birth or status'. To reinforce this, *Article 7* states that all are equal before the law and are entitled to equal protection of the law without discrimination. While implementation of human rights was designed to eliminate human wrongs such as political oppression and racism, it is important that their implementation follows on from the development of a just society (Donnelly 1985). A just society is of course an ideal:

> International human-rights law is the product of political power, pragmatic agreement and limited moral consensus. It has no deeper theoretical justification. Verbal agreement on general principles may conceal

disagreement on the meaning and policy implications of those principles. (Freeman 2002: 60)

Western societies continue to place a great deal of importance on human rights. International expectation that all societies will act in the same way toward their citizens is problematic. The development of both the *Vienna Declaration* of 1993 on minority rights and the more recent *Convention on the Rights of Persons with Disabilities* of 2006 attests to the fact that human rights are not understood universally. In effect, rights exist in a hierarchy from local customs to national and then international laws; it is normal for individuals or groups to seek resolution at the more local level to try to resolve problems. Yet it is the state (or rather those who signed up to these statutes) that has the obligation towards human rights, which leaves the way open for unseen violations in the corporate world, for example, or within the more private sphere of the family.

In order to address these concerns I turn to Nussbaum who has developed a theory of capabilities that are as universal as possible while being culturally sensitive to the quality of life of individuals (Malhotra 2008; Nussbaum 2006). These capabilities are designed to act as a litmus test for the quality of life of individuals motivating moral action because of the shared vulnerability of the human species. As Nussbaum suggests '[t]he capabilities approach is a political doctrine about basic entitlements, not a comprehensive moral doctrine. It does not even claim to be a complete political doctrine, since it simply specifies some necessary conditions for a decently just society, in the form of fundamental entitlements of all citizens' (2006: 155). Nussbaum (2006) uses the case of the disabled population in part because this segment of global society is absent from more conventional understandings of justice as triumphed by Rawls in his influential *The Theory of Justice* (1971). Rawlsian 'justice as fairness', according to Nussbaum, is not appropriate for the achievement of social justice for marginalised groups where a capabilities approach evaluates the individual in question in relation to a list related to the quality of life similar to the list outlined in international human rights conventions such as living a full life, bodily health, freedom of movement and affiliation. Also included are abstract capabilities related to the senses of imagination and reason and the capability for reason (Nussbaum 2006: 76–8). 'Capability can be regarded as a combination of an individual's personal characteristics (such as age or physiological impairment), [a] basket of purchasable goods [as a measure of their standard of living] and the individual's environment in the broadest sense' (Malhotra 2008: 85). In other words, a person's quality of life should be determined by the relationship between the physical and social environment and what their standard of living equates to in an individual context.

It is important in the context of the capability approach adopted by Nussbaum to highlight the struggle for disability rights that led to the establishment of the social model of disability which highlights the social consequences of having an impairment (see Oliver 1996). This struggle led in part to the United Nations championing the *Vienna Declaration* of 1993 on minority rights and the more recent *Convention on the Rights of Persons with Disabilities* of 2006. The problem with disability specific conventions is that they single-out 'the disabled' as a group that are in need of being helped. Many people with disabilities, including a high proportion of Canadian Paralympians, for example, do not require or accept their status as universally vulnerable people.

The documents revered and celebrated in some disability rights circles inherently lack the clout that disability activists often wish they had. For example, one of the capabilities Nussbaum highlights is the right to play, and it is fair to assume we would all agree with that requirement for a good life. Yet the simple act of playing is clearly distinct from codified professional sport such as the Paralympics. Even nations that enacted all UN human rights agreements have limited resources to police their implementation. Recent work by Friedman and Norman (2009) within the United States on legal issues surrounding the rights of Paralympians in receiving equal treatment in terms of financial and medical support compared to Olympians highlights that in terms of equality there is still a long way to go. What makes this position so unpalatable is that the tenets upon which the UN understands human rights are based are clearly inequitable.

In spite of this inequity MacIntrye (1999) reminds us that *all* human beings are vulnerable; and in fact we are all dependent rational animals and, this being the case, we should as a species be more adaptable to a common good.

> [H]ow much is involved in allegiance to a conception of the *common good* that requires both the virtues of the independent practical reasoner and the virtues of acknowledged dependence. For this is a good common to the very young and to the very old, as well as to mature adults, to the paraplegic and to the mentally backward as well as to the athlete and to those engaged in intellectual enquiry, a good that has regard to every vulnerability to which our animal identity and our animal nature, as well as our specifically human condition expose us. (MacItyre 1999: 165–6, Italics added).

It is in the pursuit of a common good that the *Universal Convention for Human Rights* and its various latter-day 'offspring' were developed, but clearly there are major problems with their implementation in practice.

While the concept of human rights developed by the UN was created to limit the power of governments, the problem is that democracy by its very nature limits the rights of minorities (Freeman 2002). In a sense, human rights in individual nations need to be balanced with other values in the social order, and even amongst human rights there can be conflicts. Yet the social case for human rights and the protection of vulnerable populations by social institutions can in turn pose a threat. Stammer (1999) suggests that we examine power relations and focuses upon the impact of institutions and social movements and their role in the distribution of it rather than simple exploring the legal formalisation of rights. In this respect the IPC and the broader Paralympic Movement specifically have a role to play. Unfortunately, of late the Paralympic Movement has embraced a commercial ethos which traditionally has been subversive with respect to human rights to the extent that economic interests and concerns are prioritised over more socially valued outcomes. The problem is that '[t]he Universal Declaration is based on the assumption that individual human rights, including the prohibition of discrimination and the right to practice one's culture, are sufficient to protect cultural minorities' (Freeman 2002: 114). This is problematic in so far as the political theory of liberal democracy has *not* been designed historically to solve the problems of cultural minorities such as the disabled, in part because classical construction of democracy presupposed a culturally unified people.

The response by the United Nations to the polemic of various human rights groups against the claims of universalism and the problems associated with cultural imperialism was the establishment of the *Vienna Declaration* of 1993 that included recognition of a number of special categories such as women, children, minorities, indigenous people, disabled persons, refugees, migrant workers, the extremely poor and the socially excluded. There is a need to recognise these holders of human-rights because these groups are more prone to human rights violations than the majority and they can get lost in the 'universality' of human rights that can so easily drift toward ideologically inappropriate forms of cultural imperialism (Freeman 2002). To further solidify the case, in 2006 the *Convention on the Rights of Persons with Disabilities* placed the spotlight on the disabled community and included *Article 30* which includes suggestions of the right to participate in cultural life including sport.

'Sport for all'

In spite of the problematic nature of the concept of human rights highlighted above, the concept appears to have salience when looking at inequitable treatment of people within the realm of sport. United Nations Educational Scientific and Cultural Organisation (UNESCO) established the *International Charter of Physical Education and Sport* in 1978 which stated in *Article 1* that the practice of physical education and sport is a right for all. It is this charter that has led to the 'sport for all' movement in the west. Human rights are also mentioned in relation to sport as a key element within the *Olympic Charter* which means they are even believed to be of concern at the high performance end of the sporting spectrum. Because of the high profile concern for human rights related to sport they seem to be a stepping-off point for talking about the poor treatment of individuals in a sporting context (see Kidd and Donnelly 2000).

Work by Kidd and Donnelly (2000) and Donnelly (2008) highlights the value of researching human rights issues as they relate to sport and see the actions of the UN as a good starting point from which to achieve 'Sport For All'. There still must be a concern that sport is a western construct and as such the promotion of sport over traditional body cultures may lead to decline of important traditions that may be just a good for people's quality of life as the practice of sport. Therefore the elevation of sport over other forms of physical education (used in the broadest sense) may not be considered a good thing in non-western contexts. Access to and availability of sports programs for the disabled in the west has been good but in developing countries the provision is mixed at best.

The development of a culture of rights has gone some way to insuring that the provision for sport for people with disabilities is comprehensive within nations such as Britain.

> This culture is represented through the growth of critical [Non-Governmental Organisations] NGOs, legally through the advent of human rights conventions and charters, informed globally through the Internet, and committed politically to challenging the cultures of secrecy and democratic exclusion within different systems of governance. (Giulianotti 2003: 361)

Within this culture then it is not surprising that UK Sport has pushed an agenda of integration within its high performance system wherever possible. It is to the process of integration that we now turn.

Integrated sport

The interdisciplinary field of disability studies has been critical of the concept of integration since it implies to some that the impaired populations are required to change in order to join the mainstream (Northway 1997). Oliver (1996) has gone so far as to suggest that integration is based on concepts of normality. In other words the concept of integration requires members of the disabled community to adopt an 'able' disposition in order to become members of the mainstream. Because of its shortcomings, Oliver dismisses integration as being heavily laden with policy rhetoric and sees the term inclusion, because of its association with politics, as more appropriate (Oliver 1996; Northway 1997). Inclusion means that members of the disability community have a choice in whether to fully embrace the mainstream:

> [E]quality (defined as 'the participation and inclusion of all groups') may sometimes be best achieved by differential treatment. This does mean that if oppressed groups so choose they can opt for groups-specific recognition in policy and provision, since within an inclusive approach difference would be accepted or included as a natural part of the whole. (Northway 1997: 166)

Following these debates there has been a shift within the literature on disability from the dichotomy of integration/segregation to another where inclusion/exclusion are seen as a more politically appropriate way to advocate the acceptance of the disabled. It is possible however to see integration as a literal intermixing that entails the culture of both groups adapting to a new cultural environment:

> Community integration is the acquiring of age, gender, and culture-appropriate roles, statuses and activities, including in(ter)dependence in decision making, and productive behaviours performed as part of multivariate relationships with family, friends, and others in natural community settings. (Dijkers 1999: 41)

In other words, integration is 'a multifaceted and difficult process, which although it could be defined at a policy level rhetoric, [is] much less easy to define in reality' (Cole 2005: 341). The difficulty when exploring the success of integration policies is that the balance between the philosophical position and the reality (in this case a cultural sport environment) is not always clear. Simply exploring the policy landscape means that any interpretation is devoid of explicit cultural influences though all policy is a cultural artifact. This being said, the aim of integration is to allow the disabled to take a full and active role within society. The ideal would be:

> [a] world in which all human beings, regardless of impairment, age, gender, social class or minority ethnic status, can co-exist as equal members of the community, secure in the knowledge that their needs will be met and that their views will be recognised, respected and valued. It will be a very different world from the one in which we now live. (Oliver and Barnes 1998: 102)

Within the context of high performance sport, this utopian vision is hard to achieve. By its very nature elite sport is selective: as Bowen suggests, 'Within professional sport, though, all but the super-able "suffer" from "exclusion or segregation"' (2002: 71). Some observers have questioned whether integration has actually been a success within an institution such as UK Sport, because 'sport isolates individuals, but only those who are *super*-able. The rest *are* left to the realm of the minor leagues, masters' leagues, local tournaments, or backyard pick-up games' (Bowen 2002: 71). This understanding of sport makes it problematic to address the issue of integration without realising that elite sport can never be completely integrated. In order to fully understand the success or failure of integration within mainstream sport at a time when human rights concerns and/or violations are regularly drawn to our attention, it is important to begin to get a sense of the culture of sport for the disabled; and so we turn to a discussion of the ethos associated with the Paralympic movement which might go so way to fleshing out the social environment that is at the heart of Nussbaum's (2006) capability theory.

Paralympic ethos

Paralympism is an ideology celebrated by the IPC that has been developed in an attempt to establish a universal ethos that extends beyond the Paralympic Games in much the same manner that Olympism has transcended the more established Olympic Games. Some scholars working within the field of sport for the disabled have argued that a philosophy of Paralympism is not needed since Olympism is appropriate for the Paralympic movement (Landry 1995; Wolf *et al.* 2008). Clearly there are examples of harmony between Paralympism and Olympism. The motto of the Barcelona '92 IXth Paralympic Games 'Sport without limits' resonates with Olympism.

The International Olympic Committee's (IOC) definition is believed by some to reflect the centrality of Coubertin's vision. The fundamental principles of the Olympic movement enshrined in the *Olympic Charters* (International Olympic Committee 2004: 9) suggest that:

> Olympism is a philosophy of life, exalting and combining in a balanced whole the qualities of body, will and mind. Blending sport with culture and education, Olympism seeks to create a way of life based on the joy of effort, the educational value of good example and respect for universal fundamental ethical principles. . ... The goal of Olympism is to place sport at the service of the harmonious development of man, with a view to promoting a peaceful society concerned with the preservation of human dignity.

Taking this at face value, 'the expression "Paralympism" appears to be somewhat superfluous, pleonastic; "Olympism" is sufficient . . . it says it all' (Landry 1995, 5). In fact during the 1956 Olympic Games 'the International Olympic Committee awarded the Fearnley Cup to the organisers of the International Stoke Mandeville Games [the antecedent of the Paralympics] for "outstanding achievement in the service of Olympic ideals"' (Goodman 1986: 157).

According to Parry, 'Olympism is a social philosophy which emphasises the role of sport in world development, international understanding, peaceful co-existence, and social and moral education' (2004: 1). As a result, compliance with it in practice can add virtue to the Paralympic movement. However, since the Paralympic movement has a distinctive cultural history and resulting habitus to match, then the need to establish an understanding of Paralympism is paramount. There are those who advocate simply the use of Olympism (Wolff *et al.* 2008) as a sign of the growing harmony between the Olympic and Paralympic Movement because discrimination of individuals regardless of ability is against the principal tenets of Olympism. In practice, however, both the Olympic and Paralympic games exclude the [Dis]abled or to put it another way 'those who can't'. Yes, Olympism may be an inclusive ideology (Wolff *et al.* 2008) but the practice of high performance sport is not (Jones and Howe 2005).

The Paralympic Movement has raised public consciousness, both trans-nationally as well as trans-culturally, with respect to the philosophical concept and meaning of a *human* performance (Howe and Jones 2005). As such it has allowed for the debate regarding western sporting practice [ethos] and places virtue at the feet of those who achieve excellence in measurable sporting terms (Landry 1995). In this respect the achievements of Paralympians will never acquire the same status as those of Olympians.

More than two decades ago Labanowich (1988) argued for the integration of the Paralympic Games into the Olympics, based upon the number of countries and athletes contesting various sports within the Paralympic Games. While there may be some validity in this move the essence of Paralympism might have been lost. To start with, de Coubertin in *The Fundamentals of the Philosophy of the Modern Olympics* highlights the degree to which physical culture may be used as a vehicle to achieve sporting excellence: 'For a hundred men to take part in physical education, you must have fifty who go in for sport. For fifty to go in for sport, you must have twenty to specialise, [and] you must have five who are capable of remarkable physical feats' (1956 [1935]: 53). This is not a situation that is commonplace in Paralympic sport. There is exceedingly tough competition to get into certain events at the Paralympic Games, notably class T54[4], the most 'able' of wheelchair racers where selection is tough if not tougher than the Olympic Games; but technology is a factor here. It is clear from data collected in the context of Paralympic sport that it is easier across the board to be selected than it is for the Olympic Games. This is the case because many of the classes of impaired athletes struggle to get enough competitors to reach the qualifying standards for the Paralympic Games. To my knowledge this has never been the case at the Olympics.

The Paralympic movement as a whole does not create a sporting aristocracy as de Coubertin believed the Olympics did; but it has created its own rituals, some a direct parroting of those used by the Olympic Movement. For example, the opening and closing ceremonies, since 1992, have been replicated to a high degree at the Paralympics assuring a full house on opening and closing nights. But the establishment of the dictum 'empower, inspire and achieve' at the heart Paralympism is distinct from the Olympic motto. In a sense the Paralympic Games cannot follow de Coubertin's vision of the cycle of Olympiad to provide the youth of any moment in time with the opportunity to compete in an international context. In stating 'The Springtime of human life is found in the young adult who may be compared to a superb machine up and ready to enter, into full activity' (de Coubertin 1956 [1935]: 53–54), de Coubertin believed that the Olympics were an ideal environment for fostering the youth [his own strong affinity with the Fascist regime in Germany during the 1930s aside]. Many athletes who compete in the Paralympic Games of the past and today are 'eligible' as a result of a traumatic occurrence in life which clearly has no fixed time in the development of the individual. Paralympians are generally older than Olympians and rehabilitation – which in a sense can be about creating another individual or a re-birth (Seymour 1998) – continues to be a feature of contemporary sport for the disabled.

While the International Paralympic Committee has distanced itself from any explicit discussion of Paralympism, relying instead on the dictum *Empower, Inspire, Achieve*, the vision of the movement is 'To Enable Paralympic Athletes to Achieve Sporting Excellence and Inspire and Excite the World'. The only official statement of Paralympism comes from the Asian Paralympic Committee[5] who clearly are enamoured with Olympism:

Paralympism is a philosophy of life which embraces the mind, body and spirit. By combining sport with education, Paralympism aims to nurture a way of life for persons with a disability based on effort, good example and respect for ethics. The ideals of Paralympism encompass both the promotion and development of "Sport For All" and "Elite Sports". Although each has differing philosophy, fundamental goals and objectives, they complement each other and stress lifelong education and experience, values, traditions and fair play, towards attaining long term individual, social, cultural and economic goals.

The Paralympic movement. like that of the Olympics. 'all benefited from the benign myths of origin rooted in reverential attitudes toward the personal qualities of their respective founding fathers and the salvational doctrine they created' (Hoberman 1995: 3).

In many respects the fledgling Paralympic movement that Ludwig Guttmann ruled over is not dissimilar to the world of corruption brought on by a distinct lack of surveillance, in part by the myth associated with Olympism (that it actually existed), how involvement with the IOC meant material reward, and a 'long history of extreme right-wing personalities and attitudes within the IOC' (see Hoberman 1995: 6).

The truth behind the Olympic movement is that the chivalric tendencies of the movement, the knightly ethos of officials and athletes alike, 'was the precise negation of socialist rationality, solidarity, and the improvement of ordinary life for the greatest number' (Hoberman 1995: 19). While de Coubertin created 'The Myth of the War experience' (Hoberman 1995: 20) – the simple idea of military heroism – many Paralympians at least in the early days lived it though they were often treated as 'less then men'. Unlike 'de Coubertin's original version of the idealised male action figure was the 'débrouillard', the dynamic 'go-getter' type (Hoberman 1995: 22). Paralympians were broadly seen as charity cases. As such it is not surprising that the Paralympic Games is seen as detrimental for the broader Disabled Persons movement. Guttmann best summed this up in 1976 when he scored an own goal in his classic pronouncement 'Mens sana in corpore sano (Healthy mind and healthy body) should read Mens sana in corpore sano et invalido! (Healthy mind and healthy body or and infirm [weak or feeble] body) (Guttmann 1976: 13). This statement highlights what the Paralympic Movement is about: providing high performance sporting opportunities for less than able bodies. Ultimately Paralympism personified in the dictum Empower, Inspire, Achieve is a goal worth pursuing, but given the direction the Paralympic Movement is heading it will be difficult to attain.

Discussion

Traditionally scholars and political organisations such as the UN have turned to human rights to gain equitable treatment of marginalised populations. It is my contention however that reliance upon state governments and international organisations such as the UN is a mistake. The act of drafting both the *Vienna Declaration* of 1993 and the more recent *Convention on the Rights of Persons with Disabilities* of 2006 and enacting them in the within national government is unlikely to achieve a more integrated society. That being said, these statutes can be said to have largely been a success in Britain if we adopt the capabilities approach triumphed by Nussbaum (2006) and focus on Paralympic athletes because they have access to sporting provision that can be seen to add to their *quality of life*.

Access to high performance sporting provision is more problematic for two reasons. Firstly, the nature of high performance sport is such that some people will always be excluded due to a lack of ability (Bowen 2002; Jones and Howe 2005); and secondly the vast number of athletes with potential to be Paralympians, and therefore part of Paralympic programmes, are not vulnerable. These are not individuals who are denied access to sporting provision. The big question that needs to be answered is whether or not the British Government is being fraudulent toward the common good by treating Paralympic athletes differently to Olympic Athletes. One argument put forward in favour of inequitable treatment of the Paralympians might be the lack of competition internationally for these individuals compared to their 'able' counterparts. In other words, there may be a belief that achieving the status of a Paralympian is less of an achievement.

The problem according to Patrick Jarvis, former president of the Canadian Paralympic Committee and one of the few former Paralympians in a position of significant power within the movement, is that:

> We get many supportive comments as Paralympians. But as soon as you start to [encroach into] their [able bodied athletes] territory, being respected just as equal athletes and you threaten to win some of their awards, a lot are still uncomfortable with [disability]. (Christie 2004)

Over the last two decades there have been both national and international statutes enacted by the British Government that have greatly improved the quality of life for people with disabilities. These statutes can be seen to eliminate overt discriminatory attitudes, to make the lives of impaired people better. Opportunities for sporting provision have been opened up, although there is some way to go before equity is achieved. However, implementation of legislation to 'protect' minority groups such as the disabled may in fact make them more vulnerable to hidden or unidentified prejudice. As Deal suggests:

> Not all forms of prejudice and discriminatory behaviour, however, are blatant and therefore easily identifiable, as subtle forms of prejudice also exist. Therefore any attempt to tackle prejudice towards disabled people must not only focus on overtly discriminatory behaviour but also recognize subtle forms of prejudice, which can be equally damaging. (2007: 94)

To the outsider the inclusion of Paralympic Games within the matrix of the 2012 Olympic Festival may be seen as a statement of a progressive world view in tune with the need for adherence to human rights. Nevertheless, integration within mainstream sporting provision has not been complete and as a result has heightened the social division between the able and the disabled. Statutes enacted by the British Government have played a part in improving the *quality of life* of vulnerable minorities, including the disabled. A degree of social justice is being achieved for the most vulnerable individuals with disabilities but few Paralympians would fall into this category. *Integration*, or the intermixing of persons previously segregated, has changed little in high performance sport settings. Any change to stop Paralympians being seen by those who understand the social world around high performance disability sport as children of a lesser god will require a fundamental shift in social attitude toward physical differences:

> Only when we acknowledge the near universality of disability and that all its dimensions (including the biomedical) are part of the social process by which the meanings of disability are negotiated, will it be possible fully to appreciate how general public policy can affect this issue. (Zola 1989: 420)

This interpretation should be considered by future policy makers, nationally and internationally, when they try to 'better' the world for marginalised populations such as the disabled. For far too long there has been an assumption that creating policy and legislation will lead to changes of practice – the staging of the 2012 Paralympic Games in London should give cause to reflect on the legitimacy of this stance.

Notes

1 The United States and Canada run a similar programs called *Wounded Warriors* and *Soldiering On* respectively.
2 This is a federation that was launched in September 2004 at the Athens Paralympic Games. It is the result of a merger of two federations, the International Stoke Mandeville Wheelchair Sports Federation (ISMWSF) and the International Sport Organisation for the Disabled (ISOD), that have been part of the Paralympic movement since its inception.
3 www.paralympic.org
4 T54 is an event classification. The 'T' says that this is a track event. The '5' says that it is an event for a wheelchair athlete and the '4' means that the athletes is a highly mobile user of a wheelchair.
5 www.asianparalympic.org/aboutus/default.asp?action=profile (last accessed 20.09.10)

References

Bailey, S. (2008) *Athlete First: A History of the Paralympic Movement*, John Wiley & Son: San Francisco.
Brittain, I. (2010) *The Paralympic Games Explained*, London: Routledge.
Bowen, J. (2002) 'The Americans with Disabilities Act and its application to sport', *Journal of the Philosophy of Sport* 29: 66–74.

Christie, J. (2004) '"Spirit in motion": Paralympians rise', *The Globe and Mail*. December 11.

Cole, B. A. (2005) 'Good faith and effort? Perspectives on educational inclusion', *Disability & Society* 20: 331–344.

Coubertin, P. de (1956 [1935]) 'The fundamentals of the philosophy of the Modern Olympics', *Bulletin de Comité International Olympique* 56: 52–54.

Daly, D. J. and Vanlandewijck, Y. (1999) 'Some criteria for evaluating the "fairness" of swimming classification', *Adapted Physical Activity Quarterly* 16: 271–289.

Deal, M. (2007) 'Aversive disablism: subtle prejudice toward disabled people', *Disability & Society* 22(1): 93–107.

Donnelly, J. (1985) *The Concept of Human Rights*, London: Croom Helm.

Donnelly, P. (2008) 'Sport and human rights', *Sport in Society* 11(4): 381–394.

Dijkers, M. (1999) 'Community integration: conceptual issues and measurement approaches in rehabilitation research', *Journal of Rehabilitation Outcome Measurements* 3(1): 39–49.

Freeman, M. (2002) *Human Rights: An Interdisciplinary Approach*, London: Routledge.

Friedman, J. L. and Norman G.C. (2009) 'The Paralympics: yet another missed opportunity for social integration', *Boston University International Law Review* 27(2): 345–366.

Giulianotti, R. (2203) 'Human rights, globalisation and sentimental education: the case of sport', *Sport in Society* 7(3): 335–369.

Goodman, S. (1986) *Spirit of Stoke Mandeville: The Story of Ludwig Guttmann*, London: Collins.

Green, M. (2004) 'Power, policy, and political priorities: elite sport development in Canada and the United Kingdom', *Sociology of Sport Journal* 21: 376–396.

Green, M. and Houlihan, B. (2005) *Elite Sport Development: Policy Learning and Political Priorities*, London: Routledge.

Guttman, L. (1976) *Textbook of Sport for the Disabled*, HM&M: Aylesbury, England.

Harris, J. (1985) *The Value of Life: An Introduction to Medical Ethics*, Routledge: New York.

Hoberman, John (1995) 'Toward a theory of Olympic internationalism', *Journal of Sports History* 22(1): 1–37

Howe, P. D. (2004) *Sport, Pain and Professionalism: Ethnographies of Injury and Risk*, London: Routledge.

Howe, P. D. (2007) 'Integration of Paralympic athletes into Athletics Canada', *International Journal of Canadian Studies* 35: 134–150.

Howe, P. D. (2008) 'From inside the newsroom: Paralympic media and the "production" of elite disability', *International Review for the Sociology of Sport* 43(2): 135–150.

Howe, P. D. and Jones, C. (2006) 'Classification of disabled athletes: (dis)empowering the Paralympic practice community', *Sociology of Sport Journal* 23: 29–46.

IPC (2003) *The Paralympian: Newsletter of the International Paralympic Committee*. No 3. Bonn, Germany.

Jones, C. and Howe, P. D. (2005) 'The conceptual boundaries of sport for the disabled: classification and athletic performance', *Journal of Philosophy of Sport* 32: 133–146.

Kidd, B. and Donnelly, P. (2000) 'Human rights in sport', *International Review for the Sociology of Sport* 35(2): 131–148.

Labanowich, S. (1988) 'A case for the integration of the disabled into the Olympic Games', *Adapted Physical Activity Quarterly* 5: 263–272.

Landry, F. (1995) 'Paralympic Games and social integration', in M. De Moragas and M. Botella (eds) *The Key of Success: The Social, Sporting, Economic and Communications Impact of Barcelona '92*. Bellaterra: Servei de Publicacions de la Universitat Autonoma de Barcelona.

LaVaque-Manty, M. (2005) 'Equal opportunity to meaningful competitions: disability rights and justice in sports', *Disability Studies Quarterly* 25(3).

Locke, J. ([1689] 1970) *Two Treaties of Government*, Cambridge: Cambridge University Press.

MacAloon, J.J (1981) *This Great Symbol: Pierre de Coubertin and the Origins of the Modern Olympic Games*, London: University of Chicago Press.

MacIntyre, A. (1999) *Dependent Rational Animals: Why Human Beings Need the Virtues*, Chicago: Open Court.

Malhotra, R. (2008) 'Expanding the frontiers of justice: reflections on the theory of capabilities, disability rights, and the politics of global equality', *Socialism and Democracy* 22(1): 83–100.

Moss, S. (2009) Jimmy Carr: 'I thought my Paralympics joke was totally acceptable', *The Guardian* November 5.

Northway, R. (1997) 'Integration and inclusion: illusion or progress in services in services for disabled people', *Social Policy and Administration* 31(2): 157–172.

Nussbaum, M. C. (2006) *Frontiers of Justice: Disability, Nationality, Species Membership*, London: Belknap Harvard.

Oliver, M. (1996) *Understanding Disability: From Theory to Practice*, Basingstoke, MacMillan.

Oliver, M. and Barnes, C. (1998) *Social Policy and Disabled People: From Exclusion to Inclusion*, London: Longman.

Parry, J. (2004) 'Olympism and its Ethic', a paper presented at the 44th International Session of the International Olympic Academy, May/June.

Rawls, J (1971) *The Theory of Justice*, Cambridge, MA: Harvard University Press.

Seymour, W. (1998) *Remaking the Body: Rehabilitation and Change*, London: Routledge.

Sherrill, C. (1999) 'Disability sport and classification theory: a new era', *Adapted Physical Activity Quarterly* 16: 206–215.

Sherrill, C. and Williams, T. (1996) 'Disability and sport: psychosocial perspectives on inclusion, integration and participation', *Sport Science Review* 5(1): 42–64.

Smith, A. and Thomas, N. (2005) 'The "inclusion" of elite athletes with disabilities in the 2002 Manchester Commonwealth Games: an exploratory analysis of British newspaper coverage', *Sport, Education and Society* 10: 49–67.

Stammer, N. (1999) 'Social movements and the social construction of human rights', *Human Rights Quarterly* 21(4): 980–1008.

Steadward, R. (1996) 'Integration and sport in the Paralympic movement', *Sport Science Review* 5: 26–41.

Vanlandewijck, Y.C. and Chappel, R. J. (1996) 'Integration and classification issues in competitive sports for athletes with disabilities', *Sport Science Review* 5: 65–88.

Wolff, E.A., Torres, C., and Hums, M.A. (2008) 'Olympism and the Olympic athlete with a disability', in O. Schantz, and K. Gilbert (eds) *The Paralympics: Elite Sport or Freak Show*, London: Meyer & Meyer.

Zola, I. K. (1989) 'Towards the necessary universalizing of disability policy', *The Milbank Memorial Fund Quarterly* 67 (Supplement 2): 401–28.

13

THE OLYMPIC MOVEMENT, ACTION SPORTS, AND THE SEARCH FOR GENERATION Y

Holly Thorpe and Belinda Wheaton

Introduction

During an International Olympic Committee (IOC) meeting in 2006, IOC president Jacques Rogge asked the International Cycling Union (ICU) to assist with the entry of skateboarding into the Olympics. Accepting Rogge's request, an ICU spokesman proclaimed: 'From our side we are committed to help the development of skateboarding' (quoted in Higgins 2007: para. 6). Newspaper headlines shortly after the meeting suggesting that 'Skateboarding could make its Olympic debut at the 2012 London Games' (Peck 2007) as a wheel-based activity under the cycling discipline, however, provoked anger amongst the transnational skateboarding community. Indeed, thousands of skateboarders from across the world responded by signing an online petition titled 'No skateboarding in the Olympics' addressed to the IOC president:

> With due respect for Olympic Athletes, we the undersigned skateboarders and advocates strongly request that the IOC NOT RECOGNIZE SKATE-BOARDING AS AN OLYMPIC SPORT, or use skateboarding to market the Olympics. . . . Skateboarding is not a 'sport' and we do not want skate-boarding exploited and transformed to fit into the Olympic program. We feel that Olympic involvement will change the face of skateboarding and its individuality and freedoms forever. We feel it would not in any way support skateboarders or skate-parks. We do not wish to be part of it and will not support the Olympics if skateboarding is added as an Olympic sport. (The Petition 2010: para. 1)

Regardless of the debates within skateboarding culture, the proposal for ICU to adopt skateboarding as a 'wheel-based' sport failed to receive the unanimous support of the various national cycling federations. Yet, despite such opposition, the continuing attempts by the IOC to create space for new 'action sports', such as skateboarding in the 2012 Summer Olympic program, point to a growing issue at the heart of the Olympic Movement in the 21st century: that is, how to remain relevant to younger generations.[1]

In this chapter we discuss the appeal of alternative, lifestyle, extreme, or action sports such as surfing, skateboarding, and snowboarding, for the Olympic movement. While attention has been given to the (sub)cultural contestation around Olympic co-optation, and their cultural politics in sports such as snowboarding (e.g., Humphreys 2003), here we focus on aspects of the cultural, economic and political rationale for the inclusion of these activities in the Olympic Games. We begin by highlighting the expansion and influence of the action sport industry. Developing in a unique historical conjuncture of mass communications, corporate sponsors, entertainment industries, and a burgeoning affluent and young demographic, action sports have diffused around the world at a phenomenal rate and far faster than established sports (Booth and Thorpe 2007; Wheaton 2004). We then discuss the success of ESPN's X Games, the self-defined 'worldwide leader' in action sports (Rinehart 2008: 175), for capturing the highly lucrative young male demographic. With its spectacular footage, distinctive sporting and cultural personalities, innovate representation styles and ubiquitous reach, the X Games has become the spiritual home of the 'extreme' or action sport concept (Rinehart 2000). We then explore how the IOC has attempted to incorporate action sports and aspects of the X Games style, shifting both the meaning of 'sport' and the representation of events at the Olympic Games. Lastly, based on our research on windsurfing, snowboarding, and BMX, we identify key themes in the inclusion of action sports into the Olympic program, and consider the impact these sports have had on the modernisation agenda in the Olympic movement.

The expansion of the action sport industry

The term 'action sports', and other related categorisations (i.e., extreme, lifestyle, alternative sports), refer to a wide range of mostly individualised activities – ranging from older 'residual' sports like climbing, surfing and skateboarding, to emergent new or hybrid activities such as parkour, wakeboarding, B.A.S.E. jumping and kite surfing (see Booth and Thorpe 2007; Wheaton 2004) – demonstrating characteristics (at least in their early phases of development) different to the traditional rule-bound, competitive, regulated western 'achievement' sport cultures. While each action sport has its own specificity, history, identity and development patterns, many of these sporting cultures appear to share a common ethos distinct from that of many traditional sports. Many core members continue to tout anti-establishment, hedonistic, individualistic and/or do-it-yourself philosophies, seeing their culture as 'completely different' from more traditional sports (skateboarder, quoted in Beal 1995: 256). As these sports continue to grow in popularity, however, they often become highly fragmented, with participants engaging in various styles of participation, demonstrating philosophical differences and various levels of skill and commitment, differences which has led to some tensions, and debate within these action sports cultures in relation to their inclusion into the Olympic Games.

Since their emergence in the 1960s, action sports have experienced unprecedented growth both in participation and in their increased visibility across public space. Surveys across Asia, Australasia, Europe and North America, have pointed to the increased popularity of non-institutionalised informal sport activities in general, and lifestyle sport specifically (c.f. Booth and Thorpe 2007; Tomlinson *et al.* 2005).[2] In 2003, for example, five of the top ten most popular sports in the United States were action sports, including inline skating, skateboarding and snowboarding.[3] In contrast, participation in traditional team-sports, such as basketball and (American) football, is declining, or slowing (Howell 2008: 476). While young, white, heterosexual males often constitute a dominant force at the core of many action sport cultures (Kusz 2004; Wheaton 2009), demographics are shifting, particularly on the margins of the sports (e.g., novices, weekend warriors); the numbers of action sport participants from different social classes and age groups, as well as females and minority groups, are growing (Thorpe 2009; Wheaton 2009).

Attracting youth: lessons from the X Games

The inclusion of action sports such as snowboarding and BMX into the Olympic program have been acclaimed by media commentators as helping to modernise the Olympic movement and attract younger audiences. However, many of the strategies employed by the IOC have been borrowed from the hugely successful extreme games (later the X Games), the brainchild of the cable television network ESPN (Entertainment and Sports Programming Network, owned by ABC, itself a division of the Walt Disney Group). The X Games sits at the centre of the global diffusion and expansion of action sport, backed by a range of transnational corporate sponsors (see Booth and Thorpe 2007; Rinehart 2000). The inaugural first summer X Games in 1995 featured 27 events in nine categories: bungee jumping, eco-challenge, in-line skating, skateboarding, skysurfing, sport climbing, street luge, cycling and water sports. Early in 1997, ESPN staged the first winter X Games (in California), drawing 38,000 spectators and televised in 198 countries and territories in 21 different languages (Pedersen and Kelly 2000). Since then new competition formats and action sport disciplines that lend themselves to television coverage have continued to emerge. Examples include boarder-cross, slope-style and big-air competitions in snowboarding, vert-ramp in skateboarding, and air-shows and biggest-wave contests in surfing.

The emergence of the X Games initially prompted much debate among grassroots practitioners who contested ESPN's co-option of their lifestyle into television–tailored 'sports' (see Beal and Wilson 2004; Rinehart 2008). Yet X Games organisers quickly learned that in order to gain the support of action sport athletes they would need to work closely with core cultural participants and industry members; mainstream sport commentators were promptly replaced by highly-respected action sport athletes whose voice and visibility gave the event credibility among athletes and young viewers. In contrast to earlier generations, many contemporary action sport athletes acknowledge mass-mediated events such as the X Games as endemic to action sport in the 21st century, and are embracing the new opportunities for increased media exposure, sponsorship and celebrity offered by the X Games (Beal and Wilson 2004). For many contemporary action sport athletes, the X Games is the ultimate forum for setting records and performing ever more technical and creative manoeuvres for international audiences.

Blurring the boundaries between music festival and sporting event, the X Games offer spectators, viewers and athletes, a unique physical, visual and virtual experience that differs from traditional sporting events (Rinehart 2008). While venues limit the number of spectators, the X Games have witnessed exponential growth in television audiences; 63 million people watched the 2002 X Games on ESPN, ESPN2 and ABC Sports Today. While the Summer X Games have traditionally attracted the largest audiences, the Winter X Games continues to gain popularity; for example the 2009 Winter X Games was televised to more than 122 countries including across Africa, Latin America, the Caribbean and the Middle East (ESPN Winter 2009). From the British/European perspective, ESPN's global dominance of action sport coverage is less evident; most events take place in North America or Asia, and are broadcast in Britain on subscription satellite sport channels, usually at off-peaks times (Wheaton 2005). Nonetheless, the global reach of the X Games continues to grow. For example, the first European Winter X-Games held in Tignes (France) in March 2010, were attended by more than 66,200 spectators, 150 athletes from around the world, 370 international journalists, and broadcast to 166 countries (live and highlights) (Winter X Games 2010: para. 1).

According to Rinehart and Sydnor (2003: 7), the television coverage of the X Games is distinct from many traditional sports in that it privileges 'discontinuous shots, short (time duration) events, quick off-centred collage-type shots, blurred frames, super slow-motion cinematography, jolts of musical accompaniment, voyeuristic body shots, [and] neon and holographic colours'. Such innovative representational styles are particularly effective at drawing younger viewers. In contrast to the aging Olympic viewership, the X Games has a considerably younger audience with a median age of 20 years (Survey Says, no date). The X Games also draws upon an array of new social media to actively engage fans. For example, during the 2009 Winter X Games viewers and spectators were given the opportunity to vote via text message to determine the winners of events such as the Ski and Snowboard Big Air competition; each competition logged more than 100,000 votes via text message in less than ten minutes (ESPN Winter 2009). Winter X Games coverage was also offered via an array of other social media including Apple iTunes, Microsoft Xbox and ESPN TV VOD, ESPN Action Sports Video, ESPN Mobile TV, and ESPN360.com.

The IOC fights back

Cognisant of the growing success of the X Games, and the diminishing numbers of young Olympic viewers, the IOC recognised the need for new strategies that would make it more appealing to the highly lucrative 14–30 age demographic 'that is still forming its consumption habits' (Zimbalist quoted in Too Many 2010: para. 10). Thus, attempting to make the Olympics more exciting for the 'youth audience' (Bennett and Lachowetz 2004; Bialik 2002; Too Many 2010), the IOC set about incorporating a selection of youth-oriented sports into the Olympic program, including windsurfing, snowboarding and BMX (bicycle motocross).

Windsurfing enters the Summer Olympic Games

The IOC's first attempt to attract younger viewers saw the inclusion of windsurfing into the 1984 Summer Games in Los Angeles. Originating during the mid 1960s, boardsailing, or windsurfing as it is more popularly known, is a hybrid sport drawing on technologies adapted from boat-sailing and surfing. During this period, windsurfing was recognised as Europe's fastest growing sport (Turner 1983), and thus held much appeal for the IOC at this particular historical moment. Windsurfing was included as a new Olympic 'boat' in the pre-existing yachting regatta; initially there was one male dominated division, but a women's division was introduced at the 1992 Barcelona Games. While some championed windsurfing as providing a more exciting, youthful, media-friendly and athletic form of sailing (Newsletter 2008), many members of the yachting fraternity did not welcome this new addition to its programme. According to multiple Olympic windsurf medallist, Barbara Kendall, the old guard of yachting saw it as 'too radical' and 'didn't understand or want anything to do with us' (personal communication, March 2010).

Ultimately, however, windsurfing did not have a particularly profound impact on the Olympic Games. The format for Olympic windsurfing is course-racing rather than the more popular, spectacular, youthful and media-friendly activities of wave sailing and freestyle preferred by many contemporary professional windsurfing competitors. In contrast, Olympic windsurf course-racing is not a good spectator sport, and does not make good television. Racing is conducted offshore making both live spectatorship and filming difficult. Indeed, even for those who understand the tactics, it can be hard to clearly identify who is winning. Despite attempts to modernise the equipment, and attract competitors from the Professional Windsurfing Association (PWA) tour (many of whom are the sport's main celebrities and ambassadors), Olympic windsurfing did not gain the support of either core windsurfers or mainstream viewers.

The lack-lustre nature of windsurfing events in the contemporary Olympic Games points to one of the difficulties facing the IOC for successfully including action sports into the Olympic program. Action sports cultures are dynamic and in a constant state of flux; to remain relevant to participants and younger viewers, sporting organisations and media agencies must remain flexible to accommodate quickly changing styles and technologies. When windsurfing was incorporated into the Games in the 1980s it was perceived as a youthful and 'extreme' sport. But, by the early 21st century, the Olympic version of the sport has become a dull, marginalised form of windsurfing, attracting little interest from either the windsurfing culture or mainstream media. The Olympic Committee continued to look elsewhere for other action sports that would appeal to younger audiences; mountain biking and canoe slalom (also known as white-water kayaking) events were both added to the Summer Olympic program in 1996. However, it has been the inclusion of action sports in the Winter Olympics, particularly snowboarding, that have been most successful in attracting younger audiences.

Snowboarding becomes an Olympic Sport

Recognising the rapid growth and huge success of snowboarding in the X Games, the IOC decided to include snowboarding in the 1998 Winter Olympic program as a discipline of skiing and under the governance of the International Ski Federation (FIS). The IOC's decision to include snowboarding under the skiing federation (FIS) rather than the International Snowboard Federation (ISF) infuriated many snowboarders (see Humphreys 2003). The world's best half-pipe rider at the time, Terje Haakonsen, was particularly vocal in his criticism of the IOC's lack of understanding of snowboarding's unique history and culture and consideration of snowboarders' needs. Haakonsen's refusal to be turned into a 'uniform-wearing, flag-bearing, walking logo' (Mellegren 1998: para. 8) gained considerable media coverage. While many core boarders and athletes supported the sentiments expressed by Haakonson, others embraced these changes: 'I want to go to the Olympics . . . be the first snowboarder to win a gold medal and be written into the history books' (Jimi Scott, quoted in Howe 1998: 151). Debates among snowboarders over the inclusion of snowboarding into the 1998 Winter Olympics were illustrative of the growing divisions and cultural fragmentation within the broader snowboarding culture during this period (see Thorpe 2007, 2009). While 'half of the companies and riders were looking forward to the Olympics as the ultimate forum that would legitimise the sport', the other half 'didn't give a damn about the Olympics because it reeked of skiing – a stuffy by-the-books sport with an attitude that was the kiss of death for snowboarding's irreverent spirit' (Richards 2003: 135). Inevitably, incorporation continued regardless of conflicting philosophies and boarders' contrasting viewpoints.

Snowboarding's debut at the 1998 Winter Olympics, however, was shrouded in controversy. When Canadian snowboarder Ross Rebagliati – the first Olympic snowboarding gold medallist – tested positive for marijuana, the event grabbed headlines around the world (Humphreys 2007). While many core snowboarders celebrated the incident as evidence of the sports counter-cultural roots and unsuitability for the Olympic Games, the IOC and television networks responded by cancelling much of the previously programmed coverage of snowboarding events. Over the next four years, however, the sporting side of snowboarding became increasingly institutionalised and professional, and the IOC, FIS and television agencies set about developing more effective strategies from representing snowboarding events and athletes, such that the coverage of snowboarding at the 2002 Winter Olympics in Salt Lake City (US) was deemed a resounding success. According to a Leisure Trends survey, 32 percent of the United States population (nearly 92 million people) watched the 2002 Olympic snowboarding half-pipe competition in which Americans won gold, silver and bronze in the men's event (this was the first US winter Olympic medal sweep since 1956) and gold in the women's event. Of those viewers 18.6 million Americans said they wanted to try snowboarding (Snowboarding And 2004). A report released by the US-based National Broadcasting Company (NBC) after the 2002 Games revealed a 23 percent increase in ratings among 18 to 34 year old viewers (Berra 2006). More recently, US snowboarder Shaun White was identified as the 'most popular' and 'recognisable athlete' attending the 2010 Winter Olympic Games in Vancouver (Ebner 2009). Further highlighting the status of snowboarding in the Winter Olympics program, the Vancouver Opening Ceremony began with a snowboarder performing a spectacular jump through the Olympic rings, and later in the ceremony many snowboarders were seen carrying the flags for their countries (i.e., Andorra, Australia, Brazil, Bulgaria, and New Zealand).

BMX comes to Beijing

The success of snowboarding prompted the IOC to consider the inclusion of other action sports into the Olympic program, and particularly the Summer Games. As one media analyst explained, while 'there's a delicate balance between chasing fads and supporting tradition. . . the Summer Games need to be open to evolving much like the Winter Games' (Paul Swangard, quoted in Sappenfield 2004: para. 7). Acknowledging the success of BMX at the X Games, and the ease at which the racing event could be incorporated in the Olympic program, the IOC announced in 2003 that BMX racing would become a medal event at the 2008 Games in Beijing (China). This initiative was strongly supported by the International Cycling Union (UCI), who offered to drop two existing cycle-track events to accommodate it. According to a UCI official, 'Olympic cycling needed some pizzazz' and BMX had 'all the right elements': 'it can be performed in an arena, it's fast and short, both men and women can do it, and the concept is something a general audience would understand and enjoy looking at' (Lindstrom, quoted in Ruibal 2008: para. 8). While many grass roots cyclists were disappointed, and petitioned against the decision, some recognised the political factors underpinning the IOC and host-nation's decision: 'China supplies 90% of the world's BMX bikes, so they were happy with the change, plus it's a 'youth sport', which they like to have in the Games' (British Olympic cycling champion Chris Hoy 2008: para. 2). In contrast to the cultural debates among snowboarders prior to the 1998 Winter Olympics, the majority of BMX participants celebrated the inclusion of their sport into the Olympic program.

Attempting to target younger viewers, as well as make the event exciting and accessible for mainstream audiences, the BMX event was touted as 'NASCAR on two wheels' (quoted in Ruibal 2008: para. 1). To ensure exciting coverage and spectacular footage, an especially large and demanding course was designed (Ruibal 2008). Recognising the potential of BMX for reaching younger audiences, NBC strongly supported the decision to 'beef up' the course, even offering to trial the larger course in their Action Sports Tour (later renamed the Dew Tour) in the lead-up to the Beijing Olympics. The NBC actively sought to 'create an audience' for the Olympic BMX events by exposing viewers to the new course, and educating viewers about the format, rules and cultural values of BMX racing, prior to its Olympic debut.

The inclusion of BMX into the Beijing Olympics was widely considered a success, particularly among spectators at the event: 'It's exciting to watch and it's so much like [snow]boarder-cross. I think it is going to do for the Summer Games what snowboarding has done for the Winter Olympics – give people a fresh new perspective. And there's a lot of carnage', exclaimed one event attendee (Gretchen Bleiler, quoted in Roenigk 2008: para. 15). In terms of television ratings, however, BMX failed to capture the imagination of younger audiences to the same extent as snowboarding. Unlike the Olympic snowboarding celebrities (such as Torah Bright and Shaun White) who participate in the same events in the X Games and the Winter Olympics, BMX racers competing at the Olympics are typically not the cultural superstars of the X Games; BMX athletes gaining the most visibility and exposure at the X Games tend to be those participating in the more freestyle-oriented events (i.e., vert, street, big air). Perhaps recognising the missed opportunity for tapping into pre-established X Games celebrity and viewership, the IOC began making moves to include freestyle or 'park' BMX into the 2012 London Olympics. In 2009, British Cycling's performance director David Brailsford informally announced: 'the information I'm getting is I'll be performance director of street BMX so I will have to go and get my hoodie and baggie shorts' (quoted in Reid 2009: para. 3). Echoing the contestation among early generations of snowboarders leading up to the 1998 Winter Olympics, however, freestyle BMX riders are divided in opinion. In the words of Mat Hoffman, cultural superstar and founder of Hoffman Sports Association, organising body for freestyle BMX events worldwide: 'No disrespect to racing or the Olympics, but. . . we created BMX freestyle to do our own thing, express our own definition of sport, and to have the freedom to express this how we please; not to have our opinions sanctioned by a higher power' (quoted in How Will 2008: para. 11).

Modernisation, media coverage and representational styles

The inclusion of action sports such as windsurfing, snowboarding and BMX, into the Olympic program have, to varying extents, helped modernise the Olympic movement. However, the IOC and affiliated television conglomerates quickly learned that merely including action sports into the Olympic program was not enough to attract, and retain younger viewers; they also had to adopt new representational styles. According to some commentators, the 'sappy' representation of the 2000 Summer Olympics in Sydney employed by the NBC to target female audiences, resulted in a 50 per cent reduction in the 18–34 male viewer category (Simpson 2002: para. 14). Attempting to regain these younger viewers, the NBC reframed the 2002 Winter Olympics as 'Fear Factor on snow and ice' emphasising 'speed, risk and edginess' (Dick Ebersol, NBC Sports president, quoted in Simpson 2002: para. 12).

The IOC and some affiliated media conglomerates began to draw heavily upon the representational styles developed by the X Games. For example, snowboarding events at the 2010 Winter Olympics included live graffiti art displays, break-dancers and beat-boxers performing in the stands, live DJs and bands during breaks in competition, interviews with snowboarding pioneers, and Olympic snow-boarding video game competitions between audience members. One journalist attributes the success of the Vancouver Olympics to the 'jazzed-up formats' of some events (e.g., half-pipe, and snowboard- and ski-cross) which, drawing upon the 'the razzmatazz and street credibility of the X Games', transformed the 'sometimes stuffy Olympic arena' into a 'party atmosphere' with 'huge, often partisan crowds' (Booth 2010: para. 3 and para. 11). Further confirming the success of these X Games-inspired innovations, a recent study revealed a 48 per cent increase among 18–24 year old Olympic viewers (Bauder 2010). Many media commentators acknowledged American snowboarder and X Games champion, Shaun White, as a key contributor to this increase in viewership. Indeed, NBC coverage of the men's snowboard half-pipe final – including White's much anticipated per-formance – drew approximately 30 million viewers in the US alone (Dillman 2010); a larger audience than the 2006 Winter Olympic opening ceremony in Turin (Italy) (Reid 2010). Recognising the success of the strategies employed during the Vancouver Olympic Games, a spokeswoman for the London Olympic Games explained: 'the popularity of the ski and snow cross in Vancouver confirms that the way sports are staged can help capture the public imagination' (quoted in Booth 2010: para. 8). Continuing, she explains 'we are drawing up detailed marketing and sport presentation plans for 2012 for each sport to ensure that they engage and inspire. . . [and] connect young people to sport' (quoted in Booth 2010: para. 8).

The inclusion and representation of action sports at the Olympic Games are attracting younger spectators and television viewers. However, many of these events are also being consumed via new forms of social media (e.g., YouTube, iPhone, Twitter). During a keynote speech on digital media at the IOC's Congress in 2009, Martin Sorrell (CEO of London-based agency WPP Group) urged the IOC to 'learn from the likes of YouTube or risk losing young viewers for life' (quoted in Baird 2009: para. 1). Continuing, he advised: 'You have to let users play with your content. . . in their own way' (para. 2). The IOC responded by offering a range of viewing formats, as well as highly interactive media forums. For example, the official website for the Olympic Movement offers a virtual exhibition of the Vancouver Winter Olympics, and also held a competition inviting online visitors to submit their own medal designs. NBC also embraced an array of new social media in their representation of the 2010 Winter Olympics, such as an online user forum, 'You Be the Judge', where users could watch and judge live performances, comparing their scores with other postings, and an 'Athlete Twitter Sheet' that allowed users to see what the athletes were saying on Twitter. Analysis of the Vancouver games suggests that these new social media were particularly appealing to younger audiences, including action sport fans. Analyzing online discussions during the Vancouver Olympics, US media analysis firm Neilsen Company identified Shaun White as the second most 'buzzed about' athlete at the Games; two other snowboarders were also included in the top ten list (Skaters And 2010).

From the perspective of the IOC, and media conglomerates and advertisers, however, the increasing popularity of these new media raises concerns about how to retain control of their product. For example, coverage of Shaun White's medal winning performance quickly became a major trending topic on Google (Current Google 2010). The IOC and NBC responded by trying to reroute information via the NBC website, and removing YouTube clips of the event. Despite their efforts to control flows of information, the 'Shaun White Double McTwist 1260 video' quickly went 'viral', with users employing technologically-savvy strategies to facilitate the sharing and downloading of 'unofficial' footage from an array of websites and social media. While the inclusion of action sports into the Olympic program has helped regain the attention of younger audiences, the relationship between the IOC, sporting bodies, media agencies, and action sports cultures and industries, remain complex and political. In the following section we further examine some of the complexities involved in modernising the Olympic movement via the inclusion of action sports.

Action sports and the politics of modernisation: some key themes

The relationship between each action sport and the IOC, as well as host organising committees, media agents, and international sporting bodies, is unique based on the activity's distinctive history, environments, geographies, identities and development patterns. Indeed, the processes of inclusion are context-specific; the reactions of cultural members are strongly influenced by the state of the sport, culture and industry, at the time of Olympic inclusion. For example, the IOC initiated the inclusion of snowboarding (1998) at the height of the sports growth; the International Cycling Federation advocated the inclusion of BMX racing (2008) when the sport and industry had reached a plateau in participation and sales; and today, as action sports industries struggle amid the current economic climate, many action sport organisations are actively lobbying to the IOC for inclusion (e.g., surfing). Unfortunately, it is beyond the scope of this chapter to explore unique processes of Olympic inclusion (or exclusion) for the various action sports. Rather, here we identify three themes in the complex processes of the Olympic incorporation. First we discuss some of the cultural and environmental differences that lead to difficulties of inclusion into the Olympic program (e.g., dynamic nature of action sports, the unique environments required for participation). Second we describe some of the ideological 'cultural clashes' that occur when action sports are incorporated into the Olympic Games. Lastly we point to some of the unique (and somewhat paradoxical) effects of the inclusion of action sports into the modern Olympic movement.

Difficulties of inclusion

As previously mentioned, contemporary action sport cultures are dynamic and in a constant state of flux; participants are regularly developing new technologies and styles of participation. To remain relevant to young viewers, the X Games responds quickly to these trends, including and deleting sports or events, and changing judging criteria, within weeks and even days. In comparison, including new sports or disciplines into the Olympic program can take many years. For example, under IOC rules, the deadline for including a completely new sport (e.g., skateboarding) into the 2012 program passed in 2005! In this time, many trends have come and gone within the skateboarding sport, culture and industry, and a whole generation of skateboarders have grown up. The IOC's detailed rules and strict regulations make it very slow to evolve, creating barriers for including rapidly evolving action sports or new disciplines into the Olympic program.

Second, many action sports cultures take place in natural environments and involve close interaction with the earth's forces, which can make them appear unsuited to both the Olympics' organisational structures, and geographical venues. Accommodating some action sports requires expensive 'artificial' environments (e.g., indoor-climbing walls, white-water pool for kayaking) which are often perceived as highly controversial investments for host cities uncertain about the extent to which such facilities will be used after the Games. Some action sports need specific natural environments that cannot be provided by the majority of venues. For example, while the IOC has expressed interest in incorporating the internationally popular action sport of surfing into the Summer Games, it recognises that such processes are complicated by the specific (and uncontrollable) environmental requirements needed for an Olympic-level surfing competition. For example, while Brazil might – depending on the size and quality of waves – be able to host a successful Olympic-standard surfing competition during the 2016 Olympic Games, it is unlikely that such an event could be hosted at the Games in Athens (2004), Beijing (2008), or London (2012). In response to numerous proposals from the IOC-recognised International Surfing Association (ISA) and National Federations, and strong support from some of surfing's biggest starts (e.g., Kelly Slater), however, the IOC has stated that inclusion of surfing as a 'new sport' in the summer program is dependent upon the development of artificial wave pools that are not only able to produce high quality waves, but must also be affordable for host cities; despite conflicting reports, such facilities remain some way off (see Aguerre 2008). Acknowledging the opportunities for economic and cultural growth facilitated by other action sports (i.e., snowboarding, BMX) inclusion into the Olympic program, some surfing companies and agencies are investing heavily into the development of such technologies.

Third, many action sports employ highly subjective criteria for judging individual performances (see Booth 2003). However, the IOC has traditionally avoided including action sport events with aesthetic components requiring unique judging criterion[4], opting instead for 'first past the post' format events (e.g., windsurf course-racing, snowboarder-cross, BMX racing) which are easier for mainstream audiences to access, and can be more easily incorporated into existing IOC structures and definitions of 'sport'. Arguably, by opting for the speed-oriented action sport events rather than the more subjective freestyle events, the IOC has distanced many action sport enthusiasts and younger viewers who prefer the more aesthetic and creative styles of participation. The exception, of course, is the highly popular Olympic snowboarding half-pipe event, which continues to excite action sport enthusiasts and mainstream viewers alike.

Ideological clashes

Despite the increasing professionalisation, commercialisation and institutionalisation of action sports, many contemporary participants continue to see themselves as different to athletes from more traditional sports, and celebrate some of the sub-cultural ethos expressed by the early pioneers. A recent study, for example, illustrated that the primary motivation of snowboarders training for the Turin Olympics was fun and pleasure (90%); secondary motives included specific snowboard atmosphere (27.5%), money benefits (22.5%), keeping fit (22.5%) and fashion (5%) (Anna, Jan and Aleksander 2007). In an interview with *Rolling Stone* two-time half-pipe gold medallist Shaun White downplays the professionalism of snowboarding: 'At the Olympics we are still the dirty ones in the bunch, the sketchy snowboard kids. I don't think I'd have it any other way' (Edwards 2006: 45). Continuing, White concedes that the Olympics are 'really awesome', but that for most snowboarders it is 'not the biggest thing in the world. . . While other athletes were wound pretty tight. . . we are pretty light-hearted about the whole situation' (Edwards 2006: para. 13). The Olympics is the pinnacle in the careers of many athletes from more traditional sports, however, among many action sport athletes, events such as the X Games, or athlete-organised competitions, continue to hold more 'cultural authenticity' (Wheaton 2005), and thus tend to be more highly valued within the action sports culture and industry.

In contrast to action sport athletes from earlier generations, many contemporary Olympic action sport athletes accept (though often begrudgingly) the strict rules and regulations established by the IOC. Nonetheless, there are instances where their anti-establishment and hedonistic ethos clash with the disciplinary, hierarchical, nationalistic Olympic regime. For example, risqué photos of US 2010 Olympic half-pipe bronze medallist Scotty Lago posing with a female fan at a post-event party, in which the female fan is captured kissing his medal held suggestively below his waist, caused public outcry. Similarly, when Japanese snowboarder

Kazuhiro Kokubo transformed his official Winter Olympic team suit into a 'hip hop fashion statement', the Japanese public decried his behaviour as unpatriotic and disrespectful. The Japanese Ski Association responded by banning Kokubo, the team manager and two coaches, from the Olympic opening ceremony, and demanding a public apology (Owens 2010: para. 10). While the general public and mass media criticised Lago and Kokubo's actions as unprofessional and decidedly un-Olympic, many core snowboarders celebrated their behaviour as evidence of the sports continued connection with its counter-cultural and anti-authoritarian roots. Commenting on these incidents, one snowboard journalist proclaimed: 'If you invite the naughty kids to the party don't be shocked when someone pisses in the punch. Snowboarders are not the typical Olympians, for better or worse' (Richards quoted in Lipton 2010: para. 2).

Many action sport participants also resist the discourse of nationalism at the Olympics, seeing it as opposing the transnational friendships they have developed with their fellow competitors, and the corporation (rather than nation-based) 'teams' with whom they train and receive financial support. As Barbara Kendall explained, in contrast to the other sailors who socialise solely with their national teams, the windsurfers had developed relationships with athletes from various nationalities, such that they were 'like a family' (personal communication, March 2010). For some committed action sport participants, this transnational sporting identity takes precedence over nationality (see also Wheaton 2005). For example, when Terje Haakonsen was asked to explain his highly controversial decision not to compete in the 1998 Winter Olympics, his response revealed stronger identification with the global snowboarding culture, and a transnational snowboarding company, than his nation:

> How can you have a sponsor for ten years and then you go to the Olympics and you can't even pack your own bags because the nation has sold you as a package? Norway is a great country to live, but it's never supported me like my sponsors. My flag should be Burton not Norway. (quoted in Reed 2005: 135)

Snowboard journalist Henning Andersen also observed a 'fundamental clash of values' at the Vancouver Winter Olympics, comparing 'the dead-serious contest of nations pitted against each other' as enforced at the Games, to the 'transnational, fun concept of snowboarding' celebrated at other international snowboarding events (Andersen 2010: para. 4). Paradoxically, while some of the values expressed by action sports participants (e.g., privileging fun, creative freedom, individual expression and personal achievement over winning, and transnational friendships) appear contradictory to contemporary discourses of Olympism, they echo some of the values endorsed in the original Olympic charter.

Unintended consequences: action sports and cosmopolitan Olympism?

Arguably, the transnational relationships endorsed by action sports athletes, and their sense of post-national global identity, are illustrative of what Giulianotti and Robertson (2007) refer to as 'intensified levels and kinds of cosmopolitanism' (p. 172). Distinct from the discourses of 'internationalism' so dominant in the contemporary Olympic movement, which are grounded in nation-state affiliation (Carrington 2004: 86), action sports see themselves as more global citizens, united by their distinct cultural values and sporting ideologies. Snowboarding journalist Jennifer Sherowski (2004), for example, proclaims: 'we belong to a planet-wide culture' that 'transcends borders and language barriers' (p. 106). While it is unlikely that the 'thin' or banal cosmopolitanism endorsed by many action sport athletes will engender a more 'universalist orientation towards, and engagement with, other cultures' (Giulianotti and Robertson 2007: 172), action sport participants' ambivalence to nationalism[5], one of the most 'deeply entrenched', 'historically claimed' and problematic aspects of the modern Olympic movement (Tomlinson 2005: 48), offers an interesting paradox requiring further scrutiny. Can, as Carrington (2004) asks in his discussion of 'cosmopolitan olympism', the Olympics stripped of its ritualistic nationalism, be constructed as a 'progressive' set of ideas and practices, a 'space within which nationalism is downplayed not reinforced?' (p. 88). If so, how might the inclusion of action sports into the Olympic program contribute to such processes? Or, put differently, will action sports become increasingly nationalistic as they are further incorporated into the Olympic program? While it is too early to draw any perceptive conclusions here, issues of power, structure, agency and socio-cultural-political context, are central to such discussions.

Lastly, in light of critiques by academics that action sports represent exclusive forms of play limited to privileged youth in the white western world (Jarvie 2006; Kusz 2004; Wheaton 2009), it may seem surprising that they are finding space in the Olympic Games which purportedly are a celebration of global and democratic participation.[6] However, many commentators suggest that these aspirations are being used selectively by the IOC to include and exclude sports, based primarily on market values, rather than Olympic ideals (e.g. Bale and Christensen 2004). Despite the expansion of alternatives to the Western achievement sports model, including a range of non-Western cultural practices, the Western neo-colonial Olympic model of sport remains firmly entrenched (Eichberg 2004). The Olympic Movements endorsement of a 'global consumer culture' over historically-rooted ideals such as 'international cooperation and universal peace' (Tomlinson 2004, quoted in Carrington 2004: 96) seems to be supported by the rationale for inclusion of action sports into the Olympic program, that is, to attract younger viewers/consumers.

Yet, another interesting consequence of the inclusion of action sports into the Olympic program is that they have (in some cases) provided greater diversity on the podium. For example, the 16 female BMX finalists at Beijing represented 13 countries, and the 16 male finalists represented 11 countries; and 188 snowboarders from 26 countries participated in 2010 Winter Olympics. Unlike many traditional Olympic sporting events, which often become dominated by a small range of nations (and thus producing highly predictable sporting spectacles), action sports offer (if only temporarily) a more level (but by no means equal) playing field. With shorter histories and less developed national infrastructure, some countries have identified action sports as 'soft sports', offering opportunities for developing Olympic medal contenders within a short period and with relatively little economic investment. During the early 2000s, for example, snowboarding and freestyle skiing were identified as offering new opportunities for China to find space on the Winter Olympic podium. As China's director of winter sports, explains:

> We don't have the foundation and the money to have the same number of clubs as in the U.S. Winter sports are very expensive compared to summer sports. . . . [But] maybe these events [freestyle skiing and snowboarding] give Chinese and Asians an advantage because of our body type, like in gymnastics and diving. (quoted in Longman 2010: para. 14)

In 2005 the Chinese National Snowboard Team, consisting of six boys and six girls, funded by a government programme with selection based solely on their athletic (rather than snowboarding) abilities, was established; by 2010, four Chinese female snowboard team members held top 10 World Cup rankings.

Conclusion

In this chapter we have examined the complex processes involved in the inclusion of action sports into the Olympic program. Attempting to modernise the Olympic movement and tap into the lucrative youth market, we have seen the IOC introduce an array of new action sports, often fast-tracking their inclusion via incorporation under existing sports with little knowledge of the unique cultural values or practical requirements of action sports participants. For example, windsurfing was included under the governing body of yachting; snowboarding was included as a discipline of skiing; and attempts continue to be made to include skateboarding as a sport under the control of the cycling federation. We also explained how, in their efforts to make the Olympic Games relevant to younger generations, the IOC and associated media agencies have drawn from the practices and representational strategies of the X Games. While the impact of the inclusion of action sports into the Olympic program has been most evident in the Winter Games, with youth audiences for the Summer Olympics on the decline, it is not surprising that the IOC is increasingly looking to new action sports (e.g., parkour or free running, skateboarding, surfing, and kite-surfing) as ways to reconnect with contemporary youth. In each of these cases, the past (i.e., windsurfing, snowboarding, BMX racing), present (i.e., BMX freestyle, skateboarding) and future (i.e., surfing, parkour, kite-surfing) discussions regarding the inclusion of action sports into the Olympic program is politically-loaded and highly controversial. The potential impacts on the action sport cultures, and on the 'mainstream' sports tasked with governing them, are complex and context-specific. As this chapter has revealed, the market-driven search for younger viewers, and the highly elusive and profitable Gen Y audience, has led to complex power struggles between at least three key agents – the IOC, media conglomerates (e.g., NBC), and action sports cultures and industries. While it is certain that action sports are increasingly shifting the representation and consumption of the Olympic Games, what is less certain is how these agents will negotiate space and control within the dynamic economic and political structures of the Olympic movement into the 21 century.

Notes

1   While the International Olympic Committee is making various efforts to appeal to younger audiences (e.g., the inaugural Youth Olympic Games held in Singapore 2010), in this chapter we focus on the inclusion of action sports to help modernise the Olympic Games and attract younger viewers.
2   Given the difficulty of capturing participation in these informal, outdoor, non association-based activities, it is likely that participation rates are growing faster than these surveys suggest (Bach, 1993). Indeed when measures such as equipment sales and media commentaries are included, it is clear that in the twenty-first century many types of action sports are attracting an ever-increasing body of followers, outpacing the expansion of traditional sports in many Western nations.
3   The National Sporting Goods Association (2007) suggested there were 12 million skateboarders in the USA, and that the number of participants grew 178% between 1995 and 2005 (cited in Howell, 2008), and snowboarding has experienced a 160 percent growth in total participation between 1995 and 2007, and a 257 percent increase in frequent participation (Action Sports, 2007).
4   Damkjaer (2004) discusses the problems of the inclusion of aesthetic sports, such as gymnastics, in the Olympics more widely, noting that while they are growing in number and visibility, they cause numerous problems for the Olympic philosophy, not least because they don't conform to the motto of 'citius, altius, fortius'.
5   It is important to note nonetheless, that there are different types of nationalism at play in sport and the Olympics, each with different effects for types of political identities (see Eichberg 2004).
6   According to the Olympic charter, in order for an event to become part of the Olympic programme it must be widely practised (for the Summer Games in at least 75 countries for men) and spread over four continents. Additionally, any changes to the programme are assessed using seven categories, including universality, popularity, costs and development of the International Federation that governs the new event or sport.

References

'Action sports: The action sports market'. (2007). Retrieved November 20, 2010, from http://activemarketinggroup.com/Assets/AMG+2009/Action+Sports.pdf
Aguerre, F. (2008) 'Surfing and the Olympics: my point of view'. Retrieved March 1 2010, from http://www.isasurf.org/OlympicSurfing.php
Andersen, H. (2010, February 19) 'An Olympic-sized rant', Method Magazine. Retrieved March 5 2010, from http://methodmag.com/node/6525
Anna, T., Jan, B., and Aleksander, T. (2007) 'Goals in sports career and motivation as the measure of professionalism in snowboarding', Medicina Sportiva, 11(1): 27–31.

Bach, L. (1993) 'Sport without facilities: the use of urban spaces by informal sports', *International Review for the Sociology of Sport* 28(3): 281–295.

Baird, D. (2009, October) 'Olympics must embrace digital and social media or lost youth audience'. Retrieved March 16 2010, from http://www.debaird.net/blendededunet/2009/10/martin-sorrell-olympics-committee-embrace-digital-social-media-or-lose-youth-audience.html#tp

Bale, J., and Christensen, M. K. (eds) (2004) *Post-Olympism? Questioning Sport in the Twenty-first Century.* Oxford: Berg Publishers.

Bauder, D. (2010, February 16) 'Olympics prove popular with TV viewers'. The Associated Press. Retrieved from ABC News, March 1 2010, http://abcnews.go.com/Sports/wire Story?id=9854780

Beal, B. (1995) 'Disqualifying the official: an exploration of social resistance through the subculture of skateboarding', *Sociology of Sport Journal* 12(3): 252–267.

Beal, B., and Wilson, C. (2004) '"Chicks dig scars"': commercialisation and the transformations of skate boarders' identities', in B. Wheaton (ed.), *Understanding Lifestyle Sports: Consumption, Identity and Difference*, London: Routledge.

Bennett, G., and Lachowetz, T. (2004) 'Marketing to lifestyles: action sports and generation Y', *Sport Marketing Quarterly* 13: 239–242.

Berra, L. (2006) 'Don't be fooled by the slouches. Snowboard goddesses Gretchen Bleiler and Lindsey Jacobellis are more than ready to become Olympic icons', *ESPN The Magazine*. Retrieved February 2 2009, from http://sports.espn.go.com/espnmag/story?id=3693536

Bialik, C. (2002) 'NBC's bid to woo young to Olympics', Retrieved March 16 2010, from http://www.medialifemagazine.com/news2002/feb02/feb04/5_fri/news3friday.html

Booth, D. (2003) 'Expression sessions: surfing, style and prestige', in R. Rinehart and S. Sydnor (eds) *To the Extreme: Alternative Sports, Inside and Out*, Albany: State University of New York Press.

Booth, D., and Thorpe, H. (2007) 'The meaning of extreme', in D. Booth and H. Thorpe (eds) *Encyclopedia of Extreme Sport*. Great Barrington: Berkshire Reference Works.

Booth, R. (2010, March 1) 'Formats jazzed-up to draw crowds at London 2012 Olympics', *The Guardian*. Retrieved May 2 2010, from http://www.guardian.co.uk/uk/2010/mar/01/olympics-2012-bmx-shanaze-read

Carrington, B. (2004) 'Cosmopolitan Olympism, humanism and the spectacle of "Race"', in J. Bale (ed.) *Post-Olympism? Questioning Sport in the Twenty-first Century*, Oxford: Berg Publishers.

Current Google insight trends: Vancouver 2010, Shaun White, Lindsey Vonn. *The Independent*. Retrieved May 12 2010, from http://www.independent.co.uk/news/media/current-google-insights-trends-vancouver-2010-shaun-white-lindsey-vonn-1907030.html

Damkjaer, S. (2004) 'Post-Olympism and the aestheticization of sport', in J. Bale (ed.) *Post-Olympism? Questioning Sport in the Twenty-first Century*, Oxford: Berg Publishers.

Dillman, L. (2010, February 21) 'Snowboarding's "X Games vibe" an unlikely but profitable fit with Olympics tradition', *LA Times*. Retrieved March 1 2010, from http://www.cleveland.com/olympics/index.ssf/2010/02/snowboardings_x_games_vibe_an.html

Ebner, D. (2009, February 11) 'US snowboarder at top of fame mountain', *Globe and Mail*. Retrieved January 5 2010, from http://www.theglobeandmail.com/sports/us-snowboarder-at-top-of-fame-mountain/article971921/

Edwards, G. (2006, March 9) 'Attack of the flying tomato', *Rolling Stone*, 995, pp. 43–45.

Eichberg, H. (2004) 'The global, the popular and the inter-popular: Olympic sport between market, state and civil society', in J. Bale (ed.) *Post-Olympism? Questioning Sport in the Twenty-first Century*, Oxford: Berg Publishers.

'ESPN Winter X Games 13 sets records across platforms'. Retrieved March 1 2010, from http:// tvbythenumbers.com/2009/02/02/espn-winter-x-games-13-sets-records-across-platforms

Giulianotti, R., and Robertson, R. (2007) 'Recovering the social: globalization, football and transnationalism', *Global Networks* 7 (2): 166–186.

Higgins, M. (2007, June 14) 'Skateboarding in Olympics: Rad or bad?', *The New York Times*. Retrieved March 1 2010, from http://www.nytimes.com/2007/06/14/sports/othersports/ 14olympics.html?_=1&pagew

'How will BMX in the Olympics affect us?' (2008, August 14). Retrieved from http://bmx. transworld.net/1000069812/features/how-will-bmx-in-the-olympics-affect

Howe, S. (1998) *(SICK) A Cultural History of Snowboarding*, New York: St. Martins Griffin.

Howell, O. (2008) 'Skateparks as neoliberal playground', *Space and Culture* 11 (4): 475–496.

Hoy, C. (2008) 'Chris Hoy gets PEZ'd! *BMX Bikes*', Retrieved March 1 2010, from http://www.bmxbikes365.com/2008_01_01_archive.html

Humphreys, D. (2003) 'Selling out snowboarding: the alternative response to commercial co-optation', in R. Rinehart and S. Sydor (eds) *To the Extreme: Alternative Sports, Inside and Out*, Albany: State University of New York Press.

Jarvie, G. (2006) *Sport, Culture and Society: An Introduction*, London: Routledge.

Kusz, K. (2004) '"Extreme America": The cultural politics of extreme sports in 1990s America', in B. Wheaton (ed.), *Understanding Lifestyle Sports: Consumption, Identity and Difference*, London: Routledge.

Lipton, N. (2010, February 26) 'High fives with Todd Richards: Olympic drag', *Yo Beat*. Retrieved March 2 2010, from http://www.yobeat.com/2010/02/26/high-fives-with-todd-richards%E2%80%94olympic-drag/

Longman, J. (2010, February 15) 'China grooms team to become a powerhouse', *The New York Times*. Retrieved March 1 2010, from http://www.nytimes.com/2010/02/15/sports/ olympics/15longman.html?fta=y&pagewa

Mellegran, D. (1998, January 7) 'AP reports Terje boycotting Nagano?', *SOL Snowboarding Online*, www.solsnowboarding.com/compete/terje.html

Newsletter, T. I. W. C. (2008) 'Windsurfing's position in the 2008 Olympics under threat'. Retrieved March 1 2010, from http://www.internationalwindsurfing.com/2008/

Owens, T. (2010, February 13) 'Japanese snowboarder banned from Olympic opening ceremony over dress code'. Retrieved March 16 2010, from http://www.terezowens.com/ japanese-snowboarder-barred-from-olympic-opening-ceremony-over-dress-code/

Peck, S. and agencies. (2007, June 8) '2012 Games could see skateboarding debut', *Telegraph.co.uk*. Retrieved May 18 2010, from http://www.telegraph.co.uk/news/uk news/1553957/2012-Games-could-see-skateboarding-debut.html

Pedersen, P. M., and Kelly, M. L. (2000) 'ESPN X Games: commercialized extreme sports for the masses', *Cyber-Journal of Sport Views and Issues* 1(1).

Reed, R. (2005) *The Way of the Snowboarder*. New York: Harry N. Abrams, Inc.

Reid, C. (2009, February 5) 'Freestyle BMX to be introduced at London 2012 Olympics'. Retrieved March 1 2010, from http://www.bikebiz.com/news/30180/Freestyle-BMX-to-be-introducted-at-London-2012

Richards, T. with Blehm, E. (2003) *P3: Pipes, Parks, and Powder*, New York: Harper Collins.

Rinehart, R. (2000) 'Emerging arriving sport: alternatives to formal sport', in J. Coakley and E. Dunning (eds), *Handbook of Sport Studies*, London: Sage.

Rinehart, R. (2008) 'ESPN's X games, contests of oppostion, resistnace, co-option, and negotiation', in M. Atkinson and K. Young (eds), *Tribal Play: Subcultural Journeys through Sport* (Vol. IV 'Research in the Sociology of Sport', Bingley: Jai.

Rinehart, R., and Sydor, S. (eds)) (2003) *To the Extreme: Alternative Sports, Inside and Out.* Albany: State University of New York Press.

Roenigk, A. (2008, August 22) 'BMX's unpredictability makes it a predictable success at Olympics', *ESPN.com*. Retrieved March 19 2010, from http://sports.espn.go.com/oly/summer08/cycling/columns/story?id=3548229

Ruibal, S. (2008, September 19) 'Hopes riding high for BMX, "NASCAR on two wheels"', *USA Today*. Retrieved March 19 2010, from http://www.usatoday.com/cleanprint/?1268911903953

Sappenfield, M. (2004, August 9) 'For X Games generation, Olympic yawn', *The Christian Science Monitor*. Retrieved March 1 2010, from http://www.csmonitor.com/2004/0809/p01s03-ussc.html

Select snow brands to show at ASR', (2004, December 2) *Transworld Business, Surf, Skate, Snow*. Retrieved from http://www.twsbiz.com

Sherowski, J. (2004, April) 'Notes from down-under', *Transworld Snowboarding*, 104–117.

Simpson, K. (2002, February 5) 'Extreme sports may represent the future of Winter Olympics'. Retrieved March 1 2010, from http://findarticles.com/p/articles/mi_qn4191/is_20020205/ai_n10001444/

Skaters and snowboarders most buzzed about athletes at Olympics', (2010, February 17). Retrieved March 16 2010, from http://blog.nielsen.com/nielsenwire/online_mobile/skaters-and-snowboarders-most-buzzed-about-athletes-at-olympics/

Snowboarding and the Olympics (2004). Retrieved January 18, 2011, from http://www.k5.com/page.asp?itemid=223

Stratford, B. (no date) 'Gary Ream doesn't speak for me'. Retrieved March 1 2010, from http://www.realskate.com/MrReam.pdf

'Survey says' (no date). Retrieved March 16 2010, from http://www.espneventmedia.com/uploads/application/XGamesIXSurveyInfo.pdf

'The Petition' (2010). Retrieved March 2 2010, from http://www.thepetitionsite.com/takeaction/656763888?ltl=1146760863

Thorpe, H. (2009) 'The psychology of extreme sport', in T. Ryba, R. Schinke and G. Tenenbaum (eds) *The Cultural Turn in Sport and Exercise Psychology*, Morgantown: Fitness Information Technology.

Thorpe, H. (2007) 'Snowboarding', in D. Booth and Thorpe (eds) *Berkshire Encyclopedia of Extreme Sport*, Berkshire, Great Barrington.

Tomlinson, A. (2005) 'Olympic survivals: the Games as a global phenomenon', in L. Allison (ed.), *The Global Politics of Sport: The Role of Global Institutions in Sport*, London: Routledge.

Tomlinson, A., Ravenscroft, N., Wheaton, B., and Gilchrist, P. (2005) *Lifestyle Sport and National Sport Policy: An Agenda for Research. Report to Sport England*.

'Too many Olympic events, or not enough?' (2010, February 23) *The New York Times*. Retrieved March 1 2010, from http://roomfordebate.blogs.nytimes.com/2010/02/23/too-many-olympic-events-or-not-enough/

Turner, S. (1983) 'Development and organisation of windsurfing', *Institute of Leisure and Amenity Management 1*, 13–15.

Wheaton, B. (ed.) (2004) *Understanding Lifestyle Sports: Consumption, Identity and Difference*, London: Routledge.

Wheaton, B. (2005) 'Selling out? The globalization and commercialisation of lifestyle sports', in L. Allison (ed.) *The Global Politics of Sport: The Role of Global Institutions in Sport*, London: Routledge.

Wheaton, B. (2009) 'The cultural politics of lifestyle sport (re)visited: beyond white male lifestyles', in J. Ormond and B. Wheaton (eds) *'On the Edge': Leisure, Consumption and the Representation of Adventure Sport* (LSA Publications Vol. 104), Eastbourne: Leisure Studies Association.

'Winter X Games Europe Tignes', (2010, March 28). Retrieved May 18, from http://ski-project.blogspot.com/

14

TEAM GB, THE BARDS OF BRITISHNESS AND A DISUNITED KINGDOM

Mark Perryman

David Hemery burning his way round the track, Mexico 1968. Mary Peters defying gravity as she hauled her frame over the high jump bar to lift pentathlon gold in Munich 1972. David Wilkie's victory in the pool, Montreal 1976. Coe and Ovett doubling up for glory, Moscow 1980. Daley Thompson acting the golden cheeky chappy, Los Angeles 1984. Beating Germany in the men's hockey final, Seoul 1988. Christie and Gunnell on the track at Barcelona 1992. Redgrave vowing he'd never be seen near a boat again after winning his fourth straight gold with Pinsent at Atlanta 1996. Redgrave doing precisely that to win his fifth and final gold, again with Pinsent at Sydney 2000. Kelly Holmes winning 800m and 1500m gold against all the odds in 2004. Hoy, Pendleton and Adlington leading Team GB's gold medal charge to fourth in the Beijing 2008 medals table.

From our late 1960s childhoods to the early twenty-first century, those of us now fifty-something can measure-out our whole lives in glowing memories of the quadrennial summer Olympics. Each and every games as likely to be remembered for the achievements of other countries' athletes, as much as for our own. 1968 for the leap beyond what had been thought the limits of human capacity by Bob Beamon. 1972 the impish Olga Korbut tilting her head at the close of her floor routine in the gymnastics hall. And so it goes on.

This is the core of the Olympian appeal. Flying in the face of ideological redoubts that position nationalism as the polar opposite of internationalism. In his classic work on the origin and spread of nationalism, *Imagined Communities*, Benedict Anderson pinpointed the persistence of the nationalist impulse notwithstanding the counterclaims of the hyper-globalisers:

> Almost every year the United Nations admits new members. And many 'old nations', once thought fully consolidated, find themselves challenged by 'sub'-nationalisms which, naturally, dream of shedding this sub-ness one happy day.

The reality is quite plain: the 'end of the era of nationalism,' so long prophesied, is not remotely in sight. Indeed, nation-ness is the most universally legitimate value in the political life of our time. (Anderson 1991: 3)

The 2012 London Olympics will take place on the cusp of this persistent irritant. One that refuses to surrender itself unconditionally to the seductive appeal of all that Team GB and its Bards of Britishness chorus line throw at us. Arthur Aughey suggests that in embracing our United Kingdom we supersede the soiled agenda of 'kith and kin' nationalism:

Britishness involved an idea of the people and of its identity rather different from that of nationalism. It was not Britishness as some peculiar spiritual substance which defined the United Kingdom. Nor was it the acknowledgement of the legitimacy of the constitutional relationship. Rather, the experience of a common loyalty to the constitution had created a new political *persona*. (Aughey 2001: 27)

Consulting my dog-eared copy of George Courtaud's best-selling *The Pocket Book of Patriotism* (Courtaud 2004) confirms any suspicions that Britishness represents a political culture founded on subjecthood rather than citizenship. There it is in back and white, 'Happy and glorious, long to reign over us', the essentials of any constitutional relationship handily summed up for easy reference in the first few lines of the National Anthem. An entirely different ethos to the French, whose anthem the *Marseillaise* comedian Rob Newman rather neatly describes as 'a rebel song named after a town with a large immigrant population. An English equivalent might be the Clash's "Guns of Brixton"' (Newman 1998: 28). Newman made that comparison a few months after a trouble-strewn English campaign at World Cup 98, in the wake of rising Scots and Welsh civic nationalism after successful devolution referendums in 1997. Thus began a decade or more of increasing separation of this United Kingdom, and a growing sense that England was no longer the same as Britain.

Political commentator Iain McWhirter at the time made this rather telling observation of a certain English attitude to this unfolding process: 'Middle England was in no mood to go to the constitutional barricades in defence of a Union which they were not convinced was under serious threat. And so, England slept through the break up of Britain' (McWhirter 1998: 49). McWhirter however was troubled by what the impact of a dawning realisation of what Scottish devolution represented for the English might foment:

England may well begin to ask questions about where she stands politically in the new order. Better to start the process now, than to allow grievances to develop which could turn the constitution into a sport for hooligans. (McWhirter 1998: 54)

The football analogy proved irresistible – in 1998, after all, Scotland not only made its customary early exit from the World Cup, but following the Scotland Act of the same year the devolved Scottish Parliament was established. Or more correctly, re-established some three hundred years after the 1707 Act of Union abolished it. McWhirter wasn't the only commentator, north or south of the border, who cast an eye at the hooliganism in England's name that stained the team's presence in Marseilles, Toulouse and Lens before expressing a fear of what shape English nationalism may now take. The process of devolution began with the Scots and Welsh referendums of 1997, was settled by the Acts which put in place their respective representative institutions, and then finally completed by the restoration of powers to Northern Ireland's Stormont. This entrenched a process that whilst not yet complete nevertheless imprints an indelible question mark on what remains of a tattered and torn Union Jack. Constitutional reformer Anthony Barnett was one of those who pinpointed the distinctions these developments have uncovered, suggesting that the Scots and Welsh 'have in common an understanding that there is a space between their nation and Britain, and they can assess the relationship between the two' (Barnett 1997: 293). As the nationalist discourse gathered pace, increasing numbers would use that space for assessment of the relationship to reject it outright, while in Northern Ireland a resurgent nationalist community sought to merge their country with another state. Amidst all of this breaking-up the English, finally, began to distinguish England from Britain. Barnett described the political thought processes this involved: 'The English are often baffled when asked how they relate their Englishness and Britishness to each other. They often fail to understand how the two can be contrasted at all. It seems like one of those puzzles that others can undo but you can't; Englishness and Britishness seem inseparable. They might prefer to be called one rather than the other but, like two sides of a coin, neither side has an independent existence from the other' (*ibid.*). Barnett suggests that the puzzle is best treated as a two-legged contest, home and away:

> At home we are English, it is the English countryside. Abroad we are British: it is the British Embassy, we do not have English passports. It is not a border that is easily recognised when crossed: it is a simultaneous experience, uniting one's being at home and one's being in the world, while giving each a separate name. (*ibid.*)

At football's Euro '96 England were pitted in the group stages against Scotland at Wembley before the inevitable exit, on penalties, at the hands of Germany in the semi-finals. Ever since, in terms of sporting nationalism at least, England has reigned victorious in any contest for popular loyalty versus Team GB which scarcely exists outside of the Olympic cycle. The confusion Barnett refers to doesn't exist in Rugby Union – one World Cup victory in England's colours in 2003, and another World Cup final appearance in 2007. In cricket there is a minor confusion involving letting the Welsh in on the act but – minus doffing our cap to Simon

Jones' magnificent contribution to the bowling attack – the Ashes win in 2005 was to all intents and purposes down to England. Confusion took a different direction in England's victorious 2009 Ashes series with the first test played in Glamorgan of all places, for five days the Welsh home of England's assault on the Aussies. And as for England's newest star of the middle order, Eoin Morgan ex-Ireland, the less said the better for a team that styles itself at the wicket as 'England', not 'British and Irish Lions', 'Cricket UK', or whatever. But of course the dominant sport by a long, long way bears no such contradictions, well, on the playing side at least. The football team is unmistakably English, with no equivalent of cricket's need for South Africans to make up the 2010–2011 Ashes squad numbers. The football team's achievements on the pitch of course however pale into something even less than insignificance compared to rugby and cricket. Yet the mere fact of consecutive qualifications for every World Cup and Euro since 1996, Euro 08 excepted, with heaped up expectations of ending more than four decades of trophyless hurt, has been more than sufficient to shape an unprecedented popularity of identification with all things England and St George. Only the Olympics, Kate and Will's Royal Wedding and the funeral processions of servicemen's coffins returning from Afghanistan fly the Union Jack with anything like the same breadth and depth of appeal.

This puzzle of the dual identification with England and Great Britain today takes place in the context of two powerful political actors, multiculturalism and globalisation. As World Cup 2010 prepared to open, writer Mike Marqusee observed the changing geography of support in England:

> For a wide variety of reasons, many people long-resident or even born and bred in this country will not be supporting England, though they'll be following the football with passion. In our cities there will be clubs, pubs and restaurants packed at various times with supporters of Argentina, Italy, Portugal, Spain, Brazil, Mexico, Ghana or Cameroon cheering on their sides. (Marqusee 2010)

The academics Les Back, Tim Crabbe and John Solomos made a similar point in their account of fans of Jamaica travelling from Brixton to follow their team at France 98 (Back, Crabbe, Solomos 2001). Whilst these commentaries on fan countercultures are important, and in part testament to the ability of multiculturalism to cope with the stresses and strains differing loyalties impose upon it, there is a danger that they become self-serving. Observations on diasporific supporter cultures become an alternative to engaging with the self-evident transformation of England's own support. The days of an all-white team ended with Viv Anderson capped in 1979; it took much longer for the make-up of the fans to alter too, but in large part this has now been achieved. England is every much a team of inner city England as of the shires: in fact far more so the former than the latter.

However any shift to a more inclusive fan culture minus the excesses of xenophobia and brutal violence is only partial. In the summer of 2004 England's penalty shoot-out defeat to Portugal at the European Championships was marked by serious rioting in Thetford and Boston and other countryside towns, including vicious assaults on Portuguese employed locally as agricultural workers. Two years later when England were knocked out of the World Cup, also by Portugal, and in a penalty shoot-out too, trouble flared again although in Boston the local paper reported this as 'nothing like on the scale seen during Euro 2004' (Whitelam 2006: 5). It was more or less the same across England. And by the time of the next tournament England qualified for, World Cup 2010, and the team's dismal performance when they were knocked out by Germany in a 4–1 thrashing, there were no reports of any such incidents at all. Is a softer variety of English patriotism emerging, or maybe we're just getting used to losing? A mixture of the two probably, coupled with the shaping of a popular cosmopolitanism that while hardly resolutely antiracist nevertheless is imbued with some kind of acceptance, in football at least, of the benefits of multiculturalism. Just before World Cup 2010 opened journalist Gary Younge put this rather neatly: 'The cry of "British Jobs for British Workers" has been drowned out by chants for players whose names the fans can barely pronounce'. He characterises the narrative of modern English football as 'the story of mass migration', linking this explicitly to the dynamic growth of the appeal of supporting to this new generation of Black and Asian fans 'because English football looks more or less like the England they inhabit' (Younge 2010).

This increasing resemblance cannot be separated in any meaningful way from the pressures of globalisation. In his book *The Third Way* the sociologist Anthony Giddens quite correctly identifies the process of globalisation as a duality: 'Globalisation "pulls away" from the nation-state in the sense that some powers nations used to possess, including those that underlay Keynesian economic management, have been weakened. However, globalisation also "pushes down" – it creates new demands and also new possibilities for regenerating local identities' (Giddens 1998: 31). London's promotion as an Olympic host city has been carefully crafted out of the second element of this process. An identity which was paid proper homage to when the joy of securing 2012 was followed twenty-four hours later by the horror of domestic suicide bombers blowing themselves up on London's buses and tube trains with the most awful of consequences. Radical geographer Doreen Massey describes the identity that was projected both in the bid and the aftermath of these bombings that became known as 7/7: 'London was being celebrated as a world city. All of these claims – to specificity, to unity, to holding out a future for the world – were built around the rich ethnic and cultural diversity of London' (Massey 2007: 5).

If London as a world city symbolises globalisation, the capital's football clubs provide one of the most potent connections between the process and the popular. Spurs vs Man City, Tottenham's first home game of the 2010–2011 Premiership season. On the back of my match programme the club handily provides a flag depicting the player's nationality alongside each of their names. The Spurs squad lists a Brazilian, a Frenchman, a Russian, a Honduran, three Croatians, a Mexican, two Cameroonians and an Italian alongside the itinerant Scots, Welsh, Irish who make up the rest of this most apparently 'English' of squads. Jermaine Defoe, Aaron Lennon and Ledley King had made the England team at the previous summer's World Cup while Michael Dawson and Peter Crouch kept the bench warm. With professional cheeky chappy 'Arry Redknapp as the team's manager, Spurs like to pass themselves off as more authentically English than most, and more especially when compared with their Francophile neighbours in the red half of North London, Arsene Wenger's Arsenal. My programme however suggests otherwise. As for Manchester City, they list two Argentines, a Togan, two Brazilians, a Paraguayan, two Spaniards, a German, a Frenchman, two Ivorians, a Nigerian, a Slovak, an Ecuadorian, two Belgians, a Dutchman and a Serb in their squad. Their manager is Italian, the club owned by Sheikh Mansour, brother of the ruler of the super oil-rich state Abu Dhabi.

Any cultural significance of popular support for Olympian Team GB is affected not only by these intersections of globalisation and localisation but also by Britain's break-up. In 2010 a Tory Prime Minister took office to preside over a United Kingdom consisting of Scotland that in 2007 elected a Scottish Nationalist to be their First Minister; Wales ruled by a Labour Party-Plaid Cymru coalition; and Northern Ireland where the constitutional nationalists, the Social Democratic and Labour Party (SDLP) were out of government, replaced by the former Irish Republican Army (IRA) men, and women, in Sinn Fein, sharing ministerial responsibilities with the Democratic Unionist Party (DUP). Scotland, Wales, Northern Ireland, not breaking away just yet, but in each country the nationalist case is both credible and popular. Brownite-Blairist Labour kind of coexisted with the tensions, and at least in Scotland and Wales they were a significant part of the process of devolved government. Which is more than anyone would claim for the Tories. In the immediate aftermath of the 2010 General Election David Runciman summed up Labour's previous, and the Tories forthcoming, plight: 'Labour can only govern England from Scotland, and the Tories can only govern Scotland from England'. Adding the tellingly accurate prediction: 'Without the possibility of uniform swings across the different parts of the United Kingdom the British Political system is unsustainable' (Runciman 2010). There is considerable substance to this claim. In the 2010 General Election the Tory share of the vote in Scotland rose by just 0.9 per cent, the Conservatives held on to their single Scottish seat while Labour enjoyed a 2.5 per cent swing in its favour and gained two extra Scottish MPs.

In Wales the Tories achieved just twenty-six per cent of the vote, ten per cent below its share across Britain as a whole, and hold only eight Welsh constituencies out of forty. The shift in the past decade to the Scottish National Party (SNP) and Plaid Cymru has of course been nowhere near as decisive as the nationalists would wish yet in a way this hardly matters. Of much greater significance is the seemingly irreversible drift to ever-increasing devolution, each move in this direction stripping bare the unreal status of a 'United Kingdom'. London 2012 will be preceded a year earlier by the Scottish Parliament and Welsh Assembly elections of 2011. In these elections the SNP secured a landslide majority in the Scottish Parliament, posing serious questions over the medium-term durability of the

Union. Yet what is almost certain is that there will be no kind of Tory recovery. In Wales a March 2011 referendum vote gave considerably more powers to its assembly. It is always unwise to start basing political outcomes on psephological forecasting, yet throughout the ten years and more of new Labour crafted devolution settlements no mainstream party, including Cameron's Conservatives, has seriously suggested the reversal of the process. Indeed, Scottish Labour, Lib-Dems and even the Conservatives trade heavily on their Scottishness, distancing themselves whenever it suits them from their Westminster counterparts, and much the same can be said of the parties in Wales too. Football, Rugby Union, Cricket have gone with the grain of this trend, indeed has played an active part in it. Team GB in many ways seeks to defy it.

The critic Richard Seymour provides a sharply written portrayal of Cameronism which the majority in Scotland and Wales at least in the forthcoming period will define themselves as in opposition to:

> What is the meaning of David Cameron? He means war. (Seymour 2010: 88)

One doesn't have to subscribe to the extremities of this analysis to recognise a crucial difference between the social turmoil of the Thatcherite 1980s and the Cameroon 2010s. In the earlier era the opposition in Scotland and Wales to Thatcher was shaped by the demand for the necessity of devolved government as a shield to protect their nations from excesses inflicted upon them by Westminster. Today those institutions already exist, nobody is seeking to abolish them, and any future turmoil will not only contribute to the strengthening of their role but in all likelihood deepen the separation they represent.

And this separation isn't simply about emergent states on England's once unrecognisable borders but a difference in politics too. Scotland and Wales in essence represent a kind of settled social-democracy that is detested by the likes of Jeremy Clarkson. 'This stupid, Fair-trade, Brown-stained, Mandelson-skewed, equal-opportunities, multicultural, carbon-neutral, trendily left, regionally assembled, big-government, mosque-drenched, all-the-pigs-are-equal, property-is-theft hellhole' (Clarkson 2009). Clarkson and his ilk represent a middle-English populism that feeds off myth and misrepresentation mixed up with ill-informed prejudice and wild-eyed exaggeration for effect. A combination made for prime time TV and best-selling books. David Cameron meanwhile offers that olive branch to those fearful of the ugliest excesses of these Clarksonite opinions. Waving his England flag for a St George's Day photo call, complete with Morris dancers, he declares, 'We should be reclaiming the flag from the BNP and saying the flag belongs to the English people, all of them. We celebrate St Patrick's Day, we celebrate St David's Day, we celebrate St Andrew's Day, yes of course we should celebrate St George's Day'. Before adding a line to reassure any reporters suspicious of what this might mean for the Union: 'English and British, Scottish and British, Welsh and British. We need to say that loudly and proudly. This is something that everyone can feel included in. People come to our country and want to feel part of our country' (Cameron 2010).

Our country. England? Great Britain? What about that sizeable chunk of the Scottish and Welsh population for whom 'our country' is Scotland and Wales minus any GB add-on, or those in Northern Ireland whose ambition is to be united with another sovereign state entirely?

When England returned from World Cup 2002 a piece of graffiti was prominently sprayed on one of the Motorway bridges which fans drove under on their way to the post-tournament August friendly at Villa Park against Portugal. 'Keep the Flags Flying'. It was a sentiment which typifies the period 1996–2010, neatly book ended by the final year of John Major as Prime Minister and the first few months of the Con-Dem coalition. Scotland and Wales have had less of a problem distinguishing their Scottishness and Welshness from the Union via a Saltire or a Dragon hung from a car window. For the English though this was relatively new. The sport-led – first football but then increasingly via rugby and cricket too – English nationalism inseparable from a popular-political momentum too. Despite the best efforts of Blairite era modernisation (see Leonard 1997; Leonard and Griffith 2002) there was no sign of this being reversed by pressure from above, in fact quite the reverse. Gordon Brown had a go, perhaps in the belief that it would help blur his rather obvious Scottishness for the English electorate (see Brown and Alexander 2007). Again to little obvious impact on a growing popular identification with England, or at the very least a distinction that England is no longer the same as Britain. To date Cameron and his allies have shown less obvious interest in the cause. This is a government at ease with the Englishness of their Conservatism, resigned to a troublesome relationship with a social-democratic neighbour over the border to the north yet confident this won't be significant enough to destabilise the Westminster coalition. In Wales politics is for the moment more fluid, the Tories have more of a base, and the nationalist argument less popular support compared to Scotland. Nevertheless the pressure towards deepening the devolution settlement of 1997, rather than reversing it, is resolute. A pressure that is almost all from Scotland and Wales rather than from England. In this sense it is a process shaped by the margins rather than the centre. Yet as a result England is changing too. No longer representing itself as all things British, there is a growing sense instead of English self-awareness, of difference. And in any event should Scotland and Wales pull further away Britain will no longer have any semblance of unity and England will finally be forced to come to terms with itself.

Of course this shift isn't complete but plenty of commentators have begun to recognise its significance, usually when St George is being worn, flown or daubed on a kid's face in expectation of World Cup success. Brian Appleyard in *The Sunday Times* has described the reasons for its significance better than most: 'The English, the inventors of modernity and latterly the most traduced and repudiated of national identities, such occasions are naturally more poignant and more significant than they are for any other nation' (Appleyard 2006). A certain type of old leftist, and some new ones too, hold their hands up in horror every four years at the sight of so much flag waving. 'Football is, perhaps, one of the last recesses or perhaps hiding places of an ancient imperial mentality', suggests Jeremy Seabrook (Seabrook 2010). While Terry Eagleton dumps on football the singular responsibility of working-class false consciousness:

> If the Cameron government is bad news for those seeking radical change, the World Cup is even worse. It reminds us of what is still likely to hold back such change long after the coalition is dead. If every right-wing think tank came up with a scheme to distract the populace from political injustice and compensate them for lives of hard labour, the solution in each case would be the same: football. (Eagleton 2010)

Weighed down by prejudices taking the place of principles, such critics are dangerously out of touch. They purposefully ignore the ways in which sport is never simply a tool for reaction or distraction. Of course it can be one, either, or both, yet it also has the potential to be something else. And this is particularly true in a state where national identity is such an enduring site of contestation. In terms of Olympics 2012, to date this particular contest has barely been discussed. The cost versus benefits argument has been pitched almost exclusively around the new stadia and facilities, investment in supporting infrastructure, the influx of tourists, promotion of London and the legacy of increased participation in sport. The writers Simon Kuper and Stefan Szymanski have an interesting argument which suggests we should look elsewhere for the principal impact of hosting the Olympics. They describe the cultural impact of a World Cup:

> People gathered together in pubs and living-rooms, a whole country suddenly caring about the same event. A World Cup is the sort of common project that otherwise barely exists in modern societies. If playing in a tournament creates social cohesion, hosting one creates even more. The inhabitants of the host country – and certainly the men – come to feel more connected to everyone else around them. Moreover, hosting probably boosts the nation's self-esteem, and so makes people feel better about themselves. (Kuper and Szymanski 2009: 273)

All sorts of claims are made for the benefits of hosting London 2012. Yet in terms of economic impact there is not a scrap of evidence from any of the previous games that they have boosted local economies: in fact in most cases the reverse. As for tourism, an authoritative report by the European Tour Operators Association (ETOA 2006) has concluded that any suggested increase in visitors is entirely cancelled out by those choosing not to holiday in a host city precisely because it is hosting a major sporting event. And things didn't look better after the same organisation updated their report following the Beijing Olympics. It concluded: 'For London the news from Beijing is concerning. If London followed the pattern

of Beijing it could see a decline of over 2.5 million visitors at a loss of £1.5 billion'
(ETOA 2009). As for the Olympics promoting London, the city is already amongst
the world's most popular tourist destinations. Letting more people know of its
attractions for a holiday is surely the least of its current problems.

Will hosting the Olympics boost participation in sport? Investigative journalist
David Conn examined the evidence:

> No previous Olympic Games or other major tournament has ever led directly
> to an increase in people taking part in sport. If anything the opposite seems
> to happen. Sport England research has shown that ordinary mortals
> watching, from their sofas, 'models of perfection' performing on the elite
> stage can actually be put off trying to do more exercise. (Conn 2008a)

This latter point is a far more convincing narrative than the fantasy that British
kids, having watched Rebecca Adlington put herself through the punishing
physical schedule which elite swimming demands, will fill the pools of Great
Britain to bursting point the following day, seeking to emulate her. Finland is a
country with almost three times the level of participation in exercise of Great
Britain: 55% of Finns exercised three times a week in 2007 compared to 21% of
Britons. Yet Finland last hosted the Olympics in 1952, the most recent global
sporting event it hosted was the inaugural World Athletics Championship in 1983,
and at the Beijing Olympics the country finished a lowly 44th in the medals table.
The Finns put their position as the healthiest nation in Europe and the developed
world down to something quite different to hosting an Olympics. Mika Pykko,
executive director of the Finnis Centre for Health Promotion, 'We are a more
equal society. We have a high level of education and generally, educated people
exercise more. We still have a challenge but historically have always been close to
nature and so the culture of walking is still there' (Conn 2008b). The contribution
of Finland's solitary 2008 Olympic gold medal to the fundamental factors that
affect mass participation in sport is judged in this deep-seated analysis to be entirely
marginal. And Team GB's erstwhile closest rival in the Olympics medal table,
Australia, concluded in a post-Beijing report that the Finns are spot-on in terms
of this non-existent causal relationship between winning medals and participation.
Instead, motivation towards physical activity exists largely outside of the emulation
of the achievements of elite athletes.

> Evidence shows that participation in physical activity is dominated by non-
> organised sport and physical recreation. Moreover, this is an increasing
> trend: aerobics and fitness activities were the biggest growth areas for parti-
> cipation between 2001 and 2008. The growth of time-poor two-income
> families leaves little time for sport. As a consequence, exercise is 'purchased'
> and 'fitted into' a schedule. People are moving towards activities that are
> able to suit lifestyle and time constraints and thus provide the most flexible
> options. Seven out of the ten growth areas in this time span were activities

such as walking, running, cycling and aerobics/gym exercise—essentially activities that can be done on an individual basis. Apart from aerobics, in 2008, participation in the five most popular sports in Australia largely took the form of non-organised involvement. There is substantial growth in the number of people engaged in non-structured physical recreational activities—such as skateboarding, skiing, golf, cycling and more informally organised competitions such as mixed indoor cricket, netball and volleyball. (Australian Government Independent Sport Panel 2009: 92)

In a supremely ironic comment on the furore in Australia which greeted this report, journalist Kevin Mitchell wrote that the analysis was being accused of 'Putting the general health of the nation over medals' (Mitchell 2009).

At best the claims of the Olympics benefiting the economy, tourism and popular participation in sport remain unproven. Its principle benefit is what has become known as the 'feel-good factor', or as Kuper and Szymanski put it, 'The likely gain in happiness from the Olympics does mean the politicians are canny to give the people bread and circuses. In post-materialist countries like Britain, the maths of hosting and happiness probably stack up' (Kuper and Szymanski 2009: 274–275). Two years before Olympics 2012 this was also the almost universal conclusion following the World Cup in South Africa. A continent hitherto almost exclusively framed inside the three reference points of civil war, AIDS and famine successfully hosted the second biggest sporting event on earth. The stadia were magnificent, the crime wave non-existent, the organisation near faultless and the people passionate and proud. In his post-tournament report journalist Richard Williams concluded,

> To South Africans of all kinds, and to their guests, the tournament really was an occasion for the shared enjoyment of a simple pleasure. For the inhabitants alone there was the more complicated satisfaction of discovering that, after being dismissed as a potential basket-case when the glow of the Rainbow Nation began to fade, they are capable of holding one of the world's biggest public events. (Williams 2010)

This effect on the country's national self-worth and its global image has real social and economic value, if it lasts. Yet London will have to coexist with the momentum towards the break-up of Britain, a process already completed in terms of the major team and spectator sports of football, rugby union, and cricket. Eric Hobsbawm's much quoted dictum 'The imagined community of millions seems more real as a team of eleven named people' (Hobsbawm 1990: 143) has applied superbly to England and St George for the past decade or so. It remains to be seen whether three and a bit weeks of August 2012 can turn a breaking-up into a making-up much beyond the raucous applause each time Team GB podiums.

References

Anderson, B. (1991) *Imagined Communities: Reflections on the Origin and Spread of Nationalism*, London: Verso.

Appleyard, B. (2006) 'It's not about football, it's bigger than that', *The Sunday Times*, 2 July.

Aughey, A. (2001) *Nationalism, Devolution and the Challenge to the United Kingdom State*, London: Pluto.

Australian Government Independent Sport Panel (2009), *The Future of Sport in Australia*.

Back, L., Crabbe, T. and Solomos, J. (2001) *The Changing Face of Football: Racism, Identity and Multiculture in the Global Game*, Oxford: Berg.

Barnett, A. (1997) *This Time, Our Constitutional Revolution*, London: Vintage.

Brown, G. and Alexander, D. (2007) *Stronger Together*, London: Fabian Society.

Cameron, D. (2010) 'David Cameron wants English to reclaim St George's Cross from BNP', *Daily Telegraph*, 24 April.

Clarkson, J. (2009) 'Get me a rope before Mandelson wipes us all out', *The Times*, 8 November.

Conn, D. (2008a) 'Games promise to generate only ripples when Britain needs to splash out', *The Guardian*, 23 July.

Conn, D. (2008b) 'Building a fit nation is no walk in the park and hosting the Olympics will not do it', *The Guardian*, 30 July.

Courtaud, G. (2004) *The Pocket Book of Patriotism*, Halstead: Halstead Books.

Eagleton. T (2010), 'Signed to solidarity FC', *The Guardian*, 16 June.

European Tour Operators Association (2006) *Olympic Report*.

European Tour Operators Association (2009) *Olympics is a Tourism Problem*.

Giddens, A. (1998) *The Third Way*, Cambridge: Polity Press.

Hobsbawm, E. (1990), *Nations and Nationalism Since 1780*, Cambridge: Cambridge University Press.

Kuper, S. and Szymanski, S. (2009) *Why England Lose*, London: Harper Collins.

Leonard, M. (1997) *Britain: Renewing Our Identity*, London: Demos.

Leonard. M. and Griffith, P. (eds) (2002) *Reclaiming Britishness*, London: Foreign Policy Centre.

Marqusee, M. (2010) 'Come on you Ghana, Brazil, Spain, Mexico, Korea, Italy. . .', *The Guardian*, 8 June.

Massey, M. (2007) *World City*, Cambridge: Polity.

McWhirter, I. (1998) 'The bulldogs that didn't bark . . . or whatever happened to England?', *Renewal* 4.

Mitchell, K. (2009) 'Australians fume as medal hopes fade', *Observer*, 22 November.

Newman, R. (1998), 'Nothing to play for', in M. Mora y Araujo and S. Kuper (eds) *Perfect Pitch: Men and Women*, London: Headline.

Runciman, D. (2010) 'Is this the end of the UK', *London Review of Books*, 27 May.

Seabrook, J. (2010) 'In defeat, there is a sense of thwarted entitlement', *The Guardian*, 29 June.

Seymour, R. (2010) *The Meaning of David Cameron*, Winchester: Zero Books.

Whitelam, P. (2006) '23 Fans arrested after World Cup exit', *Lincolnshire Echo*, 3 July.

Williams, R. (2010) 'The real legacy', *The Guardian*, 13 July.

Younge, G. (2010) 'How I finally learned to cheer for England', *New Statesman*, 7 June.

15

THE VIEW FROM THE PRESSBOX

Rose-tinted spectacle?

Rob Steen

Many academics believe, in terms of stories covered and published, that sports-writers are compliant and conservative, too frequently guilty of peddling 'soft' news at the expense of so-called investigative journalism (in itself something of a misplaced accusation: every journalist I have ever met prides him/herself on getting to the heart, i.e. truth, of every story, so long as space permits). Others, such as Raymond Boyle and Richard Haynes, whose excellent analyses of sports journalism have been greatly enhanced by interviews with leading practitioners such as Eamonn Dunphy and Richard Williams (Boyle and Haynes 2009), recognise the difficulties and compromises that face their subjects. It is not my intention, as a lecturer in sports journalism and still-practising sportswriter, to get into a slanging match. Nor does this chapter purport to be a potted history of Olympic reporting. Rather, it examines the context in which recent and contemporary sport spectacles such as the Olympics are represented by print journalists, and the professional pressures in the world of sport reporting that affect the pitch and tone of the journalistic product. The primary aim is to offer an insight into the changing nature of sports journalism, by considering how the modern press views the Olympics, how complex reporting the Games can be, and how partisan – in terms of both nationalism and sport itself – the English press is likely to be in 2012.

In addition to assessing the degree to which sport consumes newsprint in the 21st Century, I have tried to accomplish this in three specific ways, all drawing on my own experiences as a sports journalist for newspapers, magazines and websites in Britain, Australia, India and South Africa over the past 25 years: by examining international reactions to the death of a luger during the 2010 Vancouver Winter Olympics; by discussing with the investigative sports journalist Steve Downes both the pros and cons of the Olympics and the motivations, principles, ethics and other factors inherent in covering athletics in an age when the reporter, thanks to the deep shadow cast by performance-enhancing drugs, has been unable to trust the evidence of his eyes; and by trying, with the help of another experienced Olympic journalist, Matthew Engel, to anticipate how the home press will report the 2012 Games. Will they be cheerleading patriots or critical observers?

Reporting sport: the rise and spread of the back pages

The vast majority of newspaper sports coverage can be divided into three categories: The Match (previewing, reporting and analysis); The Players (stars, newcomers, contracts, transfers and injuries); and The Bosses (management, coaching, administration and regulation). There is a wide array of sporting news, feature and comment material available in England, where a uniquely broad degree of competition has long reigned in a national newspaper market. This market currently comprises nine daily UK publications (plus the *Financial Times*, which targets the international business community) and 11 Sunday titles serving three distinct audiences – tabloid/popular, midmarket and broadsheet – though shrinking page formats mean that the last of these is more accurately, if inadequately, referred to as 'upmarket', 'serious' or 'heavy'. Over the past two decades, these papers, in common with all others, have undergone seismic changes while suffering waning sales.

The latest source of disquiet has been the advent of the Internet. Where once print newspapers were the sole source of news, they are now some way back in a lengthening queue. By February 2010, average daily and Sunday circulations for those nine UK publications had both dipped below 10 million – though a further 20% of the UK population read regional and local titles exclusively, with regional morning sales up by more than 60% on a decade earlier (The Newspaper Society 2009); in 1951, Sunday sales were 30.59m (Hennessey 2007); in 1989, the year the last national paper was published in Fleet Street, daily sales were 15.4m, Sundays 17.9m (Competition Commission Report 2000). The most alarming year-on-year declines from 2009–10 were endured by the 'heavies': the *Daily Telegraph* (-9.8%), *The Independent* (-11%), *The Guardian* (-16%), and *The Times* (-16.9%) (Ponsford 2010). Not just coincidentally, all the London newspapers in Canary Wharf, King's Cross and Wapping offered their product free online during that period. In October 2009, moreover, Alexander Lebed, the Russian oligarch who had just bought the London *Evening Standard*, announced that the 180-year-old paper would become a freesheet, the first major English newspaper to follow the well-established lead of so many struggling local and regional titles. The *Standard*'s daily print run promptly soared from 250,000 to 600,000, delighting advertisers but, in some eyes, diminishing its standing.

Further marginalised by the efficiency of agents and public relations departments, editors are increasingly reliant on comment and analysis rather than fresh revelations. Sport may be perceived as frivolous by some, but it rouses the passions of millions who read the rear section of a newspaper and rarely turn to the front, so this reliance is a greater challenge for sport coverage than for any other specialist area of 21st century newsprint.

Such is the depth of interest in sport, and so magnetised are advertisers, that proprietors have permitted their editors an increasing amount of space, leading to discrete sports sections. Film, music, property, personal finance and food all have their own regular or occasional newspaper/magazine/section in British papers, but few of those interests command a weekly outlet, much less the daily ones published by *The Guardian* and *Daily Telegraph*, or, in other countries, command the entire focus as do daily sports papers such as *L'Equipe* (France), *Corriere dello Sport* (Italy) and *AS* and *Marca* (both Spain). Many titles, national and local, also produce colourful pocket guides for major events such as Wimbledon, The Ashes, a World Cup or an Olympics. This is all a far cry from when I began in the profession. Then, in the1980s, the sports desk was still dismissed, sneeringly, by other members of staff as what US sport broadcaster Howard Cosell called 'the toy department of human life', and English broadsheets confined sport to as few as three pages, one of which was invariably dominated by racecards.

At the same time, the impact of technology on the news cycle has worked with rising ferocity against papers. First came television, with its bulging portfolio of live broadcasts, specialist sports channels and rolling news programmes; then came the Internet. On the one hand, newspaper correspondents are, in theory at least, now better and more quickly informed, and at a fraction of the cost of dispatching them to the scene (an increasingly popular option, notably amid the savage staff cuts of the 2008–10 recession). However, the immediacy of it all means that the printed renditions of their reports are old news before they even hit the street. Hence the rise in columns and comment.

One positive by-product of this, though, is that the written press are more inclined than ever to cover the stories behind the action. Editors want something more, something different. Nor, unlike their counterparts in television, are they so beholden to sponsors and governing bodies that even the mildest criticism is almost invariably repressed. That this contextualisation is as likely to be conveyed by an armchair columnist as by a reporter on the spot, who may be compromised by a fear of losing accreditation and access, is irrelevant. Distance can be a boon. In the pressbox, the windows can desensitise, acting as a barrier to complete immersion, whereas the atmosphere created on the ground by the crowd and the sense of occasion may lead to the suspension, or outright surrender, of one's critical faculties. To conclude that all sports reporters are negligent of their wider responsibilities, and increasingly so in a multi-media age, would, nevertheless, be the most unjust of inferences.

Yet despite the increasing amount of physical space devoted to it, it could be argued that print coverage of sport has in fact narrowed its focus. On April 1, 2010, 23 pages out of 128 in *The Times* were devoted to athletic endeavour. Subtract 62 of those 128 pages – approximately 39 for adverts, pullouts spanning 18 pages and five for TV, radio and other listings – and sport's share (minus a page's worth of adverts) comprises a full one-third of the remainder (*The Times* 2010). Of the editorial pages, half were consumed by association football, the vast bulk filled by news stories and comment, with Wayne Rooney's latest injury attracting three pieces on its own (there were two more on the news pages). There was the inevitable rash of quotes from managers and players, every last one extracted from a previously-published story, a press conference or official statement. Amid all the opinion and conjecture lay just two match reports.

Pages 106–117 were divided between 10 further sports (while mentioning a few others in brief). The apparent pecking-order ran as follows: rugby union and league, cricket, swimming, boxing, rowing, tennis, baseball, motor racing and, bringing up the rear, horse racing. The order and selection was dictated partly by impending televised events (the Boat Race, the new baseball season, the Australian Grand Prix, the announcement of England's Twenty20 cricket squad, David Haye's first defence of his WBA world heavyweight boxing crown) and newsworthy developments (the prospect of Britain's first black representative swimmer, a row over pay differentials for the England rugby union tour of Australia, and the surreal sight of a county cricket season opening in Abu Dhabi with a floodlit match and an experimental pink ball). In all, the 22 pages contained just three match reports of any hue. Even if we include the five articles that supplemented the previous day's main live attraction, the Champions League match between Arsenal and Barcelona, that still leaves an awful lot of space to fill.

The tyranny of football was even more apparent in the midmarket *Daily Mail* and *The Sun*, the leading tabloid and bestselling daily. Of the former's 120 pages on that same April day, 80 were taken up by adverts, classifieds, listings and the Femail section; of the remainder, no less than 50% covered sport; 60% of those pages focused on football (*Daily Mail* 2010). Of the 112 pages in *The Sun* – admittedly, a paper more concerned with visual impact – approximately 45 concentrated on news or news-related features of some description, of which one-third, 15, revolved around sport. Of those, just four were not about football (and the Rooney story won two further pages at the front of the paper) (*The Sun* 2010).

Such dominance is not uncommon. A survey financed by the Danish Institute for Sports Studies and the world communication conference on sport and society, Play the Game, examined 10,000 articles about sport published in 37 newspapers in the first six months of 2005 (India, Pakistan and Malaysia were all mysteriously overlooked). The commonalities, setting aside sports of specific national interest such as baseball, were considerable. In Britain, 53.8% of the articles monitored were about football, slightly higher than the ratio in continental Europe (50.9%); in both cases, the next most popular sport (golf and cycling respectively) accounted for less than 10%, emphasising both the soccer stranglehold and the competition among the also-rans (Jorgensen 2005).

The survey's other conclusions were even more illuminating. More than half the articles monitored (58%) dealt with current events, by way of match reports, previews and results. Roughly one in 20 articles covered the economics of sport, and just one in 30 the political aspects. In fact, the proportion of stories about drugs (1.5% on average) had *declined* since the previous such survey. More predictably, men were the focus in 86% of the articles, 95% of which also happened to be written by them. 'The sports press', attested Soren Schultz Jorgensen, 'has great difficulties reporting anything that takes place outside the angle of television cameras and after the stadium spotlights have been turned off' (Jorgensen 2005: 1).

Sadly, for all that the recent tidal wave of money, allied to the impact of the recession, has bred a liberal supply of stories about political chicanery, corruption, club ownership, liquidations and broadcasting deals, and for all that they have so many pages to fill, there is little appetite among editors for prolonged investigations, preferring as they do the dependable: the daily dramas of victory and defeat, heroes and villains, underdogs and outsiders; of rebirths and small deaths, rebellion and innovation, right and wrong. Alfred Hitchcock enjoyed 'indulging in the occupation of raising goose flesh' (Muir 2010); sportswriters, as storytellers, are similarly inclined. Even so, in 2009, newsprint aplenty was expended on the moralities and ethics surrounding three long-running sagas: Caster Semenya's sexuality, Nelson Piquet Jr's intentional crash in a Grand Prix, and a falsified injury in a European rugby union match (inevitably dubbed 'Bloodgate'). Only the last of these, instructively, was of direct concern to a British audience, demonstrating the willingness of editors to look beyond their own shores. In the recent past, moreover, there has been extensive and forthright coverage of racism, cheating and financial misdeeds, coverage that would have been considerably scaled back, for space reasons, two decades earlier.

More could be done, much more, but the constraints undermining lengthy investigations can dim enthusiasm and purpose. Such stories demand time and money, and it may be many months, even years, before the fruits can be published. Having found the *Daily Mail* increasingly reluctant to accommodate him, English sports journalism's most fearless agitator, Andrew Jennings, a freelance, had to create his own website, transparencyinsport.com, to inform the world of the latest rum doings at the IOC and FIFA, and seldom receives any financial reward (Steen 2007). In addition, accreditation for major events is becoming a problem: bite the hand that feeds and privileges may be withdrawn. Furthermore, whereas access to players and officials in England was straightforward 20 years ago, the mounting contributions from broadcasters has fuelled an invasion of agents, managers and press officers, resulting in PR invective and an increasingly impenetrable wall of silence. When interviews are granted, they are increasingly done for nakedly promotional reasons, tidily summarised at the bottom of the copy – 'Wayne Gascoigne was speaking at a PermaWave hair gel convention. For more details see www.PermaWave/Gascoigne.com'.

Jennings, a news reporter for nearly 50 years, has also made TV documentaries for the BBC's Panorama and written scathing books about the IOC and FIFA. For him, hope lies with television documentaries and, especially, the Internet:

> Too many in my generation of oldies have passed on the message that it is more important to be liked by the editor and the readers/viewers/fans don't matter. It's going to be the reverse. The kids will jump sites that are lazy and not disclosing anything – the advertisers will see the hits figures and career death will follow fast for the lazy editor and the uninspired reporter who isn't

giving the readers what they want. A few well-crafted blogs could kill most current sports sections in the new world. The advertisers will follow the fans' wishes. It could happen very fast. (Steen 2007: quoted p. 64)

In 2010, four years after Jennings expressed those sentiments, and notwithstanding his predicted expansion of the global blogging community and the rising quality of TV documentaries such as ESPN's '30 for 30' series, there still seemed a strong interest in trusting those who are already respected for their knowledge and contacts, such as Henry Winter of the *Daily Telegraph* and Patrick Barclay of *The Times*. With its endless conveyor belt of free material, however, the Internet has depleted the print journalist's market value. Generating web revenue remained the newspapers' biggest concern, as evinced by Rupert Murdoch's decision to introduce a subscription service for The Times Online, emulating the *Financial Times* and the *Wall Street Journal*, a move that initially saw the number of hits, or page impressions, plunge. It should be noted that one of the most reverberant sports stories of the 21st Century, the performance-enhancing drugs ring run by San Francisco's Bay Area Laboratory Co-operative (BALCO), emerged from a small newspaper, the *San Mateo Journal*. The web has been considerably less successful in breaking sports stories than it has been in politics and showbusiness, where calculated leaks and brazen self-promotion abound.

Indeed, Boyle argues that the likes of the *Guardian*, *Daily Telegraph*, *The Scotsman* and *The Times* have developed a far more enterprising and multi-faceted approach, and quotes Jorgensen on this:

> These are newspapers that 10 years ago would look down on sport. Today they shape the market through their focus on sport. To me it is a clear sign that the market of sports journalism is going through a phase of differentiation. The classic tabloid newspapers will probably continue their one-sided focus on stars, heroes, successes and failures. But the younger generations of readers and journalists are in the process of developing a new form of sports journalism in the so-called serious end of the newspaper market. (Jorgensen 2005, quoted in Boyle 2009: 6)

Declining sales and budgets, intimidating competition from other media, and a football-centric, often blinkered outlook. Such, then, was the not entirely promising backdrop for the English sportswriter covering the build-up to London 2012.

The national interest and the death of Nodar Kumaritashvili

> There are always those in the host country who believe the Olympic Games are about their own national aggrandisement. From the whoo-whooing crowds of Los Angeles and Atlanta to the Own the Podium programme at the Vancouver Winter Olympics this year, this strikes me as graceless

behaviour in a host. Sure, the host country will win a fair collection of medals and jolly good luck to them all, but that's not what the Games are *for*. Great hosts . . . celebrate the guests, not themselves; I hope London can live up to this not terribly lofty ideal. (Barnes 2010)

Christopher Hitchens, one of journalism's most wilfully provocative polemicists, wrote an article for *Newsweek* on the eve of the 2010 Winter Olympics entitled 'Fool's Gold: How the Olympics and other international competitions breed conflict and bring out the worst in human nature' (Hitchens 2010). Responding to complaints from Ron Rossi, executive director of the US luge team in Vancouver, about the hosts' 'lack of sportsmanship' in trying to extract as much home advantage as possible, Hitchens fulminated: 'On the contrary, Mr. Rossi, what we are seeing is the very essence of sportsmanship. Whether it's the exacerbation of national rivalries that you want – as in Africa this year – or the exhibition of the most depressing traits of the human personality (guns in locker rooms, golf clubs wielded in the home, dogs maimed and tortured at stars' homes to make them fight, dope and steroids everywhere), you need only look to the wide world of sports for the most rank and vivid examples' (Hitchens 2010).

However tempting it is to man the ramparts in defence of international sport – the virtues of which include an uncommon knack for bringing together people from vastly different backgrounds in pursuit of a common and predominantly healthy passion, often generating a joy that transcends the result – this is not the place. Besides, Hitchens's one-eyed broadside was far from unjustified. That he is not a sportswriter, however, means he is more able to opine with impunity. Outsiders may have reason to believe that those paid to report on the competitive arts feel obliged – by their free admission, by their access to the corridors of power and celebrity, by their inherent determination to legitimise themselves by continually reinforcing the importance and credibility of what they are writing about, to uphold the magical elements that make sporting spectatorship such an addiction – in short, to present the Games in the best light possible. As Paul Kimmage of the *Sunday Times* pithily put it, the daily correspondents run the risk of 'spitting in the soup' (Kimmage, 2007). Many would no doubt ascribe a see-no-evil, hear-no-evil approach to all sportswriters, but it is my experience that the blinkered are in decline. The sins have become too palpable to ignore, the reasons to expose them ever more pressing.

In February 2010, Nodar Kumaritashvili, a Georgian luger, died on a training run at the Vancouver Winter Olympics. It did not help that he had been denied an adequate amount of practice by Canada's determination, as the unabashed slogan stated, to 'Own the Podium', the name given to a five-year, $120m technical program aimed at ensuring the host nation topped the medals table, more than half the cost of which was contributed by Canadian taxpayers (Starkman, 2009). Everything was done to ensure that home competitors received every possible advantage. If it was often pointed out that this was firmly within the rules, what that says about those rules is anything but flattering.

Prior to that tragic practice, Kumaritashvili had confessed to his father that the course 'terrified' him. He was by no means alone, nor remotely unjustified. Five teams dropped out following crashes, concussions and a cervical spine injury. Australia's Hannah Campbell-Pegg nearly lost control. 'To what extent are we just little lemmings that they just throw down a track and we're crash-test dummies?' she wondered. 'I mean, this is our lives' (Huffington Post 2010).

There had been a hint of things to come during the build-up to the world speed skating championships in March 2009 when various non-Canada teams were prevented from accessing the ice for pre-event practice. Along with his charges, Kevin Crockett, a former Canadian Olympic medallist who coached the Chinese team, was escorted from the Richmond Oval, one of the sites for the 2010 Olympics. Bob de Jong, Holland's Olympic champion, was admitted only after being kept out for a day. The German team claimed to have been denied access altogether. 'We were there for three days and the only thing I could do was peek through the windows to look at the venue', their coach Bart Schouten told Gerard den Elt of *AD Sportwereld*. 'The Canadians are acting like this. . .is a fort that's being intruded upon,' claimed the furious Crockett. 'There's no fair play here, there's nothing like that' (Starkman 2009).

To attribute such outpourings exclusively to nationalism would be facile. Rick Broadbent, writing in *The Times*, asked the most salient question in the aftermath of Kumaritashvili's fatal run: 'Why, if the IOC was in "deep mourning", as Jacques Rogge, the body's president said, was there not even a day of mourning after the nightmare before?' (Broadbent 2010). Other awkward questions remained unanswered, such as: 'If the track was safe, then why did the organizers [after the deadly accident] move the start 580 feet lower down and add padding to the pillars at turn 16?' (Broadbent 2010). The trenchant American author and columnist Dave Zirin also blamed the IOC, 'that sewing circle of monarchists, extortionists, and absolved fascists [which] likes to hide behind the pretense of nobility' (Zirin 2010).

> On the IOC's website, there is a quiz: 'The Ultimate goal of Olympism is to a) Organize the Olympic Games, b) encourage new world records, c) build a peaceful and better world through sport.' It's perfectly understandable if you needed three tries to answer that correctly. The answer is, of course, c— although that would certainly be news to the family of Nodar Kumaritashvili. What trumps these grand 'ethics' is the reality of what makes the IOC go 'round: television and corporate dollars. And if corporations can't come up with the money, then cities and host countries pay through the nose. (Zirin 2010)

Kumaritashvili's death highlighted how the Olympics struggles to cope with anything that threatens this purported celebration of human possibility. The ensuing criticism, moreover, contradicts the notion that the view from the press box of all things Olympian is strictly rose-tinted. Angered by the rampant commercialism and influx of drugs, spurred on by the likes of Jennings and Ian Wooldridge – both, somewhat ironically, employed by the *Daily Mail*, hardly the first newspaper one might cite as a torch-bearer for progressive thought and anti-capitalistic campaigns – journalists have increasingly depicted the Olympic movement with a mixture of celebration (at its magnitude and durability) and scepticism.

In 2009, Australia's Labour government announced, to global astonishment, that it would be cutting its Olympic funding. An infuriated John Coates, president of the Australian Olympic Committee and impending member of the IOC's executive board, protested that, since Australia had declined to sixth in the medals table in Beijing (down to 46 golds, silvers and bronzes from 58 in Sydney 2000), the nation might even fall behind Italy come 2012 without an *additional* $100m in taxpayer funding. In the *Sydney Morning Herald*, Richard Hinds took careful aim at Coates in particular and Olympism in general:

> We are told Olympic success confirms our status as a nation of great athletes. But, if it is really our facilities, coaches, medics, sports scientists – the ones now being bought by other nations – and lavish grants that make the difference, are we not merely operating one of the world's great sports factories?
>
> Which is not to say there should be no funding for Olympic sports. Indeed, those who need it most are those apparently endangered most by the Federal Government review – the archers and table tennis players, taekwondo-ists and others who don't attract the same endorsements or prizemoney as swimmers, track and field stars, basketballers and other professionals.
>
> But it is not a bad thing to ask what we are getting in return. Beyond, that is, the rather pathetic bragging rights claimed by Olympic officials and politicians when our stack of expensive medals is bigger than yours. (Hinds 2010: 2)

Wooldridge was an arch-proponent of the Olympic movement for more than three decades, yet he repeatedly expressed his contempt for Juan Antonio Samaranch, the former IOC president, lambasting 'his self-styled Excellency's exploitation of the Games as his personal court, a shadowy chamber of furtive sycophants, dubious grace and dodgy favours' (Powell 2007). On the eve of his final Olympics, the Atlanta Games of 1996, Wooldridge took enormous pride in being the 9,811[th] runner in the Olympic Torch relay chain, gleaning 'a valuable insight into the sheer joy and enthusiasm that the Games can bring to a community', yet remained unrepentant: 'I have written as cynically as anyone about the commercialism and devious politicking of the Olympic movement in recent years and do not retract a word of it' (Wooldridge 2007: 287).

In December 2009, I conducted a straw poll among a group of more than 100 first-year undergraduates at the University of Brighton, the majority of them students on the sports journalism course. Given the prevailing economic climate, did they think the Olympic Games were worth the expense? A show of hands revealed a tiny minority of approval. The message, from both this and the lengthy and passionate debate that followed, was plain: how, in the midst of a recession, can one defend spending £9bn of taxpayers' money on staging something as relatively inessential as a sporting event? Especially a sporting event whose centrepiece is track and field athletics, over which performance-enhancing drugs cast such a deep and vast shadow. Not that the fringe attractions were held up as paragons of virtue, either.

War games or Olympic Games?

Perspective is all. As Steven Downes points out somewhat defensively, that £9bn outlay is comparable to the annual capital budget for the Ministry of Defence. 'We spend that much every year,' he reasons with barely-disguised contempt, 'on warships, fighter planes and tanks' (Downes 2009). A former colleague at the *London Daily News* and the *Sunday Times*, Downes is an author and experienced athletics correspondent who has been watching the Olympics since 1964 and reporting them since 1984, and won a Royal Television Society award for his investigation into the death of Cliff Temple, the *Sunday Times* athletics correspondent. He is not, he insists, a 'fan with a typewriter', the demeaning epithet so often hurled at sports journalists. 'I don't cover athletics because I love it. I like the process and the job, the competitive process. Woodward and Bernstein always fascinated me. Growing up, I wanted to be a lawyer, then decided you could have more impact as a journalist. It was a more sexy, more relaxed, more attainable target' (Downes 2009). The attraction of athletics during the so-called doping era was nothing if not magnetic. In 1996, Downes and Duncan Mackay, athletics correspondent for *The Guardian* and *The Observer*, poured their scarring experiences and withering observations into a book, *Running Scared*, their focus trained unremittingly on drugs, fixed races and other forms of administrative corruption. To paraphrase Wiltshire's finest rock band XTC, Downes is not one to overlook the ugly underneath.

Two days after that anti-Olympian student poll, I related my class story to him. His riposte was as swift as it was certain, and nothing if not protective. 'Ask them the same question AFTER the Games', he insisted. 'Look at the change in [BBC and *Evening Standard* reporter] Andrew Gilligan's attitude during the Beijing Games. He was anti before. Maybe I'm an old romantic, but there's always been a magical quality to me' (Downes 2009).

Millions still share that view. Yet many who once felt that gripping sense of wonder – including this writer, whose memories of rising with the larks to watch the 1968 Games as a 10-year-old remain vivid and joyous, in good part because the Tommie Smith-John Carlos Black Power salute alerted him to the Gordian knot that binds sport to politics – have grown increasingly disenchanted: by the invasion of the alleged last bastion of amateurism by professionals, by the overt nationalism such occasions encourage, but mostly by performance-enhancing drugs. While Usain Bolt was mocking the world's major sprint records in Beijing, wonder, for many, took a distant second place to incredulity.

A conversation with the British sprinter Donovan Reid, a 100 metres finalist at the 1984 Los Angeles Games, reinforced Downes' belief that Bolt, by dint of his unusual physical stature, deserves the benefit of the doubt, if only for now: 'Donovan said he was a freak. We've never had a 6ft 5in sprinter like that. Biomechanics may explain it' (Downes 2009). As it did with Ed Moses, who dominated the 400 metres hurdles from the late 1970s to mid-1980s, winning 122 successive finals in addition to two Olympic golds; the American, to widespread astonishment, took just 13 strides between hurdles, sometimes as few as 12. The Bolt question is, as Downes admits, 'a public credibility test'. Ultimately, he says, 'all you can do is to rely on the evidence you have'. The philosophy is straightforward: 'You lay out the facts and let the reader decide' (Downes 2009).

That doesn't mean Downes is convinced. 'Bolt partied all night after breaking his own world 100 metres record at the 2009 World Championships in Berlin, yet he broke the 200 metres record four days later. Every fibre of me asked the question [was he clean?]. I have a hefty degree of cynicism. But I'm prepared to give him the benefit of the doubt until I find something that indicates comprehensively otherwise' (Downes 2009).

Downes cites Marion Jones, an Olympic sprint champion in 2000 who persistently denied ingesting drugs before eventually confessing her guilt in 2007, as an example of an athlete whose feats did not warrant such latitude. 'I started writing anti-Marion Jones pieces in 1998 and 1999. She had a record. She missed a drugs test at 14 or 15 and, as a consequence, missed the Games. The US Olympic Committee had a quiet word with her and her mother and then she went to college. She wasn't suspended of course. She just didn't compete' (Downes 2009).

Then there was Florence Griffith-Joyner, 'FloJo' to all and sundry. A multi-Olympic gold medallist, she died in mysterious circumstances in 1998, aged just 38, a decade after setting astounding world records in the 100 metres and 200 metres at the Seoul Games. Rivals had long accused her of using steroids and growth hormones; it was the latter, many suggested with reference to an equivocal post-mortem report, that killed her. 'That was the first time I'd seen anyone win an Olympic sprint title by a distance and still be greeted by 100,000 silent voices, hushed in disbelief', recollects Downes. 'It was the same week that Ben Johnson was disqualified from the men's 100 metres final. This was a woman who, two or three years earlier, had been an ordinary international athlete. If you're passionate about your job, this was grist to your mill' (Downes 2009). Downes, it should be noted, is among those who believe that Johnson, a Canadian, was sacrificed in order to protect Carl Lewis, an American hero.

Does Downes feel protective towards athletes? 'God, no! Although, by exposing wrongdoing, you *are* protecting the sport' (Downes 2009). Not unreasonably, he attributes the comparative lack of sustained and probing investigative reporting on the sports pages to eroding budgets rather than indolence or protectiveness. However, this does not mean that there is no media whitewashing, especially when it comes to protecting the national interest. One pertinent case in point was that of Michelle de Bruin (nee Smith), the Irish swimmer who emerged from relative obscurity to take three gold medals at the 1996 Olympics but was banned from competition for four years in 1998 after she was found to have manipulated a drug test by spiking her urine sample with alcohol. 'RTE [the Irish broadcaster] allegedly passed memos to staff saying nobody should mention the 'd-word', recalls Downes with due care:

> It took Janet Evans, the 1992 Olympic 400 metres freestyle champion, to say something at a press conference. The BBC's Hamilton Bland once [prefaced] an interview with Michelle by saying, 'We'll dismiss these allegations. . .'. Yet her husband, the discus thrower Erik de Bruin, was done for steroids, and coached her even though he couldn't swim. (Downes 2009)

Patriots or critics?

The acid test, for English sportswriters, will be London 2012. Will they be flag-waving zealots and arch-xenophobes, oblivious to all but local Olympians? Will their horizons be foreshortened and narrowed by a patriotic obligation to present the competitors, the spectators, the organisers and hence the nation itself in the most virtuous light? This may be true of many, some of them specifically instructed by editors and proprietors to peer only through the prism of nationalism, to ferment and foment the feelgood factor. Under such circumstances, can observations ever be strictly dispassionate, criticism wholly unfettered? Perhaps, perhaps not. Coverage of the funding and construction problems that have dogged preparations for London 2012 has certainly been critical, sometimes to the point of ridicule, though the dampeners have tended to be comparatively disinterested news reporters more than sportswriters.

The English press has a proud record of disobedience. In the Boer War, noted Ben MacIntyre, 'journalism was still, in many ways, an arm of the Armed Forces, happy to suspend moral judgement in the cause of empire' (MacIntyre 2010), leading to the failure to report on the British concentration camps. Yet that same conflict saw Edgar Wallace, in 1902, reveal the peace agreement to *Daily Mail* readers before it had been signed, expressly against the wishes of Lord Kitchener. A century later, the sending of troops to Afghanistan and Iraq drew much criticism. In modern times, such irreverent critical stances have been exhibited as much when tackling sportspeople as politicians (witness headlines such as 'In the name of Allah go' and 'Swedes 2 Turnips 1', let alone the more extensive verbal beatings meted out to so many national managers, captains, teams and governing bodies ever since the tabloid circulation war erupted in the 1980s). 'Alongside the acts of moral and intellectual cowardice, the laziness of thought and action,' John Simpson, the BBC World Affairs editor, has claimed, characterising the British journalist, 'there are also clear signs from time to time of a stubborn determination to tell people honestly and openly what is going on' (Simpson 2010). As yet, there has been no betrayal of that small tradition, or at least no lasting one. Yes, press releases are too often reprinted word-for-word by overworked sports desks, but those with a lofty pulpit, notably the opinion-formers of the national press, seldom tug their collective forelock to the official spoutings of the IOC and FIFA, let alone the more localised likes of the Football Association, the Rugby Football Union and the England and Wales Cricket Board. The sternest examination, though, is yet to come.

'Most sportswriters will be flag-wavers,' forecasts Matthew Engel, the well-travelled *Financial Times* columnist, a veteran of four Olympics as well as dozens of major sporting events hosted in Britain, from the Commonwealth Games to cricket World Cups:

> In the end, it's in their DNA. Many of the most thoughtful – Simon Barnes (*The Times*), Pat Collins (*Mail on Sunday*), Ian Chadband (*Sunday Telegraph*) – I know are very enthusiastic. Martin Samuel (*Daily Mail*) may be an exception. But British papers are big enough to encompass diverse views, if not always on the sports pages. There are plenty of Olymposceptics – Simon Jenkins, Camilla Cavendish, who has written very well on this in *The Times*. Not many will actually be accredited, though.
>
> Sportswriters in the end like sport and many will see this as some kind of pinnacle, for the nation and their own career. Clearly, it would be hard to cover the Olympics if all you wanted to do was say it's crap day after day. You have to be in tune with the mood of your readers to an extent. I expect I'll do what I did in Beijing: point out all the flaws beforehand then set out to enjoy the sport. Criticism is never unfettered, but there will be a mood, probably set by the ra-ra BBC. But the mood can go the other way, as it did at the 1986 Edinburgh Commonwealth Games [which was beset by financial mismanagement as well as a political boycott]. If it's going wrong, Fleet Street will pile into the story. (Engel 2010)

Engel concludes by saying, 'I think there will be a bit of irreverence and a bit of meek acceptance, but boosterism will have the upper hand. . . No-one likes a party pooper.'

The tone within the UK press, one strongly suspects, will depend on the medal count and the impact of the Coalition Government's spending cuts. In any nation hosting a major or even minor international event, the media's default position is patriotic, even blindly nationalistic. This is especially so when times are straitened and sport is looked to as a distraction and source of comfort, even inspiration and, however briefly, unity. Disappointment, therefore, can trigger all manner of shrill indignation, even wrath. The expense of an Olympic Games must be justified by glory and, at the very least, organisational competence. Broadcasters, whose job is to sell their product – the Games in all its guises – and who have far closer and more compromising links to the organisers, are more inclined to exaggerate the good and downplay, even bury, the bad; the written press is hardly so constrained.

With its uniquely competitive newspaper market, this is true of the UK, and particularly England, above all. Such journalists need not pander to the power-brokers of international sport or national governments. So, a plea to my colleagues at the sports desk: let objectivity reign.

References

Barnes, S. (2010) 'Pass the sickbay for my big Olympic losers', Times Online, 21 May. http://www.timesonline.co.uk/tol/sport/columnists/simon_barnes/article7132249.ece (accessed 29 January, 2011).

Boyle, R. and Haynes, R. (2009) *Power Play – Sport, The Media and Popular Culture* (Second Edition), Edinburgh University Press.

Broadbent, R (2010) 'Triumph overcomes tragedy after host nation takes Games to its heart', *The Times*, 1 March.

Competition Commission Report 2000 (2000), Appendix 4.2. Available at http://www.competition-commission.org.uk/rep_pub/reports/2000/fulltext/442a4.2.pdf (accessed 29 August, 2010).

Daily Mail (2010) 1 April.

Downes, S. (2009) Interview with author, 18 December.

Engel, M. (2010) Interview with author, 13 March.

The Newspaper Society (2009). Available at http://www.newspapersoc.org.uk/default.aspx?page=897 (accessed 28 August, 2010).

Hennessey, P. (2007) *Having It So Good – Britain in the Fifties*, Harmondsworth: Penguin.

Hinds, R. (2009) 'Price of gold soars on the London medal exchange', *Sydney Morning Herald*, 31 October. Available at (http://www.smh.com.au/sport/price-of-gold-soars-on-the-london-medal-exchange-20091124-jfsm.html (accessed 20 November, 2010).

Hitchens, C. (2010) 'Fool's gold: how the Olympics and other international competitions breed conflict and bring out the worst in human nature', *Newsweek*, 5 February (http://www.newsweek.com/id/233007 (accessed 29 January 2011).

The Huffington Post (2010) 'Luge slider dead in Olympics Accident', 12 February. Available at http://www.huffingtonpost.com/2010/02/12/nodar-kumaritashvili-cras_n_460474.html (accessed 5 August, 2010).

Jorgensen, S. S. (2005) 'The world's best advertising agency – the sports press', October (http://www.playthegame.org/upload//Sport_Press_Survey_English.pdf, accessed 29 January, 2011).

Kimmage, P. (2007 reprint), *Rough Ride: Behind The Wheel With A Pro Cyclist*, Random House UK.

MacIntyre, B. (2010) 'Unreliable sources by John Simpson', *The Times*, 13 March (http://entertainment.timesonline.co.uk/tol/arts_and_entertainment/books/non-fiction/article7058866.ece (accessed 29 January, 2011).

Muir, K. (2010) 'Double Take', Times Online, 2 April (http://entertainment.timesonline.co.uk/tol/arts_and_entertainment/film/film_reviews/article7084442.ece (accessed 29 January, 2011).

Ponsford, D. (2010) 'Feb ABCs: Qualities plunge but Star and Sun are up', *Press Gazette*, 12 March. Available at http://www.pressgazette.co.uk/story.asp?storycode=45172 (accessed 29 August, 2010).

Powell, J. (2007) 'Passion, humility and loyalty: Ian Wooldridge transcended sport', Mail Online, 6 March http://www.dailymail.co.uk/news/article-440333/Passion-humanity-loyalty-Ian-Wooldridge-transcended-sport.html, (accessed 29 January, 2011).

Simpson, J. (2010) *Unreliable Sources*, London: Macmillan.

Sparkman, R. (2009) 'Canada painted as bad guy in Olympic Oval fuss', *Toronto Star*, 10 March. Available at http://www.thestar.com/comment/columnists/article/599323 (accessed 13 July, 2010).

Steen, R. (2007) *Sports Journalism – A Multimedia Primer*, London: Routledge.

The Sun (2010) 1 April.

The Times (2010) 1 April.

Wooldridge, I. (2007) *Searching for Heroes – Fifty years of Sporting Encounters*, London: Hodder & Stoughton.

Zirin, D. (2010) 'Sportsmanship: The great Olympic fraud', *The Progressive*, 15 February. Available at http://www.progressive.org/zirin022510.html (accessed 10 July, 2010).

16

WATCHED BY THE GAMES

Surveillance and security at the Olympics

John Sugden

The Olympic Games stands alone as the world's greatest sporting spectacle. While in terms of spectatorship, both live and virtual, it may be outgunned by its nearest rival, the Football World Cup, as a sporting spectacle it is peerless. World Cups are awarded to nations whereas the Olympics are hosted by cities. The Games bring together the widest range of sports in (more or less) a central location and, unlike Football World Cups, the Olympics capture the attention and fire the imagination of the largest and most diverse world spectatorship. Moreover, largely of its own making, the Olympics are rich in symbolism, rooted in largely Westernised, liberal democratic traditions but susceptible to manipulation by nationalist political ideologies. The Olympics are supposed to 'stand for something' and thus they present something to stand against. As such, Olympic events are targeted by a range of individuals and groups as sites for non-violent political protest and – the primary focus of this chapter – domestic and international terrorism.

The Olympics, politics and terrorism: Mexico and Munich

While the link between politics and the modern Olympics is as old as the Games themselves, the overt targeting of the event as a means for grandstanding extrinsic, politically-related ends is relatively recent and begins in Mexico in 1968. In this context Mexico '68 is mostly remembered, not just for Bob Beaman's astonishing world record long-jump leap, but also because of African-American sprinters John Carlos's and Tommy Smith's 'black power' podium demonstration at the medal ceremony after the final of the 200 meters. At home African American track and field athletes had been radicalised by decades of unfair treatment in domestic competitions and, in an era when sport mega-events were beginning to get significant media exposure, this was a relatively benign and opportunistic way of advertising their grievance to a huge global audience (Witherspoon 2008).

Less well remembered is that in the build up to the 1968 Olympic Games thousands of students took to the streets in Mexico City to protest against President Diaz Ordaz's totalitarian Government's social and economic policies and what they perceived as the waste of resources that were being lavished on the Olympics. Matters came to a head on October 2 when, barely a week before the Games started, hundreds of student protesters were gunned down in cold blood by Mexican security forces in *Plaza de las Tres Culturas* in the *Tlateloloco* district of Mexico City. The Mexican Government's heavy-handed response was encouraged by the USA which, at this point in its history, saw a communist plot behind every popular movement for reform in Latin America. This represents a clear example of the identification of and suppression of potential disruption motivated by domestic political dissent but amplified by wider geo-politics. The world watched and did nothing as, shamefully, did the myopic Olympic Mandarins, just as they would four years later when Israeli athletes were massacred in Munich.

If there were ever any doubts that sports mega-events could provide a stage for ruthless political exploitation, the hostage taking and eventual killing of Israeli athletes and officials at the 1972 Munich Olympics removed them. To summarise, on 5 September 1972 eleven Israeli athletes and coaches were seized in the Athletes' Village and held hostage by members of Black September, a militant faction of the PLO (Palestine Liberation Organisation) which itself was the armed wing of the political movement *Fatah*, led by Yasser Arafat. The German authorities hatched a plot to lure the hostage-takers and their captives away from the Athletes' Village to a nearby military airfield on the pretext that they were being flown to a destination of their choice. Once at the airfield armed German Police attempted but failed to free the hostages who were all killed in the ensuing mêlée along with all but three of the kidnap gang. In the search for retribution, this tragedy led to one of the biggest espionage and counter terrorism operations ever mounted by *Mossad* (Israel's clandestine security service) as it systematically hunted down and killed all who had been associated with the planning and execution of the Munich debacle (Jonas 1984).

In turn for the release of the hostages Black September demanded freedom for hundreds of PLO prisoners from Israeli jails as well as the release of the joint leaders of the German-based Baader-Meinhof anti-capitalist urban terrorist organisation (Johnson 2008): the implication being that, in mounting this operation, Black September had received assistance from the Baader-Meinhof gang. This connection alone offered the first evidence that under certain circumstances domestic and international political issues could come together to threaten the security of the Olympics.

The impact of 9/11

The events of September 5 1972 in Munich made all concerned aware that from then on the Olympics were on the radar of international terrorist organisations. This was the inspiration behind the 1977 film *Black Sunday* in which a deranged Vietnam veteran teams up with rouge Palestinian terrorists and attempts to crash an airship full of high explosives into a packed stadium staging America's biggest single sporting event, the Super Bowl (Frankenheimer 1977). Despite what had happened in Munich, for most *Black Sunday* was a piece of forgettable Hollywood fantasy. The events of September 11th 2001, when Al Qaeda terrorists hijacked a number of fully-fuelled passenger airlines, two of which were flown deliberately into the upper floors of New York's Twin Towers, bringing them crashing down, killing and seriously wounding tens of thousands, made the *Black Sunday* plot appear less far-fetched. The World Trade Centre was chosen by Al Qaeda because the towers were packed with people and also because they were widely-recognised, iconic symbols of US global commercial domination. Likewise sport mega events, such as the Olympic Games and the Football World Cup, not only offer large concentrations of people but are also highly symbolic of national prestige and power.

Mathew Brzezinski (2004) argues that post-9/11 America has become a real and virtual fortress in which the security reach of the state is extensive and all-pervasive. In the immediate aftermath of the attack on the Twin Towers major sporting events hosted in the USA – the World Series, the Super Bowl and the Winter Olympics in Salt Lake City – were subject to security conditions that would not have been out of place if *Black September* had been based on a real turn of events. This has become the norm in subsequent years. The 2006 Super Bowl in Detroit offers a particular example of 'supersize security' involving one of the largest security operations in US history:

> Inside the ring of steel, fans were screened by metal and radiation detectors; special security forces and bomb disposal teams were on standby; computer linked high resolution CCTV was utilised along with real-time satellite imagery to allow instant response; and the area was guarded by 10,000 police and private security guards. (Coffee and Murakami Wood 2006: 513)

Surveillance and security around a single sporting event on this scale was unthinkable before 9/11. Henry Giroux (2008) has argued that, accelerated by the events of 9/11, the United States is rapidly evolving into a society in which the ethic of militarisation dominates at the expense of a liberal tradition of civic freedoms. Militarisation implies a condition in which a nation is either at war or preparing for war and all possible resources – social, economic, political – are mobilised to reflect this condition. The war in question is not the particular on-the-ground engagements in Iraq and Afghanistan, but the more nebulous and all-encompassing conflict between Western and Oriental values and ideologies characterised by former US President George W. Bush as a 'war on terror': a war to be waged both abroad and at home.

Supersize security is complemented by the incorporation of militarised display, memoir and metaphor in the packaging of mega sports events, particularly in the USA. Typically, shortly before a game or event commences, police and army surveillance helicopters temporarily vacate the airspace to make way for a low-level fly-past by US Air Force fighter squadrons; while on the field itself, to the accompaniment of marching bands, the pre-match show features tributes to service men and women fighting and dying overseas – by now an institutionalised feature of big-time American sports military pageantry (King 2008) and increasingly evident in the public presentation of major sports in the UK. In this regard the attractiveness of Westernised sports events for terrorists is enhanced by the fact that not only do they generate large crowds, but they also venerate and valorise the very conflicts which the terrorists stand against and use to justify their actions (Silk and Falcous 2005).

Since Munich '72 there have been no overtly geo-politically motivated attacks on the Olympic Games. There have been isolated incidents involving rogue individuals, the most serious of which was the pipe bomb blast in the Olympic Park during the Centennial Games in Atlanta 1996, attributed to Eric Robert Rudolf, who was found to have neo-Nazi leanings but no links with any global terror organisations (Johnson 2008). Despite the relative lack of terrorist involvement in the Games since Munich, international terrorism remains the number one concern for host cities. The events of September 11th 2001 turned that concern into nothing short of a moral panic, providing successive host cities and their respective governments with the licence to do almost anything in the name of counter-terrorism.

The scale and cost of Olympic Security post-9/11

'The Games must go on', famously asserted the then IOC President Avery Brundage, after the 1972 debacle in Munich. The same sentiment continued to apply after the events of September 11, 2001. But at what cost? The following analysis (see Figure 1 overleaf) by the *Wall Street Journal* (2004) starkly illustrates the impact of 9/11 on security budgets for the summer Olympic Games:

In Los Angeles in 1984 when 6,829 athletes took part and 5,720,000 tickets were sold, the average security cost was US$11,627 per athlete or $US14 per ticket. Two decades later in Athens where there were an estimated 10,500 participants, the average cost was an estimated US$142,857 per athlete or $US283 per ticket. Taking account of the increased number of participants this still represents an almost ten-fold increase in security costs in only 20 years. It can be seen clearly from the above graph the there is an extremely sharp increase from Sydney 2000 to Athens 2004 when post 9/11 the security budget leaps a staggering 800%. These figures do not account for the £93 million spent by the IOC which for the first time took out an insurance policy against the risk of the games being cancelled because of natural disasters such earthquakes, flooding and landslides, and unnatural ones, namely international terrorism (Johnson 2008). The threat of the former had not changed since the onset of the modern Olympics whereas the latter had loomed more and more ominously.

What can be bought for US$ 1.5 billion? To answer this, it is illustrative to consider the full details of the actual hardware and software deployed in and around Athens in the summer of 2004:

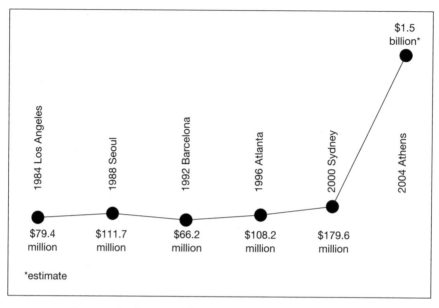

FIGURE 16.1 Securing the Summer Olympic Games

> Hundreds of CCTV cameras swept the main avenues an squares of Athens, whereas three police helicopters and a Zeppelin, equipped with more surveillance cameras hovered overhead . . . Dozens of new PAC 3 (Patriot Advanced Capability) missiles were armed and in position at three locations around the capital, including the Tatio Military Base near the athletes' Olympic Village, to provide a full defense umbrella over Athens. Security forces also received 11 state-of-the-art surveillance vans that received and monitored images from around the city . . . Authorities also got two mobile truck screening systems capable of locating explosives, weapons, or drugs in trucks and other large cargo vehicles. . . . By August 13th the Authorities had installed thousands of CCTV cameras and deployed all over Greece more than 70,000 military staff to patrol the first Summer Games since the September 11th attacks on the United States. (Samatas 2007: 224)

This extensive inventory does not take account of the NATO AWACS (Airborne Warning and Control System) surveillance airplanes circling high in Greek air space or the NATO naval vessels patrolling shipping lanes in the nearby Mediterranean Sea off the port of Piraeus.

Neither does Samatas's stock-take account for other, more shadowy, forms of scrutiny and surveillance that may have been put in place by groups and organisations not directly and transparently connected to the Athens Olympic Organising Committee. Writing in the New York Times on the eve of the 2004 Olympics, albeit with journalistic licence, Raymond Bonner comments:

Athenians hope that thoughts of running diving and setting new world records will overtake worries about security, which are driven in large part by US fears of a new Al Qaeda attack. At the moment, there are more spies than athletes at the Olympic site, and the only record set has been the cost of security – more than $1.4 billion and rising – even though no intelligence agency has reported picking up any signal that Al Qaeda is planning to ruin the Games. (Bonner 2007)

When on 5th May 2004 a hitherto unknown terrorist organisation calling itself 'Revolutionary Struggle' blew up a police station in Athens as a message to the Games organisers, concerns that the Olympics might indeed be a target for a major terrorist attack were heightened (Johnson 2008). Athens has a reputation in the NATO security community for being a hotbed of radical-left politics and anti-establishment activity. If accounts in the Greek and American press can be believed, the US did not fully trust the security regimes of Athens's Olympic Organising Committee or the Greek Government. In February 2006 the Greek Government revealed that a year earlier a sophisticated bugging device capable of recording the mobile phone conversations of dozens of targeted subscribers had been discovered. The list of those who had their conversations bugged reads like a who's-who of the Greek political elite and includes the Prime Minister, Minister of Defence, Mayor of Athens and all of the senior police and army personnel who had anything to do with Olympic security. The complex phone tap had been active from shortly before the Olympics until March 2005 when it was discovered and removed. The same month Kostas Tsalikid, a network manager from the communications technology company Vodafone, one of the few technicians with the access and capacity to plant such a device, was found hanged in his home. Although his death has been officially confirmed as suicide, there are those who are deeply suspicious of the whole affair, especially when the intercepted calls were forwarded from four cellular antennas with their coverage circles overlapping the US Embassy (Keisling 2007). The inference here is that the phone tapping was put in place at the behest of the CIA without the knowledge of the Greek authorities.

The Olympic Games and the superpanoptican

Samatas argues that in 2004 Athens was turned into a 'panoptic urban fortress'. At the centre of the intense monitoring of the Olympic City was a highly complex and web-like network of electronic surveillance gadgetry and attendant software – what Samatas refers to as the 'superpanotican'. His conceptualisation draws upon the work of Michael Foucault who himself raided 18th century political philosopher Jeremy Bentham's innovative prison design, the Panopticon – [the 'all-seeing place', derived from the Greek word *pan* (all) and *optos* (visible)] to develop a metaphor for the saturating and omnipotent nature of state-sponsored surveillance and social control in (post) modern societies (Andrews 2000). Bentham's

Panopticon was to be structured in such a way that, like a spider in the centre of its web a single guard could watch over many prisoners kept in transparent cells arranged concentrically around the observation post in such a way that the guard could see the prisoners but they could not see him. The genius of Bentham's idea lay in the fact that even if the observation post was empty the design would lead the prisoners to assume that they were being watched all of the time and this would cause them to moderate their behaviour, effectively becoming self-policing. While Bentham's design was never approved by the British government the spirit of the Panoptican lives on, as John Renne points out, saying, 'once upon a time an ethicist had a brilliant idea for a prison. Today we live in it'. It is in Bentham's native city of London, which in the first decades of the twenty first century had more public and private CCTV cameras that any other city in the world, that the concept of total surveillance comes closest to being realised (Renne 2008: 4). The presence of the Olympics there in 2012 can only accelerate this process of totalitarian intrusiveness.

Samatas also shows how for the Athens Olympics the major Western powers in the international community – Australia, France, Germany, Israel, Spain, the United Kingdom and, most importantly, the United States – were instrumental in making the Olympic Games in Athens 2004 a test-bed for the 'superpanopticonic' approach to mega-event security in the post 9/11 world. The construction and implementation of the 'superpanoticon' described above proved to be a bonanza not only for the corporate interests of the electronic surveillance industry, but also for the US military and secret service agencies with which that industry is so interdependent. Building upon C. Wright Mills'(1956) notion of the military-industrial complex, Samatas refers to this alliance as 'the security and surveillance industrial complex', a conjunction of an immense security establishment and a large high-tech surveillance and data industry.

Not surprisingly, Israel – arguably the nation at the crux of the West's confrontation with radical Islamist states and spawned terrorist organisations – has emerged as one of the world's leading global players in this 'security and surveillance industrial complex' (Brzezinski 2004). With its highly developed, militarised, hi-tech economy, coupled with a long history of counter terrorism and dealing with the threat of suicide bombers, Israel is very well placed to exploit the climate of fear that surrounds today's major sporting events as a business opportunity. As such its representatives are heavily involved in the planning and facilitation of mega-event security.

Beijing 2008

Through the murk of secrecy as thick as the smog that shrouded the Chinese capital during the 2008 Olympics, it is virtually impossible to fully ascertain the full facts regarding surveillance and security. We do know that the overall budget for the 2008 Games was more than three times that of Athens and the security budget would have been at least proportionate to that. *The Los Angeles Times* estimated that the figure was in excess of 6 billion. This is unsurprising given the little that we do know about the scale and reach of the security operation and infrastructure of militarised hi-tech hardware that put Athens in the shade (Yu *et al.* 2009). The official explanation given by the Beijing authorities for the unprecedented scale of the security operation was dominated by the themes of making the Chinese capital safe and friendly place for international visitors while at the same time countering the threat posed by international terrorism.

Given the relatively neutral position occupied by China with regard to the politics of the Middle East, the Beijing Olympics was never likely to be an obvious target for radical Islamist terror groups. Albeit from a credible source, there are even incredible suggestions that the Chinese brokered a secret deal with Al Qaeda to make sure that their Games were off-limits! In a book entitled, *The Chinese secret services: from Mao to the Olympic Games*, Frenchman Roger Faligot (2008), a respected investigative journalist and intelligence specialist claims that in 2006 Chinese spies held secret meetings with Al Qaeda in the mountains of Pakistan during which the threat of possible attacks on the Olympics were discussed. Few details of these exchanges are supplied, but Faligot writes, 'the first negotiations with Osama bin Laden's entourage are likely to have been held in Pakistan in 2006', and goes on to ask, 'what has China promised to prevent a suicide bomber from blowing himself up during the finals of the hundred meters dash? And most importantly, what confidence can we have in any commitment undertaken by Osama bin Laden? The answer will come next August in Beijing' (*ibid.*: 326). Running counter to Faligot's claims, in 2010 it was reported on the WikiLeaks website that US diplomatic correspondence in the build-up to Beijing had raised serious concerns that Ayman al-Zawahiri, Al Qaeda's second in command, had ordered attacks during the 2008 Olympics, including targeting the equestrian events in Hong Kong (Hula2010).

Truth is that if China faced 'terrorist' threats they were most likely to have been internally generated; and there is a perhaps more credible criticism that China used the Olympics and the accompanying 'threat of terrorism' as a pretext for cracking-down on domestic political dissidents, human rights activists, and ethnic/nationalist minority groups, particularly those associated with Tibet and the Uighurs in the Muslim-dominated far western region of Xinjiang (Yu *et al.* 2009). As well as this, the massive development programme undertaken in the neighbourhoods adjacent to the main Olympic venue were accompanied by massive relocation of some of Beijing's poorest citizens (Giulianotti and Klauser 2009).

Finally, in London it was reported by *The Times* that, in addition to overt security measures, Beijing was subject to saturation levels of state-sponsored spying, not just aimed at countering the threat of terrorism, but also to garner the technical and tactical intelligence of competing national Olympic teams as well as steal state and industrial secrets from the thousands of foreign government and business personnel who attended the Games (Oakshot *et al.* 2008). This serves to reinforce John MacAloon's (1997) assertion that, even before 9/11, the Olympic Games provided the perfect venue for the clandestine activities of international espionage networks.

London in the cross-hairs?

As the so-called 'war on terror' continues to cast its shadow around the world, the security operation being developed to ensure the safety of the 2012 Olympics promises to be on an unprecedented scale. There are several outstanding, over-lapping contextual issues that augment the risk of London 2012 being the site of a major terrorist incident. Firstly, London is one of the 'world cities', which in and of itself makes it an attractive prospect for tourists and terrorists alike, albeit for different reasons. Related to this, and secondly, Britain's contemporary foreign policy, its military interventions in Iraq and Afghanistan, and its continued support for Israel see it demonised as 'Little Satan' by Islamic extremists. Thirdly, in the eyes of the militants, Britain stands 'shoulder to shoulder' with 'Big Satan', the United States, and as such the London Olympics present targets at least as mouthwatering as New York's World Trade Centre. Finally, Britain's troubled history as a colonial power and its postcolonial legacy not only give it a rich multicultural heterogeneity, but also, as the bombings of July 7, 2005 remind us, make it a repository for the festering of postcolonial resentments and a potential breeding ground for Jihadist sympathisers. A confluence of happenstances not lost on those charged with the responsibility of delivering safe and secure Games in London 2012:

> On the 6th of July 2005, it was announced that London had been successful in its bid for the 2012 Games. Just 24 hours later 52 people were murdered in four terrorist attacks in London, which changed the security landscape overnight. (Ghaffur 2007)

These two stark sentences, penned in 2007 by Tarique Ghaffur, then the Assistant Commissioner of the Metropolitan Police and Security Co-ordinator for the London 2012 Olympic and Paralympics Games, capture the essence of the challenge facing London. Ghaffur goes on to suggest that London is a good choice as host because it has a wealth of experience as a terror target:

> Athens 2004 set the standard in security and surveillance for future mega-sporting events. London, with its long history of security development linked to the 'Irish Question' and with the experience of stadia security born from decades of dealing with football hooliganism, and taking account of lessons learned in Athens (and Beijing), from a practical point of view, may be better placed than most other cities to cope with the post 9/11 security demands that come with hosting the Olympic Games. (*ibid.*)

This is a perverse rationale for awarding the Games to London – a bit like arguing the case for New Orleans to host them during the hurricane season because of that city's history of dealing with violent tropical storms. Not surprisingly, given existing levels of public and private surveillance in the UK, the 'superpanoptic' approach, piloted in Athens in 2004, is at the centre of London's strategy to make safe the 2012 Olympics. With more than an echo of Athens, the London Metropolitan Police have said that the first line of security for London 2012 is to be a 'technological footprint' across London. The 'footprint' will combine and integrate 'new-build' security technologies in and around Olympic venues with existing public and private surveillance and security infrastructure, including traffic control cameras and the 500,000 + CCTV units which are estimated already to be in place in and around the metropolis.

Responding to this issue Marcus Morgan has argued that the imposition of the aforementioned 'technological footprint' would give the police along with the OSD unprecedented control over up to half a million CCTV cameras, access to DNA archives, and multiple forms of personal identification data. On top of this tens of thousands of police and privately contracted security personnel will be used and at least as much military hardware as that used in Athens in 2004 will be deployed on the ground, in the air and on the water to create a fortress around London 2012. Morgan concludes that 'the machinery is being created that is necessary to impose a highly integrated police/military apparatus in Britain's capital city, under the pretext of keeping the country safe from terrorism' (Morgan 2008: 2).

This is a theme picked up by Oscar Reyes, who, writing in the radical Journal *Red Pepper* after visiting the Athens Olympiad, observed, 'huge amounts of money were spent on equipment that didn't work. But the part that did work is now used for the surveillance of Greek society'. Then turning his attention to London 2012 he states, 'the Greatest Show on Earth, it seems, would be accompanied by one of the largest security operations ever mounted in the UK. Long after the TV cameras have moved on, the CCTV would still be watching. And that's a spectre we would be foolish to ignore'. Coaffee and Murakami Wood share Reyes's concerns, believing that an event like the 2012 Olympics may be used by government and security-related interest groups to magnify in the public mind the 'terrorist threat' and construct a 'climate of fear' to 'justify technologically driven control strategies, to counter anti-social behaviour and democratic protest, to exclude the dangerous 'other' from public space, and to introduce identity cards that link citizens to state held databases (Coaffee and Murakami Wood 2006). When it comes to human rights and civil liberties, surely contemporary China is the last place on earth that the world's oldest democracy should be looking towards for guidance.

Echoing these concerns, four years before the commencement of the 2012 London Olympics, Denis Oswald, the Chairman of the IOC's London Coordination Commission, admitted that it was difficult if not impossible to predict how much will have to be allocated to the security budget. He said, 'it's a very difficult area but if we want to have occasions like the Olympic Games, where hundreds of thousands of people meet, then you have to make sure they are safe, otherwise you just give up and the terrorists win'. This, Morgan argues, is tantamount to asking the British tax payer for a blank cheque (Morgan 2008: 2).

According to newspaper reports, estimates of the final numbers that might be written on such a cheque become more and more inflated as the opening ceremony approaches, rising to well over the $1.5 billion spent on security for the Athens Games and more than three times the estimated security bill in the original bid document (Briggs 2008). Lincoln Allison argues that no matter how sophisticated pseudo-scientific risk assessments become, unlike in the physical environment, in complex societies there are no real limits to levels of risk posed by unpredictable human forces – including terrorists (Allison 2010). This does not stop those who have vested interests in the security business using the spurious notion of 'worst case scenario' to justify the most draconian (and expensive) strategies to keep us safe in our beds. Johnson refers to this as a conflict between limited budgets versus infinite demands. Writing about risk assessments and Olympic events he argues:

> Successful security operations at recent games raise questions about whether the high levels of expenditure are proportionate to the high levels of threat . . .Given that we cannot afford to meet all potential security threats, we must allocate finite resources to address those threats that are most likely or which pose the greatest consequences. However, the dynamic political and social context for many games makes it difficult to validate the findings of any security risk assessment. There will therefore continue to be great uncertainty about the sufficiency of security measures for future Games. (Johnson 2008: 10)

On the other hand, given New York 9/11 and London 7/7 it is very difficult to argue against the need for supersize security, particularly when terror organisations themselves feed the media-amplified moral panic over mega event safety. The Olympics may not have been targeted by international terrorist organisations since 1972, but there have been serious terrorist attacks on other major sports events. In 2009 in Lahore, Pakistan, the team bus of the touring Sri Lankan cricket team was attacked by masked gunmen, believed to be members of an extreme Islamic faction with links to Al Qaeda, who killed six policemen and the coach driver and injured several cricketers before being driven off by armed police. Less than a year later a similar incident occurred during the African Cup of Nations when the Togolese National football team's bus was ambushed by guerrillas from Flec (Front for the Liberation of the Enclave of Cabinda) as it drove through Angola's disputed Province of Cabinda on its way to the competition venue. Several team officials were killed and three players were seriously injured, casting a long shadow not only over the Cup of Nations itself, but also stretching as far as South Africa where the World Cup Finals were to be held later the same year.

The terrorist threat was augmented when on the eve of the 2010 World Cup Finals an Al Qaeda spokesman declared on a North African Jihadist website that the competition was to be targeted by suicide bombers using 'undetectable explosives'. The qualifying game between England and the USA in Rustenburg on June 12 was given special mention:

How amazing could the match between the United States vs Britain (sic) be when broadcast live on air at a stadium packed with spectators the sound of an explosion rumbles through the grounds, the whole stadium is turned upside down and number of dead bodies are in their dozens and hundreds, Allah willing. (Edwards 2010)

Statements like the one quoted above from Al Qaeda, are cheap to make, but set against a history of indiscriminate public terrorist attacks by them and related groups, including sport-related targets, they serve not only to accentuate the climate of fear that surround contemporary sporting events, but also encourage vast expenditure on an intrusive security apparatus that violates principles of civil liberty and human rights and blurs the distinction between political and civil society. Thus, without even throwing so much as a whiz-bang, Al Qaeda and its ilk are in profit as are the mandarins of the security and surveillance industrial complex for whom the Olympics is just another business opportunity.

Conclusion

In December 1948, only months before London hosted the Summer Olympics for the second time, George Orwell sent to his publishers, Secker and Warburg in London, the final manuscript of his chilling novel 1984 – the story that introduced to the world the all-seeing and all-knowing tyrant 'Big Brother' and became emblematic of intrusive despotism for generations to come. Little could Orwell have known that by the time the Olympics returned to London a third time sixty four years later the reality of security and surveillance would not only have far exceeded his nightmarish imaginings, but the presence of the Olympics themselves in 2012 would have significantly accelerated the expansion of the UK's digital-state's totalitarian presence in British lives. In July 2007, Tom Wilson, Secretary to the House of Lords Constitution Committee asked, in the context of the 2012 Olympics, what would be the 'impact of surveillance and security and data collection upon the privacy of citizens and their relationship with the state?' (Wilson 2007). To date those involved in the design and activation of Olympic security for 2012 have yet to come up with a satisfactory answer. Maybe this is because we have already become so accustomed to living in an Orwellian dystopia that the terms of the question no longer have the resonance they might have once have had. As John Rennie (2008) points out, in an era in which Orwell's harrowing vision of a pervasive totalitarian state has been parodied as *Big Brother*, a popular reality TV show, and we have become used to everybody watching, photographing and filming everybody else in public and in private, when it comes to complaining about privacy and civil liberties, the game is already up. Perhaps it is time we got used to the fact that rather than us watching the Games, for the foreseeable future, it is more a case of the Games watching us.

References

Allison, L. (2010) 'London 2012 and the dirty bomb: some philosophical reflections', *The Social Affairs Unit*, 25 June. Available http://socialaffairsunit.org.uk/blog/archives/00 2010.php (accessed 12 September, 2010).

Andrews, D. (2000) 'Posting up: French post-structuralism and the critical analysis of contemporary sporting culture', in J. Coakley and E. Dunning (eds) *Handbook of Sport Studies*, London: Sage.

Bonner, R. 'Athletes and spies', *The New York Times*, Available http://www.query.nytimes.com/gst (accessed 7 June 2007).

Briggs, S. (2008) 'Security budget for 2012 Olympic Games set to break record', *The Daily Telegraph*, Available http://www.telegraph.co.uk/sport/othersports/olympics/london 2012/3550993/Security-budget-for-London-2012-set-to-break-Olympic-record-Olympics.html (accessed 15 September, 2010)

Brzezinski, M. (2004) *Fortress America. On the frontlines of Homeland Security – an inside look at the coming surveillance state*, New York: Bantam.

Coffee, J. and Murakami Wood, D. (2006) 'Security is coming home. Rethinking scale and constructing resilience in the global urban Response to terrorist risk', *International Relations* 20(4): 503–517.

Filigot, R. (2008) *The Chinese Secret Services: from Mao to the Olympic Games*, Paris: Nouveau Monde.

Frankenheimer, J. (1977) Director, *Black Sunday*, Los Angeles: Paramount.

Ghaffur, T. (2007) Assistant Commissioner Metropolitan Police, written reply to Tom Wilson, Clerk to the *Constitution Committee*, House of Lords, 8th June, 2007.

Giroux, H. (2008) 'The militarization of US higher education after 9/11', *Theory Culture & Society* 25(5): 56–82

Giulianotti, R. and Klauser, F. (2009) 'Security governance and sport mega-events: towards an interdisciplinary research agenda', *Journal of Sport and Social Issues* 34(1): 49–61.

Hula, E. (2010) 'Hong Kong terror threats during the Olympics', *Around the Rings*, http://aroundtherings.com/articles/view.aspx?id=36108 (accessed 14 January, 2010)

Jonas, G. (1984) *Vengeance*, New York: Simon and Schuster.

Johnson, C. (2008) 'Using evacuation strategies to ensure the safety and security of the 2012 Olympic venues', *Safety Science* 46(2): 302–322

Keisling, J. (2007) 'An Olympic scandal', *The Nation*. Available www.thenation.com/doc/20060320/keisling (accessed 1 May 2007).

King, S. (2008) 'Offensive lines: sport-state synergy in an era of perpetual war', *Cultural Studies – Critical Methodologies* 8(4): 527–539.

MacAloon, J. (1997) 'Politics and the Olympics: some new dimensions', *Recercat Deposit de la Recerca de Catalunya*, working paper 128.

Morgan, M. (2008) 'London Olympics terror threat used to vastly increase surveillance powers', *World Socialist Web Site*. Available http://www.wsws.org/articles/2008/may2008/lond-m03.shtml (accessed, 11 September 2020)

Oakshot, I., Sheridan, M. and Bagenal, F. (2008) 'Beijing Olympics: the spying games', *The Sunday Times*. Available http://www.timesonline.co.uk/tol/sport/olympics/article444 9148.ece (accessed, 3 September 2010)

Orwell, G. (1949) *Nineteen Eighty Four*, London: Secker and Warburg.

Renne, J. (2008) 'Here in the goldfish bowl', *Scientific American* 299(3): 4.

Reyes, O. (2008) 'The Olympics and the city', *Red Pepper*, Available http://www.red pepper.org.uk/article555.html (accessed, 11 September, 2010).

Samatas, M. (2007) 'Security and surveillance in the Athens 2004 Olympics: some lessons from a troubled story', *International Criminal Justice Review* 17(93): 220–238.

Silk, M. and Falcous, M., (2005) 'One day in September, a week in February: mobilizing American (sporting) nationalisms', *Sociology of Sport Journal* 22(4): 447–471.

Wall Street Journal, (2004) 'The cost of Olympic security', August 19, available http://www.mindfully.org/Reform/2004/Olympic-Games-Security22aug04.htm

Wilson, T. (2007) Clerk to the *Constitution Committee*, House of Lords, 8th June.

Witherspoon, K. (2008) *Before the Eyes of the World. Mexico and the 1968 Olympic Games*, Champaign: Northern Illinois University Press.

Wright Mills, C. (1956) *The Power Elite*, Oxford: Oxford University Press.

Ying. Y, Klauser. F, and Chan, G. (2009) 'Governing security at the 2008 Beijing Olympics', *International Journal for the History of Sport* 26(3): 390–405.

AFTERWORD

'No other anything . . .':
The Olympic Games yesterday
and today

John Sugden and Alan Tomlinson

> . . . no other sports festival, no other cultural event, no arts performance, no church, no political movement, no other international organisation, including the United Nations, indeed no other anything has ever managed to generate regularly scheduled and predictable performances which command anywhere the same focused global attention as do the Olympic ceremonies.
>
> John MacAloon (1996: 33)

At the end of the last chapter we were reminded of Big Brother, that literary invention of George Orwell's which has become emblematic of invisible forms of control. If Orwell had been so minded, and well enough to make the journey cross town, then in August 1948, instead of posting the manuscript for *1984*, he could have hand-delivered it to his publisher in London's Vauxhall Bridge Road before jumping on a red double-decker bus to travel north-west to the Empire Stadium Wembley to watch some of the athletics events in the 1948 Olympics. At six shillings each, in a period of post-war austerity, tickets were relatively easy to come by. For his money, at the track Orwell would have been treated to the trials and tribulations of some of the spirited amateur sportsmen and women who had come to London from 59 different countries. There were some notable absences. As retribution for its part in World War II, the host of the last pre-war Olympics in Berlin, Germany, was barred from taking part as was Japan, which, before war broke out, had won the right to host the 1940 Games in Tokyo. The Soviet Union was not there either, recovering as it was from the devastation of the conflict, and also adjudging itself to be not yet ready to take its brewing ideological struggle with the western powers onto the sports field.

Orwell had seen this coming, having written about the surrogate, war-like qualities of sport in his famous essay on the subject, *The Sporting Spirit*, published in 1946. Running counter to the much-vaunted ideals of the Olympic movement,

Orwell believed that far from bringing nations and people together, large sport events such as the Olympics fuelled aggressive nationalism and promoted xenophobia. For this reason it is highly unlikely that Orwell would have set foot in the Olympic Stadium, even if he had been *given* a ticket. While that lack of interest would have put Orwell at odds with most of his fellow citizens, neither would the vast majority of them have been watching the Games – certainly not as spectators in the stadium. Television was in its early infancy and, other than seeing newsreel recordings at the local picture house some time after the events, most would follow the progress of the Games in the newspapers or on the wireless radiogram. But in return, at least the Games would not have been watching them either. Had he taken the trip from Vauxhall to Brent, Orwell would had been no more than the proverbial ordinary 'man on a London omnibus', and in the stadium itself, his would have been just one anonymous face among those of thousands of other unremarkable, unrecognised and unregistered spectators.

Sixty four years later, while austerity was back in town and London's buses still at least resembled their 1948 ancestors, much else had changed around the staging of the 2012 Olympics, and its associated ceremonies, rituals, and cultural performances. The 1948 Austerity Olympics housed amateur competitors in ready-made facilities such as army barracks; by 1984 so-called 'amateur' superstars were emerging international celebrities; by 2008 Beijing was hosting a global elite. The most compelling and fundamental change is the way the Olympics have moved steadily and inexorably away from being an amateur, peoples', sporting festival towards a state-choreographed, commercially driven, internationally controlled, media mega-event. Of course, even at the moment of their reinvention in 1896, while founding fathers proclaimed them independent of political forces, the Olympics were framed by, and could hardly escape being tainted by, the politics of the host nation and its own international tensions (MacAloon 1981; Tomlinson 1984). For the most part however, for those and most subsequent Games up to the Second World War, planning, management and presentation of the event were left in the hands of civil society representatives, albeit from the upper classes of the host nation, along with the aristocrats of the IOC itself. The standout exception to this was Berlin in 1936. In the 1920s and 1930s totalitarian regimes in Europe had recognised the value of sporting events in wielding control and influence over the masses and stirring the pot of racialised nationalism. Stylised as the 'Nazi Olympics' the Berlin Games were seized upon by Hitler as a vehicle through which the peerless attributes of the Aryan race coupled with the orga-nisational mastery of the National Socialist Party machine could be vaunted and valorised (Kruger 2003), and its iconography commemorated in its associated imagery in posters and the like (Timmers 2008). After World War II, during the Cold War the ideological value assigned to sport by the Soviet Union and its acolytes in their contest with Western powers was taken to new heights and the Olympics were targeted as the main sporting theatre for this proxy war (Arnaud and Riordan 1998). Thus, when Moscow hosted the Games in 1980, with the benediction of the IOC, every detail of the event was planned and controlled by the Soviet political and military elite and the whole country was mobilised to ensure that the nation and its political economy were displayed in the best possible light (Edelman 2006). In the following Games in Los Angeles – boycotted tit-for-tat by the USSR as the USA had snubbed Moscow in 1980 – the USA grabbed the reins to celebrate the Games as a global festival of and tribute to Western freedoms and capitalist ideals. While the communist approach was the focus of keen criticism in the West, for what was perceived as its totalitarian model of Olympic planning and presentation, it could be argued that LA simply followed suit, the local state (California) and market tearing up the IOC rulebook to stage what many dubbed the Hamburger Games (fast-food specialist McDonald's funded the swimming facilities). The seeds for subsequent stagings of the Olympic spectacle were planted in both Moscow 1980 *and* Los Angeles 1984; at the latter, private-sector business interests, including media-moguls, took their seats at the table of Olympic governance, and the IOC drive to attract sponsors into the TOP (The Olympic Programme) scheme was intensified (for insider accounts, see Pound 2004; Payne 2005).

Thus, after Los Angeles '84 a cabal of transnational corporate mandarins joined the top brass of a 'sovereign' IOC and domestic political elite to dominate the organisation and articulation of the Olympic experience. The corporate elite, the sponsors and the broadcasters, had no formal role in the process, but were soon to make their desires, needs, and preferences known to key decision-makers. There was still a seat unoccupied at the table of Olympic governance, but not for long. Terrorism had been a growing concern for the Olympics throughout the final decades of the last century, particularly after the Black September terrorist attack on the Israeli team at the 1972 Munich Olympics. Juan Antonio Samaranch was well aware of the security problem that he was inheriting with his presidential position, and recognised the value of closed societies and dictatorships in providing and ensuring an adequately secure environment: 'For us, it is much better to go to those countries', he told Dick Pound, where there 'will never be security problems' (Pound 2004: 96). But after the September 11 attacks on New York's World Trade Centre security issues accelerated up the Olympic agenda. As they did so the view and input of the 'the security and surveillance industrial complex' (Samitas 2007) – the military, the police and related state security services – was deemed to be of paramount importance and they too joined the Olympic administrative elite. In short, in the 64 years separating London's post-war Olympiads, the Games had become far too important to leave in the hands of civil society actors and activists.

How then to make sense of a cultural and institutional phenomenon straddling history and embracing the world? Global sporting events involve the creation, management and mediation of cultural meanings for consumption by the largest reported media audiences in history. Anthropologist John MacAloon (1996: 33) contends that the Olympics are the apotheosis of this cultural form, commanding 'focused global attention' in unique fashion. MacAloon rightly calls attention to these exceptional qualities of the Olympics, though much work on the Olympics has concentrated on the Olympics as product and event, rather than the process of meaning-making underlying the getting and the staging of the Games. Contributors to this book have paid attention to the context in which the London 2012 bid was won, and the cultural politics intertwined with the branding and imaging of the Games in the crucial preparatory period before the event. In doing this, the book illuminates both the product and the event, and the underlying processes that underpin the making of the event.

For instance, audiences have traditionally admired, even revered, Olympic paraphernalia such as medals, stamps, flags, logos, posters, torches, and venues. But following a series of financial and organisational crises in the late 1970s and early 1980s, the IOC established a commission for the exploration of new sources of funding, abandoned amateurism, dramatically increased income for media rights, and adopted sponsorship (Barney et al. 2002; Wenn and Martyn 2007). Los Angeles 1984 was a pivotal moment in this transformation (Tomlinson 2006). However, in commercialising the Olympics, the IOC has also enabled and to some degree prompted audiences to interpret Olympic symbols and ideals in critical ways, and this has opened up the hermeneutic process to alternative readings and sometimes oppositional interpretations. It was widely recognised, at the count-down moment in Beijing one year before the opening of the Games, that 'rather than one strong unified message, the Beijing Olympics had already become polyphonic, multi-voiced, many themed' (Price 2008: 2); and that the narrative of the Beijing Games employed a 'pervasive cultural symbolism' in perpetuating a particular model of Chinese nationalism (deLisle 2008: 35). All Olympics have had this potential to generate interpretive controversy, on the global profile and impact of the events (Wamsley and Young 2005) and its post-modern survival and narratives (Bale and Christensen 2004): the Beijing Games provided throughout its planning period a particularly high-profile context for such political processes and cultural dynamics (Close et al. 2007). Responses to London 2012's winning bid, and to its brand-launching and development schedule and programme, have confirmed that contested meanings and readings are not confined to China/Beijing's claims and associated counter-narratives: Falcous and Silk (2010: 180) see the bidding process for London 2012, and the responses to the 7th July 2005 London bombings (these latter occurred the day after the winning of the bid in Singapore), as a process whereby corporatized narratives, carefully constructed ceremonial moments, and rituals of Britishness have been mobilised in the construction of a bogus civic multiculturalism.

Reactions to hosting the Olympics can embrace phases from expectation to mistrust, agreement to euphoria, forgetting to nostalgia (Kennett and Moragas 2006). All host cities/countries are haunted too by the prospect of underperformance, as McKay and Roderick's (2010) study of an Australian case of media obsession with failure shows. Widespread commentary and criticism in response to the 2012 logo, venue design, and the torch relay and handover ceremony for 2008, showed just how powerful and varied cultural and political responses to Olympic symbolism can be. As the myriad scandals surrounding the Olympics in Sydney 2000 and Salt Lake City 2002 showed, even the best PR firms in the world cannot prevent controversies from gaining massive momentum and even over-shadowing the Games (Lenskyj 2008; McKay, Hutchins and Mikosza 2000). UK prime minister Tony Blair promised a 'magical and memorable' Games to 'do justice to the great Olympic ideals' (Lee 2006: xiv), but the magic and the memories are cultural constructions; the making and mediation of London 2012 has been affected by factors such as how Beijing 2008 unfolded (including its 'spectacular productions' [Hubbert 2010]), how the IOC and the local organizing committee protects the brand, ongoing tensions between London and the nations and regions over legacies, an extended global economic downturn or recession, terrorist threats, and a change of UK national government.[1] In this book we have sought to show the particularities of the London case, but always within the wider context of the overarching history and sociology of the Olympic phenomenon, as the power dynamics and relations that have increasingly characterised the IOC and its various partners have squeezed the representatives of civil society to the point of suffocation.

This observation – of the appropriation of the Games from the hands of civil society actors and activists, as we put it earlier – places us firmly on the intellectual terrain of the late John Hargreaves who spent his career in critical consideration of the role played by sport in the contest between political and civil society, including, in his later theoretical and empirically focused work, matters relating to the Olympic Games. A consideration of the relevance of Hargreaves's work to much of the thinking that underpins this book is a worthy way to wrap things up. Although Hargreaves said virtually nothing on the Olympics in his major study of *Sport, Power and Culture* (Hargreaves 1986), he has instanced the Olympics in overviews of nationalism and the Games (1992) and globalisation theory (2002). More generally, his overall theoretical framework blended the historical and the sociological, the political and the cultural; and this is also the type of connected analytical and interpretive thinking that we have sought to bring to this collection of studies.

Hargreaves argued that even critical work on sport fell short for the 'inadequate way power and conflict are in general handled', and that to simply see new forms of sport as an adaptive response missed 'the complexities of the play of power' (Hargreaves 1982: 37). Hargreaves was one of the first sociologists to explicitly locate sport within the wider set of social and cultural relations in the perspective of Antonio Gramsci's conceptual concerns. He could then argue that any history of the emergence of modern sport in Britain must acknowledge the 'bringing to bear of pressure on subordinate groups: pressure ranging from outright coercion and the use of material incentives to moral exhortation' (Hargreaves 1982: 38). Popular cultural forms like sport, he proposed, must be studied for 'the way they function within an overall hegemony' (Hargreaves 1982: 51). The taken-for-grantedness of the values of the Olympics – as enshrined in its mission to 'celebrate humanity', and questioned in the early chapters of this book – is a startling example of how sport can be appropriated by elite groups in the contest for hegemony. In a more fully developed piece on hegemony, Hargreaves, quoting Raymond

Williams, stressed the importance of the theme of moral leadership in Gramsci's work, and its relation to the production of commonly taken-for-granted knowledge:

> What Gramsci stresses above all is the way a specific historical form of domination becomes sedimented and naturalized as 'common-sense' in practical consciousness, that is, in and through everyday living, so that the seemingly most innocuous values, meanings and practices reproduce a particular class hegemony . . . One of the most vital points heavily emphasised in the theory is how problematic it is for a class or group to establish and maintain its hegemony. (Hargreaves 1982a: 115)

For Hargreaves, then, sport is part of a wider process that must be understood as 'characterised by conflict and consent, coercion and struggle' (Hargreaves 1982a: 134). At the same time sport must be understood 'in its own specific terms . . . with its own meanings', never 'merely reducible to expressions of ruling class ideology' (1982a: 135). In his pathbreaking study of the history and sociology of popular sports in Britain, Hargreaves also drew upon the work of Foucault in his concluding conceptualization of the dynamics of sport and power. But running most consistently through his analysis is the Gramscian concept. Subordinate social categories 'are won over to sports rather than forced into, or manipulated into, involvement in them' (Hargreaves 1986: 7). We are not forced to cheer on Olympic competitors, nor are we morally obliged to back Olympic rhetoric. Yet many 'are won over' to both the Summer and Winter Games and eagerly anticipate the pleasures of spectatorship and even of partisan commitment. It may well be that a full interpretive framework for truly accounting for the continuing profile of the Olympics needs to draw upon the spirit of Hargreaves's blend of Gramsci and (some) Foucault.

When he turned his attention wholly to the Olympics, in his study of the politics of the 1992 Barcelona Games, Hargreaves (2000) produced a forensic analysis of the interplay of city, regional, national, and international politics. As well as embracing the broader context, he focused upon the internal politics of Spain, and the productive if tense dynamics of region/centre relations that underlay the contribution of Catalan and central Spanish (Madrid) government in the making of the Barcelona Games. Beyond the representation of Catalonia and Spain, he added, four dimensions must be recognised: a form of Olympic internationalism; a degree of Europeanisation; the influence of Americanisation; and a pervading global culture. Olympic internationalism included rituals, symbols, and parades stressing 'peace, friendship and international solidarity' (p.115) though the Iraqi team was whistled at by the audience at the opening ceremony (a reference to Iraq's invasion of Kuwait two years before), internationally known contemporary music, and world dignitaries in the tribune, including Nelson Mandela and Fidel Castro (the latter seated just below the Spanish king, clearly looking for strengthened alliances on the eve of the post-Soviet era).

Europeanisation was a project of the European Community/Commission, which had from its 1985 Adonnino Report begun to see sport as a potential source for and catalyst of European integration. In 1989 the Commission launched an Olympic programme aimed at the 1992 Barcelona Summer and Albertville Winter Games, putting 15.5 million ECUs (European Currency Units, roughly equivalent to £13.6 million) into the events, including a visual presence such as a European flag and its anthem, Beethoven's *Ode to Joy*, at ceremonies. The European Commission's president Jacques Delors also spent 5 days at the Games.

'Americanisation pervaded the Games' (p. 125), stated Hargreaves. The Hollywood-style showbiz spectacle included memorable stunts such as the igniting of the Olympic flame by an archer, and elaborate choreography for the ceremonies. Though not quite topping the medals table, the USA was represented by potent 'symbols of American capitalism – American corporate advertising' (p. 127). Overlapping with some of these forms of Americanisation were manifestations of global culture. In Barcelona's closing ceremony, 'pure pop entertainment culture took over, internationalism was superseded, and we could have been at a pop concert almost anywhere; that is, we were transported into the depthless, context-free realm of global culture' (p. 129). Mascot Cobi was whisked off during the closing ceremony 'into space in a giant shining boat' (p. 129), a Spielbergian moment of pure Hollywood translated into a kind of kitsch cosmopolitanism.

Hargreaves concluded his study with a discussion of the outcomes for the interested parties, the major agents, of their involvement in the making and staging of the Barcelona Games: 'None of the protagonists were able to determine the outcome unilaterally' (p. 131), he stated. The central state/government, the Catalan government, the municipality, and independent nationalists all had to work 'within an emergent framework of compromise' (p. 131). Alongside this, the IOC president himself was from Barcelona, with a Francoist professional past, and was himself immersed in the granting of the Games to the city, and in the overall project to rebrand Spain's fascist past. All were ready to make pacts to ensure a variety of satisfactory outcomes, within a framework of the 'promotion of a civic, multicultural Spain' (p. 163), including an enhanced recognition of Catalan distinctiveness.

Overall, Hargeaves's analysis of the Barcelona Olympic Games confirms the need to combine close-up analysis of the national context with an awareness and understanding of the international framework, identifying the negotiations and compromises at the heart of the hegemonic process; and in the Barcelona case this included the strong influence of parties and interests representing elements of the civil society. It may be that for the London 2012 event, the boundaries of influence of some of Hargreaves's major agents have shifted, perhaps to the point of erosion. Martin Shaw claims that Gramsci's core arguments about hegemony need to be reconsidered in the light of globalisation. He argues that in the post-Cold War period the conglomeration of transnational state and non-state institutional forms – in shorthand referred to as globalisation – constitutes nothing short of a 'global state' rooted in Western capitalistic values and operating worldwide at the political, economic and cultural level. Within this scenario the struggle for hegemonic dominance formerly characteristic of the nation state and its constituent elements has evolved to become a universal and one-sided contest whereby the 'global 'state', as envisaged by Shaw, is omnipresent and omnipotent both in political and civil society with only minimal room for opposition (Shaw 1999). As already argued by Carter in Chapter 4, in effect the modern Olympics is one global sovereign state apparatus that squeezes out any possibility of counter-hegemonic challenge and resistance, instead being absorbed in popular consciousness as an unquestioned social good. One of the underlying themes of this book has been to question the 'natural' value claimed for the Olympic Games, the common-sense view of its worthwhileness, and to shed light upon the differences between what the Olympic Movement claims for itself and what it actually does. In so doing, this kind of critical analysis challenges the Olympic power brokers to account for any differences.

'No other anything' compares to the Olympics, wrote MacAloon, referring to the unrivalled capacity of the Olympics to attract global attention, to its ceremonies in particular, to what can only be described as 'magnificent trivia' (Tomlinson 2005). And therein lies the drawing power of the contemporary Olympics. Controversies recur on the field of play and in the corridors of power with predictable regularity, whether this concerns knowledge control, drug use, sex and gender issues, disability policy, or, most frequently, the legacy question to which the IOC and hopeful bidders have so eagerly signed up. But as John Hargreaves would have urged, look closely at the power structures, the dormant and dominant ideologies, that fuel Olympic survivals, revivals and expansion; and the decreasing significance of influential forms of civil society in these structures. Look behind the fabulous, memorable if not magical, moments of human accomplishment of a Bolt, Redgrave, Holmes or Freeman, for the chains of power, prestige, and status that fuel and mobilise the contemporary Olympic machine. As Hargreaves noted, a more adequate handling of the dynamics of power and conflict in sporting culture, and a proper take on the complexities of the 'play of power', are prerequisites for an effective social scientific analysis of sport's place in society. It remains the task of a critical socio-cultural study of sport to interrogate the meanings of the Games, identify the stakes for which bidding and hosting cities (and the nations of which they are a part) defy economic and social logic, and analyse and interpret the broken promises as well as the utopian projections of Olympism.

With the falling curtain at the closing of London 2012, the cheering of the crowds will no doubt have been augmented faintly by the distant dry rustlings of Eric Blair . . . George Orwell . . . turning over in his grave.

Notes

1   I (AT) am grateful to Jim McKay for extended discussion of London 2012's phase of preparation, to which he brought not just the benefits of a well-travelled sociological

imagination, but the indispensable eye of the disinterested outsider and observer. This paragraph in particular draws upon our joint consideration of the London 2012 context.

References

Arnaud, P. and Riordan, J. (eds) (1998) *Sport and International Politics: The Impact of Fascism and Communism on Sport*, London: E. and F. N. Spon.

Bale, J. and Christensen, M. K. (eds) (2004) *Post-Olympism? Questioning Sport in the Twenty-first Century*, Oxford: Berg.

Barney, R. K, Wenn, S. R and Martyn, S. G. (2002) *Selling the Five Rings: The International Olympic Committee and the Rise of Olympic Commercialism*, Salt Lake City: The University of Utah Press.

Close, P., Askew, D. and Xu, X. (2007) *The Beijing Olympiad: The Political Economy of a Sporting Mega-Event*, London: Routledge.

deLisle, J. (2008) '"One world, different dreams": The contest to define the Beijing Olympics', in M.E. Price and D. Dayan (eds) *Owning the Olympics: Narratives of the New China*, Ann Arbor: The University of Michigan Press.

Edelman, R. (2006) 'Moscow 1980: Stalinism or good, clean fun.?', in A. Tomlinson and C. Young (eds) *National Identity and Global Sports Events: Culture, Politics, and Spectacle in the Olympics and the Football World Cup*, Albany NY: State University of New York Press.

Falcous, M. and Silk, M. L. (2010) 'Olympic bidding, multicultural nationalism, terror, and the epistemological violence of "Making Britain Proud"', *Studies in Ethnicity and Nationalism* 10(2): 167–86.

Hargreaves, J. (1982) 'Sport, culture and ideology', in Jennifer Hargreaves (ed.) *Sport, Culture and Ideology*, London: Routledge & Kegan Paul.

Hargreaves, J. (1982a) 'Sport and hegemony: some theoretical "problems"', in H. Cantelon and R. S. Gruneau (eds) *Sport, Culture and the Modern State*, Toronto: University of Toronto Press.

Hargreaves, J. (1986) *Sport, Power and Culture: A Social and Historical Analysis of Popular Sports in Britain*, Cambridge: Polity Press.

Hargreaves, J. (1992) 'Olympism and nationalism: some preliminary considerations', *International Review for the Sociology of Sport* 27(2): 119–35.

Hargreaves, J. (2000) *Freedom for Catalonia? Catalan Nationalism, Spanish Identity and the Barcelona Olympic Games*, Cambridge: Cambridge University Press.

Hargreaves, J. (2002) 'Globalisation theory, global sport, and nations and nationalism', in J. Sugden and A. Tomlinson (eds) *Power Games: A Critical Sociology of Sport*, London: Routledge.

Hubbert, J. (2010) 'Spectacular productions: community and commodity in the Beijing Olympics', *City & Society* 22(1): 119–42.

Kennett, C. and de Moragas, M. (2006) 'Barcelona 1992: evaluating the Olympic legacy', in A. Tomlinson and C. Young (eds) *National Identity and Global Sports Events: Culture, Politics, and Spectacle in the Olympics and the Football World Cup*, Albany NY: State University of New York Press.

Kruger, A. (2003) *The Nazi Olympics: Sport, Politics and Appeasement in the 1930s*, Champaign IL: University of Illinois Press.

Lee, M. (2006) *The Race for the 2012 Olympics: The Inside Story of How London Won the Bid*, London: Virgin Books (with Adrian Warner and David Bond).

Lenskyj, H. (2008) *Olympic Industry Resistance: Challenging Olympic Power and Propaganda*, Albany NY: State University of New York Press.

MacAloon, J. J. (1981) *This Great Symbol: Pierre de Coubertin and the Origins of the Modern Olympic Games*, Chicago: The University of Chicago Press.

MacAloon, J. J. (1996) 'Olympic ceremonies as a setting for intercultural exchange', in M. de Moragas Spa, J. J. MacAloon and M. Llinnés (eds) *Olympic Ceremonies, Historical Continuity and Cultural Exchange*, Lausanne: IOC.

McKay, J., Hutchins, B. and Mikosza, J. (2000) 'Shame and scandal in the family: Australian media narratives of the IOC/SOCOG scandal spiral', *Olympika: The International Journal of Olympic Studies* IX: 25–48.

McKay, J. and Roderick, M. (2010) '"Lay down Sally": media narratives of failure in Australian sport', *Journal of Australian Studies* 34(3): 295–315.

Orwell, G. (1970) 'The sporting spirit', in *In Front of Your Nose: The Collected Essays, Journalism and Letters of George Orwell*, Volume 4, Harmondsworth: Penguin.

Payne, M. (2005) *Olympic Turnaround: How the Olympic Games Stepped Back from the Brink of Extinction to become the World's Best Known Brand – and a Multi-billion Dollar Global Franchise*, Twyford: London Business Press.

Pound, R.W. (2004) *Inside the Olympics: A Behind-the-scenes Look at the Politics, the Scandals, and the Glory of the Games*, Canada: John Wiley & Sons Canada Ltd.

Price, M. E. (2008) 'Introduction', in M. E. Price and D. Dayan (eds) *Owning the Olympics: Narratives of the New China*, Ann Arbor: The University of Michigan Press.

Samatas, M. (2007) 'Security and surveillance in the Athens 2004 Olympics: some lessons from a troubled story', *International Criminal Justice Review* 17 (93): 220–38.

Shaw, M. (1999) 'Globality as a revolutionary transformation', in M. Shaw (ed.) *Politics and Globalisation: Knowledge, Ethics and Agency*, London: Routledge.

Timmers, M. (2008) *A Century of Olympic Posters*, London: V&A Publishing.

Tomlinson, A. (1984) 'De Coubertin and the modern Olympics', in A. Tomlinson and G. Whannel (eds) *Five-Ring Circus: Money, Power and Politics at the Olympic Games*, London: Pluto Press.

Tomlinson, A. (2005) *Sport and Leisure Cultures*, Minneapolis: University of Minnesota Press.

Tomlinson, A. (2006) 'Los Angeles 1984 and 1932: Commercializing the American Dream', in A. Tomlinson and C. Young (eds) *National Identity and Global Sports Events: Culture, Politics, and Spectacle in the Olympics and the Football World Cup*, Albany NY: State University of New York Press.

Wamsley, K. B. and Young, K. (2004) 'Coubertin's Olympic Games: The greatest show on earth', in K. B. Wamsley and K. Young (eds) *Global Olympics: Historical and Sociological Studies of the Modern Games*, Oxford: Elsevier Ltd.

Wenn, S. R. and Martyn, S. G. (2007) 'Juan Antonio Samaranch's score sheet: revenue generation and the Olympic Movement, 1980–2001', in G. P. Schaus and S. R. Wenn (eds) *Onward to the Olympics: Historical Perspectives on the Olympic Games*, Waterloo/Ontario: Wilfred Laurier University Press and The Canadian Institute in Greece.

INDEX